THE COLLABORATIVE ECONOMY AND EU LAW

'Disruptive innovation', 'the fourth industrial revolution', 'one of the ten ideas that will change the world'; the collaborative/sharing economy is shaking existing norms. It poses unprecedented challenges in terms of both material policies and governance in almost all aspects of EU law.

This book explores the application—or indeed inadequacy—of existing EU rules in the context of the collaborative economy. It analyses the novelties introduced by the collaborative economy and discusses the specific regulatory needs and instruments employed therein, most notably self-regulation. Further, it aims to elucidate the legal status of the parties involved (traders, consumers, prosumers) in these multi-sided economies, and their respective roles in the provision of services, especially with regard to liability issues. Moreover, it delves into a sector-specific examination of the relevant EU rules, especially on data protection, competition, consumer protection and labour law, and comments on the uncertainties and lacunae produced therein. It concludes with the acute question of whether fresh EU regulation would be necessary to avoid fragmentation or, on the contrary, if such regulation would create unnecessary burdens and stifle innovation.

Taking a broad perspective and pragmatic view, the book provides a comprehensive overview of the collaborative economy in the context of the EU legal landscape.

The Collaborative Economy
and EU Law

Vassilis Hatzopoulos

·H A R T·
PUBLISHING
OXFORD AND PORTLAND, OREGON
2018

Hart Publishing

An imprint of Bloomsbury Publishing Plc

Hart Publishing Ltd	Bloomsbury Publishing Plc
Kemp House	50 Bedford Square
Chawley Park	London
Cumnor Hill	WC1B 3DP
Oxford OX2 9PH	UK
UK	

www.hartpub.co.uk
www.bloomsbury.com

Published in North America (US and Canada) by
Hart Publishing
c/o International Specialized Book Services
920 NE 58th Avenue, Suite 300
Portland, OR 97213-3786
USA

www.isbs.com

HART PUBLISHING, the Hart/Stag logo, BLOOMSBURY and the
Diana logo are trademarks of Bloomsbury Publishing Plc

First published 2018

British Library Cataloguing-in-Publication Data
A catalogue record for this book is available from the British Library.

ISBN:	HB:	978-1-50991-713-6
	ePDF:	978-1-50991-714-3
	ePub:	978-1-50991-715-0

Library of Congress Cataloging-in-Publication Data

Names: Hatzopoulos, Vassilis, author.

Title: The collaborative economy and EU law / Vassilis Hatzopoulos.

Other titles: Collaborative economy and European Union law

Description: Oxford [UK] ; Portland, Oregon : Hart Publishing, 2018.

Identifiers: LCCN 2017050935 (print) | LCCN 2017048785 (ebook) | ISBN 9781509917150 (Epub) |
ISBN 9781509917136 (hardcover : alk. paper)

Subjects: LCSH: Law—Economic aspects—European Union countries. |
European Union countries—Economic policy. | Antitrust law—European Union countries. |
Economic policy—International cooperation.

Classification: LCC KJE6415 (print) | LCC KJE6415 .H38 2018 (ebook) | DDC 343.2407—dc23

LC record available at https://lccn.loc.gov/2017050935

Typeset by Compuscript Ltd, Shannon

To find out more about our authors and books visit www.hartpublishing.co.uk. Here you will find extracts,
author information, details of forthcoming events and the option to sign up for our newsletters.

To the 'A's of my life

PREFACE

The collaborative economy, or else sharing economy, peer (P2P) economy, access economy, gig economy, collaborative consumption, or on-demand economy, is a new socio-economic phenomenon, based on two-sided platforms, big data and the willingness to share. It has been suggested that '[t]he advent of the collaborative economy, in combination with artificial intelligence, big data and 3D printing, makes something like a fourth industrial revolution' (see Chapter 1). Indeed, the collaborative economy, which grows by the day, has all the characteristics which make economists talk of 'disruption'. Disruption also happens in the legal arena, where existing rules do not seem to cover new realities, and new rules do not seem forthcoming.

This book started off as an article proposal, back in the tumultuous summer (at least for my country and for the eurozone) of 2015. Brief research at the time had yielded no more than ten articles, all very interesting but of very little, if any, direct relevance for the EU. When I discussed the issue with the editors of the *CMLR* we agreed that I would write an article on the sharing economy and the EU 'provided that I found enough things to say'.

In the months which followed, literature went through a 'big bang': my files today contain no less than 500 articles, surveys and policy papers on the collaborative economy. Academic articles on the topic have been mushrooming in all disciplines: law, economics, political science, and even anthropology. The first regulatory measures, as well as the first judicial decisions, have been issued in the US and the EU. The EU Commission has published its 2016 Agenda on the Collaborative Economy. The first preliminary rulings have reached the CJEU and judgments both at the EU and the national level are forthcoming.

This swift development of the literature is directly connected to developments in the actual economy. In the last three years the collaborative economy has established itself, on both sides of the Atlantic, as one of the most dynamic segments of the new economy, and as a core driver of the Digital Single Market launched by the Juncker Commission. An idea which started off as a communitarian, non-monetised, sharing project has grown into a fully monetised, vibrant and, in some respects, wildly capitalistic marketplace. It has been observed that *Uber*, the biggest urban transportation company in the world, owns no vehicles and *Airbnb*, the world's largest accommodation provider, owns no real estate. Such big platforms have had time not only to establish themselves, but also to adapt and/or revise and diversify their initial strategies. These, and other, platforms have been making it into the news on a daily basis.

All the above developments have occurred in a legal vacuum, where platforms claim that established regulations are not fit for them, regulators hesitate to intervene for lack of a proper understanding of the ways this new economy operates and out of fear of stifling innovation, individuals are faced with all sorts of problems stemming from this new economy (from damage to property to violation of labour law rights) and courts are trying to square the circle by providing solutions without having the corresponding legal toolbox. As Judge Chhabria put it, in the *Lyft* litigation in California, 'in this case we must decide whether a multifaceted product of new technology should be fixed into either the old square or the old round hole of existing legal categories, when neither is a perfect fit' (see Chapter 5).

The developments discussed above, both material and bibliographic, pushed me beyond the article,[1] to the present, more ambitious, venture; always with the support of Ms S Roma.

The direct and immediate consequence of the speed with which the collaborative economy, and the corresponding literature, develop is that this book had to be written in a single stroke, within a very short period of time. A speedily developing topic needs to be dealt with in a speedy way; if not, the book would risk being otiose already at the time of its publication. Speedy writing also builds up some kind of momentum, whereby the author eats, sleeps and dreams about the collaborative economy. The downside of such time-constrained writing is that some thoughts or ideas which are briefly presented here—or indeed which are altogether missing—may need to be (further) developed elsewhere, or in a future edition of the book.

The book at hand is based on a considerable amount of primary sources—without pretending to be exhaustive—and on an extremely rich literature, mostly published from 2015 onwards. Many sources come from general and specialised newspapers, websites and blogs. Most sources come from the US, where the collaborative economy has made its debut and is more deeply rooted than in the EU. The objective of this book is to level up the European bibliography and to go some way towards meeting the rich bibliography already developed in the US. It pursues a twin ambition: firstly, in a positivist manner, to offer an overview of the issues raised by the collaborative economy under EU law and sketch the current legal position; secondly, in view of the issues thus raised and the problems identified, to discuss in a more normative manner whether some kind of regulation is desirable for the collaborative economy and, in the affirmative, of what kind and at what level. The two ambitions are intertwined and are present in all the chapters; however, the last chapter specifically addresses regulation issues.

One of the core interests, and indeed challenges, of the topic is that it touches upon most disciplines of law: contracts and torts, e-commerce and free movement,

---

[1] V Hatzopoulos and S Roma, 'Caring for Sharing? The Collaborative Economy under EU Law' (2017) 54 *CMLR* 81.

consumer protection, data protection, competition, labour and tax law, are all affected by the development of the collaborative economy. On this account it is a multi-disciplinary legal topic; as such, it offers the ground for the deduction of common, horizontal, conceptual tools and legal principles. The further challenge is that the collaborative economy is one of these economic and social phenomena happening outside and being completely unshaped by the EU; therefore, it is for the EU to respond to the issues raised without having any prior policy direction or engagement. In this the EU institutions and Member States need a good understanding of the challenges raised by the collaborative economy, and this book's ambition is to help in this direction.

More specifically, the aim of the present book is to outline, explore and analyse the way EU rules apply/may apply to the collaborative economy. Chapter 1 introduces the collaborative economy platforms and outlines their emergence, evolution, characteristics and classifications. Chapter 2 is pivotal, since it explores the contractual relationships which develop in the collaborative economy and examines the various legal qualifications (trader, consumer, prosumer etc) of the parties involved; it examines how these qualifications affect market access in the EU Member States and to what extent they fit into the existing legal framework for consumer protection. This makes for a long chapter, but the legal tools used are common and the different concepts build into one another. Chapter 3 explores the core role played by data in the matching functions of collaborative platforms and how the use of big data may be combined with data protection. In addition to the core role played by data, a further reason that made necessary a chapter dedicated to data, is the fact that an important reshuffle on the data protection rules is taking place on both sides of the Atlantic, but in opposing directions (more protection in the EU, less in the US under the Trump administration) and this may have important implications for collaborative platforms. Chapter 4 examines the way in which the existing tools of EU competition law may tackle the issues raised by the collaborative economy, and discusses the adjustments such tools may need: core concepts such as market definition, market power, concerted practices and abuse may need to be rethought if they are to adequately tackle rapidly evolving two-sided markets operating on the basis of complex algorithms. Chapter 5 sheds light—in a slightly dramatic tone—on the most contested aspect of the collaborative economy, that of employment and labour rights. Indeed, if the collaborative economy helps medium- and low-income individuals to top up their revenue by exploiting idle capacity, often the working hours and other conditions under which such 'crowdworkers' operate do not differ from those of the early industrial years. Chapter 6 tackles another hot, yet more technical, issue: that of dispute resolution of three-party online contracts, occasionally also having an offline performance. Judicial, alternative and online methods are discussed. Chapter 7 draws on all the previous chapters and discusses whether, when, how and at what level it is worth introducing fresh regulation for the collaborative economy. The core finding is that, while three years ago such a move would have seemed premature, the development of the collaborative economy has been so fast that, nowadays, most of the problems have been identified and many are ripe enough to be (self-) regulated; if not, legal uncertainty will loom and fragmentation will prevail, in an ever-expanding sector of the economy. Chapter 8 briefly concludes on more general issues about the future of the collaborative economy.

Taxation of collaborative activities, although a hot topic, and probably among the first ones likely to be tackled by regulators, has been left outside the scope of this book for two reasons. Firstly, other than VAT, all other taxes remain essentially within the remit of national policies and need not be discussed in a book that specifically aims to explore the interactions of the collaborative phenomenon with EU law. Secondly, as the European Parliament recognises in its 2016 Report on 'The Situation of Workers in the Collaborative Economy' (at 17) 'tax implications mainly concern enforcement' and bear no immediate relationship with the very design and functioning of collaborative markets. Similarly, intellectual property rights are not discussed in any detail, since they raise highly technical issues that are relevant only for some activities of the collaborative economy; therefore, they do not find their place in a general book dealing with horizontal issues.

The book is based on factual and legal developments as they stood in July 2017.

Sounion (Greece)
31 July 2017

ACKNOWLEDGEMENTS

This book has been a 'collaborative' venture and would not have existed without the contribution of my colleague Sofia Roma. Her help, support and overall input in the otherwise 'solitary' endeavour of writing, was beyond invaluable. Not only did she do most of the background research and editing, but also she did the first drafting of important pieces of the book under my guidance.

This book also owes its existence to Professor and dear friend Anne-Lise Sibony who, in one of our many extremely constructive discussions some years ago, foresaw the rocketing interest in the topic.

I would also like to thank Anne-Lise Sibony (again!) for her comments and constructive advice on Chapter 2 and Pablo Ibáñez Colomo for the same on Chapter 4—offered at very short notice. Of course, the usual disclaimer applies, and I remain solely responsible for all errors, omissions and misrepresentations.

Further, I would like to thank Sinead Moloney for her decision to embrace my proposal and include the book among Hart's titles, as well as Roberta Bassi and all the team working with her, for their support and efficient management of this project.

Last but not least, I would like to thank—and to apologise to—my two children, Aliki and Angelos, 10 and 7, for the time I have taken away from them in order to complete the writing of this book, and for the understanding, love and affection they have been giving me throughout. And, of course, as a parent, it would be counter-intuitive not to acknowledge the input of my own parents, in everything I have done, including this book.

CONTENTS

TABLE OF CASES

Chronological

AG Opinions

European Court of Human Rights (ECtHR)

World Trade Organisation (WTO)

National

Belgium:

France:

Italy:

Spain:

Germany:

Netherlands:

United Kingdom:

United States:

TABLE OF LEGISLATION

Regulations

Staff Working Documents

TABLE OF COMPETITION DECISIONS

EU Commission Decisions

Antitrust

Mergers & Acquisitions

State Aids

National Authorities Decisions

Spain:

United Kingdom:

TABLE OF GRAPHS AND FIGURES

LIST OF ABBREVIATIONS

ACCC	Australian Competition and Consumer Commission
ADR	alternative dispute resolution
AG	Advocate General
AGCM	Autorità Garante della Concorrenza e del Mercato
B2B	business-to-business
B2P	business-to-peer
B2C	business-to-consumer
BCR	Binding Corporate Rules
CEPS	Centre for European Policy Studies
CETA	Comprehensive Economic and Trade Agreement
CJEU	Court of Justice of the European Union
CPC	Central Product Classification
CRR/s	contracts that reference rivals
C2B	consumer-to-business
C2C	consumer-to-consumer
CNMC	Comisión Nacional de los Mercados y la Competencia
DCFR	Draft Common Frame of Reference
DFEH	Department of Fair Employment and Housing
DG	Directorate-General
DoJ	Department of Justice
DPD	Data Protection Directive
DSM	Digital Single Market
EC	European Community
ECHR	European Convention on Human Rights
ECtHR	European Court of Human Rights
EEA	European Economic Area
EESC	European Economic and Social Committee
EP	European Parliament

EU	European Union
FTC	Federal Trade Commission
GATS	General Agreement on Trade in Services
GC	General Court
GDPR	General Data Protection Regulation
GDS	global distribution systems
GPS	Global Positioning System
ILO	International Labour Organisation
IoT	Internet of Things
IP	Internet Protocol
IP	Intellectual Property
IPR	Intellectual Property Rights
JRC	Joint Research Centre
M&A/s	Merger/s & Acquisition/s
MEP	Member of the European Parliament
MFN	most favoured nation (clause)
MLM/s	Mobile Labour Market
MP/s	Member of the Parliament
MS	Member State
MTC	meet the competition (clause)
MTurk	Mechanical Turk
NSW	Non-standard work
NY	New York
ODR	online dispute resolution
OECD	Organisation for Economic Co-operation and Development
OFT	Office of Fair Trading
OLM/s	Online Labour Market
OTA/s	online travel agents
OS	operating systems
PHV	private hire vehicles
PNR	Passenger Name Record
P2B	peer-to-business
P2P	peer-to-peer

RMT	Rail, Maritime and Transport
RPM	resale price maintenance
SGEI/s	Services of general economic interest
SNCF	Société Nationale des Chemins de fer Français
SSNIP	Small but significant and non-transitory increase in price
T&C/s	Terms & Conditions
TFEU	Treaty on the Functioning of the European Union
TiSA	Trade in Services Agreement
TRIPS	Trade-Related Aspects of Intellectual Property Rights
TTIP	Transatlantic Trade and Investment Partnership
UCPD	Unfair Commercial Practices Directive
UK	United Kingdom
UN	United Nations
URSSAF	Unions de Recouvrement des Cotisations de Sécurité Sociale et d'Allocations Familiales
US	United States
VAT	Value Added Tax
WP	Working Party
WTD	Working Time Directive
WTO	World Trade Organisation

1

Introducing the Collaborative Economy

I. Introduction

The concept of sharing goods and services is far from novel. Neighbours have been borrowing tools, family has been lending money to each other, and friends have been hosted in friends' houses long before the emergence of the sharing/collaborative[1] economy model. What is truly innovative about the collaborative economy is the expansion of 'sharing' beyond an individual's social network or even region. The collaborative economy facilitates the connection between peers, while bypassing the traditional economic intermediaries. Hence, the collaborative model 'has progressed from a community practice into a profitable business model'.[2]

That seemingly simple concept of sharing among everyone who is willing to share has an inherent dynamism that is currently changing the global economic landscape. Within that context, '[t]he advent of the collaborative economy, in combination with artificial intelligence, big data and 3D printing, makes something like a fourth industrial revolution'.[3]

II. The Rise of the Collaborative Phenomenon

The collaborative economy is not merely an economic model, but also a cultural and social phenomenon, embodying the rise of the individual against the

---

[1] For a discussion of the terminology and the nuances thereby introduced see below under section III of the present chapter.

[2] M Böckmann, 'The Shared Economy: It is time to start caring about sharing; value creating factors in the shared economy' (2013) at 2.1, available at https://static1.squarespace.com/static/58d6cd33f5e231abb448d827/t/58ea595e1b10e3a416e8ab5b/1491753311257/bockmann-shared-economy.pdf.

[3] K Schwab, 'The Fourth Industrial Revolution: What It Means and How to Respond' *ForeignAffairs* (12 December 2015).

institutions, introducing the world to novel economic structures and ushering the economy into a new digital era. The appearance of the collaborative economy has been gestated for decades and has roots in technological, social, cultural and economic factors.

Firstly, technological evolution has been a key ingredient of this innovative model.[4] The technological boom characterising the twenty-first century is the reason that sharing on such a scale became possible in the first place. Indeed, the digital revolution is underway and is evolving fast. From online marketplaces to app distribution platforms to wikis to social media and even online dating platforms, almost all products, services and knowledge that one could possibly be seeking are only one click away. In this rapidly expanding digitised society, the peer-to-peer—or else collaborative—economy has started to take the centre stage by facilitating the exchange of information and services even more. Recent advances in digital technologies, such as the Internet of Things (IoT), 5G networks, cloud computing, data analytics and robotics have created a haven for online platforms to flourish and serve numerous different forms and functions. Thus the extensive use of mobile devices, equipped with elaborate apps and GPS-mapping in real time, facilitates the direct, efficient and quick match of goods/services supplied in any place and any time with someone's needs. The availability of intelligent, secure and user-friendly payment systems increases users' trust and the efficiency of the transaction online. Moreover, the massive spread of social media has established the culture of sharing (information, photos, position etc) to the general public and has played a connective role between peers. All these developments have ushered us into the 'Industry 4.0' era[5] and we are becoming prosumers, ie co-producing consumers, by actively participating in digital platforms and exploiting technological progress.

Secondly, the growth of the collaborative economy model draws on societal parameters. Urbanisation and high population concentration create a 'critical mass' of supply and demand and facilitate better matches. The collaborative economy also enables bypassing traditional middlepersons and taking control of meeting one's own needs. In fact, in their primary form, platforms intend to exercise no or little control and act rather as 'economical—technological coordination providers'.[6] Furthermore, as a social reaction to materialism, overconsumption and

---

[4] See eg A Sundararajan, 'Peer-to-Peer Businesses and the Sharing (Collaborative) Economy: Overview, Economic Effects and Regulatory Issues' (2014), available at www.smallbusiness.house.gov/uploadedfiles/1-15-2014_revised_sundararajan_testimony.pdf; J Hamari, M Sjöklint and A Ukkonen, 'The sharing economy: Why people participate in collaborative consumption' (2015) 67 *Journal of the Association for Information Science and Technology* 2047.

[5] Industry 4.0 'stands for machines (or robots) directly communicating with each other or with the remaining production staff'; see D Helbing, 'Economy 4.0 and Digital Society: The Participatory Market Society is Born' (December 2014) 10, available at http://ssrn.com/abstract=2539330.

[6] Hamari, Sjöklint and Ukkonen, 'The sharing economy' (2015).

an increasingly 'marketised' society,[7] the collaborative economy—based on sharing access and recycling—is characterised by environmental consciousness and awareness of the need for sustainability. Last but not least, the growth of the collaborative economy reflects society's desire for communication and connection,[8] since the idea behind this economic scheme is the facilitation of connection between strangers. An example of strengthening communities by sharing is the collaborative platform *Share Some Sugar*, a website where 'you can find someone in your neighbourhood or social network who is willing to lend you something that you need'.[9] Lastly, the phenomenon of the collaborative economy may be seen as a strong component of the more general trend of servitisation of modern economies, whereby added value is being created by combining services and products, and branding them altogether as 'new' or 'advanced' services or indeed 'experiences'.[10] Therefore, in the collaborative economy one is not just purchasing, for example, accommodation, but rather the experience of staying at a local's apartment.

Thirdly, the rise of collaborative economy was heavily influenced by the 'fall' of the conventional economic model. The global financial crisis and the rise of unemployment have created the need for flexibility and monetisation of idle resources. One of the main reasons for the enormous impact of the collaborative economy is its efficiency. Sharing absorbs idle capacity. Through collaborative platforms, idle objects and assets that are in a somewhat good shape can be shared and generate profit for their owner. From renting out an unused room, or a car when the owner is out of town, or tools that have been living in the toolbox, or books that have been read, the possibilities of sharing are endless, since one man's trash is another man's treasure. An example often used in the collaborative economy literature is the average use of an electric drill, which is being used 13 minutes per year, while remaining idle for the rest of the time.[11] Further, apart from objects and assets, collaborative platforms can utilise someone's time. 'Gig platforms' offer the opportunity to millions of unemployed or underemployed workers to trade labour for pay.

The combination of the above factors has resulted in the rapid growth of the collaborative economy. The collaborative model traces its roots to 1999, with the creation of *Couchsurfing*, an originally non-profit organisation aiming to match

---

[7] T Teubner, 'Thoughts on the Sharing Economy' (2014) 11 *Proceedings of the International Conference on e-Commerce* 322.

[8] Böckmann, 'The Shared Economy' (2013).

[9] Quote taken from the testimony of K Schwartz, founder of *Share Some Sugar*, available at www.collaborativeconsumption.com/2010/09/01/keara_schwartz_founder_of_share_some_sugar.

[10] For an overview of servitisation and its correlation with online platforms, see J Hojnik, 'The servitization of manufacturing: EU law implications and challenges' (2016) 53 *CMLR* 1575.

[11] DE Rauch and D Schleicher, 'Like Uber, But for Local Governmental Policy: The Future of Local Regulation of the "Sharing Economy"' (2015) *George Mason University Law & Economics*, Research Paper No 15-01, 14.

people who were looking for cheap travel with people who had an empty couch. Since then, it has evolved into a highly profitable multi-national corporation, has inspired the creation of *Airbnb* and has spread the 'sharing' phenomenon worldwide.

While the collaborative trend started in the United States, where there are already well-established companies in many sectors, it is now quickly spreading around Europe. The economic benefits of the collaborative economy for Europe are important, with its worth in Europe currently estimated at €28 billion and expected to increase to €570 billion by 2025.[12]

III. Definitions of the Collaborative Economy

Even though in 2011 the TIME magazine nominated 'Sharing Economy' as one of '10 ideas that will change the world'[13] there is still today great ambiguity as to what exactly this idea entails.[14] There is no universally accepted terminology, let alone definition. While the terms collaborative economy, sharing economy, peer (P2P) economy, access economy, gig economy, collaborative consumption and on-demand economy—among others—are mostly used interchangeably, it is arguable whether these notions reflect the same economic model,[15] especially given the plurality and diversity of the activities and the various forms that the 'sharing' scheme may take.[16]

For the purposes of the present book, the term 'collaborative economy' is preferred for three main reasons. Firstly, the term 'collaborative economy' is broader in terms of scope than the term 'sharing economy'. 'The collaborative economy refers to an economic model that focuses on providing access to products and services through renting, trading, or sharing instead of traditional ownership. The sharing economy is a subset of the collaborative economy that focuses solely on

---

[12] See *PwC*, 'Europe's five key sharing economy sectors could deliver €570 billion by 2025' (27 June 2016), available at http://press.pwc.com/News-releases/europe-s-five-key-sharing-economy-sectors-could-deliver--570-billion-by-2025/s/45858e92-e1a7-4466-a011-a7f6b9bb488f.

[13] B Walsh, 'Today's smart choice: Don't own. Share' *Time* (17 March 2011).

[14] For the linguistic history of the term 'sharing', see Teubner, 'Thoughts on the Sharing Economy' (2014) 323.

[15] R Botsman, 'Defining the Sharing Economy: What Is Collaborative Consumption—And What Isn't?' *Fast Company* (27 May 2015), available at www.fastcoexist.com/3046119/defining-the-sharing-economy-what-is-collaborative-consumption-and-what-isnt. Botsman argues that the term 'collaborative economy' reflects '[a]n economic system of decentralized networks and marketplaces that unlocks the value of underused assets by matching needs and haves, in ways that bypass traditional middlemen', such as *Etsy, Kickstarter, TaskRabbit* etc, while 'sharing economy' can be defined as '[a]n economic system based on sharing underused assets or services, for free or for a fee, directly from individuals', thus including platforms such as *Airbnb, BlaBlaCar, Cohealo* etc. She further distinguishes the terms 'collaborative consumption' and 'on-demand services'.

[16] For which see the various scenarios in Ch 2 below.

the outright sharing of assets'.[17] Thus, the more restricted term 'sharing economy' would exclude prominent platforms, such as *Uber*, which facilitate transportation services other than ride-sharing per se. Secondly, the 'sharing' business model has progressed so much in the last few years, and so much economic value has been gained by some 'sharing' platforms,[18] that the term 'sharing' has been characterised as a '"misnomer" employed to mask the essentially commercial nature of the activity on these platforms' and as a term which 'frames technology-enabled transactions as if they were altruistic or community endeavours'.[19] In other words, '[i]t has become a well-worn truism that little, if any, actual sharing occurs in the "sharing economy"'.[20] In order to take into account these developments, which in my view do not diminish the novelty or the interest of this emerging economy, I avoid the use of the term 'sharing' and opt instead for the use of 'collaborative', which is more ideologically-neutral. Thirdly, the term 'collaborative economy' is in line with the approach of the European Commission and relevant documentation, which are discussed throughout this work.

Apart from terminology, definition of this economy and framing of what it encompasses is no easy endeavour.[21] The definitions suggested by academia and institutions range from extremely broad,[22] which fail to offer sufficient delineation, to extremely narrow,[23] which exclude any business-to-peer transaction, such as through *ZipCar* and *Toys4rent*, or any transaction regarding non-physical assets.[24]

Early definitions focused on the non-commercial nature of the transactions, which were initially based more on social relations and less on monetary value,[25] while the most prominent definitions put emphasis on: (a) gaining access to goods

---

[17] W Chang, 'Growing Pains: The Role of Regulation in the Collaborative Economy' (2015) 9(1) *Intersect: The Stanford Journal of Science, Technology, and Society* 3.

[18] In December 2015 *Uber* was valued at US$62.5 billion, while in November of the same year *Airbnb* was valued at US$25.5 billion; it is also worth noting that incumbent industries have heavily invested into 'sharing' platforms; thus eg *General Motors* has invested more than US$500 million on *Uber's* competitor *Lyft*, and *Expedia* has taken over *Airbnb's* competitor *HomeAway* for US$3.9 billion; see US Federal Trade Commission (FTC) Staff Report, 'The "Sharing" Economy: Issues Facing Platforms, Participants and Regulators' (2016) 12 available at www.ftc.gov/reports/sharing-economy-issues-facing-platforms-participants-regulators-federal-trade-commission.

[19] ibid 10, with references to several articles from the daily press.

[20] J Infranca, 'Intermediary Institutions and the Sharing Economy' (2016) 90 *Tulane Law Review Online* 29, 30.

[21] For a thorough research on existing definitions of this new economy see S Oh and JY Moon, 'Calling for a shared understanding of the "sharing economy"' (2016) Proceedings of the 18th Annual International Conference on Electronic Commerce: e-Commerce in Smart connected World, Article No 35, available at http://dl.acm.org/citation.cfm?id=2971638&dl=ACM&coll=DL.

[22] See eg the activities included under the 'sharing' umbrella according to the pro-sharing organisation 'People who Share', at www.thepeoplewhoshare.com/blog/what-is-the-sharing-economy.

[23] K Frenken et al, 'Smarter regulation for the sharing economy' *The Guardian* (20 May 2015).

[24] ibid.

[25] On the emerging economy with regard to copyright see L Lessig, *Remix: Making Art and Commerce Thrive in the Hybrid Economy* (New York, The Penguin Press, 2008).

and services through sharing, bartering or renting, instead of owning;[26] (b) the creation of value through sharing facilitated by technology;[27] and (c) the innovative business model of sharing underused products and capital resources as 'crowd-based capitalism'.[28]

Thus, indicatively the 'sharing economy' has been defined as an 'econom[y] that operate[s] without money changing hands and whose goal, by and large, is not to make its participants rich';[29] as 'an economic model that has massified and commoditized ideas of collaboration and sharing to redistribute underutilized assets';[30] as 'an economic system in which assets or services are shared between private individuals, either free or for a fee, typically by means of the Internet',[31] and the list goes on.

This lack of a commonly agreed upon definition is especially problematic within the European context, since a coordinated approach between the Commission and the Member States is essential in order to avoid fragmentation of regulation across EU borders. On the above basis, the Commission opted for a rather pragmatic, if broad, approach to the definition of the term 'collaborative economy'. In its 2016 EU Agenda for the Collaborative Economy,[32] it states that the term

refers to business models where activities are facilitated by collaborative platforms that create an open marketplace for the temporary usage of goods or services often provided by private individuals. The collaborative economy involves three categories of actors: (i) service providers who share assets, resources, time and/or skills—these can be private individuals offering services on an occasional basis ('peers') or service providers acting in their professional capacity ('professional services providers'); (ii) users of these; and (iii) intermediaries that connect—via an online platform—providers with users and that facilitate transactions between them ('collaborative platforms'). Collaborative economy transactions generally do not involve a change of ownership and can be carried out for profit or not-for-profit.[33]

---

[26] R Botsman and R Rogers, *What's Mine Is Yours: How Collaborative Consumption Is Changing the Way We Live* (London, HarperCollins, 2011); see also by the same authors, 'Beyond Zipcar: Collaborative Consumption' (2010) *Harvard Business Review*, available at https://hbr.org/2010/10/beyond-zipcar-collaborative-consumption.

[27] L Gansky, *The Mesh: Why the Future of Business is Sharing* (New York, Portfolio Penguin, 2010).

[28] A Sundararajan, *The Sharing Economy: The End of Employment and the Rise of Crowd-Based Capitalism* (Cambridge, MIT Press, 2016).

[29] NA John, 'Sharing and Web 2.0: The emergence of a keyword' (2013) 15 *New Media & Society* 167.

[30] EE Erving, 'The Sharing Economy: Exploring the Intersection of Collaborative Consumption and Capitalism' (2014) Scripps College, Scripps Senior Theses, Paper No 409, available at http://scholarship.claremont.edu/scripps_theses/409/.

[31] See the definition given by English Oxford Living Dictionaries, available at https://en.oxforddictionaries.com/definition/sharing_economy.

[32] Communication from the Commission, 'A European Agenda for the collaborative economy', COM(2016) 356 final; the various ideas introduced by this Communication are discussed in the relevant chapters of this book, while a horizontal evaluation of this initiative is proposed in Ch 7.

[33] ibid at 1; it should be noted that in 2015 the Commission had defined the collaborative economy as 'a complex ecosystem of on-demand services and temporary use of assets based on exchanges via online platforms'; see Commission Communication, 'Upgrading the Single Market: More opportunities for people and business', COM(2015) 550 final at 2.1.

The Commission has implicitly offered further guidance on which platforms belong, in its view, in the collaborative economy by contrast and comparison with other online platforms; in that regard, it provided an indicative list of examples of online platforms which are differentiated from collaborative ones:

> Typical examples [of online platforms] include general internet search engines (e.g. Google, Bing), specialised search tools (e.g. Google Shopping, Kelkoo, Twenga, Google Local, TripAdvisor, Yelp,), location-based business directories or some maps (e.g. Google or Bing Maps), news aggregators (e.g. Google News), online market places (e.g. Amazon, eBay, Allegro, Booking.com), audio-visual and music platforms (e.g. Deezer, Spotify, Netflix, Canal play, Apple TV), video sharing platforms (e.g. YouTube, Dailymotion), payment systems (e.g. PayPal, Apple Pay), social networks (e.g. Facebook, Linkedin, Twitter, Tuenti), app stores (e.g. Apple App Store, Google Play) or collaborative economy platforms (e.g. AirBnB, Uber, Taskrabbit, Bla-bla car).[34]

For present purposes, the Commission's above definition of the collaborative economy will be followed and refined, as necessary. Hence, the term 'collaborative economy' will encompass those stricto sensu collaborative economy platforms, which facilitate: (a) access, as opposed to transfer of ownership; and (b) the conclusion of a transaction (contract) between two other parties (a tripartite relationship); (c) which parties are mostly—but not exclusively[35]—peers, regardless of whether these are prosumers or service providers. For the purposes of the present book, even when a transaction involves the (provisional) delivery of a good, it will be called a 'service', consisting in making possible (through lending, renting, exchanging or else) the use of the given good. As put elsewhere '[s]haring is contrary to ownership. As a consequence, Sharing Economy companies transform anything into a service'.[36]

In view of the above definition, e-commerce platforms such as *eBay* or *Etsy* do not fall within the scope of the present book, since they promote transfer of material ownership. Further, content provider platforms, such as *Spotify*, *Netflix*[37]

---

[34] See European Commission, Open consultation on the '[r]egulatory environment for platforms, online intermediaries, data and cloud computing and the collaborative economy' (2016) 5, available at https://ec.europa.eu/digital-single-market/en/news/public-consultation-regulatory-environment-platforms-online-intermediaries-data-and-cloud. The Commission has not yet reached a conclusion on the definition of online platforms.

[35] Incumbents are steadily getting involved and are starting to establish themselves in the collaborative economy. Thus, businesses become more and more active in collaborative platforms, and are changing the groups' dynamics. Therefore, the characteristic of 'peer' economy could be misleading, as it is slowly fading in favour of an escalating presence of businesses, professionals and incumbents in the collaborative economy.

[36] V Demary, 'Competition in the Sharing Economy' (2015) *Cologne Institute for Economic Research*, IW Policy Paper No 19, 14, available at www.iwkoeln.de/en/studies/beitrag/vera-demary-competition-in-the-sharing-economy-235445.

[37] If direct interaction between multiple sides of users is necessary for defining a multi-sided platform, then businesses such as *Netflix* cannot be considered as such; see A Hagiu and J Wright, 'Marketplace or Reseller?' (2014) 61 *Management Science* 184.

and *YouTube* will not be considered as part of the collaborative economy, since no contract is concluded between the peers.[38] Platforms where content is shared by third parties who do not own and/or do not have the right to share such content (eg *LimeWire, BitTorrent*) will not be discussed, as besides the questions discussed in the present book, such platforms may be plainly illegal, as they raise acute copyright issues. Social media will be excluded as well, since even though they connect peers, the objective of such platforms is fundamentally different to that of 'collaborative' ones, and thus any element of transaction is absent from the former. Similarly, platforms promoting traditional, already established businesses, as comparison websites (*Booking.com, TripAdvisor* etc) do for restaurants, hotels etc, are outside the scope of the present book, which aims to explore the innovative phenomenon of the peer-centric economy. Finally, *Wikis* will also be excluded, since they only convey information and do not entail the temporary use of any good or service.[39]

IV. Main Characteristics of the Collaborative Economy

A. Online Platforms' Intermediation

The collaborative economy becomes a reality through the connecting role of collaborative platforms. The latter belong in the extended family of online platforms, ie broadly speaking, digital businesses that provide a meeting place for two or more different (groups of) users over the Internet.[40] What qualifies as an online platform is a hotly debated issue, with the Commission defining one as 'an undertaking operating in two (or multi)-sided markets, which uses the Internet to enable interactions between two or more distinct but interdependent groups of users so as to generate value for at least one of the groups'.[41] It has further noted that '[c]ertain platforms also qualify as Intermediary service providers'.[42]

---

[38] This is in line with the Commission's view, according to which *Netflix* is not a two-sided platform but rather 'a retailer of films because there is no direct interaction between buyers and sellers and no affiliation costs on either side'; see also B Martins, 'An economic policy perspective on online platforms' (2016) *JRC Technical Reports, Institute for prospective technological studies*, Digital economy Working Paper No 5, 15; the inclusion of *Netflix* in the list of online platform examples has also been questioned in the UK House of Lords, 'Online Platforms and the Digital Single Market' (2016) 10th Report of Session 2015–16, paras 55–58. For an overview of the *Netflix* phenomenon, see L Davies, 'Netflix and the Coalition for an Open Internet' in D Smith-Rowsey (ed), *The Netflix Effect: Technology and Entertainment in the 21st Century* (New York, Bloomsbury Academic, 2016).

[39] Occasional reference to the above will be made for reasons of comparison or analogy with collaborative platforms.

[40] See the UK House of Lords, 'Online Platforms and the Digital Single Market' (2016) para 1.

[41] In the context of its open consultation on the '[r]egulatory environment for platforms, online intermediaries, data and cloud computing and the collaborative economy' (2016) 5.

[42] The terminology chosen is somehow puzzling, since it is not clear whether the Commission consciously opts for the narrower term of intermediary service provider as within the meaning of

As online platforms, collaborative platforms bear all the characteristics of the former, ie the multi-sided nature of the market, the purpose of intermediation and the interdependence (through network effects) between the groups of users.[43]

i. Multi-sided Markets

Online platforms are multi-sided markets. Examples of offline multi-sided models are markets (shopping malls and stock exchange) or newspapers printing classified ads; they gather both sellers and buyers at the same place, thus facilitating their direct interaction. Similarly, in the digital context, different groups of users are brought together by the platform operator in order to facilitate an interaction between them (eg exchange of information, a commercial transaction, a social connection etc). Depending on the platform's business model and objective, users can be buyers of products or services, sellers, advertisers, software developers, and so on.

While many theories and definitions of multi-sided markets have been expressed by economic theorists,[44] for present purposes the following definition will be followed: a multi-sided market has 'a) two or more groups of customers, b) who need each other in some way, c) but who cannot capture the value from their mutual attraction on their own; and d) rely on the catalyst (platform) to facilitate value creating transactions between them'.[45]

Arts 12–14 (mere conduit, cashing and hosting) of the E-Commerce Directive (European Parliament and Council Directive 2000/31/EC of 8 June 2000 on certain legal aspects of information society services, in particular electronic commerce, in the Internal Market [2000] OJ L 178/1), or whether it means that some online platforms (or some activities of the one platform) cannot even qualify as information society service providers in the first place. For an analysis of when a collaborative platform qualifies as an information society service provider see Ch 2 below.

[43] The Commission has also identified some further key characteristics that online platforms share: the capacity to facilitate, and extract value, from direct interactions or transactions between users; the ability to collect, use and process a large amount of personal and non-personal data; the capacity to create and benefit from 'network effects'; the ability to create and shape new markets and also disrupt traditional ones through the participation of individuals and the processing of information; and reliance on information technology as the means to achieve all of the above. See Commission Staff Working Document, 'Online Platforms' SWD(2016) 172 final, at 2.1.

[44] The literature on multi-sided markets is very rich; see inter alia pioneers JC Rochet and J Tirole, 'Platform Competition in Two-Sided Markets' (2003) 1 *Journal of the European Economic Association* 990; by the same authors, 'Two-Sided Markets: A Progress Report' (2006) 37 *The RAND Journal of Economics* 645; D Evans and R Schmalensee, 'The Antitrust Analysis of Multi-sided Platform Businesses' (2012) *National Bureau of Economic Research*, Working Paper No 18783, available at http://chicagounbound.uchicago.edu/cgi/viewcontent.cgi?article=1482&context=law_and_economics; G Weyl, 'A Price Theory of Multi-Sided Platforms' (2010) 100 *American Economic Review* 1642; Organisation for Economic Co-operation and Development (OECD), 'Two-Sided Markets' (2009) DAF/COMP 20; D Evans (ed), 'Platform Economics: Essays on Multi-Sided Businesses' (2011) Competition Policy International (CPI), available at http://ssrn.com/abstract=1974020; D Auer and N Petit, 'Two-Sided Markets and the Challenge of Turning Economic Theory into Antitrust Policy' (2015) 60 *The Antitrust Bulletin* 426; for further literature and analysis on multi-sided platforms see Ch 4 below.

[45] Evans and Schmalenese, 'The Antitrust Analysis of Multi-sided Platform Businesses' (2012) 7.

Further, a multi-sided market may be defined with regard to its price structure. In multi-sided markets, the price structure is non-neutral in the sense that '[a] market is two-sided if the platform can affect the volume of transactions by charging more to one side of the market and reducing the price paid by the other side by an equal amount; in other words, the price structure matters, and platforms must design it so as to bring both sides on board'.[46] In other words, multi-sided markets create value by coordinating multiple groups of users and by ensuring that there are enough 'players' on each side.

ii. Network Effects—Externalities

Network effects, based on interdependence between the groups of users, are arguably the most important characteristic of platforms. Cross-market effects are created through the connection of distinct groups of users. Utility and demand of users on one side of the market are (generally) positively linked to utility and demand of users on another side of the market. Two types of network effects are produced in multi-sided markets; direct and indirect.

Direct network effects work within each group, in the sense that consumers or suppliers are influenced by the presence of other consumers or suppliers respectively. Users are attracted by the opportunity for social interaction with each other, as is the case with social networks. Potential *Facebook* users may be more inclined to join the platform if more people they know are already on *Facebook*. Inversely, any additional user will enhance the experience of all existing users. Similarly, and more importantly, consumers are generally attracted by the presence of other consumers. For example, buyers on *Amazon* bookstore benefit from other buyers' experience, through the recommendations lists compiled on the basis of previous purchases.

Negative network effects may also occur: while the presence of multiple suppliers typically increases the quality and quantity of products or services offered through the platform, thus making the platform more attractive to prospective consumers, the competition between the suppliers may create negative network effects within the group of suppliers.

Indirect network effects accrue between—as opposed to within—the different (groups of) users of the platform and can be explained with the 'chicken and egg' metaphor: more buyers attract more sellers. The market becomes more valuable for each group of users when there are more users on the other group. Therefore, the role of the platform is to gather as many users as possible at both ends. Accordingly, the value of the platform increases not only when it has attracted many consumers, but also when it has many suppliers. Two types of indirect network effects (externalities) have been identified by economists: usage externalities and membership externalities.[47] *Usage externalities* exist when two types of users gain

---

[46] Rochet and Tirole, 'Two-Sided Markets: A Progress Report' (2006) 648.
[47] See Rochet and Tirole (2006) (n 44).

more value from using the platform to find matches and conclude a transaction with the other side. For instance, those seeking short-term accommodation on *Airbnb* gain value from finding those offering short-term accommodation on the platform and from eventually achieving the match. *Membership externalities* exist when the users on the one side gain more value when the number of users on the other side increases.[48] For example, advertisers gain more value the more consumers are on the other side of the market, since in that way their 'audience', and hence pool of prospective customers, is greater.

In order to achieve an effective balance between the interdependent groups of users, the platform, more often than not, will charge more on one side of the market while reducing the price paid by the other side of users by an equal amount.[49] Thus, indirect network effects result in the non-neutral price structure of the multi-sided market: '[n]etwork effects generate externalities: the user gets more (or less) than what he pays for. As a result, prices no longer correspond to actual benefits or costs. The price paid for access to the network no longer matches the marginal cost or marginal benefit of joining it.'[50] For example, several credit cards are offered to consumers for free, while the cost of issuing and managing credit cards is shouldered by the merchants.

Given that every group of users creates externalities, both direct and indirect, for the other users of the platform, the platform's role is to internalise such externalities, thus increasing its own value and that of (at least one group of) its users.

iii. Matching through Algorithms

As already noted above, the core role of an online platform (or, indeed, any multi-sided market) is to bring together the different groups of users it attracts. It plays an intermediary role. It creates value by connecting distinct groups of users and reducing interaction costs among those. Without the aid of the platform, the different types of users (eg suppliers and consumers) would find it (more) difficult and particularly costly to even find each other, let alone conclude transactions.

What is more, in digital platforms the pools of users on each side are exponentially greater, thus increasing the possibilities of better matches. Matching in the digital context is facilitated by matching or search algorithms, in which platforms must invest in order to increase their value; the more efficient and effective the matching, the more users will be attracted to the platform. Algorithms, therefore, are not only used by general search engines, such as *Google*. Specialised algorithms are also used by platforms, such as *Amazon*, *eBay*, *Facebook*, *Booking.com*, *Airbnb*, and so on, for providing search rankings and recommendations according to the consumers'/users' preferences within the site or more general profile.

---

[48] Evans and Schmalenese (2012) (n 44) 11.
[49] Rochet and Tirole (2006) (n 44).
[50] Martins, 'An economic policy perspective on online platforms' (2016) 11.

The results of the algorithms' matching (often) appear in search rankings, which have become the main tool to facilitate online matching. Two issues are highlighted with regard to search rankings: firstly, search rankings inherently entail the 'superstar economics' effect, which may lead to lock-in of popular products. Consumers tend to look at and trust only the higher-ranked products, which means that popular products tend to become even more popular. This practice may give an (excessive) advantage to popular products, which may even lead to monopoly-like situations and increases in those products' prices. Secondly, 'search rankings may not necessarily reflect user preferences'.[51] While consumers would expect 'natural' or 'organic' search results, according to their query, the neutrality of the search results may be compromised, if not absent. For example, 'paid placements' and promotion of own products[52] may mislead consumers, as may any 'editing' of the results by the platform. Further, the criteria for the matching or recommendations or search ranking often lack the transparency needed.

Last but not least, the matching role of platforms is more efficient with the aggregation and analysis of data. Thus, platforms collect information about products and consumers' preferences in order to provide the most matchable results and thus improve the users' experience. Since matching through algorithms reduces search (transaction) costs and the more the information the better the matching, it follows that the input of large amount of data in platforms (algorithms) reduces the search costs for users.

iv. All-importance of Data

The 'datafication' of all aspects of life, and the aggregation of large amounts of data has led to talk of a 'big data revolution'. Online platforms observe and collect personal data, concerning the age, gender, residence, employment, professional capacities and qualifications, dietary or other preferences, health conditions, medications, economic details and much more of both the users and the providers of collaborative services. They also observe and collect data on the users' commercial and other behaviour or even acquire data from data brokers. Indeed, their function is to match the needs of the former with the goods/services on offer from the latter. The more information they possess, the better the matches they provide.[53] Thus, the aggregation of information by platforms puts them at a competitive advantage. This advantage is expressed in the form of information asymmetries towards both the suppliers and the final consumers.[54]

---

[51] Martins (n 38) 22.

[52] Such a behaviour may violate antitrust laws, in the form of abuse of dominance, as seen in the Commission's decision to fine *Google* €2.42 billion for giving an illegal advantage to its own products, namely its comparison shopping service. This is further discussed in terms of competition law in Ch 4 below.

[53] In this sense, under EU data protection legislation (for which see Ch 3 below), they are 'data controllers'—in that they command the type of data processing that should be done—and are typically also 'data processors', in that they do the processing themselves.

[54] For the solution to the problem of information asymmetries see Ch 7 below.

Moreover, personal data are not only collected and used by the platform, but are also traded to advertisers or other online platforms. Personal data have a value of their own. In this context, while participation in online platforms, such as *Facebook* or *Airbnb*, is seemingly free of charge, personal data are input in the platform by the individual as an exchange for the platform's services. Data therefore becomes a form of 'currency'.[55]

The issues raised by data collection and process under EU data protection and competition law are discussed below in Chapters 3 and 4 respectively.

B. Peer-to-peer Transactions

Most collaborative endeavours reflect transactions between individuals (peer-to-peer), connected through digital platforms.[56] This means three things: firstly, that individuals have the opportunity to bypass traditional middlepersons and assume control for having their own needs met; secondly, that one's social network is endlessly expanded, since collaborative platforms allow for total strangers to share rides, meals, rooms etc; and thirdly, that the roles of consumers and suppliers are entirely revisited. The relationship between buyers and sellers as we know it is disrupted. Consequently, the persons formerly known as 'consumers' can now get what they need from each other, while detracting control and value away from big centralised firms. As already mentioned above, however, though the collaborative economy may still be peer-centric, its identity is undergoing a shift. Traditional businesses and professionals become increasingly involved in the collaborative economy by supplying their services therein as well, a tendency which is likely to gain in momentum once the collaborative economy is properly regulated.[57]

C. Shift from Ownership to Accessibility

A key characteristic of the novel scheme of the collaborative economy is the shift from ownership to accessibility.[58] During the last decade, the focus of individuals has shifted from gathering assets to gathering experiences, so the value of assets

---

[55] This was acknowledged in the Commission, 'Proposal for a Directive of the European Parliament and of the Council on certain aspects concerning contracts for the supply of digital content' COM(2015) 634 final; the draft Digital Content Directive introduces the concept of 'freemium' and recognises that personal data given to a platform may constitute 'remuneration' for the services thereby provided, thus bringing the whole transaction under the EU rules on services (Art 56 TFEU ff). See Ch 3 below.

[56] Although business-to-peer transactions, such as *Zipcar*, may also be included in the 'collaborative economy' family.

[57] S Miller, 'First Principles for Regulating the Sharing Economy' (2016) 53 *Harvard Journal on Legislation* 147, 164.

[58] While some argue that transactions that transfer ownership may still be included in the 'collaborative economy umbrella', such as *eBay*, *Etsy* etc.

is decreasing, while at the same time the value of access to goods and services is increasing.

Through sharing, individuals gain access to expensive and luxury goods, which suddenly become affordable. Thus, the collaborative economy opens new profit markets for new customer groups and businesses and allows for a more effective use of resources. It further represents an innovative complement to a production economy in the form of a use-based economy. It also offers a way out of the economic and financial crisis, by enabling people to exchange things for others that they need.

D. Reputation Rating Mechanisms—Self Regulation

Ebay established, more than 15 years ago, a digital 'reputation system' which allows buyers and sellers to provide feedback on their transactions. This peer-review system has been exceptionally useful in the collaborative economy, since it diminishes the inherent risks of dealing with the unknown and distant individual, bypasses the reputation mechanism of businesses, and increases trust among users. Reputation rating mechanisms are just one, of several, means of self-regulation which are available to collaborative platforms. These are further discussed in Chapter 7 below.

V. Market Sectors

The collaborative economy has been developing at a galloping pace in the last few years to cover every imaginable economic activity.[59] In some areas it has already attained some degree of maturity (see section A below), while in others its potential remains to materialise (see section B).

A. Main Market Sectors

i. Transportation

Urban transportation through collaborative businesses could take various forms, namely car rental, ride-sharing, car-sharing, driving services, bicycle sharing and so forth. Platforms such as *Turo* and *Getaround* allow individuals—car

---

[59] For a collaborative economy sector-based graphic see J Owyang, 'Honeycomb 3.0: The Collaborative Economy Market Expansion' (2016) available at www.web-strategist.com/blog/2016/03/10/honeycomb-3-0-the-collaborative-economy-market-expansion-sxsw; see also an interesting 'Collaborative Consumption Directory' on the basis of sector, location or business model, available at www.collaborativeconsumption.com/directory/.

owners—to become entrepreneurs by offering their own vehicles to their peers as short-term car rentals, and allow people who need a car to rent one per hour or per day from others nearby. *Zimride* connects people from the same school, university, company, etc who can *share a ride* to/from the same location. *Zimride* sells ride-share networks to organisations, such as universities and companies and offers free membership for passengers/users; thus it becomes a service offered by institutions to their workers, students etc. Platforms such as *Uber* and *Lyft* allow individuals who own a car (outside the taxi industry) to provide *driving services* (or share their cars) in point-to-point chauffeured urban transportation, for a fee. Last but not least, *BlaBlaCar* allows people who are travelling to some long-distance destination to find passengers with whom to share their ride and its cost; they offer ride-sharing services. From all the above models and players, *Uber* is by far the most important, and the one which has provoked the most controversy in different jurisdictions.

ii. Accommodation

Airbnb is undoubtedly one of the most popular collaborative businesses. It currently operates in 191 countries, counting more than 160 million users.[60] *Airbnb* allows individuals to become entrepreneurs by offering part or all of their living space to their peers as short-term accommodation. Thus visitors (consumers), instead of participating in the traditional hotel industry or in regions with no hotel presence,[61] may choose to pay to be hosted at an individual's home. Rates are determined by hosts (suppliers) and *Airbnb* withholds a charging fee per transaction.[62] *Airbnb* allows peers to list on the platform a spare room in their home, an empty apartment, a house they don't use, a boat, or even a tree-house. Furthermore, in November 2016 *Airbnb* expanded its company profile by allowing individuals to provide local tours and experiences, along with accommodation, on the platform. So far it exercises minimal regulatory control,[63] depending mostly on some identification procedures and an online reputation system (rating stars).[64]

Similarly, collaborative businesses such as *Couchsurfing* or home-swap platforms (eg *HomeExchange*) promote short-term accommodation at private individuals' homes (or just couches), but without payment for the accommodation per se.

---

[60] See *Airbnb*, 'About Us' at www.Airbnb.com/about/about-us?locale=en; up from 60 million one year earlier.

[61] Interestingly enough '76% of Airbnb properties are outside the main hotel districts', suggesting complementarity of collaborative and incumbent businesses; see G Zervas, D Proserpio and J Byers, 'The rise of the sharing economy: Estimating the impact of Airbnb on the hotel industry' (2016) *Boston University School of Management*, Research Paper No 2013-16, 2.

[62] ibid 8.

[63] For the legal battles that *Airbnb* is dealing with, see Ch 7 below.

[64] Note, though, that following complaints about racism and discrimination against potential visitors, *Airbnb* is also embracing a non-discrimination policy; see *Airbnb*, 'Airbnb's Nondiscrimination Policy: Our Commitment to Inclusion and Respect', available at www.airbnb.com/help/article/1405/airbnb-s-nondiscrimination-policy--our-commitment-to-inclusion-and-respect.

These platforms usually charge a membership fee[65] to the platform and connect those interested.

iii. Freelance Labour

The collaborative economy—also referred to as 'gig economy'—offers unemployed or underemployed people the opportunity to trade labour for pay. 'Crowdworkers' may engage in a myriad of tasks or services provided online, such as writing, designing logos or translating documents on platforms such as *Fiverr*, *MechanicalTurk*, *Upwork* and *Freelancer*; alternatively they may perform errands or tasks offline, on a local basis, such as dog sitting on *DogVacay*, assembling furniture on *AskforTask* or watering the neighbour's lawn on *Taskrabbit*.

Moreover, apart from working in exchange for pay, some collaborative platforms, such as *Skillharbour*, operate as 'time banks', by facilitating the exchange of services between peers in a non-monetary relation. Individuals can pool and trade time and skills, bypassing money as a measure of value. Everyone's time and work is valued equally, and one hour of work equals one time-dollar: an individual could clean a garden in exchange for a massage, or teach a yoga class in exchange for learning Portuguese. Almost any skill is an asset and could be traded for another skill in this time-based model. 'Crowdworking' is further analysed in Chapter 5 below.

iv. Finance

Collaborative platforms also engage in financial services, such as crowdfunding and fundraising, money lending, investing, virtual currencies, etc, the most popular among which is crowdfunding. Crowdfunding platforms (eg *Kickstarter* and *Indiegogo*) facilitate raising monetary contributions through a campaign, with the objective of funding someone's project, venture or idea. Crowdfunding has been used to fund both for-profit entrepreneurial ventures, artistic and creative projects and non-profit or community-oriented social projects.

In a 2014 Communication specifically addressing crowdfunding, the Commission distinguished three main forms of crowdfunding,[66] while two years later, in a Staff Working Document, this number had gone up to five.[67] These are: (a) investment-based crowdfunding, in which companies issue equity or debt instruments to crowd-investors through a platform; (b) lending-based crowdfunding, also known as crowdlending, in which companies or individuals seek to

---

[65] While registration at *Couchsurfing* is free, verification of users comes upon payment of an annual fee; see https://support.couchsurfing.org/hc/en-us/articles/214633027-Verification-Payment-Questions.

[66] Communication from the Commission, 'Unleashing the potential of Crowdfunding in the European Union', COM(2014) 172 final.

[67] Commission Staff Working Document, 'Crowdfunding in the EU Capital Markets Union', SWD(2016) 154 final.

obtain funds from the public through platforms in the form of a loan agreement; (c) invoice trading crowdfunding, whereby businesses sell unpaid invoices and receivables, individually or in bundle, to a pool of investors through an online platform; (d) reward based crowdfunding, also known as crowd sponsoring, where individuals donate to a project or business with expectations of receiving in return a symbolic or else non-financial reward, at a later stage; and (e) donation based crowdfunding, where individuals donate amounts to meet a larger funding aim of a specific charitable project while receiving no financial or material return. From the above, forms (d) and (e) are closest to the 'sharing' ideal, although they do not entail stricto sensu a temporary transfer of ownership, but rather a definitive one. The other three forms do entail some kind of temporary transfer of ownership (of the funds), but are more 'to be seen as one part of the broader universe of financial technology innovations (FinTech)'[68] rather than as part of the 'collaborative economy'. As the Commission itself notes,[69] the relevant EU regulatory framework includes: the Directives on Prospectus,[70] Payment Services,[71] Markets in Financial Instruments,[72] Capital Requirements (CRD IV),[73] Alternative Investment Fund Managers,[74] Consumer Credit[75] and Distance Marketing of Financial Services[76] and the Regulations on Capital Requirements,[77] European Venture

---

[68] ibid 12.

[69] COM(2014) 172 final, 7.

[70] European Parliament and Council Directive 2003/71/EC of 4 November 2003 on the prospectus to be published when securities are offered to the public or admitted to trading and amending Directive 2001/34/EC [2003] OJ L 345/64.

[71] European Parliament and Council Directive 2007/64/EC of 13 November 2007 on payment services in the internal market amending Directives 97/7/EC, 2002/65/EC, 2005/60/EC and 2006/48/EC and repealing Directive 97/5/EC (Payment Services Directive) [2007] OJ L319/1. The Payment Services Directive might apply also to crowd-sponsoring, where the business model adopted is such that it falls under the scope of this instrument.

[72] European Parliament and Council Directive 2004/39/EC of 21 April 2004 on markets in financial instruments amending Council Directives 85/611/EEC and 93/6/EEC and Directive 2000/12/EC of the European Parliament and of the Council and repealing Council Directive 93/22/EEC [2004] OJ L 145/1.

[73] European Parliament and Council Directive 2013/36/EU of 26 June 2013 on access to the activity of credit institutions and the prudential supervision of credit institutions and investment firms, amending Directive 2002/87/EC and repealing Directives 2006/48/EC and 2006/49/EC [2013] OJ L176/338.

[74] European Parliament and Council Directive 2011/61/EU of 8 June 2011 on Alternative Investment Fund Managers and amending Directives 2003/41/EC and 2009/65/EC and Regulations (EC) No 1060/2009 and (EU) No 1095/2010 [2011] OJ L 174/1.

[75] European Parliament and Council Directive 2008/48/EC of 23 April 2008 on credit agreements for consumers and repealing Council Directive 87/102/EEC [2008] OJ L133/66.

[76] European Parliament and Council Directive 2002/65/EC of 23 September 2002 concerning the distance marketing of consumer financial services and amending Council Directive 90/619/EEC and Directives 97/7/EC and 98/27/EC [2002] OJ L271/16.

[77] European Parliament and Council Regulation (EU) No 575/2013 of 26 June 2013 on prudential requirements for credit institutions and investment firms and amending Regulation (EU) No 648/2012 [2013] OJ L176/1.

Capital and European Social Entrepreneurship Funds.[78] The technicalities of these instruments surpass the scope of the present book and this is why crowdfunding is only exceptionally discussed in the remainder of the book.

B. Up-and-Coming Market Sectors

i. Energy

'The sharing economy is coming to the power industry. In the future, we may buy energy from each other, just as we now rent homes from each other on Airbnb'.[79] The collaborative economy has been active in 'sharing' utilities since its early stages, especially with the distribution among peers of wi-fi, through platforms such as *Fon* and *Open Garden*. This has paved the way for initiatives of 'sharing' in the energy sector. The global energy system is built on the basis that supply must follow demand. The electricity production and distribution facilities have, therefore, been built to meet peak demand, meaning that for the rest of the time part of the infrastructure sits idle. Further, small individual generators, such as rooftop solar panels and small-scale wind farms are increasing and have even become common in certain parts of the world. 'Energy efficiency, demand response (demand flexibility), distributed generation such as rooftop solar, distributed storage such as batteries, smart thermostats, heat pumps and more can become the front lines of a sharing economy revolution for the grid'.[80] On top of the above, the growing culture of renewable energy and the Internet of Things technology, allowing peers to take more initiative in their use of energy according to their needs, make for perfect conditions for the collaborative economy model to expand into the energy sector.

As was suggested at the World Economic Forum in a report on the future of electricity, '[u]nder the right price signals and market design, customers will be able to produce their own electricity, store it and then consume it at a cheaper time or sell it back to the grid. Such a system will even allow peer-to-peer decentralized transactions'.[81] Indeed, *Siemens* and start-up company, *LO3 Energy*, have initiated a pilot project, where they are using blockchain technology to allow for

---

[78] European Parliament and Council Regulation Regulation (EU) No 345/2013 of 17 April 2013 on European venture capital funds [2013] OJ L115/1; European Parliament and Council Regulation (EU) No 346/2013 of 17 April 2013 on European social entrepreneurship funds [2013] OJ L 115/18.

[79] B Schiller, 'The Sharing Economy Takes On Electricity, So You Can Buy Your Power From Neighbors' *Fast Company* (30 September 2014), available at www.fastcompany.com/3036271/the-sharing-economy-takes-on-electricity-so-you-can-buy-your-power-from-neighbors.

[80] R Torben, 'Will the sharing economy approach enter the energy market' (13 February 2017), available at www.torbenrick.eu/blog/technology/sharing-economy-approach-enter-the-energy-market.

[81] See A May, 'Power to the People: How the Sharing Economy Will Transform the Electricity Industry' *World Economic Forum* (10 March 2017), available at www.weforum.org/press/2017/03/power-to-the-people-how-the-sharing-economy-will-transform-the-electricity-industry.

peer-to-peer sharing of energy resources in Brooklyn, allowing 'neighbours to purchase power from each other's rooftop solar panels'.[82] Further, *Mosaic* and *SunShare* are solar lending platforms which connect individuals with solar contractors and providers in order to collaborate on solar installations within communities. Similarly, *Vandebron*—a start-up platform from the Netherlands—allows for consumers to buy energy directly from independent small producers, such as farmers with wind turbines or solar panels. 'The idea behind the platform is to connect people with a surplus of energy with people who are interested in buying sustainable energy directly from the source'.[83] Lastly, the collaborative model could potentially be applied in battery energy storage systems; this 'can be done either by splitting the capacity to different users (horizontal sharing), by assigning the different applications at different times of the day (vertical sharing) or a mixture thereof'.[84]

ii. Health

In the last few years, tele-medicine has witnessed a rapid growth. 'In contrast to traditional, office-based services, patients may access medical services in an "on-demand" fashion, engaging in instant message exchanges, video chats, and remote exams'.[85] This is facilitated by collaborative platforms connecting doctors with patients. Further, wellness and other non-core health related services, such as care-giving or providing psychological support and fitness advice, are beginning to flourish. Thus, *Heal* matches patients with doctors performing on-demand house calls, *Care* connects families with caregivers providing adult and senior care, child care etc, *Cohealo* promotes sharing of medical equipment across health systems' facilities, *PatientsLikeMe* connects patients who share their health experiences, *Spuce* provides telemedicine, *Eaze* facilitates the delivery of medical marijuana, *Uber* (*UberHealth*) occasionally delivers wellness packs and free nurse-administered flu shots, and the list goes on.[86] Similarly, collaborative platforms, such as *Kindly* and *PopExpert* offer wellness services by connecting individuals with wellness coaches and experts.

[82] L Briggs, 'Energy may be ripe for the sharing economy, thanks to Bitcoin's blockchain technology' *Energy Post* (9 December 2016), available at http://energypost.eu/energy-may-ripe-sharing-economy-thanks-bitcoins-blockchain-technology.

[83] 'How the Sharing Economy Is Disrupting the Energy Sector' *Thinque* (20 May 2016), available at https://blog.thinque.com.au/how-the-sharing-economy-is-disrupting-the-energy-sector.

[84] P Lombardi and F Schwabe, 'Sharing Economy as a new business model for energy storage systems' (2017) 188 *Applied Energy* 485, 487.

[85] BJ Miller, DW Moore and CW Schmidt Jr, 'Telemedicine and the Sharing Economy: The "Uber" for Healthcare' (2016) 22 *American Journal of Managed Care* 420, 421.

[86] See *PwC*, 'Uber … for Healthcare? Health Sharing Economy Business Model Examples' (13 May 2015), available at www.pwc.com/ca/en/healthcare/publications/pwc-health-sharing-economy-business-model-examples-2015-05-en.pdf.

C. Other

From renting out tools that have been living in the toolbox on *1000 Tools*, or books that have been already read on *Bookshare*,[87] the possibilities of sharing are endless, giving individuals access to expensive and luxury goods that suddenly become affordable. Thus, while someone could not afford to own a yacht or a couture dress, temporary access to those can be gained through platforms such as *GetMyBoat* and *Girl Meets Dress* respectively. Further, collaborative platforms support food services provided by either professional or amateur chefs. An example of the former case is *Eatro*, a platform for 'ordering wholesome meals delivered quickly to your door from top local chefs'. *BonAppetour*, on the other hand, is a platform connecting locals with travellers who wish to dine at the locals' homes.

VI. Conclusion

The collaborative economy has grown exponentially in these last few years. From a simple idea based on community interest and mutual help, it has become a fully-blown business model full of dynamism, variants and complexities. As such it exerts a disruptive effect on the economy and, more largely into society. In the US the effects of such disruption have been materialising for some time and reflection on those has already started. In the EU, on the other hand, the collaborative economy is a more recent phenomenon, no less disruptive. In the following chapters the ways in which the collaborative economy is received in EU law are explored.

---

[87] A peer-to-peer book lending platform based in Brazil.

2

Market Access and Consumer Protection in the Collaborative Economy

I. Introduction

The fact that the collaborative economy is based on online platforms bringing together two (or more) parties has already been discussed in the first chapter of this book. The three parties typically involved in a collaborative relationship are: (a) the platform which intermediates between (b) the user[1] and (c) the supplier[2] of the underlying service. Each one of these parties derives rights and obligations both from national and EU law. The legal qualifications under the former indirectly inform the applicability of rules under the latter, to the extent that different EU rules will apply to different contractual setups; despite the EU's important inroads into contract law, this is still, to a large extent, a matter of national law. However, the role of national contract law should not overshadow the fact that the core concepts of EU internal market law, such as that of 'service provider', 'trader' and 'consumer', have an autonomous meaning under EU law, thus impregnating national legal orders.

The objective of the present chapter is to show how national contract law (section II) and EU internal market law go hand in hand and, how, each through its own instruments, define the conditions for market access (section III) and consumer protection (section IV) in the collaborative economy. Indeed, the nexus between market access and consumer protection is not only technical/legal in the way it is explained in the following pages, but is also substantive/economic: enhanced market access favours innovation, widening the span of services and/

---

[1] The term 'user' is preferred to the more technical term 'consumer', because the latter makes direct reference to the relevant EU legislation, discussed in section IV of this chapter; 'user' is wider than 'consumer' given that it also encompasses professional users who would not qualify as 'consumers'.

[2] The term 'service *supplier*' is preferred to the more commonly used 'service *provider*', because the latter makes direct reference to the EU Treaty freedoms (especially Arts 56 and 57 TFEU), thus implying that the underlying activity is economic and the 'provider' a 'trader' (in the sense of EU consumer law)—two assumptions that are not necessarily true in the framework of the collaborative economy.

or prices available to consumers, thus being altogether beneficial to them and protective of their interests. This substantive link between market access and consumer protection also explains that the two are defined by reference to common legal criteria, as explained below.

II. Contractual Links in a Collaborative Relation

In a collaborative situation there may be several contractual relationships between the three parties involved. Depending on the specifics of each case, these relationships may correspond to one of the scenarios discussed in section A; the criteria distinguishing between the scenarios are discussed in section B.

A. The Scenarios

Scenario 1: The Platform as an Intermediary

In this case the platform concludes two contracts for digital services, one with the consumer and one with the supplier. With the former the contract is one of intermediation in order to have access to the underlying services, while with the latter, the contract is one of promotion, advertisement and intermediation for the said services. In the contract between the supplier and the platform, consideration typically takes the form of a subscription fee (as is the case with *HomeAway*) or a commission for each transaction concluded (as is the case with *Airbnb*), or both. On top, or instead, of the above methods, consideration may come in the form of use by the platform of consumers' personal or other data, the displaying of different publicity messages to consumers, or any combination thereof. The two latter situations correspond to what has come to be commonly known as 'freemium' and has been recognised as valid consideration for the conclusion of a contract both by the Court in *Papasavvas*[3] and by the EU legislature in the draft Digital Single Market Directives.[4]

A third contract is concluded, for the provision of the underlying service, between the supplier and the consumer. The latter pays the price of the contract (consideration) to the former, typically with the intermediation of the platform.

---

[3] Case C-291/13 *Papasavvas* EU:C:2014:2209, where a free online newspaper paid only by advertisements was held to be an information society service.

[4] See Commission, 'Proposal for a Directive of the European Parliament and of the Council on certain aspects concerning contracts for the supply of digital content' COM(2015) 634 final, Art 3(1); see also Commission, 'Proposal for a Directive of the European Parliament and of the Council on certain aspects concerning contracts for the online and other distance sales of goods' COM(2015) 635 final, Art 3(2).

In this first scenario the supplier is responsible for any damage accruing from the ill-execution of the underlying service, while the platform is, in principle, only responsible for the electronic services. The platform could, however, be held liable for the supplier's conduct on the basis of vicarious liability—*responsabilité du fait d'autrui*[5]—for independent contractors under the 'apparent authority' doctrine, where either the platform or the supplier manifest an agency relationship which the victim reasonably relied upon. It is interesting to note in this respect that the Draft Common Frame Reference of European Private Law, Article VI-3:201 dealing with this bears the title 'Accountability of damage caused by employees *and representatives*' (emphasis added) thus specifically extending vicarious liability to people who do not have an employment relationship with the 'principal', but are 'similarly engaged' by them.[6] Home-sharing platforms, such as *Airbnb*, *Home-Away* and the like, would fit within this category. Also, ride-sharing platforms such as *BlaBlaCar* could be brought into this scenario.

Scenario 2: The Platform as (Double) Service Provider

In this case the platform delivers both the digital[7] and the underlying service. This happens when the platform plays a predominant role in defining and/or delivering the underlying service. The customer only 'sees' the platform as its co-contractor and pays directly to it—or to the supplier at a price and/or by the method determined by the platform. The contractual relationship between the platform and the supplier is one of employment or another kind of collaboration in which the platform has a dominant role. With due reservations made in respect of the many pending cases on both sides of the Atlantic,[8] car-sharing platforms such as *Uber* and *Lyft* would seem to fall within this category.

Under this setup, the platform is responsible for any damage suffered by the consumer either directly under the contract terms, or indirectly by way of vicarious liability based on *respondeat superior*, ie the idea that employers should be liable for the wrongdoings of their employees inasmuch as they exert control over the means and methods followed by the latter.

---

[5] Although the conditions for, and results of, indirect, strict and vicarious liability are not strictly speaking the same under common and continental law, for the purposes of the present description, reference to the broad categories/systems of tort liability is enough.

[6] See C von Bar et al (eds), *Principles, Definitions and Model Rules of European Private Law: Draft Common Frame of Reference (DCFR)*, outline edn, prepared by the Study Group on a European Civil Code and the Research Group on EC Private Law (Acquis Group) (Munich, European Law Publishers, 2009) 401, available at http://ec.europa.eu/justice/policies/civil/docs/dcfr_outline_edition_en.pdf; however, liability would be excluded under the *Principles of European Tort Law* proposed by the European Group of Tort Law, available at http://civil.udg.edu/php/biblioteca/items/283/PETL.pdf, since under Art 6:102, 'Liability for auxiliaries' para 2 it is expressly stipulated that 'an independent contractor is not regarded as an auxiliary for the purposes of this article'.

[7] In the previous scenario this was called 'intermediation service', a term which is not appropriate here given that the underlying service is also provided by the platform.

[8] For which see Chs 5 and 7.

Scenario 3: The Supplier as (Main) Service Provider

In this case the core contract for the underlying service is concluded between the supplier and the consumer. The platform serves as an e-shop or a mere promotional outlet (billboard) for the supplier. The platform does not enter into any contractual relationship with the consumer or, if it does, such contract is concluded on behalf and for the account of the supplier. Here, the principal-agent relationship which exists is the opposite from the one discussed under the previous scenario. Consequently, it is very difficult to envisage the platform being held liable for the wrongdoings of the supplier.

This scenario corresponds to the situation where: (a) the underlying service is clearly distinguishable from the intermediation service; and (b) the platform is just one among many means of advertising the supplier's services to consumers. Platforms such as *Booking.com* would fall into this category. Therefore, core collaborative economy activities, where the offer by peers is made possible by the very existence of the platform and is intimately connected to it, are unlikely to fall within this scenario.

Graph. 1: Contractual Relationships in the Collaborative Economy—Scenarios 1, 2 and 3

Scenario 4: The Platform and the Supplier as a Single Entity

Scenario 4 is a variant (or combination) of scenarios 2 and 3: the relationship between the platform and the supplier is so close (and/or difficult to identify) that they are considered together as a single contracting entity; together they enter in a contractual relationship with the consumer. Under tort law, this would correspond to the situations where the 'joint enterprise' liability would be said to exist, in the sense that 'the actor who benefits from the enterprise should also bear the burdens of it, regardless of precautions taken'.[9]

If car-sharing platforms (such as *Uber* and *Lyft*) were not found to be the employers of their drivers, then their situation could fit under this scenario; similarly, if home-sharing platforms (such as *Airbnb* and *HomeAway*) were found to participate in an active and determinant way to the conclusion of the agreement between the peers, they could be accommodated under this scenario.

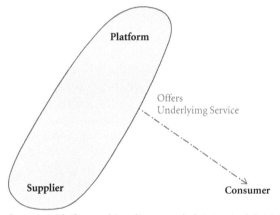

Scenario 4: Platform and Supplier are so closly interwined that it is impossible to distinguish who does what—seen as a single provider

Graph. 2: Contractual Relationships in the Collaborative Economy—Scenario 4

Scenario 5: A Special Contractual Category for Two-sided Platforms

This scenario is an 'artificial' one, in the sense that the legislator (EU or national) recognises the special nature of the collaborative three-party relationship and sets special rules for it, specifically allocating the rights and liabilities of the parties involved. Such an approach, recognising the *de facto* central role of platforms in the collaborative economy, could be justified in legal terms, but not necessarily in economic terms—especially if it were imposed at a time where the collaborative economy in Europe is in its infancy.

---

[9] A McPeak, 'Sharing Tort Liability in the New Sharing Economy' (2016) 49 *Connecticut Law Review* 171, 192, available at https://ssrn.com/abstract=2776429.

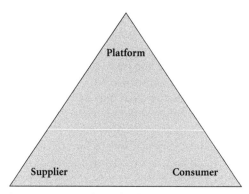

Scenario 5: A special (regulated) three-way relationship

Graph. 3: Contractual Relationships in the Collaborative Economy—Scenario 5

The distinction between the above scenarios is a fine one and depends on the facts of each case. The most likely scenarios in the collaborative context are 1 and 2, since scenarios 3 and 4 suppose that the supplier has equal, at least, power with the platform. Most platforms claim scenario 1, ie that they are mere intermediaries, that they bear no responsibility for the actual content of the goods/services delivered and therefore, that the only contract they partake in is the intermediation one. This has several advantages for the platforms. In particular, (a) they do not need to be authorised for the specific underlying activity (such as eg passenger transport, credit operations etc); (b) they cannot be held responsible for any ill-execution of the underlying contract or for damage accruing therefrom; and (c) they can claim to be fully absolved from any liability, including for misrepresentation, offensive or illegal content, under Articles 13–15 of the E-commerce Directive.[10]

B. The Criteria for Determining the Parties' Roles in Collaborative Three-way Relations

It is true that the way platforms present their role—and that of the suppliers—to the consumers may have an impact on the kind of contract which is concluded: the stronger and the more visible the statements to the effect that platforms are mere intermediaries and that the underlying service is provided by a third party, the higher the probability that they are not considered to partake in the contract for the underlying service. The legal effects of the above statements, however, will need to be assessed against the actual participation of the platform to the delivery of the underlying service: the more active the platform's role in the delivery of the underlying service, the less likely that their 'disclaimers' will be of any legal

---

[10] For the application of the E-commerce Directive see section III.A below.

value. If the platform's role is decisive and the supplier only acts as an 'execution agent', the underlying service shall be deemed to be provided by the former. This may be ascertained on the basis of two separate, but interrelated, questions. The first question relates to the platform's input in, and influence on, the provision of the underlying service; the second has to do with the existence of an employment relationship between the platform and the supplier. Indeed, it is the nuances of the answers to these two questions that will determine, in each case, which one of the four scenarios above is to be followed (the fifth being artificially imposed through regulation).

i. Who is Responsible for Defining and Delivering the Underlying Service?

From the very definition of the concept of 'sharing economy' it follows that most platforms do not own the assets they put at the disposition of their clients, nor do they provide directly the underlying service themselves; in this sense they only offer electronic intermediation services. This simple assertion, however, should be revisited in view of the fact that several platforms are more or less involved in the type/quality/conditions of the underlying service provision. Thus, for example, *Uber* and many of the transportation platforms[11] impose conditions on the types of cars that may be used (only passenger cars, of a certain age, etc), the facilities that should be offered (bottle of water, wi-fi connection, bluetooth connection for the passenger's music etc) and, most importantly, fix the price paid by the passenger; some of them, including *Uber*, pay the drivers for their services. Platforms are, therefore, directly involved in the provision of transportation services and are unlikely to qualify as mere providers of online services. The position in relation to *Uber* has given rise to great controversy and to opposing judicial decisions in the various Member States, and even more contradictory decisions in the US.[12] The question has been brought, and is pending, before the CJEU.[13] *BlaBlaCar*, on the other hand, a ride-sharing company (which matches individuals driving to some long-distance destination with other individuals wishing to go to that same destination), has been held by the Madrid Commercial Tribunal to be a mere intermediary, not in competition with traditional coach or train services.[14] Transportation services are not the only ones where the platforms play a very important role. Financial services is another area in which the platforms' actions may be going beyond mere intermediation.[15] Home-sharing platforms, on the

---

[11] The examples which follow are not necessarily taken from *Uber*, but rather illustrate the practices of various transportation platforms.

[12] For the different solutions reached in different jurisdictions see Ch 7 below.

[13] Case C-434/15 *Asociación Profesional Elite Taxi v Uber Systems Spain* EU:C:2017:364.

[14] *Confebus v BlablaCar* SJM M 6/2017 (2 February 2017) ECLI:ES:JMM:2017:6.

[15] A preliminary question referred to the Court by a Finnish Court in relation to a crowdfunding platform has been removed from the Court's register following an order by the President of the Court: see Case C-311/15 *TrustBuddy* EU:C:2015:759.

other hand, are much closer to qualifying as mere intermediaries. For one thing, these platforms do not have any relationship akin to employment with home-owners, nor do they (typically) exert any control over the facilities put on offer. On the contrary, they are open to any type of accommodation (from single beds in shared rooms to entire houses and to luxurious estates; and from barges and sailing-boats to tree-houses) and they make it clear that it is the responsibility of the home-owners to define and deliver the level of service they deem appropriate. Price is also determined by the home-owners. Several of these platforms, however, are less passive than the previous passage assumes: they offer advice to home-owners as to how to be good hosts, put at their disposition professional photographers, propose set-term contracts, withhold a security deposit, take insurance on behalf of both parties and even, on the basis of the big data they dispose of, propose the 'ideal' price for different locations at different periods of the year.[16] While it is difficult to hold that platforms which do all the above are mere intermediaries, it may, nonetheless, be said that all the above services are indeed ancillary to the main service which is that of the intermediation.

The Commission's Communication on a European Agenda for the collaborative economy[17] proposes some clarifications in this respect. While acknowledging that the question of whether a collaborative platform also provides the underlying service may only be resolved on a case-by-case basis, it sets out three criteria: (a) whether the platform imposes (as opposed to proposes) the price; (b) whether it decides on other key contractual terms; and (c) whether it owns the key assets used to provide the underlying service. When these criteria are cumulatively met, then, according to the Commission, there would be 'strong indications' that the platform also offers the underlying service. This is an extremely demanding test (especially if it is only to offer 'strong indications'), since even where the platform does actively decide on key contractual terms, it will rarely *impose* a price and even more rarely, if ever, will it possess the assets required to offer the underlying service. Possession of the assets by the platform is likely to run counter to two of the very defining concepts of the collaborative economy, ie (i) sharing goods and services; and (ii) two-sided markets. Thus, according to the above criteria, in most cases, the platform will not be participating in the underlying service. What is more, according to the Commission, other, secondary criteria that may be taken into account are: whether the platform incurs the costs and assumes all the risks related to the service and if an employment relationship exists with the person providing the service; mere assistance, on the other hand, for the performance of ancillary tasks (such as the ones described above for home-renting platforms) does not mean that the platform exerts significant control over either the choice of providers or the manner in which the underlying service is being offered.[18]

---

[16] On the issue of price fixing see Ch 4 below.
[17] Communication from the Commission, 'A European Agenda for the collaborative economy', COM(2016) 356 final.
[18] ibid 6–7.

The extremely demanding test set by the Commission in order to reach the conclusion that a platform actively participates in the underlying service, and thus is subject to the corresponding regulatory and liability burdens, is consistent with the Commission's pro-collaborative attitude. It is, however, creating a big loophole in the protection of consumers, who will be deprived of any remedy against the platforms and will only be able to claim their rights against the suppliers: in the best case, the supplier will be a 'trader' within the meaning of consumer protection law and will have the financial means to face the consumer's claim. If the consumer is less lucky, the supplier will qualify as a 'trader' but will not be able to shoulder the consumer's claim and, in the worst case scenario, the supplier will be a mere 'prosumer' and consumer protection will be altogether inapplicable. At the same time, the Commission's very demanding conditions for holding a platform liable for the underlying services runs in the direct opposite direction from the EU legislature's approach in the neighbouring area of package travelling, where the core burden of consumer protection is specifically attributed to the intermediary.[19]

In view of the above, it is unlikely that the courts, or indeed the CJEU (in the pending *Uber* case) will follow the Commission's approach. This is especially true in view of Advocate General Szpunar's Opinion, where he plainly dismissed both the ownership (of the cars) and the employment criteria as being relevant.[20] Instead, he put the focus on the facts that *Uber*: (a) makes the transport service possible in the first place;[21] and (b) controls the economically significant aspects of the transport service, ie price, safety conditions, supply, conduct of drivers and, ultimately, possible exclusion from the platform.[22] The fact that most of the above are controlled in an indirect and non-binding manner did not make the learned Advocate General shy away from concluding that *Uber* was the provider of the main service.[23] In view of the likely judicial outcome in the *Uber* case and the criticisms presented above, the criteria proposed by the Commission may still be considered as relevant, but instead of being viewed as cumulative and sufficient conditions, they should be evaluated as part of a multi-tiered test (*faisceau d'indices*), in tandem with all the other criteria discussed in the previous paragraphs.

The complete opposite scenario may not be altogether excluded: the supplier may be the dominant party both in determining and delivering the underlying service and in fixing the conditions for its promotion and distribution through the platform (scenario 3 above). Such a scenario is only possible where the supplier is a powerful undertaking and already possesses such a strong branding that it can outweigh the platform's own branding and its capacity to reach consumers around

---

[19] For which see briefly sections IV.A.iv and IV.B.i below.
[20] Opinion of AG Szpunar in Case C-434/15 *Asociación Profesional Elite Taxi* EU:C:2017:364, paras 54 and 55.
[21] ibid paras 43 and 44.
[22] ibid para 51.
[23] ibid paras 47 and 48.

the globe. This scenario hardly fits into the logic of the collaborative economy as it now stands, but may become commonplace with the rapid spread of two-sided platforms and their increased use as a means of distributing goods and services. Indeed, while the collaborative paradigm is based on individual prosumers sharing their idle capacity, platforms are increasingly being used also by the incumbents to promote their own services—whether in the traditional version or face-lifted for the new environment.[24] This, eventually, may lead to the denaturation of the collaborative paradigm, but in an environment as fluid as the one discussed here 'it is tough to make provisions, especially about the future'.[25]

ii. Is there an Employment Relationship?

If the supplier is in an employment relationship with the platform, then it is clear that it is the latter which enters into a contract with the consumer. The conditions, criteria and consequences of finding an employment relationship in the collaborative framework are discussed at length in Chapter 5 below.

* * *

From the above analysis of contract law, it becomes apparent that participants in the collaborative economy may, depending on the fact-set and the legal qualifications applying to them, find themselves subject to different contractual relationships and may qualify as advertisers, suppliers, employees and so on. These qualifications, in turn, trigger different sets of EU rules which are more or less favourable to opening up market access in Europe. It is to these rules that the discussion now turns.

III. Market Access in the Collaborative Economy

Market access is the building block of any economic integration project. While it has always been at the core of the internal market, in the last decade the Court has expressly acknowledged its importance, transforming it thus into the 'slogan' of the internal market.[26]

Market access under the EU rules benefits only those service providers which have their seat or are otherwise connected to one Member State. Although secondary establishment in a Member State 'may be done by means merely of an office managed by a person who is independent but authorised to act on a

---

[24] SR Miller, 'First Principles for Regulating the Sharing Economy' (2016) 53 *Harvard Journal on Legislation* 147, available at https://ssrn.com/abstract=2568016.

[25] A well-known quotation attributed to Yogi Berra; see www.goodreads.com/quotes/261863-it-s-tough-to-make-predictions-especially-about-the-future.

[26] See J Snell, 'The Notion of Market Access: A Concept or a Slogan?' (2010) 47 *CMLR* 437.

permanent basis for the operator, as would be the case with an agency', this lax condition is not satisfied by 'a mere provider of computer support services in the host Member State'.[27] This is a condition which needs be ascertained in the area of the collaborative economy, as the technical, fiscal and other arrangements may vary greatly from case to case. A further question which calls for a—non obvious—answer is whether suppliers who have no connection whatsoever with the EU may, nonetheless, claim the benefit of free movement rules merely because they provide their underlying service through a platform 'established' in the EU.

Platforms and providers that are completely unconnected to the EU—a vast majority at the present phase of development of the collaborative economy—will need to claim market access under the WTO GATS or any other bilateral or regional agreement binding the EU and the State where the platform is based, such as, eg the CETA or the EU/Singapore Free Trade Agreement.[28]

Platforms and suppliers that do come within the territorial scope of application of EU law may claim market access under the general Treaty rules (see section D below), the Professional Qualifications Directive (see section C), the Services Directive (see section B) and the E-commerce Directive (see section A). Platforms, in particular, are likely to invoke these texts in reverse order.

A. The E-commerce Directive

The E-commerce Directive[29] is *lex specialis* in relation to the Services Directive and other horizontal EU rules, such as eg Directive 2005/36 on professional qualifications. It only applies to information society services, ie 'any service normally provided for remuneration, at a distance, by electronic means and at the individual request of a recipient of services'.[30] The provision of such services in the EU is, in principle, not subject to any prior authorisation in the providers' home State (Article 4(1)) and benefits from the 'internal market clause' (Article 3(2)), according to which all other (host) Member States are precluded from raising any obstacles. Therefore, the E-commerce Directive is the ideal 'market access opener' both in the home and in the host Member States, and collaborative platforms may greatly benefit from it.

---

[27] Case C-347/09 *Dickinger and Oemer* EU:C:2011:582, paras 35 and 37.

[28] On market access under the GATS and other trade agreements, see briefly section E below.

[29] European Parliament and Council Directive 2000/31/EC of 8 June 2000 on certain legal aspects of information society services, in particular electronic commerce, in the Internal Market (Directive on electronic commerce) [2000] OJ L 178/1.

[30] Art 2(a) of the Directive refers to the definition given in the 'notification' Directive 98/34/EC, nowadays replaced by Directive 2015/1535/EU [2015] OJ L241/1. This latter text explains the elements of the above definition as follows: (i) 'at a distance' means that the service is provided without the parties being simultaneously present; (ii) 'by electronic means' means that the service is sent initially and received at its destination by means of electronic equipment for the processing (including digital compression) and storage of data, and entirely transmitted, conveyed and received by wire, by radio, by optical means or by other electromagnetic means, (iii) 'at the individual request of a recipient of services' means that the service is provided through the transmission of data on individual request.

Host State authorities may legitimately deviate from the internal market clause only in situations justified by public policy, public health, public security and consumer protection objectives.[31] According to the E-commerce Directive, the above reasons only justify measures imposed for services 'imported' from some other Member State, but they do not allow the 'home' Member State (or the one in which eg a US-based platform will make its establishment within the EU) to impose any prior authorisation requirement or equivalent restriction. This does not mean that the home Member State may not supervise information society providers established in its territory; on the contrary, it is held responsible to supervise them 'on behalf' of all other Member States.[32]

Platforms will be able to benefit from this facilitated access only to the extent that they qualify as 'service providers' within the meaning of Article 57 TFEU,[33] and that their activity is limited to the provision of electronic services, ie mere intermediation, and does not extend to affecting/participating in the provision of the underlying service. Thus, the discussion above on the respective roles of the platform and the supplier is highly relevant. Indeed, going back to the scenarios discussed above, platforms could claim market access under the E-commerce Directive under scenario 1 and scenario 3, ie in the cases where they only act as e-intermediaries and have no involvement in the provision of the underlying service. On the other hand, as soon as a platform is found to be directly involved in the provision of the underlying service, it would cease being a provider of digital services and would qualify as an 'offline' service provider. It is unclear whether a principle of 'severability' exists, whereby digital services may be distinguished from offline ones, and the platform could remain subject to the E-commerce Directive in respect of the former. Advocate General Szpunar, in his Opinion in *Asociación Profesional Elite Taxi (Uber Spain)*, hints to the negative, since he proposes that in 'composite services'[34] provided or controlled by the platform 'it is necessary to identify the main component of the supply envisaged, that is to say, the component which gives it meaning in economic terms'.[35] This view, which makes sure that no artificial legal partitioning of unitary economic activities takes place, if adopted by the Court, would typically lead the e-intermediation service to be treated together with—and under the rules applicable to—the underlying material service; by the same token, however, the enhanced market access foreseen in favour of information society undertakings will not be available to most platforms.

---

[31] See Art 3(4).

[32] See recital 22 of the Directive; we shall return later to the issue of the grounds that may be invoked by the Member States in order to regulate collaborative economy activities: see Ch 7.

[33] For which see section B below on the Services Directive.

[34] Opinion of AG Szpunar in Case C-434/15 *Asociación Profesional Elite Taxi* (n 20); this term is used by the AG at para 28.

[35] ibid para 35.

B. The Services Directive

The Services Directive[36] is, so far, the only horizontal liberalisation instrument in the field of services. Those platforms which do not fall under the E-commerce Directive and which, on the basis of the underlying activity they pursue, need to be authorised, have all the interest to try to file their authorisation request under the Services Directive. Indeed, this Directive sets a liberal and transparent framework for the delivery of authorisations for those service providers who come within its scope,[37] while facilitating the trans-border provision of such services.[38] At the same time, it codifies some obligations for service providers, essentially in terms of information which needs to be provided to the consumers,[39] and of professional liability insurance.[40]

In order to fall within the ambit of the Services Directive, an entity should qualify as a service provider within the meaning of Article 57 TFEU and not fall within one of the many exceptions of the Directive. The advantages, in terms of market access, offered by the Services Directive are briefly discussed in sections ii and iii below.

Those who do not come within the scope of the Services Directive (see the discussion in section i below) are not altogether devoid of any protection, since they can still claim all the substantial rights recognised by the Court as directly stemming from Articles 56 and 57 TFEU. At the procedural level, those platforms and/or suppliers who do not come under the Services Directive may, nonetheless, claim the application of the principle of transparency and non-discrimination developed by the Court in recent years—a case law which, as explained elsewhere,[41] may be a source of important safeguards and (even) rights.

i. Scope—Sectors Excluded from the Services Directive

As stated above, and developed at length elsewhere,[42] several sectors are excluded from the scope of the Services Directive. Transportation services, financial services,

---

[36] European Parliament and Council Directive 2006/123/EC of 12 December 2006 on services in the internal market (Services Directive) [2006] OJ L 376/36.

[37] Arts 9–15.

[38] Art 16.

[39] Services Directive 2006/123, Art 22.

[40] ibid Art 23.

[41] See V Hatzopoulos, 'The Allocation of Limited Authorisations under EU Internal Market Rules' in P Adrianse, F van Omeren, W de Ouden and J Wolswinkel (eds), *Scarcity and the State* (Cambridge, Intersentia, 2016); see also, by the same author, 'Des marchés publics à la délivrance des autorisations: Spill-over all over?' in I Govaere and D Hanf (eds), *Scrutinizing Internal and External Dimensions of European Law—Les dimensions internes et externes du droit européen à l'épreuve—Liber Amicorum Paul Demaret*, Tome 1 (Bruxelles, P.I.E.-Peter Lang, 2013); and, more extensively, by the same author, 'Du principe de non-discrimination (au niveau européen) au principe de bonne administration (au niveau national)?' (2016) *Cahiers de droit européen* 311.

[42] V Hatzopoulos, 'Assessing the Services Directive' in C Barnard (ed), *Cambridge Yearbook of European Law 2007–2008*, Vol 10 (Oxford, Hart Publishing, 2008).

healthcare services, temporary work agencies, social services such as social hous-ing and childcare are some of the activities which, while being excluded from the Directive, are relevant for the collaborative economy. It is necessary to evaluate for each collaborative activity whether and to what extent it falls within these exceptions.

Given that exceptions to the Treaty freedoms and to secondary legislation implementing them should be interpreted restrictively, it is by no means guar-anteed that any activity in the above sectors will be excluded from the scope of the Services Directive. For instance, given that in *Femarbel* the Court held that only those core health-related activities which are performed by health profes-sionals are excluded from the Directive;[43] most health-related services offered over platforms[44] would still come under the Services Directive, to the extent that they do not correspond to core health activities but essentially revolve around non-specialised services, general advice, psychological support and the like.[45] On the other hand, the Court has given an ambiguous interpretation to the concept of transport services, by including hot air balloon rides[46] but exclud-ing short cruises on the canals of Amsterdam.[47] In a judgment which may prove extremely topical for *Uber* and other platforms in the field of transport, the Court held that the activity of technical control of vehicles, although not a transporta-tion service in itself, comes within the Directive's exception covering the larger category of 'services in the field of transport'.[48] Thus, it may be that other ancil-lary activities, such as eg the logistical support offered by collaborative platforms in this field—if we assume that platforms are not themselves transportation undertakings[49]—takes them outside the scope of the Services Directive. If this were true, platforms active in the field of transportation would, either directly (as transportation undertakings) or indirectly (as offering ancillary services) be excluded from the Directive's scope.[50] Determining whether this is so or whether, on the contrary, the platforms do come within the ambit of the Directive, would still require an evaluation of the degree of connection between the 'ancillary' ser-vices offered by the platform and the 'main' transportation services at stake.

---

[43] Case C-57/12 *Fédération des maisons de repos privées de Belgique (Femarbel) ASBL v Commission communautaire commune de Brussels-Capitale* EU:2013:517.

[44] Such as eg *Cohealo*, which helps health systems share medical equipment across facilities, or *Macmillan Cancer Support*, which brings into contact and supports cancer patients (see www.macmillan.org.uk/about-us).

[45] See also Case C-539/11 *Ottica New Line di Accardi Vincenzo* EU:C:2013:591, where the Court found that the authorisation of an optician's shop did not come under the rules of the Services Directive.

[46] Case C-382/08 *Neukirchinger* EU:C:2011:27.

[47] Joined Cases C-340/14 and C-341/14 *Trijber* EU:C:2015:641.

[48] Case C-168/14 *Grupo Itevelesa et al* EU:C:2015:685, paras 48–50.

[49] For which see above nn 11–22 and the corresponding text.

[50] See also in this sense the Opinion of AG Szpunar in Case C-434/15 *Asociación Profesional Elite Taxi* (n 20), paras 68 and 70.

ii. Impact of the Services Directive on Collaborative Platforms

Collaborative platforms serve as intermediaries between those who are looking for specific services and those who may be offering them. They act as brokers. Their very function is to allow offer and demand to meet (offer being sometimes created by the platforms themselves).[51] This brings them, in principle, within the traditional definition of a trader. Given that most platforms either charge a subscription fee or claim a commission for each contract concluded with their intermediation, their activity is overarchingly economic. Even in the cases where the use of a platform is apparently free, it will be typically making money either from publicity or from the secondary use of the users' data (freemium).[52] In view of the extremely wide definition of remuneration accepted by the Court,[53] and the fact that remuneration may be provided by a party other than the recipient (the so called triangular situations, typically in the field of advertising and publicity),[54] almost all collaborative platforms will qualify as service providers in the sense of Article 57 TFEU.[55] This broad vision is also confirmed in the draft Digital Single Market Directives, where it is specifically stipulated that remuneration exists where 'a price is to be paid or the consumer actively provides counter-performance other than money in the form of personal data or any other data'.[56] Only the rare small-size platforms operating at the local/community level, which only serve social/solidarity purposes, such as for example sharing libraries, will elude this qualification. These will in principle fall outside the scope of the EU rules, primary and secondary; by the same token they are likely to evade the bulk of locally applicable restrictions and rules, as they will have a very specific, not-for-profit object and a very limited geographic coverage. These will not be further considered here. All platforms contemplated by the present book, therefore, are service providers in the sense of Article 57 TFEU and the Services Directive.

Under the Services Directive, the requirement for a prior authorisation is not altogether excluded (unlike under the E-commerce Directive), but Member States need to show that such prior authorisation regimes that are maintained are justified, necessary and proportionate.[57] Justifications may stem from overriding reasons of public interest (including public order, security and health).[58]

---

[51] Given that they actually 'create' this new kind of offer; see Ch 1 above.

[52] Eg through data trade, targeted advertising, personalised services etc.

[53] Joined Cases C-51/96 and C-191/97 *Deliège* EU:C:2000:199.

[54] See *Deliège* as above, but more importantly Case C-353/89 *Commission v The Netherlands (mediawet)* EU:C:1991:325.

[55] See Case C-291/13 *Papasavvas* EU:C:2014:2209, where a free online newspaper paid only by advertisements was held to be an information society service.

[56] See COM(2015) 634 final, Art 3(1) for the supply of digital content and COM(2015) 635 final, Art 3(2) for the distant sale of goods.

[57] Services Directive 2006/123, Art 9.

[58] For the confusions between overriding reasons of general interest and express treaty provisions see V Hatzopoulos, 'Justifications to restrictions to free movement: Towards a single normative framework?' in M Andenas, T Bekkedal and L Pantaleo (eds), *The Reach of Free Movement* (The Hague, TMC Asser Press/Springer, 2017).

Given that both the imposition of an authorisation in the first place, and the conditions attached thereto, are subject to the requirements of non-discrimination, objectivity and transparency, the question of identifying similar and/or comparable activities—both between platforms themselves (eg *Uber* and *Lyft*) and between platforms and real-world activities (eg *Uber* and cab services)—is central. In this respect, the 'market definition' under competition law[59] may be helpful, although not conclusive.

Where an authorisation is required, it should be delivered according to non-discriminatory, objective and transparent criteria, known in advance, within reasonable time and be of indeterminate temporal and geographic coverage.[60] It may not contain any of the requirements blacklisted in Article 14 of the Directive and may only exceptionally contain requirements from the grey list of Article 15.

Several practices prohibited under Article 14 may be relevant for platforms. Therefore, for instance, it may be worth asking whether the restriction imposed by several national legislators on the number of days that *Airbnb* hosts may rent out their housing is compatible with the prohibition of an economic needs test. Similarly, the compatibility of certain existing national legislations with the prohibition of 'direct or indirect involvement of competing operators, including within consultative bodies, in the granting of authorisations or in the adoption of the other decisions of the competent authorities' may also raise acute questions: while the incumbent traditional industries, such as hoteliers, taxi drivers and bankers are organised and do find their way, directly or indirectly, to the decision-makers, platforms and, even more, suppliers, typically lack such organised representation. The obligation to offer a financial guarantee or to take out insurance in the territory of the Member State where the service is offered may also raise questions.

Measures from the grey list may also be problematic. For instance, the prohibition of minimum and/or maximum prices could possibly run contrary to any commitments regarding prices given by platforms to national competition authorities.[61] Similarly, the rule that platforms may not be obliged to 'supply other specific services jointly with its service' could already be suffering under the different rules imposed by national legislators in the home-sharing sector, according to which home-owners are obliged to offer or abstain from offering specific services (such as eg welcoming/reception, cleaning, laundry etc).[62]

A further question is whether the platforms may invoke restrictions imposed on the suppliers of the underlying service, such as, for example, whether *Airbnb* may complain about the limited number of days that its hosts are allowed to rent out

---

[59] For which see Ch 4 below.
[60] Services Directive 2006/123, Arts 10–13.
[61] Given that the use of algorithms makes any potential collusion difficult to prove, competition authorities may be tempted to discuss prices with platforms either in the framework of proposed mergers or in a classic 101 TFEU action for resale price maintenance; for the issue of price parallelism and algorithms, see Ch 4 below.
[62] For the different national rules, see Ch 7 below.

their housing. Indeed, housing is a field where restrictions are typically imposed on the home-owners rather than on the platforms; and while the latter may be well equipped to react, both at the political and at the legal level, the former typically lack such resources. This brings up the more general question whether platforms should be allowed to raise market access claims on behalf of their suppliers. A positive reply, although sensible, is not granted under the current case law. Indeed, in *Schnitzer* the Court has held that the recipient of a service may claim protection for his service provider,[63] while in the *Gambelli/Placanica* saga,[64] and most explicitly in *Costa and Cifone*,[65] the Court has held that the (international) platform may claim protection for, and on behalf of, its (local) agents in the state where access is sought. Similarly, in *Las*, the Court admitted that the employer was entitled to claim rights under Article 45 TFEU, on behalf of his employees, in relation to the language in which the employment contract had to be concluded.[66] However, *Schnitzer* only covers the relationship between the consumer (not the platform) and the supplier, while *Las* and *Costa and Cifone* cover the situations where the supplier is the employee or the agent, respectively, of the platform. All other scenarios, including the (relatively) rare cases where the supplier of the underlying service is not a service provider,[67] remain to be adjudicated upon.

Once authorised in one Member State, a platform may pursue its activities in all other Member States by virtue of Article 16 of the Services Directive. In principle, service provision should be unfettered, unless by restrictions justified by public order, public security, public health or the protection of the environment.[68] Where the underlying service is not executed online but materialises in a specific Member State (the host Member State) and most risks are connected with the actual service, rather than with the electronic/intermediation, the host State will, more often than not, be justified to invoke such exceptions to the principle of Article 16 of the Services Directive.[69] Thus, for instance, a short-term housing contract concluded between *Airbnb* and a Belgian host for a stay in Greece, is subject to all the Greek regulations connected with the public order, security, health and the protection of the environment. The greater the remoteness between the platform and the underlying service supplier, the less likely it is that the authorisation conditions of the former will be relevant for the activity of the latter. If, in the previous example, the Belgian tourist had reserved his/her stay with *Hilton Hotels*, zoning restrictions and fire extinguishing systems would have been checked at the authorisation of

---

[63] Case C-215/01 *Schnitzer* EU:C:2003:662.

[64] Case C-243/01 *Gambelli et al* EU:C:2003:597; Joined Cases C-338/04, C-359/04 and C-360/04 *Placanica* EU:C:2006:71;

[65] Joined Cases C-72/10 and C-77/10 *Costa and Cifone* EU:C:2012:80.

[66] Case C-202/11 *Las* EU:C:2013:239.

[67] For this distinction see section iii below.

[68] The extent to which Member States may be precluded from invoking other overriding reasons of general interest by virtue of Art 16 of the Services Directive is disputed among scholars: see Hatzopoulos, 'Justifications to restrictions to free movement: Towards a single normative framework?' (2017).

[69] For the reasons which the national authorities may invoke in order to limit platforms' activities, see Ch 7 below.

the Hotel; since however, *Airbnb* as a platform is authorised on completely different criteria, such interests need to be taken into account on a case-by-case basis. Therefore, compared to 'traditional' services, those offered through collaborative platforms are more likely to be subject to locally-imposed protective measures.

Further, Article 22 of the Services Directive requires all service providers to make easily accessible, including by electronic means, substantial information concerning the service provider. This information obligation arising under the Services Directive should be seen together with all the information requirements imposed by the consumer protection Directives.[70] An important legal issue arising for platforms is that, as stated in the previous sentence, the above information obligations concern 'the provider'. It is unclear whether the 'provider' concerned is that of the electronic (intermediation) service, the supplier of the underlying service, or both. Given that the above obligation comes under Chapter V of the Directive on the 'Quality of Services', and is intended to make sure that professional and other rules are respected, it would be counter-intuitive if it only covered the electronic service. Thus the question of determining whether it is the platform or the supplier who defines the service and who is responsible for its actual delivery, becomes crucial once again. Platforms wishing to be on the safe side, however, should provide information concerning both themselves and the suppliers of the underlying service, while respecting data protection rules.[71] Most platforms, however, do not currently follow such a practice.

iii. *Impact of the Services Directive on the Suppliers of the Underlying Service*

Suppliers of the underlying services would, more often than not, qualify as 'service providers' under Article 57 TFEU and the Services Directive. This qualification is given to any natural or legal person who offers any self-employed economic activity, normally provided for remuneration;[72] no requirement of frequency, duration or requirement that the providers act within their trade, etc is to be found either in the case law or in the Directive. Indeed, the Court has qualified as service providers anyone from amateur athletes[73] to retired university professors.[74] In view of the very wide concept of remuneration followed by the Court, any activity which has a broadly economic character, even if pursued on a one-off basis by a non-professional, will qualify as a service—and the person providing it a 'service provider'.

The only activities which the Court holds not to constitute services are those who are either intimately connected to the exercise of official authority or are

---

[70] Which are discussed later in this chapter; see section D.i. below.
[71] For which see Ch 3.
[72] Services Directive 2006/123, Art 4(2).
[73] *Deliège* (n 53).
[74] Case C-281/06 *Jundt* EU:C:2007:816.

governed by solidarity.[75] These are typically exercised by public entities or private bodies entrusted by the public authorities, and it is highly unlikely that the activity exercised by any individual service supplier comes under this category. Therefore, most, if not all, suppliers of the underlying service will also qualify as 'service providers' in the sense of the Services Directive and of Article 57 TFEU.

A question mark remains in relation to genuine 'sharing' activities, such as house-swapping (eg *Love Home Swap*, which advertises using the moto 'You go to theirs. They come to yours'), ride-sharing where the passenger only pays a fraction of the petrol consumed (eg *BlaBlaCar*) and other similar activities, where not only is there no apparent remuneration but, moreover, the intent of engaging in any economic activity at all seems to be lacking.

Thus, the concept of 'service provider' is much larger than that of 'trader' under the Consumer Rights and the Unfair Commercial Practices Directives, since it embraces professional service providers acting within their trade ('traders'), professionals acting outside their trade and non-professional, occasional, or even one-off service providers, also termed 'prosumers'.[76]

All service providers, professionals and prosumers alike, will be able to claim market access under the Services Directive on the same terms as platforms. Three points may differ, however, depending on the above distinction. Firstly, service providers who only act occasionally and not on a professional basis, should not be subject to any requirement of authorisation; or if an authorisation were required it should be subject to lighter requirements than the equivalent for 'professionals' in order to satisfy the requirement of proportionality.[77] Thus, for instance, people active in the short-term accommodation sector may be subject to the same rules as hoteliers if they rent out their premises in a repeated and systematic manner, subject to lighter regulation (concerning eg health, safety and security) or no regulation at all if they are occasional flat/couch swappers. Secondly, the extensive information obligation,[78] as well as, thirdly, the professional liability insurance[79] foreseen by the Services Directive, may also prove to be disproportionate where the provider is only a prosumer occasionally offering services through a platform.

It is worth noting that the idea of having special—lighter—standards for operators in the collaborative economy has been mooted by several parties, not only in relation to the suppliers, but also in relation to the platforms themselves. Thus, for instance, the Italian Competition Authority in a position paper published in September 2015 in relation to the review of the competition legislation, suggested

---

[75] For an extensive discussion of the distinction between economic and non-economic activities under the Court's case law see V Hatzopoulos, 'The Economic Constitution of the EU Treaty and the limits between economic and non-economic activities' (2012) 23 *EBLRev* 973.

[76] For which see section D.i below.

[77] See in that sense also Commission Staff Working Document, 'A Single Market Strategy for Europe—Analysis and Evidence' SWD(2015) 202 final, 5.

[78] Services Directive 2006/123, Art 22.

[79] ibid Art 23.

that *Uber* and its drivers should be seen as a *tertius genus* (in relation to traditional taxis and to chauffeured cars), and be subject to a regulation 'as light as possible'.[80]

C. Regulated Professions

Collaborative economy activities may sometimes fall within a regulated profession. For instance, being a tourist guide is an activity that is regulated in several countries. Similarly, the provision of financial services and, under certain circumstances, financial advice, is also regulated, both at Member State and EU level. Other collaborative activities may not directly correspond to a regulated profession as such, but may be on its periphery, such as in the field of healthcare, psychoanalysis and psychotherapy, or social assistance. An issue yet unexplored is whether, to what extent and how service providers should comply with the national requirements on regulated professions.

The starting point should be that regulated professions remain regulated no matter how/how often they are carried out. Thus, collaborative service providers offering some regulated activity through a platform should do so in accordance with the rules applicable within the (host) Member State where the service is provided. Typically even the occasional (or even the one-off) exercise of such a regulated profession is prohibited and may give rise to criminal and/or administrative action against the 'counterfeiter'. Therefore, in principle, the obligation to comply with the relevant regulations should apply to all those who qualify as service providers, even if they do not qualify as traders or, else, professionals.

This, however, may be counter-intuitive for people who are willing to give up some of their time, skills and expertise in order to help their fellow men and women, especially when they do so for no immediate return.[81] Therefore, a question may be raised whether a different, more relaxed, approach should be taken in relation to collaborative services which are offered for free (even if the platform makes money from advertising or otherwise).

A further element attenuating the general rule that regulated professions should only be exercised by the corresponding professionals could reside on the (non) use of the relevant professional title—possibly combined with the (in)frequent manner in which such services are provided: should a person who occasionally offers psychological support, while stating that s/he is neither a psychologist nor a psychoanalyst, be prevented from doing so?

---

[80] For a discussion of this document and other developments under Italian law see A de Franceschi, 'The Adequacy of Italian Law for the Platform Economy' (2016) 5 *EuCML* 56.

[81] In that regard see *JustAnswer*, a collaborative platform connecting experts such as doctors, lawyers, vets, mechanics etc, with people with questions/problems.

For those who do act 'professionally', a different issue is raised as to how they may make use of their qualifications in order to lawfully offer services in other Member States. Directive 2005/36[82] contains a Title II on (non-established) occasional service providers who may, in principle, rely on their home qualifications and title, without having to go through the recognition procedure. Such service providers may not be required to obtain any authorisation or to register with any professional body of the host State. They may be required, however, to inform the competent authority of their presence in the territory. On this occasion, they may be required to prove their nationality, the fact that they are legally established in another Member State, their qualifications and other more case-specific issues; exceptionally their qualifications may be checked by the host Member State when they are to exercise an activity with public health or safety implications.[83]

It is clear that these obligations may not apply, as such, to a service provider who is not resident in the host Member State, but only offers services over the Internet. It might be good practice, however, if the above information could be made public by means of the collaborative platform.

D. Other Relevant Rules

The rules discussed above (under the E-commerce Directive, Services Directive and Professional Qualifications Directive) are three specific pieces of internal market legislation that are likely to apply to activities delivered in the collaborative framework. However, these rules are not necessarily applicable to all activities in the collaborative economy, and when they are applicable they are not necessarily the only rules that apply.

i. Rules Not Necessarily Applicable

As explained in the previous paragraphs, the E-commerce Directive only applies to electronic services offered at a distance, while the Professional Qualifications Directive only applies to regulated professions. The Services Directive, for its part, suffers a great many exceptions. Therefore, several activities, as discussed above, may be excluded by one, the other, or indeed all the above rules. This does not mean that such activities evade EU law altogether, since they remain subject to the basic Treaty rules. Thus, the platforms and suppliers involved in such services may still claim market access, equal treatment and fair administration, as developed by the CJEU under the primary law.

---

[82] European Parliament and Council Directive 2005/36/EC of 7 September 2005 on the recognition of professional qualifications (Professional Qualifications Directive) [2005] OJ L 255/22, as amended by Directive 2013/55/EU OJ L 354/132.
[83] ibid Art 7.

ii. Other Rules also Applicable

In addition to the rules discussed above, the EU has also developed sector-specific rules in some areas, such as, for instance, transport, financial and insurance services and the network-bound industries. Subject to the legal qualifications discussed above, these rules do apply in the collaborative framework. These are not discussed in any detail here. The remaining bulk of internal market rules, on data protection and consumer protection, are discussed in the following sections.

E. Market Access under WTO Law and Other Free Trade Agreements

As the US has a clear lead over the EU in the development of the collaborative economy, most platforms are currently situated in that country. Many decide to set up a seat or other form of establishment within the EU, while other, typically smaller ones, operate directly from the US. The latter, pending the conclusion of the TTIP, have to rely on the GATS and are thus faced with a formidable legal tangle.

Under the GATS there are four modes of service delivery. Mode 1 is for the transborder provision of services, where only the service crosses the border; mode 2 is for consumption abroad, where only the recipient moves; mode 3 is for the establishment of foreign companies and their subsidiaries; and mode 4 is for the provisional posting of service providers. For each one of these four modes, GATS signatories have scheduled liberalisation commitments on the basis of a detailed classification of services inspired by the Central Product Classification (CPC) developed under the auspices of the UN. This classification has 12 main categories, over 60 sub-categories and several hundred sub-sub-categories of services.[84] On each one of those, signatory States have offered different levels of engagements concerning Market Access (GATS, Article XVI) and National Treatment (GATS, Article XVII). States have been much more willing to offer engagements under mode 1, which does not imply any physical movement, especially so at a time when the number of services likely to be offered at a distance was much more limited. On the other hand they have been much more hesitant in opening up sectors of the 'real' economy.

---

[84] The GATS classification corresponds to an abridged/simplified version of the UN CPC, which contains thousands of categories disaggregated down to five-digit classifications followed by unnumbered sub/sub-categories; on the relationship between the classification of services used in the GATS and the CPC see WTO, *United States—Measures Affecting the Cross-Border Supply of Gambling and Betting Services (US/Antigua Gambling)*—Report of the Appellate Body (7 April 2005) WT/DS285/AB/R, paras 196–213, available at https://docs.wto.org/dol2fe/Pages/FE_Search/ExportFile.aspx?id=57247&filename=Q/WT/DS/285ABR.pdf.

In view of the fact that States have offered different engagements for the different modes and the different categories and sub-categories of services, the collaborative platform, for each of the services it offers, may be subject to three different modes and thus to three corresponding degrees of market access: (a) if, according to the criteria set out above,[85] it only offers e-services, then it is only subject to the commitments under mode 1; (b) if it also participates in the underlying service but the underlying service is offered by providers of the host State, then the platform may claim market access according to the commitments offered under mode 3; (c) if, finally, the platform participates in the underlying service and the underlying service is offered by providers who temporarily cross the borders, then it may claim market access under mode 4. These three options (with the uncertainties they embody) multiplied by the number of service categories and the uncertainties connected to the scheduling of commitments under the GATS, make market access of foreign collaborative platforms precarious, to say the least.

Collaborative platforms established in Canada or in other countries with which the EU has concluded modern preferential agreements, such as the CETA, may be in a better position. Market access under the CETA, just like under the GATS, is based on positive lists of schedules (ie only the items and/or areas which are listed are subject to liberalisation), but it is more trader-friendly in several ways:[86] (a) once accepted into the host State, service providers enjoy national treatment on the basis of negative lists of schedules (ie national treatment covers all sectors/ activities, apart from those specifically excluded); (b) the rules on transparency and internal regulation have a much stronger bite than the ones of the GATS; (c) there are common disciplines in many specific areas (such as eg transport, financial services, e-commerce, intellectual property) which could facilitate specific services; (d) a mechanism is put in place to facilitate mutual recognition and the creation of common standards and rules; and (e) there is an investor-State dispute settlement mechanism. If the above is accurate, then it may be that collaborative economy platforms established in Canada, in Singapore or other third countries which have concluded a comprehensive trade agreement with the EU stand better chances of market access in the EU, than those established in the US.

F. Conclusion

Collaborative platforms' market access under EU law is greatly facilitated by the E-commerce Directive, by the Services Directive, by primary law on free movement and, occasionally by sector-specific legislation. In order to determine which

---

[85] Under section B.ii.
[86] This is not the place to discuss the merits (and possible shortcomings) of the CETA concluded between Canada and the EU.

of the above rules apply in any given circumstance, three basic questions need to be answered, in the following order: (a) is the platform a service provider?; (b) is the platform only offering digital (intermediation) service or is it directly involved in the provision or the definition of the underlying service?; and (c) in which service sector is the platform active and which specific piece of EU legislation applies to it? All these questions—and question (b) in particular—revolve around the same major qualifications discussed earlier, concerning the contractual links that exist between the parties in the triangular situation. The same core questions above are raised in different contexts (E-commerce Directive, Services Directive, primary law, sector specific legislation) and may, thus, yield different—or even opposing—answers.

IV. Consumer Protection

As discussed above, the collaborative economy creates new services and makes new experiences available to consumers, while giving them the opportunity, by exploiting their idle capacity, to occasionally transform themselves into prosumers or even traders. Overall, this is clearly beneficial to consumers.

By allowing consumers to shift sides, thus blurring the traditional production/consumption paradigm, the collaborative economy questions the traditional consumer protection model based on the dichotomy of traders versus consumers. This dichotomy is absolutely crucial in order to determine the precise scope of application of consumer protection rules (see section A below). Once their scope has been defined, the actual impact of consumer protection rules on the participants in collaborative economy is discussed (see section B below). The finding that consumer protection rules as they stand are ill-suited for the collaborative economy, combined with the self-regulatory possibilities offered to platforms and with behavioural hindsight gathered in recent years on this topic, leads to a reflection on whether the collaborative economy could be the perfect test-bed for a new paradigm of consumer protection law (see section C below).

A. Scope of Application of Consumer Protection Rules in the Collaborative Economy

EU consumer protection rules raise, once again, questions similar to the above, but again from a slightly different perspective.

Consumer protection in the EU is essentially secured through (in chronological order of adoption) the Unfair Contracts Terms Directive,[87] the Unfair Commercial

---

[87] Council Directive 93/13/EC of 5 April 1993 on unfair terms in consumer contracts (Unfair Terms Directive) [1993] OJ L 95/29.

Practices Directive,[88] the Consumer Rights Directive,[89] the Directive on alternative dispute resolution and the Regulation on online dispute resolution.[90] These will be further complemented by the forthcoming Digital Single Market Directives, especially the one on digital content.[91] Moreover, collaborative platforms which are held to directly partake in the provision of the underlying service are also subject to any sector-specific regulations, liability regime, codes of conduct etc applicable to the activity exercised by them.

The web of rules set by these texts is designed to level the playing field for traders by harmonising rules that protect consumers against traders, sellers or suppliers.[92] In other words, all the above legislation applies neither to consumer-to-consumer or C2C relations (also referred to as peer-to-peer or P2P) nor to business-to-business or B2B relations. As already explained, the existence of a C2C relationship is one of the main characteristics of collaborative activities (while B2B is not excluded). Thus, in order to understand the way consumer protection law applies to collaborative platforms, it is crucial to assess which of the three parties typically involved in collaborative economy activities qualifies as a trader, ie 'acting for purposes relating to his trade, business, craft or profession' and which is a consumer, ie acting outside his trade, business, craft or profession.[93] This is discussed in sections i, ii and iii below for platforms, consumers and suppliers, respectively. The mishaps there identified lead to a brief discussion of the idea of a 'Platform Directive', in section iv.

i. Platforms

a. General

The fact that collaborative platforms typically exercise economic activities[94] does not necessarily mean that they always qualify as traders. In the former test the

---

[88] European Parliament and Council Directive 2005/29/EC of 11 May 2005 concerning unfair business-to-consumer commercial practices in the internal market and amending Council Directive 84/450/EEC, Directives 97/7/EC, 98/27/EC and 2002/65/EC of the European Parliament and of the Council and Regulation (EC) No 2006/2004 of the European Parliament and of the Council (Unfair Commercial Practices Directive-UCPD) [2005] OJ L 149/22.

[89] European Parliament and Council Directive 2011/83/EU of 25 October 2011 on consumer rights, amending Council Directive 93/13/EEC and Directive 1999/44/EC of the European Parliament and of the Council and repealing Council Directive 85/577/EEC and Directive 97/7/EC of the European Parliament and of the Council [2011] OJ L 304/64.

[90] European Parliament and Council Directive 2013/11/EU of 21 May 2013 on alternative dispute resolution for consumer disputes and amending Regulation (EC) No 2006/2004 and Directive 2009/22/EC (Directive on consumer ADR) [2013] OJ L 165/63; European Parliament and Council Regulation (EU) No 524/2013 of 21 May 2013 on online dispute resolution for consumer disputes and amending Regulation (EC) No 2006/2004 and Directive 2009/22/EC (Regulation on consumer ODR) [2013] OJ L165/1.

[91] COM(2015) 634 final.

[92] Different terms are used in different Directives depending on their subject matter ('suppliers' is the term used in the draft Digital Content Directive, Art 2(3)), but are defined in the same way; the term 'traders' is used here for purposes of consistency.

[93] Unfair Terms Directive 93/13, Art 2(a) and (b).

[94] See above under section III.B.ii.

focus is on the nature of the activity, while in the latter it is on the kind of trade, profession etc exercised by the operator and on whether they gain some—direct or indirect—revenue from it. What is more, the fact that the definition of trader found in the above-mentioned Directives uses the term 'purpose' brings in an element of intent and allows for some subjectivity to be incorporated into the definition of a trader—and of a consumer.

The Commission proposes that 'according to a case-by-case assessment, a platform may be acting for purposes relating to its business, whenever, for example, it charges a commission on the transactions between suppliers and users, provides additional paid services or draws revenues from targeted advertising'.[95] It is from this perspective, for example, that the Italian Consumer and Competition Authority, upheld by the Administrative Court of Lazio, held that *TripAdvisor* qualifies as a 'trader' although it does not directly charge for its services.[96] Although it is conceivable that a platform carries out some economic activity which is outside the scope of its trade etc or that it offers some communitarian, social or other non-commercial activity, more often than not, collaborative platforms will qualify as 'traders'.

b. The E-commerce Exclusion of Liability

Traders or not, platforms may be exempted from any liability, civil or criminal, on the basis of the E-commerce Directive, for content over which they have no control. Therfore, in cases where the e-service provider serves as a 'mere conduit' for illegal content (Article 12), offers 'caching' services (Article 13) or provides 'hosting' (Article 14), without in any way participating in the creation, transformation or else the modification and active dissemination of the illegal information, such provider is exempt from liability.[97] Since 'mere conduit' and 'caching' suppose that the information is stored only in a temporary and transient manner necessary for the electronic process to take place, and given that most platforms store information for longer and process it in order to perform their matching function, it is essentially Article 14 on 'hosting' that is relevant here.

According to the Court,

> in order to establish whether the liability of a referencing service provider may be limited under Article 14 of Directive 2000/31, it is necessary to examine whether the role played

---

[95] See Commission Staff Working Document, 'Guidance on the implementation/application of Directive 2005/29/EC on Unfair Commercial Practices' SWD(2016) 163 final, 124.

[96] *TripAdvisor* Autorità Garante della Concorrenza e del Mercato, Decision No PS9345 of 19 December 2014, paras 87–89. This specific part of the decision by the AGCM was confirmed by the Tribunale Amministrativo Regionale per il Lazio, Sezione I, Sentenza No 9355 of 13 July 2015. The case is taken from the above-mentioned Communication, which is a sign that the Commission endorses this reasoning.

[97] For the finding that a social networking platform (which is not very dissimilar from collaborative platforms) offers hosting services see Case C-360/10 *SABAM v Netlog* EU:C:2012:85.

by that service provider is neutral, in the sense that its conduct is merely technical, automatic and passive, pointing to a lack of knowledge or control of the data which it stores.[98]

On the other hand, 'the operator plays such [an active] role when it provides assistance which entails, in particular, optimising the presentation of the offers for sale in question or promoting them'.[99]

Thus, it becomes crucial to know whether a platform actively intermediates between the parties (by drafting terms or clauses of their contract, by deciding on the price etc) or whether, on the contrary, it only serves as a passive 'bulletin board' for information over which it has no control whatsoever.[100]

As the Commission has put it 'the exemption from liability applies on the condition that the collaborative platform does not play an active role which would give it the knowledge of, control over or awareness of the illegal information'.[101]

The Dutch Supreme Court has held that an active platform (in the area of accommodation) is characterised by the fact that the provider and the client may not get into direct contact but have to go through the platform for their transaction to be concluded. Conversely, where the platform only provides the necessary contact details of the accommodation provider, then it will be considered a mere bulletin board.[102] Further to this criterion, one may say that a platform which is being paid for the actual conclusion of a contract (by way of a commission) rather than for making public the service and contact details of its provider (by way of a registration fee, subscription or advertisement) is more likely to qualify as 'active'.[103]

The appreciation of the neutrality of the platform in view of assessing its liability in many respects resembles the evaluation, discussed above, of whether it provides merely e-services or, whether it is also involved in the provision of the

---

[98] Joined Cases C-236/08 to C-238/08 *Google France v Louis Vuitton* EU:C:2010:159, para 114.

[99] Case C-324/09 *L'Oreal v eBay* EU:C:2011:474, para 123; illustrations of the application of the above rules are provided by the French decision of the Court of Cassation, Commercial Chamber in *PublicitéSté Pewterpassion.com c/ Sté Leguide.com* 11-27729 of 4 December 2012, where the Court held that a platform which top ranked products against remuneration was indirectly promoting such products and could not claim Art 14 liability exclusion, while the German Federal Court of Justice, in *Hotelbewertungsportal* I ZR 94/13 of 19 March 2015, held a platform not liable for the demeaning review put up by one of its users concerning the services received through the intermediation of the said platform. For a thorough discussion of the liability issues raised by the combination of the E-commerce Directive with the Unfair Commercial Practices Directive, see SWD(2016) 163 final, 119 ff.

[100] The term 'bulletin board' is taken from R Koolhoven et al, 'Impulse Paper on specific Liability Issues raised by the collaborative economy in the accommodation sector, Paris-Amsterdam-Barcelona', upon request by the Commission (2016) 12 available at http://ec.europa.eu/growth/single-market/strategy/collaborative-economy_el.

[101] Commission Report 'on the adequacy of national expert resources for complying with the regulatory functions pursuant to Article 27(4) of Directive 2013/30/EU' COM(2016) 318 final, 7–8.

[102] *Duinzigt* Hoge Raad 16 October 2015, NL:HR:2015:3099, Prejudiciele beslissing op vraag van NL:RBDHA:2015:1437.

[103] In this sense see also Koolhoven et al 'Impulse Paper on specific Liability Issues raised by the collaborative economy in the accommodation sector, Paris-Amsterdam-Barcelona' (2016) (n 100) 15.

underlying service.[104] Indeed, if the platform is considered to be itself offering the underlying service, then the E-commerce Directive and its Article 14 are altogether inapplicable (at least to the services exceeding the e-service). If, on the other hand, it is established that the platform is only an e-provider, then the applicability of Article 14 may be assessed on the basis of the criteria discussed above.

Thus, a gradation may be established along the following lines: when the platform participates to the provision of the underlying service, the E-commerce Directive is inapplicable; when the platform plays an active role in determining the content of the underlying service (which may be offered by a third party) then the E-commerce Directive may apply but the exclusion of liability foreseen in Article 14 may not. The exclusion of liability shall apply where the platform does neither of the above and has a passive or neutral role both in the definition and in the provision of the underlying service.

'Neutral' platforms only benefit from the liability exemption as long as they reasonably ignore the illegal information. As soon as they get to know of it, they need to remove or disable access to it. According to the Court, the platform may no longer benefit from the exclusion when it has 'been aware of facts or circumstances on the basis of which a diligent economic operator should have identified the illegality in question and acted in accordance'.[105] A diligent platform provider must, therefore, not only respond to notifications from users, but should also implement an effective notice-and-take-down policy.[106]

Platform liability for content over which it has not control, has also occupied the European Court of Human Rights, under the perspective of Article 10 of the European Convention on Human Rights (ECHR), on freedom of expression.[107] In two recent decisions the Strasbourg Court has drawn a very fine, if obscure, dividing line. In *Delfi v Estonia* the Court condoned with national courts which required platforms to monitor and delete users' online expression which involved threats and hate speech.[108] In *MTE v Hungary*, on the other hand, the Court concluded that similar national judgments which, however, only involved trade defamation, did violate Article 10 of the Convention as they harmed the defendant's ability to provide a 'platform for third parties to exercise their freedom of expression by posting comments'.[109] On the face of it, it would seem that the Strasbourg Court, on the basis of Article 10 of the ECHR, follows an approach similar to

---

[104] See section II.B.i above.

[105] Case C-324/09 *L'Oreal v eBay*, para 120; it should be noted, however, that no general obligation to monitor the content of the hosted material may be imposed on the e-service provider, see Art 15(1) of the E-commerce Directive.

[106] It is yet a different issue whether and to what extent national private law on agency, an issue typically regulated by the national civil codes, will apply to 'passive' platforms.

[107] ECHR, Art 10.

[108] *Delfi v Estonia*, ECtHR, Application 64569/09, Judgment of 16 June 2015, ECLI:CE:ECHR:2015: 0616JUD006456909.

[109] *MTE v Hungary*, ECtHR, Application 22947/13, Judgment of 2 February 2016, ECLI:CE:ECHR: 2016:0202JUD002294713.

the one followed by Article 14 of the E-commerce Directive. A reservation would be made in extreme cases violating core fundamental rights, such as the right to life and to dignity. The distinction between acceptable and unacceptable content would be based on a 'know it when you see it' basis, as only clearly intolerable content would be illegal.[110] In practice, however, this would mean that platforms should put into place monitoring mechanisms, a solution diametrically opposed to the one currently in force under Article 14 of the E-commerce Directive. The ECtHR's judgments are not directly relevant for platforms coming under the scope of Article 14 of the E-commerce Directive, as the latter would clearly be *lex specialis* to the Convention. The judgments may be of importance, however: (a) for platforms which are not covered by the Directive; (b) as an input in the ongoing discussions for the revision of the E-commerce Directive; and (c) as a source of inspiration for an '*interpretation conforme*' by the CJEU of the E-commerce Directive, in order to bring it into line with the ECtHR's case law. In this latter scenario, the liability exclusion foreseen by the Directive would be set aside in cases of extreme violations.

Liability under the E-commerce Directive may exist towards the consumers of e-services as well as towards third parties.[111] In other words, the question whether the subject of the illegal information (the plaintiff) is or is not a consumer is irrelevant. The above developments hold true both in relation to the service recipients (who would typically qualify as consumers) and to service providers (who occasionally would qualify as traders themselves).[112]

ii. Consumers

In a similar, but inverse, manner, most users of the platforms' services will qualify as 'consumers' and will, thus, be able to claim protection. Being at the receiving end, both of the electronic service offered by the platform and of the underlying service offered by the service provider (alone or jointly with the platform) or the platform (with the supplier as its employee),[113] these users will typically qualify as 'consumers'; although it may not be excluded that some of them make use of the platform's services within (ie not outside) their own trade etc. For instance, most users of business, financial and work-space collaborative services would probably not qualify as consumers, since they are likely to be using those in the course of their own trade. The development of the collaborative economy is likely to set it adrift from its initial 'sharing' culture and give rise to more B2B (rather than C2C) transactions. Conversely, the fact that the users of a collaborative platform make

---

[110] D Keller, 'Policy Debates Over EU Platform Liability Laws: New Human Rights Case Law in the Real World' *The Center for Internet and Society, Stanford Law School Blog* (14 April 2016), available at https://cyberlaw.stanford.edu/blog/2016/04/policy-debates-over-eu-platform-liability-laws-new-human-rights-case-law-real-world.

[111] See eg Case C-131/12 *Google Spain v AEDP and Mario Costeja Gonzales* EU:C:2014:317.

[112] For the peers providing the service see section iii below.

[113] See section II.A above.

their living through some trade activity does not automatically mean that they enter the specific transaction in their capacity as trader. This has been expressly recognised by the Court in relation to lawyers:[114] in his dealings with his clients a lawyer is a trader,[115] while in his dealings with a credit institution the lawyer is a consumer, provided that the credit in question is not used for his professional activity; this is so even if the lawyer in question specialises in commercial law, displays a high level of technical knowledge and secures the loan taken by collaterals offered by his law firm.[116]

Subject to the above qualifications, the fact remains that most platform users will qualify as 'consumers' and will be protected as such.

iii. Suppliers

More delicate is the qualification of the supplier of the underlying service. This, however, is a core issue, given that the supplier's qualification as a trader or as a consumer is crucial for the application of the consumer protection rules. Indeed, if the supplier of the underlying service is a trader, then the collaborative platform will be in a B2B relation with him/her and it will not have to comply with any of the obligations discussed below in section B, which only apply to B2C situations.

In most cases, the providers of the underlying service offer collaborative services occasionally, in their spare time, on top of their main employment (or unemployment benefit).[117] In most cases, therefore, the collaborative activity does not become the main 'trade, business, craft or profession' of the individuals concerned. This could be otherwise if the collaborative activity comes within the broader professional activity of the person concerned, in which case it could be said that it constitutes a diversified expression of the trade etc already exercised (this would be the case with hoteliers promoting their rooms through *Airbnb*). The same could be true for inactive, unemployed or underemployed people who, after a while, come to depend economically on their collaborative activity.

Inspired by the practice followed in several Member States, the Commission suggests that 'thresholds, established in a reasonable way, can be a useful proxy and

---

[114] See Case C-110/14 *Costea v Volksbank* EU:C:2015:538, para 20, where the Court notes that 'one and the same person can act as a consumer in certain transactions and as a seller or supplier in others'.

[115] Case C-537/13 *Šiba* EU:C:2015:14, para 23.

[116] See Case C-110/14 *Costea*.

[117] See eg the data published in Commission Staff Working Document 'European agenda for the collaborative economy—supporting analysis' SWD(2016) 184 final, 37–38, where it is stated that: (a) income from collaborative activities account for less than quarter of the household income for 39% of participants and for less than half of the household income for another 58%; and (b) many 'participants' never performed a task for the platform they are registered with; even in the US, where the collaborative economy is well ahead of that in Europe, only 33% of the participants gain their principal income from the collaborative economy: see WP De Groen and I Maseli, 'The Impact of the Collaborative Economy on the Labour market' (2016) Centre for European Policy Studies (CEPS) Special Report, 10, available at http://ec.europa.eu/DocsRoom/documents/16953/attachments/1/translations.

can help create a clear regulatory framework to the benefit of non-professional providers'.[118] The Commission proposes that a combination of the following would be determinant: (a) the frequency of the services, ie whether the services are offered regularly or on a purely marginal and accessory basis; (b) the profit seeking motive, as opposed to the aim of exchanging assets or skills, and even (in a more questionable manner) the fact that they simply obtain cost compensation; (c) the level of turnover from the activity concerned, and whether such turnover is higher/lower than that obtained from other activities pursued by the same person (in the sense that if some other activity is more lucrative, that other activity is likely to qualify as the trade etc of the provider).[119]

The first two criteria proposed by the Commission (regularly versus purely occasional; profit seeking versus with aim of exchanging skills) only resolve clear cut extreme cases, and are unhelpful in most mainstream situations. The same is true for the third criterion, since the comparison of levels of turnover from different activities may only be helpful if the differences are great; however, the majority of collaborative participants decide to partake in this new economy precisely because the revenue generated thereby is important for them. In other words, people are unlikely to put their spare rooms for rent, to start driving passengers around the city or to offer their personal skills if the moneys thus gained do not substantially add to their other revenues. This is not to say that the Commission's approach of using sets of criteria is flawed; such criteria, however, need to be defined in a more precise/useful manner. The Commission's approach of defining the absolute outer limits and leaving it to national administrations and jurisdictions to flesh them out, although extremely prudent, is also quite unhelpful.

iv. Towards a 'Platform Directive'?

The above difficulties have pushed several authors to question 'whether the intervention of a professional intermediary or platform should affect the qualification of the contract concluded between the actual service provider and the recipient'.[120] The idea put forward is that, in a transaction where at least one party (of the three) is a trader, there should always be consumer protection. The issue of intermediaries' liability, when proposing contracts with non-professionals, also occurs in an offline context, as it may often be unclear for consumers whether their counterpart is a professional or a non-professional. In the latter case, intermediaries wishing to evade any responsibility should clearly inform consumers that they are not protected by consumer laws. Even if they do so, however, they are not sure of

---

[118] ibid. It should be assumed that the term 'non-professional' provider is to be contrasted with a 'professional' service provider, ie a 'trader' or, in the most recent texts a 'supplier'.
[119] COM(2016) 356 final, 9.
[120] E Terryn, 'The sharing economy in Belgium—a case for regulation?' (2016) 5 *EuCML* 45, 50.

being absolved of any responsibility; indeed a clause to that effect included in the draft Consumer Protection Directive[121] has been dropped from the final text.[122]

The situation may be even more unclear in relation to online platforms, given that they extend the suppliers' offer to an indeterminate number of people, which could rule out the possibility of claiming that the offer of the underlying services is 'occasional' and its provider is non-professional. This is, for example, the tipping point under Belgian law, concerning peer-to-peer lending of money: while it is legally done on a private basis, the mere use of an internet platform bestows a public character to the appeal for repayable funds, for which a banking licence is needed, which private persons lack.[123] It may be convincingly argued that a formalistic and rigid solution applied in an area as delicate as 'financial services' need not be transposed to other more mainstream areas, such as housing, and even less so, tool-sharing, cooking and the like. In Denmark, however, the same solution is followed in an all-encompassing manner: 'If two private parties enter into a contract with the assistance of an active third party (an intermediary), the contract between the seller and the buyer is considered a B2C contract if the customer is a consumer. The seller or service provider then has to apply [sic] with the consumer regulation and the third party has certain obligations such as a duty to inform the buyer (the customer) in accordance with consumer protection regulation'.[124] Other Member States may be following other, similar-but-different, approaches, thus resulting in important fragmentation both at the level of consumer protection and at the level of the obligations and liabilities imposed on platforms and suppliers of the underlying services.

In view of the above, and in order to avoid the complexities of vicarious liability under tort law briefly mentioned above,[125] some commentators have suggested that liability arising from the activity of collaborative platforms should be specifically regulated in the form of a 'Platform Directive'.[126] Such a Directive, specifically aimed at tripartite contractual relations, would not be all that original in the framework of EU law: the old Commercial Agents Directive seeks to protect the agent against the principal,[127] while the recently revised Package Travel Directive[128]

---

[121] See Commission, 'Proposal for a Directive of the European Parliament and of the Council on consumer rights' COM(2008) 614, Art 7.

[122] European Parliament and Council Directive 2011/83/EU of 25 October 2011 on consumer rights, amending Council Directive 93/13/EEC and Directive 1999/44/EC of the European Parliament and of the Council and repealing Council Directive 85/577/EEC and Directive 97/7/EC of the European Parliament and of the Council [2011] OJ L 304/64.

[123] Terryn, 'The sharing economy in Belgium—a case for regulation?' (2016) with further references.

[124] MJ Sorensen, 'Private Law Perspectives on Platform Services: Uber—A business model in search of a new contractual legal frame?' (2016) 5 *EuCML* 15, 17.

[125] See section II above.

[126] C Busch et al, 'The Rise of the Platform Economy: A New Challenge for EU Consumer Law?' (2016) 5 *EuCML* 3.

[127] Council Directive 86/653/EEC of 18 December 1986 on the coordination of the laws of the Member States relating to self-employed commercial agents [1986] OJ L 382/17.

[128] European Parliament and Council Directive (EU) 2015/2302 of 25 November 2015 on package travel and linked travel arrangements, amending Regulation (EC) No 2006/2004 and Directive 2011/83/EU of the European Parliament and of the Council and repealing Council Directive 90/314/EEC (Package Travel Directive) [2015] OJ L 326/1.

seeks to better protect consumers by putting most of the burden on the intermediary. The proposed Platform Directive could either establish some clearer criteria for identifying the responsible party in different situations, or impose rules of strict liability irrespective of the underlying contractual relations, or (better) combine the two approaches.

Indeed, several arguments may be invoked in favour of such a regulated allocation of liability. Firstly, some of the requirements laid down in consumer protection legislation, such as 'extensive information disclosures, rights of withdrawal, secure payments, transparent confirmation processes and adequate dispute resolution services',[129] or data protection, could be an extremely heavy burden for peers to bear. 'It is not only a matter of differences in expertise, experience and scale. It is also a question about feasibility, fairness and the reasonable expectations that peer consumers might harbour in relation to peer providers'.[130] Secondly, aggrieved consumers may find it difficult or impossible to seek redress from suppliers. 'For example, they may not be able to easily contact peer providers residing in another country or speaking another language. Or, peer providers may simply not able to cover the claims, eg because of a lack of financial resources'.[131] Turning to a notable and sizeable business, such as the platform, instead of an individual who occasionally rents out his/her apartment or performs odd jobs, seems indeed more sensible.[132] Thirdly, in view of the immense role and control of certain platforms (especially in the transportation sector), suppliers have a very limited involvement in the performance of the underlying service and it would therefore be unfair for them to be held liable for factors determined by the platform. 'Peer providers may not have control over the timing, format and presentation of disclosures about the goods or services they offer and limited influence in the way that pricing, payments and disputes are addressed'.[133] All in all, peers cannot be expected to show the same level of professional diligence, care and quality as platforms can.

Together with reducing fragmentation and levelling the playing field, the interests of the consumer should be the overarching principle of such a Directive. Therefore, it may be necessary to derogate from regular dispute resolution rules and create a more favourable set of choices for the consumer, as discussed in Chapter 6.

Some national jurisdictions have already shown flexibility in lightening the standard of care imposed on non-professional sellers,[134] while the new Package

---

[129] Organisation for Economic Co-operation and Development (OECD), 'Protecting Consumers in Peer Platform Markets, Exploring the Issues' (2016) OECD Digital Economy Papers No 253, 20–21, available at www.oecd-ilibrary.org/science-and-technology/protecting-consumers-in-peer-platform-markets_5jlwvz39m1zw-en.

[130] ibid.

[131] ibid 22.

[132] On the issues—and difficulties—raised by dispute resolution, see Ch 6 below.

[133] ibid 21.

[134] For example, Hungary, Norway and the Netherlands, while others, such as Finland, Italy and Spain, have excluded any possibility to differentiate: see OECD, 'Protecting Consumers in Peer Platform Markets, Exploring the Issues' (2016) 21.

Travel Directive has explicitly allowed Member States to allocate liability of non-performance of the obligations arising from the package travel contract to the intermediary.[135] Similarly, the OECD suggests a model of co-operative (shared) responsibility, whereby 'the burden of offering a reasonable level of consumer protection is a shared one', with practices that include 'effective reputation, monitoring and feedback mechanisms, educating and informing peers, to make sure peers properly inform other peers, establish secure ways of communication and mediation, and make sure peers can be identified in case matters go wrong'.[136] Indeed, many platforms have already introduced such initiatives through self-regulation.

In addition to the relations between the consumer and the platform/supplier, such a Platform Directive could also clarify the relations between the platform and the supplier of the underlying service. Indeed, if the latter is not a professional but rather a prosumer, then consumer protection law also applies in this relationship, as the prosumer may have all the rights awarded to traditional 'consumers' against the platform.

Finally, as discussed in Chapter 6 on dispute resolution, under the Rome I Regulation[137] and the Brussels I Regulation (recast),[138] consumers benefit from special rules on the designation of applicable law and competent jurisdictions. Like consumer protection law, the applicability of these Regulations relies on the uncertain qualification of one of the parties as a consumer. Thus, while it certainly applies to the relationship between the platform and the consumer (B2C), it also applies to the relationship between the platform and the non-professional supplier (prosumer, again B2C), while it may not apply to the relations of the latter with the consumer (C2C). The proposed Platform Directive could also take a position in this respect, thus enhancing legal certainty.

Last but not least, it need not be stressed that if the proposed Platform Directive did set the criteria for determining which party is responsible for which part of the service finally offered to the consumer, it would greatly facilitate the questions surrounding market access and the eventual applicability of other texts of EU secondary legislation, such as the E-commerce and Services Directives (as well as national legislation).[139] It could also resolve many of the conundrums that non-EU platforms have to face under the GATS rules and commitments.[140]

The adoption of the Platform Directive corresponds to scenario 5, briefly discussed above.[141] Is the adoption of such a Directive a good idea?

---

[135] Art 13(1), which reads: 'Member States may maintain or introduce in their national law provisions under which the retailer is also responsible for the performance of the package'.

[136] OECD (n 129) 23.

[137] European Parliament and Council Regulation (EC) No 593/2008 of 17 June 2008 on the law applicable to contractual obligations (Rome I) [2008] OJ L 177/6.

[138] European Parliament and Council Regulation (EU) No 1215/2012 of 12 December 2012 on jurisdiction and the recognition and enforcement of judgments in civil and commercial matters (Brussels I Regulation (recast)) [2012] OJ L 351/1.

[139] Discussed in sections III.A and III.B above.

[140] For which see section III.E above.

[141] See section II.A above.

Table 1: Applicability of core EU rules on the different scenarios of the collaborative economy

Scenario	Consumer protection rules (including Rome I Regulation)				Services Directive		E-commerce Directive
	Consumer protection applies to supplier		Consumer protection applies to consumer		By platform	By supplier	By platform
					Supplier = Irrelevant	Supplier = Irrelevant	Supplier = Irrelevant
Specifics	Supplier = Trader	Supplier = Prosumer	Supplier = Trader	Supplier = Prosumer			
1	(B2B) NO	(B2C) YES for the e-service, unless exempted under E-Commerce Directive, Arts 14–15	(B2C) YES for the e-service (platform) (B2C) YES for the underlying service (supplier)	(B2C) YES for the e-service (platform) (C2C) NO for the underlying service (supplier)[142]	YES, unless exception[143]	YES	YES
2	(B2B) NO	Prosumer = Worker NO since s/he is under employment or other subordination relation	Supplier = Irrelevant Consumer can claim for both e- and underlying service from platform		YES, unless exception[144]	NO since subordination	NO since provider of the underlying service
3	(B2B) NO	(B2C) YES[145]	(B2C) YES	(C2C) NO[146]	YES, unless exception[147]	YES, unless exception[148]	YES, in its relation with the supplier
4	NA	NA	YES, against both supplier and platform		YES, unless exception[149]	YES, unless exception[150]	NO
5	Special rules (Platform Directive)						

[142] But: Danish model, whereby the existence of platform triggers consumer protection law?
[143] But: E-commerce Directive more favourable.
[144] But: no possibility to claim the application of the E-commerce Directive.
[145] But: unlikely scenario.
[146] But: Danish model, whereby the existence of platform triggers consumer protection law?
[147] But: E-commerce Directive more favourable.
[148] But: obligations should be alleviated if the supplier is not a trader?
[149] But: no possibility to claim the application of the E-commerce Directive.
[150] But: no possibility to claim the application of the E-commerce Directive.

In the preceding table, I have attempted to codify the different possibilities discussed above, all of them depending on uncertain and unclear legal tests, such as: when is a platform a mere intermediary and when is it a full service provider?; when is a supplier a professional and when is s/he a consumer?; when does a professional also qualify as a consumer? These questions, difficult to answer even in the traditional economy, become even more blurred in the disruptive environment of the collaborative economy. Some authors even question whether they are adapted at all for this new environment. It comes as no surprise that the table above depicts a great amount of legal uncertainty, depending both on the specifics of each case and on the legal systems and legal traditions of the different Member States.

The table assumes that the platform is a trader and follows the five main scenarios discussed above in section II.A. It has two parts. The column on the left examines the circumstances in which consumer protection rules (including the favourable choice of law of the Rome I Regulation) may be claimed by the supplier (against the platform) and by the consumer (against the platform and the supplier) respectively. It can clearly be observed that the level of protection, especially of the consumer, varies considerably depending on the kind of contractual links identified (scenarios 1 to 5) and the legal qualification of the supplier, as a trader or a prosumer.

The two columns on the right examine the circumstances under which the platform and the supplier may use the Services Directive and/or the E-commerce Directive in order to gain market access. It is based on the assumption that the supplier—trader or prosumer—qualifies as 'service provider'. Here again, important differences surface.

In view of the radically differing solutions which may ensue from delicate—and thus uncertain—legal qualifications, it would seem that the adoption of a Platform Directive would, in principle, be a good idea. However, one should not underestimate the variety and complexity of the legal issues involved, and not overestimate the capacity of the EU legislature—or any legislature for that matter—to come up with meaningful and satisfactory answers thereto. Thus, it may be worth asking, in view of the general guidance already offered by the Commission in its 2016 collaborative economy package,[151] what the added value of a Directive would be. Should the adoption of such a Directive be a priority in the current circumstances or, on the contrary, would it be preferable to let the collaborative economy reach maturity first, before adopting a hard law instrument in this area? This issue is further discussed in Chapter 7 below.

B. How Can Platforms/Suppliers Abide by Consumer Protection Rules: Obligations and Recommendations

Platforms, insofar as they are traders, must abide by consumer protection rules with regard to their intermediary services and, potentially, with regard to the underlying service provided.

---

[151] For which see section II.B.i above.

i. Obligations Deriving from the Intermediation Services

Regardless of whether the platform is party to the contract between the supplier and the consumer and the obligations arising therefrom, platforms must abide by consumer protection laws with regard to their intermediary services. Collaborative platforms offer a variety of services to their consumers (both suppliers and consumers) arising from their role as intermediaries. These services can be: (a) pre-transaction services, such as information, advice on safety, criminal records check, verification of the identity of users, review/reputation system, matching of demand and supply (including recommendations and advertising of suppliers, geo-location etc), photos, guidance and so on; (b) transaction services, such as laying out Terms and Conditions, price recommendation or setting and payment services; and (c) post-transaction services, such as insurance, tax assistance, compliance monitoring and action, complaints handling, and the like.[152]

In view of the ambiguous roles of the three parties involved and the complex relationships shaped, as discussed above, the first and foremost pre-contractual information duty of platforms would be to take appropriate measures enabling the consumers to 'clearly understand who their contracting party is'.[153] As mentioned above, consumer protection legislation does not apply if the contracting party is a peer (ie not a professional or else a 'trader'). Therefore, the platform should inform consumers that they will only be protected by EU consumer and marketing laws insofar as their supplier is a 'trader'.[154] This is especially so since platforms often use confusing terminology. For example *Airbnb* calls its users 'hosts' and 'guests', thus potentially leaving the parties wondering whether consumer laws apply.[155] Such an information obligation derives from the professional diligence and transparency requirements under the UCPD.[156] In particular, concerning the status of the suppliers, in order to avoid omitting material information, the collaborative platform should,

> under Articles 6(1)(f) and 7(1) and (2) of the UCPD, enable relevant third party traders to indicate to users that they are traders, and the platform should inform consumers whether and if so what criteria it applies to select the suppliers operating through it and whether and if so what checks it performs in relation to their reliability.[157]

Platforms should also enable suppliers that qualify as traders to abide by the consumer protection acquis, 'for example by designing their web structures to make it possible for third party traders to identify themselves as such to platforms users'.[158]

---

[152] See European Commission, 'Exploratory study of consumer issues in online peer-to-peer platform markets' Task 1 Report (2017), Figure 9 at 47, available at http://ec.europa.eu/newsroom/document.cfm?doc_id=45250.

[153] See SWD(2016) 163 final, 127 with regard to e-commerce platforms (marketplaces) in general. The same applies to collaborative platforms.

[154] See COM(2016) 356 final, 10.

[155] OECD (n 129) 20.

[156] UCPD 2005/29, Arts 5(2), 2(h), 6 and 7.

[157] See SWD(2016) 163 final, 132.

[158] See COM(2016) 356 final, 10.

Further, platforms should inform potential consumers about their intended contractual role. If platforms wish to only act (and appear) as mere intermediaries, instead of suppliers of the underlying service, they should disclose the limitation of the service provided to the consumer in order to avoid liability being pointed at them. While a specific provision obliging platforms to disclose their intended role was dropped from the draft Consumers Rights Directive,[159] a legal basis can arguably be found in Article 6(1)(a) of the existing Consumer Rights Directive.[160] If the platform omits or fails to inform the consumer that the contracting party will be other than the platform itself, it can be faced with its own liability deriving from the provision of the underlying service, such as non-performance and the like.

In *Wathelet*,[161] where an offline intermediary (garage) had failed to inform the consumer that it was acting merely as an intermediary and that the seller was actually a private individual, the Court clarified that a professional intermediary can itself be considered party to the contract between two consumers, if it does not adequately inform the buyer (consumer) about the identity of the seller (supplier).[162] In a similar way, a Danish High Court, in a case concerning a consumer buying a flight ticket from an airline (supplier) through an online travel agency (intermediary), found that

> the consumer had reason to assume that he had bought the ticket directly from the travel agency, given that the latter had been his only contact point during the purchase, had received the payment and provided the tickets. The general impression provided by the webpage of the travel agency also made it reasonable for the consumer to assume that he was buying the tickets directly from them.[163]

While in the collaborative economy suppliers usually are more apparent to the consumer than the airline in the above case, the consumer may be confused, especially in cases where the platform exercises control. The criteria referred to in the Danish judgment (only contact point, receipt of payment) could apply to most collaborative platforms.

It should be noted, nonetheless, that clear and precise paperwork may not prevail over reality: however detailed and clear the legal status of the parties involved may be on paper, it may be completely ignored—and even turned onto its head—by courts when the mismatch between paper and reality is too great. This approach was followed by the Central London Employment Tribunal in the UK *Uber* case, where not only did it set aside *Uber's* contractual terms negating any employment

---

[159] Art 7.

[160] The provision requires the trader to provide consumers with clear and comprehensible information about 'the main characteristics of the goods or services'. On the applicability of this provision in the case of platforms see Busch et al, 'The Rise of the Platform Economy: A New Challenge for EU Consumer Law?' (2016) 5.

[161] Case C-149/15 *Wathelet* EU:C:2016:840.

[162] Under European Parliament and Council Directive 1999/44/EC of 25 May 1999 on certain aspects of the sale of consumer goods and associated guarantees (Consumer Sales Directive) [1999] OJ L 171/12.

[163] See SWD(2016) 163 final, 128.

relationship with its drivers, but also found that such relationship was established by virtue of a separate, unwritten contract, which was not subject to the jurisdiction clauses of the main contract.[164]

Moreover, platform operators should offer pre-contractual information regarding the services offered via the platform. While such an obligation is ambiguous under existing consumer protection legislation, the recently revised Package Travel Directive, imposing an information duty on both the intermediary and the supplier, could be showing the way for collaborative platforms as well. In any case, platform operators should be wary of how they present and advertise the services provided through the platform. For instance, the *Tribunal correctionnel de Paris* fined the French subsidiary of *Uber* for misleading commercial practices on the grounds of presenting its *UberPOP* service as ride-sharing, even though it was in reality a taxi service.[165]

In any event, some collaborative platforms, in the pre-contractual stage, advertise or else promote the services offered through their platforms, and even promote and propose to consumers certain suppliers that they consider a good match. Such behaviour on the part of the platform can create reasonable expectations for the quality and specific characteristics of the services and thus determine the conformity (or lack thereof) of the services with the contract.[166] Conversely, platforms might have a duty towards consumers to remove suppliers who have been known not to perform their contract obligations, or at least inform them about the risk. Indeed, the biggest platforms, such as *Airbnb* and *Uber*, regulate—to some extent—the quality of the services offered by monitoring the performance of their suppliers, and ban them from using the platform if there is poor performance or bad behaviour.[167] Such a practice, of discontinuing problematic suppliers, could satisfy the professional diligence test foreseen in Article 5 of the UCPD and thus prevent an unfair practice from being characterised as such. Such a practice, however, does raise acute problems under labour law, as discussed in Chapter 5.

Platforms also act as communication intermediaries, with most communications between peers necessarily going through the platform. Thus, the responsibility for promptly directing and forwarding messages to the parties concerned belongs to platforms. A similar obligation has already been provided in the recent Package Travel Directive.[168]

---

[164] Case Nos 2202551/2015 & Others, *Aslam, Farrar and Others v Uber*, Judgment of 28 October 2016, para 92, available at www.judiciary.gov.uk/judgments/mr-y-aslam-mr-j-farrar-and-others-v-uber/; this case is discussed in some detail in Ch 5.

[165] *Uber France / DGCCRF et autres*; upheld by the *Cour d'appel de Paris* in Judgment PI4084000776 of 7 December 2015, available at www.legalis.net/jurisprudences/cour-dappel-de-paris-pole-4-chambre-10-arret-du-7-decembre-2015. For more on the legal battles of *Uber* see Ch 7 below.

[166] See in that regard eg Consumer Sales Directive 1999/44, Art 2(2)(d); see also COM (2015) 635 final, Art 5(c), for the distant sale of goods.

[167] See Ch 7 below.

[168] Art 15.

Another pre-contractual duty for platforms derives from the review/reputation system employed:

> When publishing user reviews, a platform operator is required to provide truthful information on the main characteristics of its services in accordance with Articles 6(1)(b) and 7(4)(a) UCPD. In particular, the platform should not mislead its users as to the origin of the reviews: it should avoid creating the impression that reviews posted through it originate from real users, when it cannot adequately ensure this.[169]

Without amounting to a general monitoring obligation,[170] platforms should take appropriate measures to ensure the truthfulness of the reviews posted. In that regard, *TripAdvisor* was fined by the Italian Consumer and Competition Authority for publishing misleading reviews. The platform had not performed controls to establish whether the reviews were authentic and that they had not been orchestrated in order to influence the rankings.[171] Further, the online posting of only a selection of reviews by the platform operator could constitute an unfair practice in the form of misleading omission. Reviews and reputation systems also generate data-related concerns:

> If the platform deletes such data, the supplier's sales may dramatically decrease. It is, therefore, not implausible to assume that platforms are under an obligation to carefully manage their reputation system and that they may be liable for damages if a supplier suffers a reputational loss because of insufficient data security.[172]

Similarly, obligations for platforms by virtue of their intermediary role arise during the transaction. Therefore, lawful Terms and Conditions, safe payment methods, and (when the platform exerts control over the pricing) fair pricing, among others, should be provided by platforms to consumers. Especially with regard to prices, collaborative platforms often run on a dynamic pricing model in order to achieve balance between supply and demand (see eg *Uber's* infamous surge pricing), use complex algorithms that determine or recommend prices, set prices that include various (and sometimes obscure) fees and charges, and employ drip pricing. Such practices are highly likely to constitute misleading actions or omissions under the UCPD.[173] Indeed, for instance, *Uber's* surge pricing in correlation with the platform's underlying use of data, such as the battery level on the consumers' phones,[174] may be contrary to the professional diligence requirement.[175] On the other hand, *Airbnb* was found by the Australian Competition and Consumer Commission (ACCC) to mislead consumers through drip pricing.[176] The ACCC

---

[169] See SWD(2016) 163 final, 139.
[170] See Art 15(1) of the E-commerce Directive.
[171] The fine was, however, cancelled by the Tribunale Amministrativo Regionale per il Lazio, Sezione I, Sentenza No 9355 of 13 July 2015.
[172] Busch et al (n 126) 8.
[173] UCPD 2005/29, Arts 6(1)(d) and 7(4)(c).
[174] For which see Ch 3 below.
[175] UCPD 2005/29, Art 5.
[176] ACCC also found *eDreams* to be misleading consumers for similar reasons; see ACCC, 'Airbnb and eDreams give undertakings to ACCC for improved pricing practices' Media Release 194/15 of 13 October 2015, available at www.accc.gov.au/media-release/airbnb-and-edreams-give-undertakings-to-accc-for-improved-pricing-practices.

stated that the company had failed to disclose mandatory fees, such as cleaning and service fees, on key pages (search results pages and accommodation listing pages) and thus 'engaged in misleading and deceptive conduct'.[177]

After the transaction between the peers is concluded, platforms should provide information about alternative dispute resolution for consumer issues,[178] and offer any complementary services, such as insurance[179] or tax assistance.

ii. Obligations Deriving from the Underlying Service—Whose Responsibility?

Apart from their responsibilities as intermediaries, platforms may be faced with liability deriving from the performance of the underlying service. This could happen either on the basis of generally applicable principles of tort law, or on the basis of the special tripartite relationship materialising in the collaborative context.[180] Indeed, in the collaborative economy suppliers could be 'sharing' liability with the platform or, more exceptionally, the platform could bear all liability by itself. As explained above, the latter situation could materialise both for substantive reasons (notably when the suppliers are found to be the platform's employees) and for more formalistic reasons (notably when the platform fails to clarify its role as a mere intermediary and the consumer reasonably presumes that the platform is its contracting party).[181] The conditions under which each type of responsibility may materialise have been discussed in previous sections of this chapter and need not be repeated.

C. The Collaborative Economy as a Disruption to Consumer Protection Law

So far (in sections A and B above) we have assumed that existing consumer protection rules should be applied to the collaborative economy. In the present section this assumption will be questioned.

The collaborative economy has had disruptive effects not only at the economic level, but also at the social, by making possible and even generalising social conduct that was simply unthinkable few years ago: people take rides with drivers completely unknown to them, let into their houses complete strangers with whom they can hardly communicate, and lend money to people the creditworthiness of whom they have no means to evaluate.

> This could be interpreted as a sign that the consumer is not really interested in consumer protection … Easy access and cheap price may blind consumers from the risks associated with using a platform service. We might also view this development as a phase in which

---

[177] ibid.
[178] See Ch 6 below.
[179] This may entail further forms of liability for the platform.
[180] See the discussion of the different scenarios in section II.A as well as the discussion of a Platform Directive in section IV.A.iv above.
[181] See section IV.B.i above.

we are entering into a new market paradigm where previous virtues (consumer protection, quality etc) are replaced by other virtues (cheap prices, easy access, the 'sharing experience', authenticity).[182]

Therefore, the question may be raised whether traditional consumer protection law is, as such, appropriate for the collaborative economy. Indeed, several factors may, if taken together, point towards an alternative, more personalised, consumer protection regime for the collaborative economy.

Firstly, there is the increasingly rich literature on the role that behavioural sciences may/should play in defining legal rules and standards.[183] Consumer protection is *par excellence* an area which could benefit from behavioural insights.[184] The relevance of behavioural insights for consumer law is not specific to the collaborative economy, but the ongoing re-think of consumer protection along behavioural lines needs to be taken into account when dealing with the collaborative economy. According to the behavioural approach, there is no such thing as an 'average consumer';[185] or if the 'average consumer' as a normative standard were to be used it should refer not to one who is 'reasonably circumspect and attentive', which is the standard followed by the CJEU,[186] but rather to one who is only boundedly rational and can only dedicate finite resources to making choices.[187] Therefore the benchmark used by the legislature and courts when assessing consumers' needs is fundamentally flawed. This is so because consumers have a finite capacity to process information,[188] so overloading them with information is useless or bluntly counter-productive: 'complex and numerous information requirements may even induce an "information overload" and lead to dysfunctions, confusion or paralysis in consumer choices'.[189] Further, consumers are subject to a number of cognitive biases[190] and empirically demonstrate a dramatic heterogeneity of judgement and decision behaviour. Indeed, 'different consumers will manifest different deviations from rationality, depending on factors such as their cognitive ability, thinking style, risk-taking propensity, personality traits,

---

[182] MJ Sorensen, 'Private Law Perspectives on Platform Services' (2016) 5 *EuCML* 15, 19.

[183] See A Tor, 'The Methodology of the Behavioral Analysis of Law' (2008) 4 *Haifa Law Review* 237, available at http://weblaw.haifa.ac.il/he/Faculty/Tor/Publications/The%20Methodology%20of%20 the%20Behavioral%20Analysis%20of%20Law.pdf; see more recently G Helleringer and AL Sibony, 'European Consumer Protection Through the Behavioral Lens' (2017) *Columbia Journal of European Law* 607, with an extensive bibliography.

[184] See A Tor, 'Some Challenges Facing a Behaviorally-Informed Approach to the Directive on Unfair Commercial Practices' in T Tóth (ed), *Unfair Commercial Practices: The Long Road to Harmonized Law Enforcement* (Budapest, Pázmány Press, 2014); Helleringer and Sibony, 'European Consumer Protection Through the Behavioral Lens' (2017).

[185] See, inter alia, A Nordhausen Scholes, 'Behavioural Economics and the Autonomous Consumer' in C Barnard, MW Gehring and I Solanke (eds), *Cambridge Yearbook of European Legal Studies 2011–2012*, Vol 14 (Oxford, Hart Publishing, 2012).

[186] Case C-210/96 *Gut Springenheide* EU:C:1998:369, para 31.

[187] See R Incadrona and C Poncibó, 'The average consumer, the unfair commercial practices directive and the cognitive revolution' (2007) 30 *Journal of Consumer Policy* 21.

[188] Helleringer and Sibony (n 183).

[189] Incadrona and Poncibó, 'The average consumer, the unfair commercial practices directive and the cognitive revolution' (2007) 32.

[190] ibid 31.

and more'.[191] Furthermore, 'the same consumer tends to behave differently when buying durable technical products with a high unit price ... than when doing routine shopping'.[192] The 'mood congruence' effect also plays an important role, since when the consumer is in a good mood s/he tends to remember positive things about a product, while the opposite is true when the consumer's mood is low.[193]

Secondly, specifically in the collaborative economy, which is all new, disruptive and under constant mutation, an important normative concept used in the area of consumer law may also be absent: what are the 'legitimate expectations'—a core legal benchmark used by the UCPD in order to identify unfair practices—of the user of a service such as *Uber*, *Airbnb* or *Indiegogo*, which is scarcely regulated, if not borderline illegal in most places? The commercial adjustments (such as eg *Airbnb* having introduced the home-owners' insurance scheme,[194] or, more recently, having introduced an anti-discrimination policy[195]) and service modifications (such as *Uber* imposing stricter conditions on the recruitment of its drivers, or training them, etc) have specifically been made in order to respond to 'legitimate expectations' which, however, were not there (or were not acknowledged as such) during the first phases of development of the collaborative services. Thus, 'legitimate expectations' in the field of the collaborative economy may be more of a moving target than a fixed benchmark; what is more, experienced digitally literate users may have different legitimate expectations to digitally challenged users.

Thirdly, there is the issue of information. EU consumer protection law is, to a large extent, based on the disclosure of information. 'Numerous mandatory disclosures illustrate an apparent act of faith that EU consumers are capable of making informed decisions so long as the relevant—if abundant—information is presented to them in a comprehensive manner'.[196] However, it has been rightly noted that

> even if the law often looks as if it has been drafted for the one-in-a-thousand rational consumer, this has more to do with the internal market rationale that underpins EU law on information than with an assumption that consumers are rational.[197]

There are at least two reasons which explain the EU's attachment to disclosure. For one thing, information requirements have been one of the core instruments in pursuing the free movement of goods and services under internal market law: national regulations which forebode the usage of popular commercial names, such as pasta, beer or Cassis,[198] or which prescribed specific shapes for specific

---

[191] Tor, 'Some Challenges Facing a Behaviorally-Informed Approach to the Directive on Unfair Commercial Practices' (2014) 16–17.
[192] Incadrona and Poncibó (n 187) 33.
[193] ibid.
[194] For which see *Airbnb*, 'How does homeowner's insurance work with Airbnb?', available at www.airbnb.com/help/article/296/how-does-homeowner-s-insurance-work-with-airbnb.
[195] For which see *Airbnb*, 'Airbnb's Nondiscrimination Policy: Our Commitment to Inclusion and Respect', available at www.airbnb.com/help/article/1405/airbnb-s-nondiscrimination-policy--our-commitment-to-inclusion-and-respect.
[196] Helleringer and Sibony (n 183) 11.
[197] Helleringer and Sibony (n 183) 7.
[198] Case 407/85 *Glocken* EU:C:1988:401; Case 178/84 *Commission v Germany (bier purity)*, EU:C:1987:126, and Case 120/78 *Rewe Central (Cassis de Dijon)* EU:C:1979:42, respectively.

product packaging,[199] were to be set aside, replaced by adequate labelling. Therefore, adequate information given to the consumer was the 'proportionate' alternative to national regulations held disproportionately burdensome: instead of changing the commercial name, shape or content of the products, traders had only to offer enough elements for the consumer to make an informed choice. The EU legislature, for its part, when it enacted the first consumer protection Directives back in the 1980s, did so upon the general internal market legal basis, following the requirement of unanimity in the Council. In this framework information requirements, which have the additional advantage of being respectful of national private law systems, were the easiest way forward.[200] However, the efficiency of consumer 'protection through information' has been robustly questioned,[201] in view of the empirical finding that consumers do not read.[202] Accordingly, the EU obsession with disclosure has been accused of expressing 'the hypocrite's version of consumer protection'.[203] Irrespective of whether this critique is exaggerated,[204] it is worth noting that the above-mentioned EU rationale for insisting on information disclosure, ie that of securing market access to goods and services of other Member States, does not apply in the same way in the field of the collaborative economy. As explained above, market access for platforms is automatically secured through the E-commerce Directive or, at least, enhanced by the Services Directive. Therefore, to conclude this first point on the value of information disclosure, it may be said that: (a) as a means of protecting consumers it is being contested; and (b) as a means of serving the internal market it is being set aside by other, more 'aggressive' rules securing market access.

A second point concerning the value of information is that, under the complex three-party relationships developing in the collaborative context, it is not always clear *whose* information should be provided to the consumer: is it enough to provide information about the platform? Surely not, at least where the supplier of the underlying service is clearly distinguishable from it and occupies a decisive role in the delivery of the service. Is it, then, enough to get the prescribed information concerning the individual supplier just minutes before the actual 'consumption' of the service (as it is the case for example with *Uber* drivers); and in circumstances where it is sure that the information will not be read by the consumer?

The value of mandatory information is further diminished by the fact that its disclosure is supposed to make up for the information asymmetries existing

---

[199] Case 261/81 *Rau v De Smedt* EU:C:1982:382.

[200] For a more extensive discussion of these ideas see Helleringer and Sibony (n 183) 12.

[201] O Bar-Gil and O Ben-Sahar, 'Regulatory Techniques in Consumer Protection: A critique of European Consumer Contract Law' (2013) 50 *CMLRev* 109.

[202] O Ben-Sahar, 'The Myth of the "Opportunity to Read" in Contract Law' (2009) 5 *European Review of Contract Law* 1; for a more recent survey, specifically conducted in the EU, see the European Commission's 'Study on consumers' attitudes towards Terms and Conditions (T&Cs)', Final Report (2016), available at http://ec.europa.eu/consumers/consumer_evidence/behavioural_research/docs/terms_and_conditions_final_report_en.pdf; briefly presented, together with its accompanying documents, at http://ec.europa.eu/consumers/consumer_evidence/behavioural_research/consumers_attitudes_terms_conditions/index_en.htm; this study finds that less than one in ten users of e-shopping sites do actually read the Terms and Conditions.

[203] Helleringer and Sibony (n 183) 16, discuss—and rebut—this view.

[204] ibid: this in fact is one of the main points of the authors.

between the trader and the consumer. In the collaborative context, it is not altogether certain that such asymmetries exist in the first place, given that suppliers may themselves be prosumers, as opposed to traders. Furthermore, such asymmetries are, to a large extent, alleviated by the use of rating systems—a means of self-regulation put to work by most collaborative platforms.[205] Such rating systems are typically better designed than mandatory disclosure to attract consumers' attention, more user-friendly and convey important information in a summary and concise way. Therefore, provided that the fairness of reviews is secured,[206] from this perspective the added value of general mandatory information disclosure is to be questioned.

Fourthly, legal and behavioural scholarship has put forward the idea that the efficiency of law in general and consumer protection in particular could be enhanced if impersonal default rules, having general application to all traders and consumers, were progressively replaced by either personalised default rules or, in more rare situations, active choices by the parties involved.[207] According to Sunstein 'personalized default rules are the wave of the future', since they alleviate the injustice and/or inefficiency inherent in the application of general catch-all rules to dissimilar situations, while giving a sense to the individuals' natural inertia and their unlikeliness to make active choices.[208]

Default rules are rules which apply in the absence of a specific choice made by the individual, such as eg a rule stating that, unless there is an express objection on their part, individuals shall (or shall not) become organ donors. Individualised default rules are such rules which apply differently to different categories of people. These may be tailored either on the basis of a single variable, such as gender, age, weight, in which case we talk of 'crude personalised default rules', or on the basis of many characteristics, including past behaviour in similar circumstances, in which case we talk of 'granular personalised default rules'.[209] Some level of personalisation of the rules, especially crude, can be envisaged under traditional law-making, eg different rules for minors/elders, for men and women and so on. However, personalisation is greatly enhanced, if not altogether made possible—if we are talking about granular—by big data analytics.[210] This is so because 'patterns of purchases, mouse clicks, credit payments, and social network ties reveal fundamental aspects of individuals' personalities and values'.[211] Or, to put it in a more prosaic manner, 'the iPhones, not the eyes, turn out to be the windows into the soul'.[212]

---

[205] For the issue of ratings/reviews systems see Ch 7 below.
[206] This topic is discussed in Ch 7 below.
[207] See CR Sunstein, 'Impersonal Default Rules vs Active Choices vs Personalized Default Rules: A Triptych' (2012) (unpublished manuscript, on file with author), available at http://nrs.harvard.edu/urn-3:HUL.InstRepos:9876090.
[208] ibid 6.
[209] A Porat and LJ Strahilevitz, 'Personalizing Default Rules and Disclosure with Big Data' (2014) 112 *Michigan Law Review* 1417, 1434.
[210] Big data analytics may, but do not necessarily, violate data protection rules, for which see Ch 3 below, since they are typically used in anonymised, statistical data.
[211] Porat and Strahilievitz, 'Personalizing Default Rules and Disclosure with Big Data' (2014) 1436.
[212] ibid 1439.

Collaborative platforms do just that: they gather and manipulate big data concerning their consumers and suppliers, with whom they interact through smart phones, tablets and computers, in order to match offer with demand. For platforms, the use of big data is at the core of their activities. Their very function requires them to know the age, gender, past purchases and reviews, habits, preferences, predilections and particularities of their customers in order to propose to them the most suitable service. With time, platforms also acquire knowledge of prior behaviours and the reactions of their customers. It seems somehow incongruous for the operator who knows everything about you when offering a service to pretend that s/he knows nothing when it comes to determining the standard of protection or the information which is relevant (personalised disclosure) due for that same service. In other words, if the personification of rules were to start in some segment of the economy, the collaborative sector would be the prime candidate.

Personalised rules may concern both information disclosure obligations and substantive levels of protection.[213] In particular in relation to disclosure obligations, in view of the particularities discussed above, ie the all-important role of rating mechanisms and the clear inefficacy of communicating information on the actual supplier a few moments before the consumption of the service, it may be that, in order to secure the required level of consumer protection, different rules should apply; such rules should, by any means, take into account the particular characteristics of each consumer or set of consumers.

In practice this could happen in several ways, with either the legislature or the platforms in the forefront. As a first and timid step, platforms could be allowed to propose to their users different levels of disclosure, depending on the latter's personal characteristics.[214] A similar logic is already followed in the area of financial services, where according to the MiFiD, credit institutions may only propose financial products in line with the consumer's experience rating, established at the start of every credit relation. Such personalised disclosure could be agreed at the beginning or, indeed, at a later stage of the use of the platform, and could be proposed as a voluntary substitute for the mandatory disclosure obligations stemming from consumer protection laws. Substitution would be voluntary in the sense that the user/consumer could opt in to it, or remain covered by the 'traditional' disclosure obligations, which would then work as a 'negative default'. It is submitted that if the use of personalised consumer protection rules were to be tried, the collaborative economy segment of the economy would be the place to start.

---

[213] ibid 1470; see also Helleringer and Sibony (n 183) 17 ff, arguing in favour of personalised disclosure of information, taking into account the general context, the medium used, timing, and other factors relevant to the consumer.

[214] It is interesting to note that the UK House of Lords in its 10th Report of Session 2015–16, 'Online Platforms and the Digital Single Market', proposes a similar approach to be followed in the field of data protection, with the use of 'kite-marks' including 'a graded scale indicating levels of data protection', para 235; it is even more interesting to note how well the two ideas, ie grading of data protection and grading of information disclosure, feed into each other.

3

Data in the Collaborative Economy

I. Introduction: The Role of Data in the Collaborative Economy

Data are inherently significant for the very existence and function of collaborative platforms. Collaborative platforms collect and process a great amount of data concerning the age, gender, residence, employment, professional capacities and qualifications, dietary or other preferences, health condition, medications, location, economic details and much more of both the recipient and the supplier of the underlying service. The more information at the disposal of the platform, the better the intermediary (matching) services it can provide to its users.

While collaborative start-ups were initially characterised by their small size, locality and low-key philosophy, many collaborative platforms have developed into major digital players with millions of users and significant business value. Thus, while big data may be irrelevant for the former, who lack the volume of participants and the resources to invest in technical data analytics tools, they are certainly significant for the latter.

In the sphere of the 'data economy' three stages of big data processing usually take place by collaborative platforms: acquisition, analysis and application.[1] Platforms employ various means of acquiring users' personal data. They actively acquire data by requiring potential users to enter certain personal data, such as name, photo, ID, and so on, in order to be given access to the platform in the first place or to log in through an already existing social media account, thus connecting the dots in creating a complete digital profile ('mandatory data'). Once they become users of the platform, both suppliers and consumers continue to actively add a significant amount of personal data (location, cultural preferences, financial status, medical conditions etc), which are necessary for the provision of the underlying service, the increase of trust among peers and the development of

---

[1] See M Oostveen and K Irion, 'The Golden Age of Personal Data: How to Regulate an Enabling Fundamental Right?' in M Bakhoum et al (eds), *Personal Data in Competition, Consumer Protection and IP Law—Towards a Holistic Approach?* (Berlin, Springer, forthcoming); also (2016) Amsterdam Law School Legal Studies Research Paper No 68; and (2016) Institute for Information Law Research Paper No 6, available at https://ssrn.com/abstract=2885701, 8.

their 'branding' in the case of suppliers ('voluntary/self-presentation data'). In that regard, '[p]rivacy in data sharing is two-fold: data exchanges take place between users and platform-organizations, and between users and peer-users'.[2]

Further, collaborative platforms are in a position and have the capacity to 'passively collect' personal data as well. Passive collection of data can occur even without the users' knowledge, through the users' web browsers (eg IP address), through cookies placed by the platform on their devices, or simply through the mere use of the platform (time spent at each section, search within the platform, etc).[3] What is more, when used in the form of a mobile app, collaborative platforms require access to the user's ID, contacts, location, SMS, phone calls, photos, camera, etc, to which the users must consent if they wish to use the relevant app via their smartphone ('technical data'). This information can be accessed by platforms at all times, even when the app is not being used.[4]

Additionally, in the 'data economy'[5] platforms can acquire individuals' personal data either from the data subjects themselves, from data brokers, through the sale and/or exchange of data between companies, or else through mergers and acquisitions.[6] Lastly, the combination and analysis of existing datasets either concerning one individual, 'such as personal data on physical fitness with shopping behaviour'[7] of that one user, or the combination of personal data of one user with personal data of others, can create new data.[8]

In the second phase of processing data, collaborative platforms typically proceed to the analysis of the data collected. Technological advances have led to sophisticated and self-learning algorithms, and other big analytics tools, able to process and yield conclusions on a large volume and variety of data at high speeds. Data mining by intelligent computer algorithms in existing databases can

---

[2] G Ranzini et al, 'Privacy in the Sharing Economy' (2017) Report from the EU H2020 Research Project Ps2Share: Participation, Privacy, and Power in the Sharing Economy, 3, available at https://ssrn.com/abstract=2960942.

[3] See the testimony of *Skyscanner* in the UK House of Lords, 'Online Platforms and the Digital Single Market' (2016) 10th Report of Session 2015–16, para 209.

[4] ibid para 211.

[5] The term is taken from Commission Communication, 'Building a European Data Economy' COM (2017) 9 final; The data economy 'measures the overall impacts of the data market—ie the marketplace where digital data is exchanged as products or services derived from raw data—on the economy as a whole. It involves the generation, collection, storage, processing, distribution, analysis, elaboration, delivery, and exploitation of data enabled by digital technologies (European Data Market study, SMART 2013/0063, IDC, 2016)' fn 1.

[6] It has been estimated that the number of big-data-related mergers doubled between 2008 and 2013 from 55 to 134. See European Data Protection Supervisor, 'Report of Workshop on Privacy, Consumers, Competition and Big Data' (11 July 2014) 1, available at https://secure.edps.europa.eu/EDPSWEB/webdav/site/mySite/shared/Documents/Consultation/Big%20data/14-07-11_EDPS_Report_Workshop_Big_data_EN.pdf. For further discussion see Ch 4 on competition, below.

[7] See Oostveen and Irion, 'The Golden Age of Personal Data: How to Regulate an Enabling Fundamental Right?' (2017) 9.

[8] C Twigg-Flesner, 'Disruptive Technology—Disrupted Law? How the Digital Revolution Affects (Contract) Law' in A De Franceschi (ed), *European Contract Law and the Digital Single Market, The Implications of the Digital Revolution* (Cambridge, Intersentia, 2016) 41.

elucidate hidden patterns either automatically and independently or upon specific hypotheses and queries inserted.[9] Thus, for example, recommendations for similar products or services on a platform, such as *Airbnb's* 'For You' section, are the result of data mining of previous preferences and analysis of patterns in the commercial behaviour of the user.

Lastly, 'knowledge is applied and algorithmic decisions are made'.[10] The information acquired and analysed is applied through the various uses of personal data. The main use of the personal data collected is the facilitation of the platform's function and purpose, that is, to provide matches. *Uber*, for example, would not be able to provide its services without knowledge of the consumer's location and *Eatro* without knowledge of the customer's food allergies or dietary preferences. More data available to the platform lead to better matches and therefore to higher quality services. Secondarily, collaborative platforms may use personal data for targeted advertising or promoting sponsored content, according to the user's interests, quests and overall commercial and otherwise behaviour. Even more, targeted personalised content may derive from a psychological profile put together and attributed to the user on the basis of the personal data collected, instead of simply his/her preferences and behaviour online.[11] This rather intrusive approach would be even more relevant (and tempting) as collaborative platforms are expanding their scope and are following the trend of servitisation.[12] Since *Airbnb* has begun offering 'experiences' as well as accommodation and *Uber* has become active in delivering products, knowledge of the psychological motivations of consumers would be even more valuable to the platforms. Further, collected personal data may be sold to other companies and produce direct revenue for the collaborative platforms. Alternatively, personal data may be shared with governments and municipalities in the context of public procurement or the provision of services of general economic interest (SGEIs).[13] *Uber* has already concluded agreements for sharing its data with public authorities, 'which will provide new insights to help manage urban growth, relieve traffic congestion, expand public transportation, and reduce greenhouse gas emissions'.[14]

---

[9] For a comprehensive and easy to understand overview of data mining technologies see IH Witten et al, *Data Mining: Practical Machine Learning Tools and Techniques*, 4th edn (Cambridge, MA, Morgan Kaufmann, 2017).

[10] Oostveen and Irion (n 1) 9.

[11] See eg S Liu and A Matilla, 'Airbnb: Online targeted advertising, sense of power, and consumer decisions' (2017) 60 *International Journal of Hospitality Management* 33. According to the study: 'Airbnb distinguishes itself from traditional hotels by offering guests a "feeling at home" (e.g., belongingness) and an "atypical place to stay" (eg uniqueness). In this research, we examine the interaction effect of advertising appeal (belongingness vs uniqueness) and an individual's sense of power (low vs high) on click-through intention and purchase intention. The findings suggest that powerless individuals respond more favorably to the belongingness appeal, whereas powerful individuals react more positively to the uniqueness appeal'.

[12] For an overview of servitisation and its correlation with online platforms, see J Hojnik, 'The servitization of manufacturing: EU law implications and challenges' (2016) 53 *CMLR* 1575.

[13] For which see Ch 7 below.

[14] P Bajpai, 'How Uber is Selling all Your Ride Data' *Investopedia* (9 March 2016), available at www.investopedia.com/articles/investing/030916/how-uber-uses-its-data-bank.asp.

The aforementioned 'data process' leads to two primary conclusions on the nature and role of personal data in the collaborative economy. Firstly, data constitute a 'tradeable commodity'.[15] However, data per se are not protected, nor are they treated as valuable commodities themselves by legislation. On the contrary, data protection only covers the protection of the person from any damage deriving from the use of their personal data, whereas there is no data property right, ie right to participate in the economic value of the data as such.

Secondly, personal data can act as 'consideration'.[16] Article 3(1) of the Commission's draft Digital Content Directive explicitly provides for the conclusion of contracts where 'the supplier supplies digital content to the consumer or undertakes to do so and, in exchange, a price is to be paid or the consumer actively provides counter-performance other than money in the form of personal data or any other data'.[17] In line with the acknowledgment of the monetary value of data, several businesses have started to offer discounted services to their consumers on the condition that they agree to be tracked online and/or to receive targeted advertisements.[18] While collaborative platforms' users may be under the impression that participation to the platform is free of charge, in reality their personal (and/or non-personal) data act as currency. This alone depicts a lack of transparency with regard to personal data in the digital era.

Indeed, the various complex uses of personal data by platforms are vague and unknown to users. While the majority of users distrust major platforms as to the acquisition and processing of their personal data,[19] they participate in online platforms by inserting valuable and occasionally sensitive personal data, accepting that their course onwards will remain a mystery to them perpetually. In that regard, privacy is being traded off in exchange for users' participation in the collaborative economy.[20]

II. Personal Data Protection versus Big Data Economy

In order to appreciate how data protection law applies in the collaborative economy one needs to inquire about the applicable rules and scope of protection

---

[15] See H Zech, 'Data as a Tradeable Commodity' and A De Franceschi, 'Data as a Tradeable Commodity and the New Instruments for their Protection' in A De Franceschi (ed), *European Contract Law and the Digital Single Market, The Implications of the Digital Revolution* (Cambridge, Intersentia, 2016).

[16] C Langhanke and M Schmidt-Kessel, 'Consumer Data as Consideration' (2015) 4 *EuCML* 218.

[17] Commission, 'Proposal for a Directive of the European Parliament and of the Council on certain aspects concerning contracts for the supply of digital content' COM(2015) 634 final. The introduction of the concept of 'freemium' is relevant in the collaborative economy as well, even though the draft Directive does not generally apply to most collaborative services.

[18] See I Graef, 'Market Definition and Market Power in Data: The Case of Online Platforms' (2015) 38 *World Competition* 473, fn 5 therein and the corresponding text.

[19] UK House of Lords, 'Online Platforms and the Digital Single Market' (2016) paras 207–208.

[20] G Ranzini et al, 'Privacy in the Sharing Economy' (2017) 2.

(section A), examine the way core rules on personal data apply in this new context (section B), the same as rules on digital privacy (section C), before turning to data flows between the EU and third countries (section D).

A. Applicable Rules—Scope of Data Protection

The right to privacy and personal data[21] constitute fundamental rights, and as such are protected by Article 8 of the European Convention on Human Rights (ECHR) (right to privacy),[22] by Articles 7 and 8 of the Charter of Fundamental Rights of the European Union (Charter) (respect for private and family life and protection of personal data respectively), and are enshrined in Article 16(1) of the Treaty on the Functioning of the European Union (TFEU). Further, data protection has been endorsed by the Council of Europe with the adoption of the Convention for the Protection of Individuals with regard to Automatic Processing of Personal Data (also known as Convention 108).[23]

The main instrument and cornerstone of data protection in the EU is currently the Data Protection Directive (DPD),[24] soon to be replaced by the General Data Protection Regulation (GDPR) which will enter into force in May 2018. Next to the GDPR, the 'e-Privacy Directive'[25] also applies to personal data and protects them from unlawful processing as long as they are being transmitted through

---

[21] While the right to privacy and the right to data protection constitute two separate rights, they overlap. '"Data protection" is broader than "privacy protection" because it also concerns other fundamental rights and freedoms, and all kinds of data regardless of their relationship with privacy, and at the same time more limited because it merely concerns the processing of personal information, with other aspects of privacy protection being disregarded'; see European Data Protection Supervisor, P Hustinx, 'EU Data Protection Law: The Review of Directive 95/46/EC and the Proposed General Data Protection Regulation' (2014) *Collected Courses of the European University Institute's Academy of European Law*, 24th Session on European Union Law, 1–12 July 2013, 5, available at www.statewatch. org/news/2014/sep/eu-2014-09-edps-data-protection-article.pdf. Thus, both rights are discussed intertwined in this chapter.

[22] The ECtHR has decided that the right to privacy entails, inter alia, the protection of personal data from unlawful processing: see *Leander v Sweden*, ECtHR, Application 9248/81, Judgment of 26 March 1987, ECLI:CE:ECHR:1987:0326JUD000924881, para 48; see also *S and Marper v United Kingdom*, ECtHR, Application 30562/04 and 30566/04, Judgment of 4 December 2008, ECLI:CE:ECHR:2008: 1204JUD003056204, para 67: 'The mere storing of data relating to the private life of an individual amounts to an interference within the meaning of Article 8 [of the European Convention on Human Rights, which guarantees the right to respect for private and family life, home and correspondence]'.

[23] Council of Europe, 'Convention for the Protection of Individuals with regard to Automatic Processing of Personal Data' (Treaty No 108). An in-depth analysis of the specific provisions of the Conventions and the Charter would surpass the scope of the present book and is therefore omitted. In what follows, focus is given to the EU data protection legal framework. However, reference to relevant ECtHR jurisprudence is made when appropriate.

[24] European Parliament and Council Directive 95/46/EC of 24 October 1995 on protection of individuals with regard to the processing of personal data and on the free movement of such data [1995] OJ L 281/31 (Data Protection Directive—DPD).

[25] European Parliament and Council Directive 2002/58/EC of 12 July 2012 concerning the processing of personal data and the protection of privacy in the electronic communications sector (e-Privacy Directive) [2002] OJ L 201/37.

some means of communication. As part of the reform of the EU privacy rules, a draft Regulation on Privacy and Electronic Communications has also been proposed[26] in order to reinforce security and trust in the Digital Single Market (DSM). The new e-Privacy Regulation is supposed to enter into force on the same date as the GDPR. Hence, as of May 2018 the EU will have a new legal framework both for data and for privacy protection.

With regard to the scope of the data protection framework, the first and foremost delineation to be made is that it only covers personal data.[27] However, even after the recent data protection legislation reform, there are still ambiguities as to what exactly constitutes personal data and therefore as to what should be protected. The GDPR expanded the definition of 'personal data',[28] by adding online identifiers, device identifiers, cookie IDs and IP addresses, following the CJEU's jurisprudence.[29] It therefore defined 'personal data' as:

> any information relating to an identified or identifiable natural person ('data subject'); an identifiable natural person is one who can be identified, directly or indirectly, in particular by reference to an identifier such as a name, an identification number, location data, an online identifier or to one or more factors specific to the physical, physiological, genetic, mental, economic, cultural or social identity of that natural person.[30]

Although the addition is welcome, the definition still leaves open the question of non-personal data, anonymised data and meta-data (ie 'data about data') which, even though not personal data per se, if combined with other non-personal data can indeed pinpoint one single natural person. Further, collaborative platforms may use even seemingly useless non-personal data for personalised treatment of their users: *Uber* revealed that 'desperate customers with smartphones on low battery are willing to pay even ten times more for a car ride than usual'.[31] The pricing policy could, therefore, possibly be altered accordingly, thus influencing the consumer, even though information on battery retention is not considered as 'personal data'. Since the collection, processing and use of all the above-mentioned data is unregulated, the effectiveness of the data protection regime is questionable.

---

[26] See Commission, 'Proposal for a Regulation of the European Parliament and of the Council concerning the respect for private life and the protection of personal data in electronic communications and repealing Directive 2002/58/EC' (e-Privacy Regulation) COM(2017) 10 final.

[27] Non-personal data may be protected under competition and/or intellectual property rules. Such rules are briefly touched upon in this chapter in order to provide a thorough overview.

[28] For further analysis on the concept of 'personal data' see Article 29 Data Protection Working Party, 'Opinion 4/2007 on the concept of personal data', adopted on 20 June 2007 (WP136).

[29] Case C-582/14 *Breyer v Bundesrepublik Deutschland* EU:C:2016:779 and previously Case C-70/10, *Scarlet v SABAM* EU:C:2011:771.

[30] GDPR, Art 4(1).

[31] O Zezulka, 'The Digital Footprint and Principles of Personality Protection in the European Union' (2016) *Prague Law* Working Papers Series No 2016/III/2, 3, available at https://ssrn.com/abstract=2896864; see also B Carson, 'You're more likely to order a pricey Uber ride if your phone is about to die' *Business Insider* (12 September 2016), available at www.businessinsider.com/people-with-low-phone-batteries-more-likely-to-accept-uber-surge-pricing-2016-5.

Collaborative platforms will typically be both 'data controllers' and 'data processors'.[32] As such they must comply with the applicable data protection regime and any other relevant legislation. The liability exemption of the E-commerce Directive[33] which covers caching, mere conduit and hosting[34] does not exclude the collaborative platform's liability arising under the applicable personal data protection legislation, in so far as the platform's own activities are concerned. Similarly to platforms (but on a much smaller scale), suppliers also collect information about their customers in order to provide the underlying service. In that regard, they could be considered as 'data controllers' themselves and thus bear the obligations of the data protection regime, provided that they do not fall under the 'household exemption'.[35] While this exemption does not cover collaborative platforms, which process data for commercial purposes or even for charitable, non-profit purposes,[36] it may be relevant with regard to suppliers of the underlying service. The exemption of personal or household activity requires that the processing has 'no connection to a professional or commercial activity. Personal or household activities could include correspondence and the holding of addresses, or social networking and online activity undertaken within the context of such activities'.[37] However, collaborative services are significantly different from social networking or online activity in general and the suppliers of the underlying service provide the collaborative services precisely for economic/commercial purposes, be it on an occasional or professional basis. It is, therefore, unclear whether the data protection obligations are meant to apply to those individuals as well, even though their processing[38] would probably be very limited, if not exhausted by the mere collection of the personal data of their customers.

---

[32] See the definitions in DPD, Art 2(d) and (e) and GDPR, Art 4(7) and (8). Data controllers determine the purposes for which and manner in which personal data are to be processed, while data processors conduct the processing on behalf of the data controllers; the latter bear fewer responsibilities than the former. On some occasions, collaborative platforms may outsource the data processing to other organisations, in which case the data processor will be different from the data controller. For more on the role of the two, see Information Commissioner's Office, 'Data controllers and data processors: What the difference is and what the governance implications are' (2014), available at www.ico.org. uk/media/for-organisations/documents/1546/data-controllers-and-data-processors-dp-guidance.pdf.

[33] European Parliament and Council Directive 2000/31/EC of 8 June 2000 on certain legal aspects of information society services, in particular electronic commerce, in the Internal Market (Directive on electronic commerce) [2000] OJ L 178/1.

[34] Art 14 of the E-commerce Directive, for which see Ch 2 above.

[35] DPD, Art 3(2) and GDPR, Art 2(2)(c). The Working Party has already opined that '[t]he users of such networks, uploading personal data also of third parties, would qualify as controllers provided that their activities are not subject to the so-called "household exception"'; see Article 29 Data Protection Working Party, 'Opinion 1/2010 on the concepts of "controller" and "processor"', adopted on 16 February 2010 (WP169) 21.

[36] The scope of application of the DPD has been interpreted broadly by the Court to include church or charitable foundations: see Joined Cases C-465/00, C-138/01 and C-139/01 *Österreichischer Rundfunk* EU:C:2003:294, paras 41–43; and Case C-101/01 *Bodil Lindqvist* EU:C:2003:596, paras 39–41.

[37] See GDPR, Recital 18.

[38] Indeed it is difficult to imagine why the owner of an *Airbnb* flat would need to keep a full record of travellers hosted therein; the same is even more true for *Uber* drivers and their passengers.

On the other side, in general both suppliers and consumers will be data subjects, since the platform processes the data of both groups. Indeed, suppliers will be protected by the data protection acquis, regardless of whether they qualify as traders, service providers under Article 57 TFEU and the Services Directive, or mere prosumers.[39] However, only natural persons can be data subjects and therefore claim protection under the EU data protection regime.[40] The application of data protection regulations thus depends on whether the data are 'consumer generated' or 'company generated'.[41] The GDPR clearly states that

> [t]his Regulation does not cover the processing of personal data which concerns legal persons and in particular undertakings established as legal persons, including the name and the form of the legal person and the contact details of the legal person.[42]

Therefore, if the supplier (and/or the recipient on rare occasions) of the underlying service is a company, as is the case in B2B relations,[43] then the company data cannot be protected at all by data protection legislation; it may, nonetheless, fall to be considered under intellectual property or competition rules.[44]

Last but not least, the territorial applicability of data protection rules is under review. While the Directive currently in force only applies to collaborative platforms established in the EU or having some 'means of processing' in the form of automated equipment or otherwise in an EU Member State,[45] the GDPR extends the scope of application to all collaborative platforms established *outside* the EU to the extent that their data subject is established in the EU or to the extent that they monitor the behaviour of EU data subjects.[46] Such broadening of the territorial scope of application of the new Regulation was necessary in order to take into account the annulment, by the Court, of the 'Safe Harbour Agreement'.[47] This is likely to affect most collaborative platforms: apart from the biggest platforms that maintain some kind of establishment in the EU and are therefore already subject to EU data protection rules, the majority of platforms will now have to commit to significant expenditure to adapt their technical and legal structures in line with the GDPR requirements, or else stop serving EU data subjects.

---

[39] See Ch 2 above.

[40] However, some national jurisdictions (eg Austria, Denmark and Italy) have extended the application of data protection rules to legal persons as well. Similarly, the Commission has examined the applicability of the data protection rules to legal persons. See D Korff, 'Study on the protection of the rights and interests of legal persons with regard to the processing of personal data relating to such persons' prepared for the Commission (2000), available at http://ec.europa.eu/justice/policies/privacy/docs/studies/legal_en.pdf. In any case, the GDPR reiterates the applicability of data protection only to natural persons.

[41] Zech, 'Data as a Tradeable Commodity' (2016) 59.

[42] GDPR, Recital 14.

[43] Eg through platforms such as *Kwipped* or *Cohealo*.

[44] For which see sections III.B, and III.C below and Ch 4 respectively.

[45] DPD, Art 4.

[46] GDPR, Art 3.

[47] The CJEU ruled the 'Safe Harbour' framework invalid with its judgment in Case C-362/14 *Maximillian Schrems v Data Protection Commissioner* EU:C:2015:650.

B. Personal Data Protection in the Collaborative Economy

EU rules on data protection may be presented as revolving around three core pillars: (i) definition of the conditions which have to be met for data processing to take place; (ii) imposition of specific obligations to data controllers; and (iii) recognition of specific rights in favour of data subjects.

i. Process of Personal Data—By the Rulebook

The processing of personal data is defined as

> any operation or set of operations which is performed upon personal data, whether or not by automatic means, such as collection, recording, organization, storage, adaptation or alteration, retrieval, consultation, use, disclosure by transmission, dissemination or otherwise making available, alignment or combination, blocking, erasure or destruction.[48]

Therefore, any use of personal data, even mere collection, whether active or passive, constitutes processing and must comply with the Directive's (soon Regulation's) rules for it to be lawful.

The data protection rules provide six reasons for legitimate processing of personal data,[49] out of which consent takes the centre stage.

a. Consent

Consent is usually required by platforms as a sine qua non condition for participation to the platform. In most cases, it is given by the data subjects (ie users in both sides of the platform) by agreeing with the platform's Terms and Conditions, which include the relevant data processing provisions.[50] Thus, prima facie, the condition of consent is fulfilled by the majority of collaborative platforms. However, consent is valid only when it meets certain requirements. The GDPR clarifies the requirements for valid consent, ie 'freely given, specific, informed and unambiguous indication of the data subject's wishes by which he or she, by a statement or by a clear affirmative action, signifies agreement to the processing of personal data relating to him or her'.[51] Consent, therefore, needs to be clear and *explicit*, ie given by affirmative action, a requirement previously reserved only for sensitive data.[52] This welcome clarification, however, does not specifically address issues that could come up in the context of the collaborative economy.

---

[48] DPD, Art 2(b) and GDPR, Art 4(2).

[49] DPD, Art 7 and GDPR, Art 6.

[50] In practice, platforms require the entry of personal data, such as name, e-mail address etc, for signing up and note that signing up signifies agreement with the Terms and Conditions, which are accessible through a separate link. Usually access to the Terms and Conditions is not necessary for successful signing up, thus creating ambiguity as to whether the user actually read and agreed to the platform's data processing terms.

[51] GDPR, Art 4(11).

[52] Even though the term 'explicit' was not maintained for general data processing in the final form of the GDPR, the requirements included in the definition of consent, and especially that of a clear affirmative action, will have the same effects as if the provision required for 'explicit' or else express consent.

Consent must be given by affirmative action prior to any data processing by the platform.[53] However, in the automatic digital environment, it is unclear when exactly platforms begin collecting data. For example, geolocation data, the IP address and other online identifiers, as well as information on the user's behaviour (eg sections visited, time spent etc) can be instantly known to platforms, before any consent is given or even considered.

Consent must also be given 'freely' for it to be valid. This means that the consent given is the result of the freely and independently formed will of the user. As clarified by the Working Party 'free consent means a voluntary decision, by an individual in possession of all of his faculties, taken in the absence of coercion of any kind, be it social, financial, psychological or other'.[54] The GDPR also explained that where there is a 'clear imbalance' between the controller and the data subject (such as in the case of an employer and an employee), consent is presumed not to be freely given.[55] Further, '[c]onsent is presumed not to be freely given if it does not allow separate consent to be given to different personal data processing operations'.[56] This criterion, in the context of the collaborative economy, raises complex issues challenging its observance in practice. Firstly, 'most content and services offered by online platforms are offered on a "take it or leave it" basis',[57] which in many cases means that consent is in reality coerced. Truly, individuals are unable to negotiate the Terms and Conditions of their participation in the collaborative platform. They are, thus, obliged to either abstain from the collaborative services altogether or to provide their consent and conform to almost any data processing performed by the platform. This is especially significant in cases where the platform maintains a monopoly, or has established considerable market power, or even in cases of collaboration of the platform with public authorities. If, for instance, the government has allocated an SGEI to the collaborative platform,[58] it is hard to imagine how one could deny consent to their data processing and therefore lose access to the service provided. Secondly, the freely given consent requirement could be problematic in terms of personal data acting as consideration for access to the platform and the services provided therein. '[I]t is not usually possible to force someone to permit another person to have access to personal data. This could be a problem where a trader requires personal data to be made available before digital content is supplied …'.[59] Data processing, instead of being a free decision of the user, thus becomes a contractual obligation, linked to the

[53] Article 29 Data Protection Working Party, 'Opinion 15/2011 on the definition of consent', adopted on 13 July 2011 (WP187), 9.

[54] Article 29 Data Protection Working Party, 'Working Document on the processing of personal data relating to health in electronic health records (EHR)', adopted on 15 February 2007 (WP131) 8.

[55] GDPR, Recital 43.

[56] ibid.

[57] UK House of Lords Report (n 3) para 218.

[58] For a brief discussion of this scenario see Ch 7 below.

[59] Twigg-Flesner, 'Disruptive Technology—Disrupted Law? How the Digital Revolution Affects (Contract) Law' (2016) 41.

receipt of the platform's services. Withdrawal of consent may cause even more complex contract law issues, when data have been given as consideration (instead of money) for the receipt of the platform's services. It could be that withdrawal of consent for the data processing leads to discontinuation of the services provided by the platform in exchange for access to the personal data. On the other hand, if withdrawal is not possible, then the consent cannot be considered as free. Thirdly, concerning the suppliers of the underlying service, it is presumed that consent cannot be considered as free in cases where the data subject is under the influence of the data controller, such as in situations of employment. Indeed, the Working Party has identified that

> although not necessarily always, the data subject can be in a situation of dependence on the data controller—due to the nature of the relationship or to special circumstances—and might fear that he could be treated differently if he does not consent to the data processing.[60]

It has further explained that

> … where consent is required from a worker, and there is a real or potential relevant prejudice that arises from not consenting, the consent is not valid in terms of satisfying either Article 7 or Article 8 as it is not freely given. If it is not possible for the worker to refuse it is not consent. … An area of difficulty is where the giving of consent is a condition of employment. The worker is in theory able to refuse consent but the consequence may be the loss of a job opportunity. In such circumstances consent is not freely given and is therefore not valid. The situation is even clearer cut where, as is often the case, all employers impose the same or a similar condition of employment.[61]

The analysis of consent in the context of working environments is especially relevant for providers offering the underlying services through a collaborative platform. Although the relationship between suppliers and platform is yet to be defined, several indications point to an employment relationship and some national jurisdictions have already adjudicated so.[62] Nonetheless, even if an employment relationship is absent, the fact that participation in the collaborative services is contingent upon consent for data processing may mean that consent is not free and therefore not valid. As quoted above, the mere potential of missing out on a source of income can constitute a determining factor for compelled agreement to the data processing. This may be especially true considering that the collaborative economy is largely seen as a solution to lack of (traditional) employment or insufficient income from traditional employment. In any case, the line between simply a financial (or otherwise) incentive and unfree assent to data processing is hazy and needs to be examined on a case-by-case basis.

---

[60] Article 29 Data Protection Working Party, 'Opinion 15/2011 on the definition of consent' 13.
[61] Article 29 Data Protection Working Party, 'Opinion 8/2001 on the processing of personal data in the employment context', adopted on 13 September 2001 (WP48); quote taken from WP, 'Opinion 15/2011' (n 53) 13–14.
[62] See Ch 5.

Further, consent must also be specific in terms of the scope and consequences of the data processing. It is common practice for platforms to include the consent requirement in lengthy, all-inclusive Terms and Conditions. However, distinct consent for different purposes is needed. If a platform wishes to process the user's personal data for the provision of services, for targeted advertising and for selling to third parties, it must inform so the data subject and gain consent for each of these purposes.[63] Despite the standard practice, this has been clarified in the context of location data:

> (the) definition explicitly rules out consent being given as part of accepting the general terms and conditions for the electronic communications service offered. ... Depending on the type of service offered, consent may relate to a specific operation or may constitute agreement to being located on an ongoing basis.[64]

Thus, participation to the platform and consequently access to the collaborative services should not be contingent upon the general acceptance of all the data processing terms included in the platform's policies, especially since some of those are neither necessary nor relevant to the provision of the platform's service. As in the example of social networks,

> [t]he user should be put in a position to give free and specific consent to receiving behavioural advertising, independently of his access to the social network service. A pop-up box could be used to offer the user such a possibility.[65]

In any case, a 'take it or leave it' option cannot be considered as valid consent, especially considering that the data subject may wish his/her data to be processed for the purposes of participation in the collaborative platform, but disagree with the commercial use of the data.

Lastly, consent must be 'informed'. Informed consent presupposes transparency and provision of all the information necessary at the time that consent is being sought.[66] That necessary information includes the nature of the data collected, the purposes of the processing, the recipient of the data in cases of data transfers, the rights of the data subject and so on. The observance of the 'informed consent' criterion depends on two factors: the quality of the information provided (ie whether it is written clearly, easily understandable, etc) and its accessibility. In practice, the platforms' policies to which the user must agree prior to gaining access to the services are almost always complex, technical, lengthy and generally incomprehensible to the average individual. What is more, the fact that users do

---

[63] See GDPR, Recital 43.

[64] Article 29 Data Protection Working Party, 'Opinion on the use of location data with a view to providing value-added services', adopted in November 2005 (WP115); quote taken from 'Opinion 15/2011 on the definition of consent' (n 53) 18.

[65] 'Opinion 15/2011 on the definition of consent' (n 53) 18.

[66] Similar to the obligation of informed consent is the obligation of information of Arts 10–11 of the DPD and Arts 13–14 of the GDPR.

not complain or protest those Terms, along with the fact that most platforms use similar language and policies, gives little incentive for platforms to provide more transparent and easily understandable information. The majority of collaborative platforms' users are, therefore, unaware of the complex process of data collection, analysis and applications. Indicatively, according to a 2016 Eurobarometer survey on online platforms, 56 per cent of responding consumers replied that they had not read the terms and conditions of online platforms;[67] it is a separate question what proportion of the remaining 44 per cent has understood them. Thus, the consent, while clear and affirmative, might not necessarily be informed. However, the heavy fines introduced by the GDPR for breach of the transparency provisions and a potential failure to obtain explicit consent could motivate platforms to change their information policies. Further, potential users are more likely to opt for platforms with clearer and more user-friendly data protection policies, thus enhancing competition among platforms; since collaborative platforms already compete on elements other than price, such as innovation, quality of services, friendliness and a culture of bringing peers to the centre stage, competition on the basis of their data policies is likely to be forthcoming.

b. Other Grounds Justifying Data Processing

Apart from consent, data processing may nonetheless be lawful, on the basis of one of the five other alternative grounds, which, however, are subject to a strict 'necessity test'. Data processing by platforms could be lawful even without the data subject's consent:

(a) if such processing is necessary for the performance of a contract to which the data subject is party;[68] this legal ground could prove to be significant for collaborative platforms, given that the aggregation and processing of personal data is necessary for the matching of the users (consumers and suppliers of the service) and for the provision of the underlying service itself. However, platforms cannot extend the legitimacy under this condition to justify data processing beyond what is necessary for the specific contract. It is therefore questionable whether, for example, the observation of the user's behaviour and interests for the purpose of targeted advertising can be considered to fall under the performance of their contractual obligations;

(b) if the processing is necessary for compliance with a legal obligation.[69] Such legal obligation for collaborative platforms could derive, for example, from tax law. For instance, *Airbnb* has been cooperating with public authorities for

---

[67] European Commission, 'Special Eurobarometer 447 on online platforms' (2016), available at http://ec.europa.eu/information_society/newsroom/image/document/2016-24/ebs_447_en_16136.pdf.
[68] DPD, Art 7(b) and GDPR, Art 6(b).
[69] DPD, Art 7(c) and GDPR, Art 6(c).

tax collection purposes and has been compelled to share personal data with authorities.[70] Further collaborative platforms could be enjoined to reveal personal data in the course of investigating—and even preventing—criminal acts;[71]

(c) if the processing is necessary for the performance of government tasks ('the performance of a task carried out in the public interest or in the exercise of official authority vested in the controller').[72] This issue may be relevant with regard to SGEI missions entrusted to collaborative platforms. The 'necessity' and 'proportionality' tests are particularly important in mitigating processing of personal data in this context;

(d) processing of personal data without the data subject's consent can be lawful on the grounds of protection of his/her vital interests.[73] This reason is unlikely to apply to collaborative platforms, at least at the present stage of their development;

(e) finally, data processing is allowed when it is necessary for the protection of the legitimate interests of the data controller, provided that such interests are not overridden by the data subject's interest.[74] This criterion, along with consent, is the most likely to be invoked by platforms and at the same time is the most salient one. The GDPR Recitals introduce some examples of processing that could be legitimate under this criterion, such as direct marketing or preventing fraud,[75] ensuring network and information security,[76] reporting

---

[70] Indicatively, it is estimated that 'Airbnb has already provided non-anonymized data about every San Francisco Airbnb host to the San Francisco Treasurer/Tax Collector (TTX)'. The platform also claims it was compelled to hand over confidential, personal data to 'bureaucrats who will sift through it in search of potential violations of local planning and zoning laws'; see JC Wong, 'Airbnb Is Already Sharing Non-Anonymized User Data with SF', *SF Weekly* (12 November 2015), available at http://archives. sfweekly.com/thesnitch/2015/11/12/airbnb-was-already-sharing-non-anonymized-user-data-with-sf; see also *Airbnb citizen*, 'Protecting the Privacy of the Airbnb Community' (21 April 2015) at https:// www.airbnbcitizen.com/protecting-the-privacy-of-the-airbnb-community. Even more so, in Belgium, *Airbnb* has commenced proceedings against an order obliging it to provide information on hosts to authorities for tax collection purposes (pending at the time of writing); see M Lauwers, 'Airbnb veut préserver la vie privée de ses hôtes' *L'Echo* (20 July 2017).

[71] It has been argued that in the area of security, 'platforms seem to reinforce the traditional function of the State' through the means of data collection and surveillance, which can prove useful to governments for fighting crime and terrorism; see A Strowel and W Vergote, 'Digital Platforms: To Regulate or Not To Regulate? Message to Regulators: Fix the Economics First, Then Focus on the Right Regulation' (2015) Written Evidence (OPL0087) found in UK House of Lords, 'Online platforms and the Digital Single Market: oral and written evidence' 788, available at www.parliament. uk/documents/lords-committees/eu-internal-market-subcommittee/online-platforms/OnlinePlat-formsWrittenEvVolumePublished.pdf. For more on the issue of provision of platform data to governments see US Federal Trade Commission (FTC) Staff Report, 'The "Sharing" Economy: Issues Facing Platforms, Participants and Regulators' (2016) 63–65, available at www.ftc.gov/reports/sharing-economy-issues-facing-platforms-participants-regulators-federal-trade-commission.

[72] DPD, Art 7(e) and GDPR, Art 6(e).

[73] DPD, Art 7(d) and GDPR, Art 6(d).

[74] DDP, Art 7(f) and GDPR, Art 6(f).

[75] GDPR, Recital 47.

[76] GDPR, Recital 49.

criminal acts or threats to the competent authority,[77] and transmitting personal data, including client and employee data, within a group for internal administration purposes.[78] All these reasons—and many more—may be invoked by collaborative platforms. However, this criterion certainly does not give platforms a 'free pass', but rather, it would probably be difficult to pass the balancing test. Firstly, the balancing test should be documented, so that the assessment made can be examined by the courts, and it must include a broad range of factors taken into account. Secondly, it has been found by the Working Party that certain forms of processing, such as behavioural advertising and data brokering, cannot possibly be legitimised on this legal ground. Thirdly, the platforms' legitimate interests must not conflict with either the data subjects' rights or their interests, regardless of whether these are legitimate or not.[79] In view of the above, the Court recently ruled in *Rīgas* that not all 'legitimate interests' can be used to justify the data subject's personal data processing, even when a public authority has deemed such processing 'necessary'.[80] This judgment, if nothing else, sets the tone that under the GDPR this criterion will be interpreted strictly. In any case, the notion of 'legitimate interests' is largely open to interpretation and therefore might pose a challenge in striking a fair balance of interests between the platforms and their users.

If none of the above grounds exist, the data processing will be in breach of the data protection laws.

c. Sensitive Data

Collaborative platforms are in a position to possess (and process) a wide range of users' personal information, including sensitive data, such as racial or ethnic origin and religious beliefs.

Platforms like *Airbnb* have been accused of tolerating discrimination on the basis of racial and ethnic origin, which is revealed by the users' photos and general profiles on the platform.[81] Similarly, information on users' sex lives can be

---

[77] GDPR, Recital 50.

[78] GDPR, Recital 48.

[79] More specifically see Article 29 Data Protection Working Party, 'Opinion 06/2014 on the notion of legitimate interests of the data controller under Article 7 of Directive 95/46/EC', adopted on 9 April 2014 (WP217).

[80] Case C-13/16 *Rīgas satiksme* EU:C:2017:336. This legal ground has also been interpreted by the Court upon references for preliminary ruling with regard to its direct effect in national jurisdictions in Joined Cases C-468/10 and C-469/10 *ASNEF* EU:C:2011:777; and again in Case C-582/14 *Breyer* EU:C:2016:779. The Court clarified that Art 7(f) precludes Member States from excluding, categorically and in general, the possibility of processing certain categories of personal data without allowing the opposing rights and interests at issue to be balanced against each other in a particular case (paras 47–48 of the former and para 62 of the latter). Further, the request for a preliminary ruling interpreting Art 7(f) is pending in Case C-40/17 *Fashion ID* [2017] OJ C 112/22.

[81] For the anti-discrimination policy employed by *Airbnb* see Ch 7 below.

available to collaborative platforms.[82] Alternatively, platforms can form conclusions about the users' sex lives based on non-sensitive personal data.[83] Further, collaborative platforms collect and process information directly or indirectly relating to the users' health and wellness. Platforms providing services in the food market sector instantly come across the users' dietary preferences and allergies. Transportation platforms require their drivers to undergo medical checks in order to assess whether they are medically fit to partner with the platform.[84] Accommodation platforms receive information on users' disabilities or special conditions and health habits, such as smoking. Further, collaborative platforms' users often provide their social security number and other relevant documentation to platforms they wish to participate in. Also, the provision of some collaborative services is directly linked to the area of healthcare.[85]

This means that collaborative platforms process data similar to medical records, including illnesses, disabilities, medications, test results, medical history, allergies, mental health information and so on. Additionally, the combination of individual health or non-health data can create a detailed medical profile. It is, therefore, important to know which data constitute health data and consequently fall under the greater protection of sensitive data (Article 8 of the DPD and Article 9 of the GDPR). In this respect the broad view adopted by the Data Protection Working Party as to what constitutes health data should demand the platforms' attention:

> information such as the fact that a woman has broken her leg (Lindqvist), that a person is wearing glasses or contact lenses, data about a person's intellectual and emotional capacity (such as IQ), information about smoking and drinking habits, data on allergies disclosed to private entities (such as airlines) or to public bodies (such as schools); data on health conditions to be used in an emergency (for example information that a child taking part in a summer camp or similar event suffers from asthma); membership of an individual in a patient support group (e.g. cancer support group), Weight Watchers, Alcoholics Anonymous or other self-help and support groups with a health-related

---

[82] *Uber* was sued before French courts for accidentally revealing an affair of an *Uber* passenger to his wife, due to a bug in the app, which sent notifications even after logging-out; see E Braun, 'Un Français demande 45 millions d'euros à Uber pour avoir précipité son divorce' *Le Figaro* (8 February 2017).

[83] An example of this is the notorious *Uber*'s 'Rides of Glory' scandal. *Uber* proudly showed on its website that its employees could make conclusions about the customers' use of *Uber* for one-night stands. The company even used this knowledge to convey sex research and statistics and promote itself through the so-called 'Rides of Glory'. The post was soon deleted from the website; see D Perry, 'Sex and Uber's "Rides of Glory": The company tracks your one-night stands—and much more' *The Oregonian/Oregon Live* (20 November 2014), available at www.oregonlive.com/today/index.ssf/2014/11/sex_the_single_girl_and_ubers.html. See also A Ramasastry, 'Too Much Sharing in the Sharing Economy? Uber's Use of Our Passenger Data Highlights the Perils of Data Collection via Geolocation' *Verdict* (10 February 2015), available at https://verdict.justia.com/2015/02/10/much-sharing-sharing-economy.

[84] See eg *Uber*'s medical check requirement at www.uber.com/drive/denver/resources/colorado-medical-checks.

[85] See the growth of the collaborative economy in the health sector discussed in Ch 1 above. For further reading on the digitisation of healthcare see C Thuemmler and C Bai (eds), *Health 4.0: How Virtualization and Big Data are Revolutionizing Healthcare* (Switzerland, Springer International Publishing, 2017).

objective; and the mere mentioning of the fact that somebody is ill in an employment context are all data concerning the health of individual data subjects.[86]

Moreover, even the most innocuous non-health data, when collected over a significant period of time, combined and analysed, can reveal health-related information and can thus qualify as health data.[87] In these cases, collaborative platforms must comply with the stricter regulation of sensitive data processing laid out in Articles 8 and 9 of the DPD and the GDPR respectively.

ii. *Obligations of Data Controllers*

Apart from legitimate processing, the DPD and the GDPR ensure protection of data by imposing certain obligations upon data controllers.

The rules impose several general principles on data quality:[88] lawful and fair processing;[89] purpose specification and limitation;[90] data quality principles, ie relevancy and accuracy of data;[91] limited retention of data; exemption for scientific research and statistics ('storage limitation');[92] integrity and confidentiality;[93] and accountability.[94]

Most prominently, the data quality principles, ie relevancy and accuracy, must be preserved by data controllers in all processing acts. The relevancy principle requires platforms to process only adequate, relevant and not excessive data in relation to the purposes for which they are collected and/or further processed. Anonymisation and pseudonymisation techniques could be useful for the observance of the principle. According to the data accuracy principle, platforms shall not use data without taking steps to ensure with reasonable certainty that the data are accurate and up to date. In certain collaborative services, regular checking of data accuracy is essential, because of the potential damages, such as for instance in the case of crowdfunding (crowd-investing), where inaccurate data could lead to financial losses for the users and liability for the entrepreneurs and the platform itself. However, this obligation may be particularly burdensome for those 'passive' small platforms that act as mere communication boards. In that regard, this obligation may clash with the prohibition to impose a general obligation on providers

---

[86] Article 29 Data Protection Working Party Annex—health data in apps and devices, attached to the Working Party's letter dated 5 February 2015 responding to the Commission's request to clarify the scope of the definition of data concerning health in relation to lifestyle and wellbeing apps.

[87] Health data can therefore be: (a) inherently or clearly medical data; (b) raw sensor data that can be used independently or combined to yield conclusions about the actual health status or health risk of a person; and/or (c) conclusions drawn about a person's health status or health risk (irrespective of their accuracy).

[88] DPD, Art 6 and GDPR, Art 5.

[89] DPD, Art 6(1)(a) and GDPR, Art 5(1)(a).

[90] DPD, Art 6(1)(b) and GDPR, Art 5(1)(b).

[91] DPD, Art 6(1)(c) and (d) and GDPR, Art 5(1)(c) and (d).

[92] DPD, Art 6(1)(e) and GDPR, Art 5(1)(e).

[93] GDPR, Art 5(1)(f).

[94] DPD, Art 6(2) and GDPR, Art 5(2).

to monitor, according with the E-commerce Directive,[95] if this latter text is found to be applicable.[96]

With regard to the principle of limited retention of data, platforms are obliged to either delete data as soon as they are no longer needed for the purposes for which they were collected, or retain the information upon anonymisation or pseudonymisation. The limitation stands with the GDPR thus raising questions about its somewhat 'conservative' approach:

> the proportionality notion that a minimum of data should be stored for as short a time as possible, can be considered limiting for the innovation process ... The progress of technology is going in the opposite direction, ie to store and process as much personal data as possible and deliver services based on insights gained.[97]

So far, the Court has applied the principle of data retention quite strictly in the technological context and has even declared the Data Retention Directive invalid. In its landmark judgments, *Digital Rights Ireland*,[98] *Google Spain*[99] and *Schrems*,[100] the Court recognised the primacy of the fundamental right to privacy and personal data over the right of storing and processing data.

A novelty introduced by the GDPR is the idea of data protection 'by default' or 'by design',[101] meaning that the default settings/characteristics of any site, service or electronic product should be the ones most protective of privacy. In this way, transparency is increased and users gain more control over their personal data. This requirement implies technical as well as substantial alterations of the current processing activities by platforms. It therefore imposes a significant burden on collaborative platforms, which must ensure that data protection compliance is included in the systems (software, algorithms etc) used for their data processing activities. In addition, they are required, by default, to process only the minimum amount of personal data necessary.

Last but not least, the data protection regime is based on the principle of accountability of data controllers. This key principle can potentially bring data protection from 'theory to practice'.[102] It focuses on the role and responsibility of data controllers (mainly collaborative platforms) and places upon them the

---

[95] E-commerce Directive, Art 15; for the role of this Directive in regulating platforms' liability see Ch 2 above.

[96] D Keller, 'Intermediary Liability and User Content under Europe's New Data Protection Law' (8 October 2015) *The Center for Internet and Society, Stanford Law School, Blog*, available at https://cyberlaw.stanford.edu/blog/2015/10/intermediary-liability-and-user-content-under-europe%E2%80%99s-new-data-protection-law.

[97] M Westerlund and J Enkvist, 'Platform Privacy: The Missing Piece of Data Protection Legislation' (2016) 7 *Journal of Intellectual Property, Information Technology and Electronic Commerce Law* 1, para 1.

[98] Joined Cases C-293/12 and C-594/12 *Digital Rights Ireland* EU:C:2014:238, in which the Court rendered the Data Retention Directive invalid.

[99] Case C-131/12 *Google Spain* EU:C:2014:317.

[100] Case C-362/14 *Schrems* (n 47).

[101] Art 23.

[102] Article 29 Data Protection Working Party, 'Opinion 3/2010 on the principle of accountability', adopted on 13 July 2010 (WP173) 3.

burden of the observance of data protection rules in practice. Based on this provision, platforms have the front seat in the implementation of data protection law, thus performing the role of the 'parent', by enacting data protective measures and initiatives to ensure the effective application of the rules laid down by regulators. The Working Party in its Opinion on the future of privacy, whereby it evaluated the Directive, suggested strengthening the controllers' accountability principle by introducing a general accountability provision.[103] The GDPR brings about greater responsibilities, heavier duties and higher fines for controllers, thus strengthening their accountability.

The OECD privacy guidelines explain that '[a] data controller should be accountable for complying with measures which give effect to the principles stated above'.[104] In other words, the accountability principle translates to an obligation of platforms to *(pro)actively* put in place appropriate and effective measures that will ensure the implementation of the above-mentioned principles and more generally safeguard data protection during their processing, and not merely react to shortcomings in practice. Thus, the accountability principle renders platforms responsible for the observance of data protection rules in practice. The Working Party provided an indicative, non-exhaustive list of such measures that controllers could take, such as offering adequate data-related training and education to staff members, allocating sufficient resources for privacy management, setting up binding data protection policies and so on.[105] In any case, the measures enacted by each platform should be 'tailored' to the specific characteristics of the business, such as scale of the platform, nature of the data processed (sensitive data or general data), and the like. Thus, one can talk of some kind of 'guided self-regulation'.

If all the above obligations are heavy for those small platforms, which presumably are data controllers, they will be impossible to bear for suppliers (providers of the underlying service and prosumers), even though they technically may qualify as data controllers as well.[106] Further clarifications on the role of suppliers and their obligations with regard to the data rules are very much needed.

iii. Rights of Data Subjects

Data subjects are awarded with a series of rights against data controllers. The GDPR reinforces the control that data subjects have over their personal data by introducing further rights.

---

[103] ibid 6–10. See also Article 29 Data Protection Working Party, Working Party on Police and Justice, 'The Future of Privacy: Joint contribution to the Consultation of the European Commission on the legal framework for the fundamental right to protection of personal data', adopted on 1 December 2009 (WP168) 18–21.

[104] Organisation for Economic Co-operation and Development (OECD), 'Guidelines on the Protection of Privacy and Transborder Flows of Personal Data', available at www.oecd.org/sti/ieconomy/oecdguidelinesontheprotectionofprivacyandtransborderflowsofpersonaldata.htm#part2.

[105] Similarly, see OECD, 'The OECD Privacy Framework' (2013) 16, available at www.oecd.org/sti/ieconomy/oecd_privacy_framework.pdf.

[106] See section II.A above.

a. Right of Access

Data subjects have the right of access. This right includes the right to obtain from the data controller information about the processing of their data (purposes of processing, categories of data concerned, recipients of data etc), as well as the rectification, erasure[107] or blocking of data if their processing violates the data protection regime or if the data are inaccurate or incomplete, and notification of third parties to whom the data have been disclosed of such rectification, erasure or blocking.[108] Under the GDPR, data subjects will also have the more extensive right to restrict processing, ie to restrict the use of their personal data only to limited purposes, for a number of reasons, such as contested accuracy of the data, unlawful processing, data not needed for the original purpose etc.[109] The data subject's request for access may be restricted due to overriding interests, such as national security, defence and so on.[110] However, the Court has interpreted the right of access in the sense that it should not be unduly restricted by time limits and that data subjects should be given the right of access for past data processing operations as well. Otherwise, the right to rectify, erase or block (ie stop the use of) data or the right to object to personal data processing would be ineffective.[111]

This means that collaborative platforms' participants shall have the right to access their data by requesting (and receiving) information on aspects of their data processing, such as the purposes of the processing, the categories of personal data concerned, the recipients of the data, the envisaged period of the data storage and so on.[112] The GDPR introduces further mandatory categories of information to be provided upon data subjects' requests for access, thus placing a heavier administrative burden upon platforms. In the event that the platform has violated the EU data protection rules, or if the data are incomplete or inaccurate, the platform user would have the right to rectify, erase or block those data. Requests to access data kept in platforms' records have apparently seen the light in the collaborative economy. An example of such requests involves *Uber* drivers seeking access to information kept in *Uber's* secret records upon deactivation of their accounts.[113] On another note, if those data are already published on the platform, such as eg in the form of peer reviews, it could prove to be difficult to have the data deleted.

b. Right to be Forgotten

The right of erasure, or else the 'right to be forgotten' was recognised by the CJEU in *Google Spain*,[114] and is consolidated in the GDPR, though not unconditionally.

---

[107] This is further analysed immediately below.
[108] DPD, Art 12 and GDPR, Arts 15–18.
[109] GDPR, Art 18.
[110] DPD, Art 13 and GDPR, Art 23.
[111] Case C-553/07 *College van burgemeester en wethouders van Rotterdam v MEE Rijkeboer* EU:C:2009:293.
[112] GDPR, Art 15.
[113] See www.ridesharingdriver.com/fired-uber-drivers-get-deactivated-and-reactivated.
[114] Case C-131/12 *Google Spain* (n 99).

Erasure of data may be requested only on the following (disjunctive) grounds: (a) data no longer necessary for the purposes initially collected or processed; (b) withdrawal of data subject's consent, where no other legal ground justifies the processing; (c) data subject objects to processing that has been considered necessary for the performance of public interest tasks or official authority vested in the controller or for the purposes of the legitimate interests pursued by the controller or by a third party, or for direct marketing purposes; (d) personal data have been unlawfully processed; (e) obligation to erase stemming from a legal obligation under Union or Member State law; (f) personal data collected upon a child's consent.[115]

In view of the recognition of data as 'consideration' by the recent draft Digital Content Directive ('freemium'),[116] three points need to be made with regard to the right to erasure. Firstly, if the economic value of personal data is indeed assignable to third parties, is the right to erasure allocated to the third party as well, even though it is intended to protect the personality element of the right? In other words, does the data subject lose the right to erasure because of the 'sale' of the data to a third party and accordingly does acquisition of data by the third party mean simultaneous acquisition of the corresponding rights, such as the right to erasure? Secondly, considering that personal data (may) act as counter-performance for participation in the collaborative platform, does erasure of personal data mean expulsion from the platform? Or, alternatively, does the platform gain (permanent) ownership of the data once provided? Thirdly, it bears remembering that in the collaborative economy the interdependence of parties is significant. Therefore, erasure of the personal data of an individual user may cause a chain-reaction, influence a great number of participants and disrupt the collaborative ecosystem. In the collaborative economy '… your online reputation and profile are not just your data; that data reflects a lot of other user feedback on you that has been generated solely through that marketplace and by others …'.[117] It is quite unclear what will happen, for example, with the posted peer reviews of an individual requesting the erasure of his/her personal data from the platform, insofar as most collaborative platforms recognise in their Terms and Conditions that any user-generated content remains the user's property. Indeed, '[a] complete allocation of one's own data (semantically defined by reference to their own personality) would be inconsistent with the constitutionally protected freedom of expression and information'.[118] However, platforms retain wide-scope licences to basically treat the content as they wish.[119]

---

[115] GDPR, Art 17(1).
[116] As noted above (n 17).
[117] UK House of Lords Report (n 3), para 246.
[118] Zech (n 15) 67.
[119] For example *Uber's* Terms state: '… Any User Content provided by you remains your property. However, by providing User Content to Uber, you grant Uber a worldwide, perpetual, irrevocable, transferable, royalty-free license, with the right to sublicense, to use, copy, modify, create derivative works of, distribute, publicly display, publicly perform, and otherwise exploit in any manner such User

c. Profiling

Further, data subjects have the right not to be subject to decisions based solely on automated processing, or else to 'profiling',[120] ie

> any form of automated processing of personal data consisting of the use of personal data to evaluate certain personal aspects relating to a natural person, in particular to analyse or predict aspects concerning that natural person's performance at work, economic situation, health, personal preferences, interests, reliability, behaviour, location or movements.[121]

This is particularly interesting in the collaborative economy, considering that its function is largely based on big data analytics and algorithms. The role of algorithms and other technological proxies in the effective functioning of collaborative platforms is crucial, considering the myriad of automated (or semi-automated) decisions taking place by using personal data, such as scanning of messages' content and flagging of suspicious activities, decision-making concerning the provider's 'job performance' based on the reviews received, location data and matching of suppliers with users of eg driving services, automated payment or withholding of such payment at the end of the service provided (or failure of provision) and so on.[122] Objection of the data subject to automated decisions could create difficulties in the provision of the collaborative services, as well as causing a decrease in speed and increase in costs for the platform, since the automated decisions would have to be manually processed. Further, if the objection to automated decisions is legitimate, the data in question must not be further used by the controller, although past processing of those data remains legitimate nonetheless.

d. Data Portability

The GDPR introduces a new right of data portability, ie the right of data subjects to receive their personal data in a structured, commonly used machine-readable format, and transfer their personal data from one controller to another.[123] This will be a cause of extra burdens for electronic platforms, since the transferability of myriads of data included in complex datasets is likely to prove to be a challenging task for them. Even more so, data portability means that similar platforms would have to build their applications in a similar manner, in order to make such portability possible in the first place. This raises standards and may create barriers

---

Content in all formats and distribution channels now known or hereafter devised (including in connection with the Services and Uber's business and on third-party sites and services), without further notice to or consent from you, and without the requirement of payment to you or any other person or entity'; see www.uber.com/legal/terms/us.

[120] DPD, Art 15 and GDPR, Art 22.
[121] GDPR, Art 4(4).
[122] On the issue of automatic decision-making through algorithms, see also Ch 5, where the idea of 'algocracy' is discussed.
[123] GDPR, Art 20.

for new businesses to enter the market. Also, similar to the right to be forgotten, data portability raises complex questions about data ownership.

C. Digital Privacy in the Collaborative Economy

The proposed e-Privacy Regulation is *lex specialis* to the GDPR and will complement it as regards electronic communications data that qualify as personal data.[124] The proposal's broad definition of 'electronic communications services' means that all services including an element of communication, even if ancillary to the main service, will fall in the scope of the e-Privacy Regulation.[125] Collaborative platforms will thus be subject to this Regulation as well as to the GDPR, insofar as they provide a means for peer-messaging. For instance, *Airbnb* users communicate via the platform in order to fix details of the hosting service, availability of the listed property, time of meeting, location of keys, directions to the house and so on. Thus, communications will be protected by both the GDPR and the e-Privacy Regulation, while personal data not associated with any messaging, communication, and the like will be protected only by the GDPR, as described above. More specifically, with regard to the e-Privacy Regulation, this instrument regulates the use of: (a) electronic communications *content*, ie data relating to online communications, such as messages between users, reviews, etc, including text, voice, videos, images and sound; and (b) electronic communications *meta-data*, such as location data of both the user generating the communication and the user receiving the message, date, time, duration and the type of the communication.

The e-Privacy Regulation poses a general prohibition on interference with electronic communications data, such as by listening, tapping, storing, monitoring, scanning or through other kinds of interception, surveillance or processing of electronic communications data, by persons other than the end-users.[126]

However, collaborative platforms often scan the content of users' communications in order to better self-regulate the environment, ie to secure truthful reviews, to avoid scams and combat fraud, abuse and violation of their policies in general. Exceptions to the rule may be justified:

(a) for the sole purpose of the provision of a specific service to an end-user, if the end-user or end-users concerned have given their consent to the processing of his or her electronic communications content and the provision of that service cannot be fulfilled

---

[124] Art 1(3) of the proposed e-Privacy Regulation.

[125] The e-Privacy Regulation broadens the scope significantly in relation to the (soon to be) repealed Directive. The Regulation will apply to 'the processing of electronic communications data carried out in connection with the provision and the use of electronic communications services and to information related to the terminal equipment of end-users' (Art 2(1) of the proposed e-Privacy Regulation). Thus, e-privacy rules will also apply to new players providing electronic communications services therein forth, such as over-the-top service providers, as *WhatsApp*, *Facebook Messenger* and *Skype*, but also other online platforms that include online communication, such as e-commerce platforms, dating apps, video game websites and collaborative platforms.

[126] See the proposed e-Privacy Regulation, Art 5.

without the processing of such content; or (b) if all end-users concerned have given their consent to the processing of their electronic communications content for one or more specified purposes that cannot be fulfilled by processing information that is made anonymous, and the provider has consulted the supervisory authority.[127]

Similarly, meta-data (eg time, location of the communication etc) can be used: (a) when necessary for mandatory quality of service requirements, billing, calculating interconnection payments, detecting and/or stopping fraudulent, or abusive use of, or subscription to, electronic communications services; or (b) when the end user's consent has been given for one or more purposes that cannot be fulfilled if the information is rendered anonymous.[128] Consent therefore plays a fundamental role here as well, thus making it important for platforms obtain users' consent specifically relating to the processing of their communications' content and meta-data. The comments already made about consent under the GDPR are also relevant in the present context.

D. Transborder Data Flows

The collaborative economy enables transactions between peers from different parts of the world, thus inherently entailing an element of universality. In *Fiverr*, for instance, a peer from an EU Member State can offer freelance services for a peer located elsewhere, a community project in New York can be funded by peers located in the EU through *Indiegogo*, and so on. In order to enable such transactions, it is sometimes necessary for the collaborative platforms to perform cross-border data transfers. Further, collaborative platforms are often headquartered or based in the US and simultaneously are affiliated with an EU Member State. Therefore platforms may process personal data concerning EU data subjects by operating from outside the EU. Alternatively, personal data collected by a platform operating within the EU can later be transferred to a third country, where perhaps the parent company is located.

In order to ensure a high level of protection for the EU data subjects regardless of the location of the processing, EU data protection law: (a) enjoys a broad scope of application;[129] and (b) restricts personal data transfers to third countries.

Both the DPD[130] and the GDPR[131] introduce a general prohibition on transfers of personal data to third countries unless specific conditions are met.[132] The prohibition may be lifted provided that the transfer is made to a country with an adequate level of data protection[133] or where the foreign controller has

---

[127] ibid Art 6(3).
[128] ibid Art 6(2).
[129] For which see section II.A above.
[130] DPD, Art 25 ff.
[131] GDPR, Art 44 ff.
[132] The area of free data flow has been extended by the 'Agreement on the European Economic Area (EEA)' [1994] OJ L 1/3.
[133] DPD, Art 25 and GDPR, Art 45.

implemented adequate safeguards for the data transfer with respect to the right of privacy and corresponding rights, ie standard contractual clauses (pre-) approved by the Commission, or Binding Corporate Rules (BCRs).[134] Alternatively, an exemption or derogation from the prohibition, such as consent, performance of contract, important public interest ground, vital interests of the data subject, etc may apply.

The Commission's adequacy decisions have caused controversy and have been the subject of judicial review. The 'Safe Harbour' decision, ie the Commission's decision of 2000 that the US data protection regime was adequate within the meaning of the DPD,[135] was ruled retroactively invalid by the CJEU with its landmark judgment in *Schrems*.[136] The Court interpreted the term 'adequate level of protection' as 'essentially equivalent' to that guaranteed within the EU and thus found that the requirement was not met by the Safe Harbour principles. The decision was largely based on the fact that the Safe Harbour principles were applicable solely to self-certified US organisations receiving personal data from the EU, while the US public authorities were not required to comply with them,[137] as well as the fact that the Safe Harbour decision enabled interference founded on national security and public interest requirements or on domestic legislation of the US.[138]

In order to ensure some extra-territorial application of the EU rules in a more effective manner than it did with the Safe Harbour agreement, the EU has adopted the EU-US 'Privacy Shield' framework. The EU-US Privacy Shield imposes stronger obligations on US companies to protect Europeans' personal data, includes safeguards on US government access to data, ensures effective protection and redress for individuals and provides for annual joint review to monitor the implementation of the agreement.

However, the Privacy Shield too has faced criticism and its future remains uncertain at the time of writing. The Working Party, in its relevant Opinion,[139] pointed out three points of concern: (i) that the decision does not oblige organisations to delete data if they are no longer necessary; (ii) the US administration not fully excluding the continued collection of massive and indiscriminate data; and lastly (iii) both the powers and the position of the Ombudsperson need clarification in order to ensure independence and effectiveness. Thus, despite the somewhat increased data safety thresholds included in the revised agreement, the EU-US Privacy Shield has been brought before the CJEU for annulment.[140]

---

[134] DPD, Art 26(2) and GDPR, Art 47.

[135] Commission Decision 2000/520/EC of 26 July 2000 pursuant to Directive 95/46/EC of the European Parliament and of the Council on the adequacy of the protection provided by the safe harbour privacy principles and related frequently asked questions issued by the US Department of Commerce [2000] OJ L 215/7.

[136] Case C-362/14 *Schrems* (n 47).

[137] ibid para 82.

[138] ibid para 87.

[139] Article 29 Data Protection Working Party, 'Opinion 01/2016 on the EU—U.S. Privacy Shield draft adequacy decision', adopted on 13 April 2016, (WP238).

[140] Case T-670/16 *Digital Rights Ireland v Commission* [2016] OJ C 410/26.

The action came as no surprise, considering the controversy over the US privacy regime and surveillance methods. At the time of writing the case was pending before the CJEU. While data transfers conducted under the Privacy Shield are meanwhile valid, if the CJEU annuls the agreement, as with its predecessor, it might be that the Commission would find itself in a dead-end and that transatlantic data transfers might grind to a halt.

To make matters worse for the EU-US data transfer agreement, the Trump administration fundamentally altered the online privacy regime in the US, by allowing internet service providers to share users' personal information, including location data, without the data subject's consent, with marketers and other third parties.[141] It is hard to imagine how such a regime could be perceived as equivalent with the European one as analysed above. It is equally hard to imagine how the Commission could insist on the EU-US Privacy Shield implementation following the *Schrems* judgment which noted that:

> in the light of the fact that the level of protection ensured by a third country is liable to change, it is incumbent upon the Commission, after it has adopted a decision pursuant to Article 25(6) of Directive 95/46, to check periodically whether the finding relating to the adequacy of the level of protection ensured by the third country in question is still factually and legally justified. Such a check is required, in any event, when evidence gives rise to a doubt in that regard.[142]

And while in the EU the Court and legislature have been struggling for a higher level of data protection, the idea has been mooted that the EU data protection regime, even before its reinforcement by the GDPR, could fall foul of the EU's obligations under the GATS.[143] According to this view, it is not so much the rules themselves, but rather their inconsistent (and somehow political) application by the Commission's adequacy decisions, that could trigger the GATS rules on the Most Favoured Nation (Article II), on National Treatment (Article XVII) and on Internal Regulation (Article VI); the same inconsistent application would prevent the *chapeau* of Article XIV to be satisfied, thus ruling out the justification of such discriminatory practices.[144] Therefore, according to this view, it would be recommended that the Commission follows clearer criteria and a more transparent procedure when issuing its adequacy decisions.[145]

However desirable this may be, it is my view that even under the current conditions, any tentative claim based on the above GATS rules would have thin chances

---

[141] D Lee, 'Anger as US internet privacy law scrapped', *BBC News* (29 March 2017).

[142] Case C-362/14 *Schrems* (n 47). Quote taken from the CJEU Judgment's Summary, available at http://eur-lex.europa.eu/legal-content/EN/SUM/?uri=CELEX:62014CJ0362&qid=1491246083807.

[143] S Yakovleva and K Irion, 'The Best of Both Worlds? Free Trade in Services, and EU Law on Privacy and Data Protection' (2016) 2 *European Data Protection Law Review* 191; *Amsterdam Law School Research Paper No 65*; *Institute for Information Law Research Paper No 5*; available at https://ssrn.com/abstract=2877168.

[144] ibid 24 ff.

[145] ibid 25 ff.

of succeeding: given that the discrimination test followed by the GATS is a substantive one (ie treat equally situations which are equal and differently situations which are different) and that the burden of proof is on the plaintiff, it will be extremely difficult to effectively compare the data protection regimes of different WTO States and positively to show that they ensure an equal level of data protection; especially so since the CJEU in *Schrems* has held that protection should be 'essentially equivalent' to that offered by the EU.[146]

Direct recognition of privacy and data protection is also found in the new generation of the international free trade agreements (CETA, TTIP, TiSA).[147] However, these have been heavily criticised for potentially reducing data protection for EU citizens and risking the privacy and data protection standards gained. Article 16.4 of the CETA points to 'international standards of data protection' which should be taken into account by all parties in the adoption/application of rules for the protection of personal information of users engaged in electronic commerce. While the EU Commission officially denies that the EU privacy and data protection rules may be risked by the international trade agreements[148] and declares that data protection as a fundamental right is not included in the negotiations for such agreements, it is entirely possible that the trade agreements will eventually allow for circumvention of such rules.

Last but not least, 'Brexit' raises data transfer issues, since the UK after becoming a third country will not be part of the (then into force) GDPR and will have to either seek an adequacy decision or make sure that its data controllers and processors offer adequate safeguards.[149] In view of the fact that the UK is the second biggest exporter of services in the world (after the US) and that three-quarters of its cross-border data flows are with EU countries, the adoption of an adequacy decision by the Commission would be preferable. Such a decision, however, which would compel the UK to as high a standard of protection as the GDPR, could only be negotiated after the completion of Brexit, thus making necessary the negotiation of transitional measures. All the above add to the complexity of the—already complex—data transfer regime put into place by the EU to protect its citizens within and without its territory.

---

[146] See above n 136 and the corresponding text.

[147] For the interrelation of free trade in services and EU data protection law, see Yakovleva and Irion, 'The Best of Both Worlds? Free Trade in Services, and EU Law on Privacy and Data Protection' (2016); see also C Kuner, *Transborder Data Flows and Data Privacy Law* (Oxford, Oxford University Press, 2013); see also C Stupp, 'European Commission paralysed over data flows in TiSA trade deal' *Euractiv* (11 October 2016), available at www.euractiv.com/section/trade-society/news/european-commission-paralysed-over-data-flows-in-tisa-trade-deal.

[148] See Q&A for TiSA on the protection of 'people's data' at http://ec.europa.eu/trade/policy/in-focus/tisa/questions-and-answers/.

[149] See UK House of Lords, 'Brexit: the EU data protection package' (2017) 3rd Report of Session 2017–19, available at https://publications.parliament.uk/pa/ld201719/ldselect/ldeucom/7/702.htm.

III. Data Protection under Other EU Rules

At least three sets of rules need to be reviewed here in correlation with data protection: consumer protection law (section A), intellectual property law (section B), and competition law (section C).

A. Data Protection and Consumer Protection Law

The consumers' protection directives provide for the protection of consumers' data. These instruments thus complement the data protection regime and may be used as a secondary legal basis in data protection-based claims, or even a primary one in cases of gaps in the data protection regime.

Most prominently, under the Unfair Commercial Practices Directive (UCPD)[150] if the data controller ('trader' in terms of consumer protection law) fails to inform the consumer that his/her personal data will be used for commercial purposes as well as for the provision of the services, the former's behaviour would constitute misleading omission of material information.[151] The Unfair Contract Terms Directive[152] provides for minimum protection rules against standard terms in contracts. Platforms must, therefore, comply with this instrument as well in the drafting of the standard Terms and Conditions to be accepted by peers. These must not cause great imbalance between the platform's and the users' rights to the detriment of the latter, with regard to data processing, or else they may be deemed unfair under consumer protection legislation. It goes without saying that the above rules only apply in favour of consumers in C2B relations, where the other party is a trader; therefore, the discussion in Chapter 2 of this book is fully relevant here as well.

B. Data Protection and Intellectual Property Law

i. Protection of Platforms' Databases

Apart from the users of collaborative economy (ie suppliers of the underlying service and final consumers), the platform itself may also claim protection of the

---

[150] European Parliament and Council Directive 2005/29/EC of 11 May 2005 concerning unfair business-to-consumer commercial practices in the internal market and amending Council Directive 84/450/EEC, Directives 97/7/EC, 98/27/EC and 2002/65/EC of the European Parliament and of the Council and Regulation (EC) No 2006/2004 of the European Parliament and of the Council (Unfair Commercial Practices Directive-UCPD) [2005] OJ L 149/22.

[151] Under Art 7(2) and No 22 of Annex I of the UCPD. See Commission Staff Working Document, 'Guidance on the implementation/application of Directive 2005/29/EC on Unfair Commercial Practices' SWD(2016) 163 final, 27.

[152] Council Directive 93/13/EC of 5 April 1993 on unfair terms in consumer contracts (Unfair Terms Directive) [1993] OJ L 95/29.

data it has collected, analysed and generated. While the creators of most personal data acquired by the platform are the data subjects, ie the users, the platform is the creator of the database based on those personal data. According to the Database Directive,[153] a database is defined as 'a collection of independent works, data or other materials[154] arranged in a systematic or methodical way and individually accessible by electronic or other means'.[155] Therefore, the collection of data in the possession of the collaborative platforms will qualify as a database and thus be protected under the Database Directive. The latter provides for both the protection of the *database structure* under copyright rules (Article 3 ff) and the *database content* as a sui generis right attributed to the created database (Article 7 ff).

Protection under copyright rules is contingent upon the selection or arrangement of the database contents constituting the author's own intellectual creation.[156] The CJEU in *Football Dataco* highlighted the element of 'originality' and the 'free creative choices' in the creation of the database as crucial indications for finding an intellectual creation.[157] It also clarified that the 'originality' requirement is not met 'when the setting up of the database is dictated by technical considerations, rules or constraints which leave no room for creative freedom'.[158] Even though the collection and organisation of data by collaborative platforms takes place through automated means, namely algorithms and other automated machine-learning proxies, such collection may still be considered as an intellectual creation and qualify for copyright protection under the Database Directive.[159] For instance, feeding the algorithm/machine with conscious and intentional queries and hypotheses by the platforms' employees in order to yield a pre-determined

---

[153] European Parliament and Council Directive 96/9/EC of 11 March 1996 on the legal protection of databases (Database Directive) [1996] OJ L 77/20.

[154] 'Independence means that the individual data can be used on their own'; see Case C-338/02 *Fixtures Marketing* EU:C:2004:696. This condition, however, squares badly with big data: as already explained above (section II.A), even the most seemingly insignificant piece of data can lead to valuable conclusions and can influence a large number of platform users, through analysis and/or combination with other data. Hence, in view of the development of big data databases and algorithms, the Court's future jurisprudence may need to address this lacuna in the interpretation of the 'independence' criterion of the database definition. On this issue see also Zech (n 15) 71–72.

[155] Database Directive, Art 1(2).

[156] ibid Art 3(1).

[157] Case C-604/10 *Football Dataco* EU:C:2012:115. The Court (para 38) interpreted the 'selection or arrangement' as 'making free and creative choices and thus stamp[ing] his "personal touch"'. See also Recital 16 of the Directive, where it is stated that: '… no criterion other than originality in the sense of the author's intellectual creation should be applied to determine the eligibility of the database for copyright protection, and in particular no aesthetic or qualitative criteria should be applied'.

[158] ibid para 39.

[159] See Graef, 'Market Definition and Market Power in Data: The Case of Online Platforms' (2015) 480–481; see also Commission Staff Working Document on the free flow of data and emerging issues of the European data economy, SWD(2017) 2 final, 19, where the Commission stated: 'Machine-generated and industrial data do not benefit from protection by other intellectual property rights as they are deemed not to be the result of an intellectual effort. Results of data integration, analytics, etc. can be protected, on the other hand, as a result of a protection given to the intellectual effort made into the design of the data integration process or the analytics algorithm (software)'.

type of results can fulfil the criterion of 'free creative choices'[160] that indicate an intellectual creation. Even if copyright protection is for some reason not granted to databases of collaborative platforms, these may still claim the sui generis database protection right. The right of Article 7 ff is contingent upon qualitative and/or quantitative substantial investment on behalf of the platform,[161] therefore recognising the economic value of data and thus protecting the result of the investment as opposed to the intellectual creation.[162] The investment refers to the obtaining, verification or presentation of the contents of the database. The Court has made a distinction between investment in *creating* and *obtaining* data and has interpreted the 'investment' criterion narrowly to cover only the latter:

> With regard to the distinction between creating and obtaining data, the Court of Justice argued that activities which are 'indivisibly linked' to the creation of data cannot be taken into account for the purposes of assessing substantial investment in the obtaining of the contents of the database.[163]

Any platform-*produced* data are, therefore, not considered to be an investment and thus do not qualify for the sui generis protection.[164] However, as already discussed, collaborative platforms produce fresh data themselves by extracting information from, and combining of, existing user-generated data. This means that the sui generis database protection right is of limited applicability only to those data obtained, presented or verified. The fact that platforms create data themselves does not of itself mean that they may not claim the sui generis protection so long as they have invested in obtaining data as well.[165]

Provided that the above conditions for the attribution of the sui generis right are met by collaborative platforms, the latter shall receive protection against the

> repeated and systematic extraction and/or re-utilization of insubstantial parts of the contents of the database implying acts which conflict with a normal exploitation of that database or which unreasonably prejudice the legitimate interests of the maker of the database.[166]

---

[160] As was required by the Court in Case C-604/10 *Football Dataco* (n 157).

[161] See Art 7(1): '… in either the obtaining, verification or presentation of the contents to prevent extraction and/or re-utilization of the whole or of a substantial part, evaluated qualitatively and/or quantitatively, of the contents of that database'.

[162] See Zech (n 15) 70.

[163] I Graef, *EU Competition Law, Data Protection and Online Platforms: Data as Essential Facility*, International Competition Law Series Vol 68 (Kluwer Law International, 2016) ch 5, para 136 therein.

[164] See Case C-46/02 *Fixtures Marketing Ltd v Oy Veikkaus Ab* EU:C:2004:694, para 34; Case C-203/02 *The British Horseracing Board Ltd and Others v William Hill Organization Ltd* EU:C:2004:695, para 31; Case C-338/02 *Fixtures Marketing Ltd v Svenska Spel AB* EU:C:2004:696, para 24; Case C-444/02 *Fixtures Marketing Ltd v Organismos prognostikon agonon podosfairou AE (OPAP)* EU:C:2004:697, para 40.

[165] See Case C-46/02 *Fixtures Marketing v Oy Veikkaus Ab* paras 39–40; Case C-203/02 *The British Horseracing Board*, paras 35–36; Case C-338/02, *Fixtures Marketing v Svenska Spel AB*, paras 29–30; and Case C-444/02 *Fixtures Marketing Ltd v Organismos prognostikon agonon podosfairou AE (OPAP)*, paras 45–46; data originally created by the platform could, as mentioned above, be covered by copyright.

[166] Database Directive, Art 7(5).

Thus, exclusivity rights are conferred upon the database as a whole, whereas the individual parts (data) of the data collection do not gain any exclusivity rights and therefore are not protected.

ii. *Protection of Platforms' Trade Secrets*

In addition to protection of the database, the unauthorised extraction and/or re-utilisation of data gathered by collaborative platforms, as well as platforms' algorithms, can be prevented on the basis of trade secrets protection.

Article 2 of the freshly adopted Directive on trade secrets[167] defines 'trade secret' by three elements: firstly, the information must be confidential; secondly, it should have commercial value because of its confidentiality; and thirdly, the trade secret holder should have made reasonable efforts to keep it confidential.[168] All these criteria are likely to be met by collaborative platforms. While some of the 'volunteered data', such as name and age, may not qualify as confidential information in this age of extensive digital footprints,[169] other, such as dietary preferences, medical conditions, location, etc constitute privileged information of the collaborative platform and therefore should be considered as secret. Further, passively collected data, such as the users' commercial, and other, behaviour and preferences, as well as meta-data produced by collaborative platforms would certainly qualify as 'secret'.

As for the second criterion, the commercial value of personal data for collaborative platforms in general has been analysed above. The confidentiality of users' personal data is of direct economic interest for platforms, which manage to improve their services—and thus gain more market value—by using exactly that confidential information. For example, *Airbnb* predicts which renters and guests would be the best match on the basis of their personal data, which are fed into various algorithms and analysed. The company claims that technology has improved matches by four per cent.[170] Therefore, *Airbnb* has a profound interest in keeping the personal data and its algorithms secret from its competitors, as these are a significant source of profit for the company. The same is true for most collaborative platforms.

Thus, the third criterion will be fulfilled as well, since platforms usually go to great lengths in order to keep the data they have aggregated and their algorithms secret from their competitors. Confidentiality agreements and legal actions in cases of alleged extraction of corporate secrets constitute standard practice. In the US, *Uber* and *Lyft* have exchanged (and settled for the most part) legal actions over

---

[167] European Parliament and Council Directive (EU) 2016/943 of 8 June 2016 on the protection of undisclosed know-how and business information (trade secrets) against their unlawful acquisition, use and disclosure [2016] OJ L 157/1.

[168] This definition follows the definition of 'undisclosed information' in the Trade-Related Aspects of Intellectual Property Rights (TRIPS) Agreement.

[169] See Graef (n 18) 482.

[170] J Clark, 'Big Data Knows When You're Going to Quit Your Job Before You Do' *Bloomberg* (30 December 2014).

data breaches. *Lyft* had sued a former officer for allegedly breaking his confidentiality agreement when he left his position with *Lyft* and proceeded to work for *Uber*. During the legal proceedings, he revealed that *Lyft* had 'discovered a method to "hack into Uber's computer systems and gain access to Uber confidential information".[171] On the other hand, *Uber*, after finding out that 50,000 of its drivers' names and their licence numbers had been hacked, brought legal action to identify the culprit.[172]

Further, the confidential information regarded as trade secrets can be 'commercial data such as information on customers and suppliers, business plans or market research and strategies'.[173] Personal data included in lists of clients/customers or internal datasets containing research or other data may also constitute trade secrets.[174] In view of the above, users' data as well as platforms' algorithms and own datasets will most probably qualify as trade secrets.

As such, they shall be protected against unlawful acquisition, disclosure and use from competitors. However, trade secrets holders do not have exclusive rights over the information covered by the trade secrets, which means that competitors are free to develop and use the same, similar or alternative solutions. Therefore, most collaborative platforms use similar algorithms and tools and extract similar pieces of information from users.

C. Data and Competition

The intersection between data protection and competition law has received growing attention with the increased use of data in the online environment, thus creating the need for a holistic regulatory approach.[175]

The massive accumulation of data by collaborative platforms gives rise to antitrust concerns. Indeed, big data can enhance market power, lock-in platforms' users, create barriers to entry and even lead to dominance. Data are so inherently important for platforms that they may constitute essential facilities. All these questions relate to how data affect competition rules and are addressed, in the context of competition law, in the following chapter.

---

[171] J Menn and D Levine, 'Uber, Lyft settlement did not require either side to pay—sources' *Reuters* (1 July 2016).

[172] ibid.

[173] Recital 2 of the Directive on trade secrets.

[174] Annex 21 of the Commission Staff Working Document, 'Impact Assessment, Accompanying the document proposal for a Directive of the European Parliament and of the Council on the protection of undisclosed know-how and business information (trade secrets) against their unlawful acquisition, use and disclosure' SWD(2013) 471 final, 254.

[175] The EDPS commenced in 2014 a process of synergy between competition law, data and consumer protection. In its Opinion on coherent enforcement of fundamental rights in the age of big data (Opinion 8/2016), the EDPS recommends establishing a Digital Clearing House for enforcement in the EU digital sector, a voluntary network of regulatory bodies to voluntarily share information, and suggests that this should be supplemented by guidance on how regulators could coherently apply competition, data protection and consumer protection rules protecting the individual.

With regard to the effect of competition law in data protection, one observation must be made. The GDPR introduced the right to data portability, as a means to foster competition. Data portability prevents lock-in of users due to high switching costs, enhances multi-homing and restricts a platform's market power and potential dominance. Simultaneously, the right to data portability empowers data subjects to have more control over their data, protects them from having their data stored in 'silos' and from being 'locked-in' a specific platform. Data portability, connected as it is with the possibility of multi-homing, therefore benefits both data protection of data subjects and competition between platforms.

IV. Conclusions

The role of data in the collaborative platforms and the protection of the personal data of users comes as part of a broader evolution of EU data protection and privacy law ushered in by the growth of online activity. EU regulators have replaced outdated legislation (DPD and e-Privacy Directive) with more modern, forceful and user-centric legislation. Thus, overall, the new GDPR reinforces data protection, places more control on the hands of data subjects themselves, imposes obligations on data controllers (such as platforms), focuses on principles and promises greater harmonisation within the Union, since the rules are dressed in the form of a Regulation. However, the flexibility embedded in the GDPR, intended to avoid stifling technological progress, leaves significant issues unanswered. These questions are likely to be raised in an acute manner in relation to collaborative platforms where, contrary to traditional e-commerce platforms (typically selling goods), personal data is 'of the essence' for the very service provided: the dietary needs of the *Eatro* user, the gender/age/appearance of the *Uber* driver and the location and route of the *Uber* rider, as well as the financial details of the project creator in *Kickstarter* are all determinants of the very collaborative service offered through the platform. The situation is made even more complex by the triangular relations developed with the help of collaborative platforms and the automated transfer and exchange of data between the parties. So much so that it is worth asking whether the GDPR is completely agnostic to the issues raised by the collaborative economy, and whether it will have to be reviewed in order to accommodate them.

On the other side of the spectrum, the courts seem to be ruling in favour of the data subject in landmark cases. Indeed, the clash between data protection and other rights has already been brought to the courts.[176] For instance, the freedom

---

[176] The ECtHR also plays a prominent role in the clash of the data protection and privacy rights with other rights. For instance, see *Delfi v Estonia*, ECtHR, Application 64569/09, Judgment of 16 June 2015, ECLI:CE:ECHR:2015:0616JUD006456909; and *MTE v Hungary*, ECtHR, Application 22947/13, Judgment of 2 February 2016, ECLI:CE:ECHR:2016:0202JUD002294713, whereby the right to private life (Art 8 ECHR) clashed with the freedom of expression (Art 10 ECHR).

of expression in the realm of the digital economy has already been adjudicated on by the CJEU. In the famous *Digital Rights Ireland* case,[177] the Data Retention Directive[178] was declared invalid by the Court for it interfered in a particularly serious manner with the rights to respect for private life and protection of personal data. While the interference did indeed satisfy an objective of general interest, ie public security and the fight against serious crime, it was found to be non-compliant with the principle of proportionality, and it was, therefore, characterised by the Court as a non-justified interference. More specifically, the Court found that:

> the fact that data are retained and subsequently used without the subscriber or registered user being informed is likely to generate in the minds of the persons concerned the feeling that their private lives are the subject of constant surveillance.[179]

It also found that:

> the retention of the data in question might have an effect on the use, by subscribers or registered users, of the means of communication covered by that directive and, consequently, on their exercise of the freedom of expression guaranteed by Article 11 of the Charter.[180]

In other words, '[t]he Court found that surveillance, whether by governments or companies, constitutes a serious interference with the fundamental rights to privacy and data protection that has a potentially chilling effect on the freedom of expression'.[181] This may hold true for collaborative platforms, especially in terms of passive collection of personal data and monitoring the user's activity and behaviour. Moreover, aggressive and intrusive targeting, personalised advertising and profiling may negatively influence the user's autonomy, freedom of expression and even freedom of thought (Article 10 of the Charter).

On the other hand, data protection may clash with the somewhat neglected right to conduct business.[182] It is true that collaborative platforms rely heavily on the collection and processing of personal data for achieving their purposes. Contrasting rights are even more relevant in the collaborative economy, considering the triangular-shaped relations. In a simple case scenario, the revelation of personal data, and even sensitive ones (eg ethnicity), in the posted peer reviews, opens the floor to friction between: (a) the right of expression and information for the party posting the review and the rest of the users; (b) the right to privacy and

---

[177] Joined Cases C-293/12 and C-594/12 *Digital Rights Ireland* (n 98).
[178] European Parliament and Council Directive 2006/24/EC of 15 March 2006 on the retention of data generated or processed in connection with the provision of publicly available electronic communications services or of public communications networks and amending Directive 2002/58/EC [2006] OJ L 105/54.
[179] Joined Cases C-293/12 and C-594/12 *Digital Rights Ireland* (n 98) para 37.
[180] ibid para 28.
[181] Oostveen and Irion (n 1) 7.
[182] While the battle between data protection and the right to conduct business in the digital era has not yet reached the European courts, the battle between the latter and the 'neighbouring' right to intellectual property has in Case C-314/12 *Telekabel* EU:C:2014:192.

personal data protection for the data subject; and (c) the right to conduct business for the platform itself.

As in any case of conflicts between fundamental rights protected by the European legal order, a *fair balance* must be struck through the means of interpretation.[183] It might be that the European Courts might be transforming into constitutional courts in the field of digital law or even proceed to controversial, if not manipulative, interpretations.[184] For the time being, the CJEU appears to favour data protection and the free movement of data in relation to the above-mentioned 'other' rights.[185] Notably, the Court has already invalidated four EU legislative acts with regard to data protection and privacy, while judgment on a fifth one is still pending: Council Decisions 2004/496 and 2004/535 on the conclusion of an Agreement between the EC and the US on the processing and transfer of PNR (Passenger Name Record) data by Air Carriers to the US were annulled; EU Regulations 1290/2005 and 259/2008 on the publication of information on beneficiaries of European agricultural funds were partly invalidated for failure to observe the principle of proportionality with regard to the personal data published; Directive 2006/24 on the retention of data generated or processed in connection with the provision of publicly available electronic communications services or of public communications networks was declared invalid, as it interfered seriously with the privacy and data protection rights; the Safe Harbour decision was also declared void, as explained above; lastly, the EU-US Privacy Shield agreement,[186] adopted to replace the annulled Safe Harbour decision, is currently under challenge before the CJEU.[187] In the near future, the European Courts' standing is bound to have an even greater impact, with the growing importance of data.[188]

While the judicial treatment of the rights to data protection and privacy in the digital context at large remains to be seen, the intensive data extraction and the extensive data usage made by collaborative platforms seems generally at odds with the protective framework put into place by the EU legislature and judiciary. Indeed, in view of the above, regulatory gaps and grey areas in personal data protection still exist at the European level despite the recent reform, thus jeopardising

---

[183]   See Case C-275/06 *Promusicae* EU:C:2008:54.

[184]   See O Pollicino, 'The ambition of the Court of Justice of the European Union to be a Constitutional Court in the field of digital law', and B Van der Sloot, 'The ECtHR as constitutional court in the age of Big Data', both in E Psychogiopoulou (ed), *European Courts, New Technologies and Fundamental Rights, Workshop Proceedings* (Hellenic Foundation for European & Foreign Policy, 2017) at 6–7 and 19–20 respectively.

[185]   Oostveen and Irion (n 1) 7–8.

[186]   For which see section II.D above.

[187]   Respectively: Joined Cases C-317/04 and C-318/04 *European Parliament v Council of the European Union and European Parliament v European Commission* EU:C:2006:346; Joined Cases C-92/09 and C-93/09 *Volker und Markus Schecke GbR, Hartmut Eifert v Land Hessen* EU:C:2010:662; Joined Cases C-293/12 and C-594/12 *Digital Rights Ireland* (n 98); Case C-362/14 *Schrems* (n 47); pending is Case T-670/16 *Digital Rights Ireland v Commission* (n 140), with regard to the EU-US Privacy Shield.

[188]   For an overview of the CJEU's role on data protection and privacy, see K Irion, 'Special Regard: The Court of Justice and the fundamental rights to privacy and data protection', in U Faber et al (eds), *Festschrift fur Wolfhard Kohte* (Baden-Baden, Nomos, 2016); Institute for Information Law Research Paper No 4; Amsterdam Law School Research Paper No 35; available at https://ssrn.com/abstract=2836910.

effective data protection. Clarifications and adjustments in order to tackle real issues arising from the collaborative economy are very much needed. For instance, the role of suppliers and their obligations, potentially as data controllers, needs to be elucidated. The same is true for the role of data as counter-performance, as important questions arise in terms of both contract law and data protection. Further, the economic value of personal data needs to be taken into consideration in the context of competition law. The question whether the accumulation of big data can constitute a competitive advantage or even an essential facility remains unanswered.[189] Further, the interrelation of data protection and intellectual property rules must be assessed holistically by regulators; while data portability is essential in order to avoid entry barriers and to promote fair competition between platforms, intellectual property rules (trade secrets and database protection) may hinder its application. Ex ante regulation and guidance by the Commission is necessary to adapt data protection rules in the collaborative economy.

Further, information and empowerment of data subjects is key for the effective protection of their personal data. Platform users are already more active than the average consumer. It is only fit that they actively choose how their data will be processed once 'trained' to become more mindful about their control over their data. In line with the self-regulation culture enshrined in the collaborative economy, platforms could give data subjects the option of data processing every step of the way, through pop-up boxes and comprehensible questions, instead of lengthy, all-inclusive Terms and Conditions. Further, platforms' privacy notices could be supported by 'kite-marks', ie visual symbols explaining the effects of their decisions.[190] '[S]uch kite-marks should include a graded scale indicating levels of data protection, similar to the traffic light system used in labelling for food products',[191] so that platform' users know instantly the level of data protection provided by the platform. This could also enhance competition between platforms on the basis of the quality of data protection offered to their potential users. While such a user-centric approach might seem tiring at first, the benefits for both competition and data protection may be prime.

---

[189] For an analysis of this in the context of competition law see the following chapter.
[190] This view is also suggested in the UK House of Lords Report (n 3) paras 237–39.
[191] ibid para 235.

4

The Collaborative Economy
and EU Competition Law

I. Introduction

There is no doubt that collaborative platforms offer new services—or a wider variety of pre-existing ones—in a way that is generally beneficial to consumers. Thus, for instance, tourists nowadays have a much wider variety of accommodation choices, at a much wider array of prices. Moreover, the supplementary supply of accommodation makes sure that hotel prices do not skyrocket even during high-season or peak events and can prevent abusive practices; it allows for extra demand to be covered when permanent facilities are not enough.[1] Therefore, the overall balance of the collaborative economy towards consumer welfare seems clearly positive.

Indeed, collaborative platforms have revived competition in long uncontested or even closed markets, such as the taxi industry. Even more so, collaborative platforms enjoy, for the most part, regulatory benefits, thus creating concerns about competition on an unlevel playing field. On the other hand, traditional players use their longstanding (dominant) position to lobby for regulation that would block the entry of collaborative platforms. Indeed, some collaborative services have been banned altogether in certain EU Member States.[2]

In the realm of vivid competition of collaborative platforms with traditional businesses and with other collaborative platforms facilitating similar services, the literature has identified several important challenges to the application of competition law as we know it. The disruptive nature, the role of collaborative platforms as multi-sided (mostly two-sided) markets, the network effects produced, the use of sophisticated algorithms and the plurality of the various peer-based business

---

[1] It has been calculated that approximately 30% of visitors to the 2014 World Cup in Rio de Janeiro were able to find accommodation through some collaborative platform.

[2] *Uber, BlaBlaCar* and *Airbnb* have submitted complaints to the Commission against France, Germany, Spain and Hungary for the transport sector; and against Spain, Germany, Belgium and France, for the accommodation sector. On the possible legal claims see D Geradin, 'Should Uber be Allowed to Compete in Europe? And if so How?' (2015) *Competition Policy International*, available at www.competitionpolicyinternational.com/assets/Europe-Column-New-Format.pdf.

models employed in the collaborative economy test the applicability and sufficiency of existing competition rules, originally intended to regulate traditional markets. This is true both in the area of antitrust (see section II below) and of state aids (see section III below).

II. Antitrust

In order to appreciate the way antitrust rules apply in the collaborative economy, it is necessary to examine how the latter affects the concept of 'undertaking' (see section A), market definition (see section B) and market power (see section C), before turning into the actual practices prohibited under Article 101 TFEU (see section D) and Article 102 TFEU (see section E).

A. Collaborative Participants as Undertakings

The term 'undertakings' has been interpreted by the Court quite broadly, in the sense that it 'encompasses every entity engaged in an economic activity, regardless of the legal status of the entity or the way in which it is financed'.[3] As explained above,[4] most collaborative platforms pursue economic activities, with the exception of those small, non-for-profit platforms which act mostly in restricted communal contexts.[5] As per the CJEU's jurisprudence, any activity consisting in offering goods and services on a given market is an economic activity.[6] Therefore the vast majority of suppliers of the underlying services perform economic activities.

Thus, the collaborative economy entails two types of economic activity: (a) the intermediation for the matching of supply and demand by the platform; and (b) the supply of the underlying service by individuals. Since platforms and suppliers pursue distinct economic activities they constitute, prima facie, two separate, distinct undertakings. However, it is possible that some collaborative platforms do not act merely as digital intermediaries, but rather perform, or substantially participate in, the underlying service as well. For example, *Uber* could

---

[3] Case C-41/90 *Höfner and Elser v Macrotron* EU:C:1991:161, para 21.

[4] See Ch 2 above.

[5] Even those organisations not having a profit-motive or an economic purpose, may still qualify as 'undertakings', provided that they carry out some commercial or economic activity; for the lack of profit-motive see Case 209/78 *Van Landewyck v Commission* EU:C:1980:248, para 88; Case C-244/94 *FFSA v Ministère de l'Agriculture and de la Pêche* EU:C:1995:392, para 21; and Case C-67/96 *Albany* EU:C:1999:430, para 85; for the lack of economic purpose see Case 155/73 *Italy v Sacchi* EU:C:1974:40, paras 13–14.

[6] See Case C-180/98 *Pavlov* EU:C:2000:428, para 75; Case C-35/96 *Commission v Italy* EU:C:1998:303, para 36; and Case 118/85 *Commission v Italy* EU:C:1987:283, para 7.

be found to provide services no different from those of traditional taxi operators by performing the (single) economic activity of intermediation *and* supply of transport,[7] and thus qualify as a single undertaking along with its drivers.[8] On the contrary, as described above, *Airbnb* is much less involved in the provision of the accommodation services, which translates into its offering only the intermediation service while, the '*Airbnb* hosts' offer the actual accommodation services.[9] This is a matter of a case-by-case evaluation, whereby the determination of the economic activity/ies and consequently the undertaking/s will be contingent upon the degree of control asserted by the platforms, the activeness of their role in the supply, the involvement in the quality/type/conditions of the underlying service and so on. Therefore, the test and indicia concerning the characterisation of the contractual relationships between platforms and suppliers discussed in Chapter 2 above, are, in principle,[10] relevant for competition law purposes as well.

Individuals providing collaborative services, even if mere prosumers, may very well qualify as single undertakings when providing the underlying services.[11] For the most part, they perform economic activities, bear their own financial risks, and even more so they typically use their own assets, skills and resources. Therefore, but for extreme cases where the platform's control is so exorbitant as to exclude any initiative and risk-taking by the suppliers, these should be considered as undertakings.

However, employees[12] or agents who act on behalf of their principal and do not assume any financial risk[13] are generally not undertakings. Therefore, the question of the employment status (or lack thereof) is a key one to resolve. An 'employee' for the purposes of Articles 101 and 102 TFEU is generally defined in the same way as a 'worker' under Article 39 TFEU.[14] The issue of whether individuals providing collaborative services are 'workers' in the context of employment law is, as

---

[7] G Lougher and S Kalmanowicz, 'EU Competition Law in the Sharing Economy' (2016) 7 *Journal of European Competition Law & Practice* 87, 90; see also the discussion in Chs 2 and 7 of this book.

[8] If *Uber* and its drivers were to be considered as a single undertaking their relations would not raise any competition issues, but rather labour law issues; for an eloquent description of this dilemma see J Nowag, 'UBER Between Labour and Competition Law' (2016) 3 *Lund Student EU Law Review* 95; see also Ch 5 below on labour law.

[9] See above under Ch 2.

[10] As explained in the following paras, a supplier who qualifies as a 'worker' under contract and labour law, could, nonetheless, qualify as an undertaking under competition law.

[11] The Court has found that individuals can qualify as undertakings: see Case 258/78 *Nungesser v Commission* EU:C:1982:211 and Case 35/83 *BAT v Commission* EU:C:1985:32. Even more so, inventors, opera singers, barristers and farmers have already been qualified as such; see respectively *Reuter/BASF* (Case COMP/28.996) [1976] OJ L254/40; *RAI/UNITEL* (Case COMP/29.599) [1978] OJ L157/39; Case C-309/99 *Wouters* EU:C:2002:98; and *French Beef* (Case COMP/38.279) [2003] OJ L 209/12. Moreover, the CJEU has held that an entity may be an undertaking for *some* of its activities, while not being one for others: see eg Case C-475/99 *Ambulanz Glöckner* EU:C:2001:577.

[12] Case C-22/98 *Becu* EU:C:1999:419.

[13] See Commission, 'Guidelines on Vertical Restraints' [2010] OJ C 130/1, paras 12–21.

[14] ibid para 26.

yet, unresolved.[15] However, there are reasons to argue that even those suppliers who qualify as 'workers' within the labour law context, may still be considered as separate undertakings under competition law.[16]

In *Becu*, Advocate General Colomer explained that for an employee to be considered an undertaking separate from his employer, the employee would have to be capable of exerting sufficient competitive significance and to retain 'a certain degree of—essentially economic—autonomy'.[17] The main criterion for this is 'the ability to take on financial risks':[18]

> This is not the case of someone with the status of an employee, as it is the employer that owns the assets necessary to participate on the market. An essential element of ownership of an asset is the right to exclude others from using it.

This '… "translates into authority over people" as the employer controls the assets the employee intends to work with'.[19]

In the collaborative economy, the platforms typically do not own any assets, but it is rather the suppliers who provide the assets necessary for the performance of the activity. Even more so, suppliers provide complementary resources and invest time and their own money to prepare for the provision of services; *Uber* drivers pay for petrol, cleaning and car service costs, insurance, amenities, and the like, and *Airbnb* hosts pay for property tax, apartment maintenance, taking photos of the property, equipment, supplies and luxuries, and so on. The main criterion for considering that employees are integrated into the entity of their employers, ie lack of financial risks, is therefore reversed in the collaborative economy.

Further, Advocate General Jacobs in *Brentjens*, distinguished employees from undertakings as follows: 'Employees normally do not bear the direct commercial risk of a given transaction. They are subject to the orders of their employer. They do not offer services to different clients, but work for a single employer'.[20]

Unlike the traditional 'employee', suppliers in the collaborative economy: (a) do bear a direct commercial risk, as they are only remunerated for each transaction they conduct (ie not with a salary); (b) frequently invest in the provision of services with their own assets and resources; (c) do not take orders from the platform, but rather choose freely and independently whether they will take a ride, rent out an apartment at a specific time, perform a gig and so on; and (d) provide their

---

[15] See Ch 5 below on labour law.

[16] In support of the view that employees could be undertakings see C Townley, 'The Concept of an "Undertaking": The Boundaries of the Corporation—A Discussion of Agency, Employees and Subsidiaries' in G Amato and CD Ehlermann (eds), *EC Competition Law—A Critical Assessment* (Oxford, Hart Publishing, 2007).

[17] Case C-22/98 *Becu* EU:C:1998:133, para 47; Similarly see AG Jacobs in Joined Cases C-115/97 to C-117/97 Brentjens EU:C:1999:434, para 215, where he distinguishes employees from undertakings.

[18] Case C-22/98 *Becu* EU:C:1998:133, para 53.

[19] O Odudu and D Bailey, 'The Single Economic Entity Doctrine in EU Competition Law' (2014) 51 *CMLR* 1721, 1736, notes omitted.

[20] Joined Cases C-115/97 to C-117/97 *Brentjens* (n 17) para 215.

services to different clients and can 'multi-home', ie offer their services through various platforms.

Suppliers of the underlying services through collaborative platforms will thus, more often than not, qualify as individual undertakings under competition law, as opposed to one single economic unit along with the platform. Further, in view of the disruptive nature of the collaborative economy and the unique nature and status of collaborative suppliers, it may be worth re-examining the limits of the concept of an 'undertaking' to include those borderline suppliers who may be classified as 'employees' under labour laws.[21] This, however, would come at a normative price: the same terms (and the criteria associated therewith) would have different meanings (different outcomes) in different fields of the law and there would be situations where both competition and labour law would apply to the same factual situations. If this were to hold true, the collaborative phenomenon would be disruptive not only of economic realities, but also of legal categories.

B. Market Definition

Defining the relevant market in the collaborative economy is no easy task.[22] In accordance with the discussion of the economic activities accruing in the collaborative economy,[23] at least two distinct relevant markets are identified: (a) the platform intermediation; and (b) the underlying services market. However, in certain circumstances it is possible that the intermediation service is so closely intertwined with the provision of the underlying service that the platform together with its suppliers would operate in a single relevant product market. Platforms may be active in either the intermediation relevant market only, or both the intermediation and the underlying service relevant markets. In this latter case, when the platform's control over the underlying service is so comprehensive that the intermediation service itself is of only incidental importance, the relevant market in terms of competition law could be only that of the underlying service. It is under this perspective that Advocate General Szpunar in *Asociación Profesional Elite Taxi (Uber Spain)* found that *Uber* is active in the relevant market for urban transport services and that the intermediation services were only ancillary to the core service, which is that of urban transportation.[24]

---

[21] This idea of questioning the traditional concept of employee within the collaborative economy is also briefly discussed by G Lougher and S Kalmanowicz, 'EU Competition Law in the Sharing Economy' (2016) 91.

[22] For a more extensive discussion of this issue see F Russo and ML Stasi, 'Defining the relevant market in the sharing economy' (2016) 5 *Internet Policy Review* 1.

[23] See section II.A immediately above.

[24] Opinion of AG Szpunar in Case C-434/15 *Asociación Profesional Elite Taxi* EU:C:2017:364, para 61.

i. Defining the Market for Platform Intermediation

a. Two-sided Markets

Collaborative platforms are active in the product market for platform intermediation. This market is inherently two-sided: the platform gets money and gathers market-share both in the market of suppliers and in the market of final consumers. While the two markets are strongly interconnected by means of the externalities produced,[25] participants in each market segment may have opposing interests (the supplier strives for higher income, while the consumer for lower prices). Hence, the question: do platforms operate on one (two-sided) or two separate relevant markets and, if the former is true, which market segment is relevant and how is it to be taken into account?[26]

Ambivalent EU and National Practice

Two-sided markets have been treated inconsistently by the Commission. During merger assessments, it has found that two-sided markets constitute one single market, as opposed to two separate markets. This was the case in *Travelport/ Worldspan*,[27] where these two-sided platforms connected two separate customer sides, ie travel agents and travel service providers, by operating a global distribution system (GDS);[28] the Commission found one two-sided relevant market for 'electronic travel distribution services through a GDS'. Similarly, in the *Google/ DoubleClick* case,[29] the Commission found a single two-sided relevant market for online advertising intermediation services, as the two-sided platforms connected publishers with advertisers; the Commission did not examine the possibility that separate markets could have existed for publishers and advertisers, but rather addressed only 'the reality of an intermediation market, which it considered separate from the direct sales channel'.[30] Thus, no reasoning was provided why the Commission found one single two-sided market rather than two separate ones.[31] However, with regard to the market for payment cards, in the more recent *MasterCard*[32] and *Visa Europe* cases,[33] the Commission changed its approach by

---

[25] For a brief discussion on multi-sided markets and externalities see Ch 1 above.

[26] On two-sided markets under competition law, see L Filistrucchi et al, 'Market Definition in Two-Sided Markets: Theory and Practice' (2014) 10 *Journal of Competition Law and Economics* 292.

[27] *Travelport/Worldspan* (Case COMP/M.4523) [2007] OJ L 314/21.

[28] A tool that allows travel agents to gather information and make reservations (for airlines, cars, hotels) from travel service providers.

[29] *Google/DoubleClick* (Case COMP/M.4731) [2008] OJ C 184/10.

[30] L Filistrucchi et al, 'Market Definition in Two-Sided Markets: Theory and Practice' (2014) 308.

[31] Further insight into the two-sided market/s is expected in the context of the ongoing antitrust cases the Commission opened against *Google* in November 2010.

[32] *MasterCard* (Case COMP/34.579), *EuroCommerce* (Case COMP/36.518), *Commercial Cards* (Case COMP/38.580) [2009] OJ C 264/8.

[33] *Visa Europe MIF* (Case COMP/39.398) [2011] OJ C 79/8.

finding two interrelated markets.[34] Broadly speaking, in *MasterCard* the Commission's position was based on the arguments that defining a single two-sided market: (a) would not sufficiently accommodate the complex vertical structure of the market; (b) would not reflect that the relevant product is not merely payment services, but also other acquiring and issuing services; and (c) would be inconsistent with previous practice in market definition of two-sided markets, such as newspapers.[35] This approach has been fiercely criticised by academia.[36]

In its investigation against *Google* for abuse of its dominant position with regard to *Google's* search engine, the Press Releases and Commission's statements indicate that the Commission distinguishes between a market for online search advertising on the advertisers' side and a market for web search on the users' side. As no decision has been published at the time of writing, it remains to be seen whether the Commission will treat those separately or as one two-sided market.[37]

At the national level, the approach of two separate markets was adopted by the Spanish National Authority for Markets and Competition (Comisión Nacional de los Mercados y la Competencia, CNMC) in the recent assessment of the *Just Eat/ La Nevera Roja* merger.[38] The CNMC said that the two interdependent 'demand-sides', ie (a) restaurants; and (b) final consumers, give rise to two separate, interdependent markets.[39] In the first one—the market where the platforms offer their intermediation services to restaurants—online platforms compete with each other in offering restaurants better management, advertising and a marketing channel to attract more customers for their food deliveries. In this market, the management of food orders directly from restaurants themselves was not included. In the second market, however,—the market where the platforms offer their intermediation services to consumers—the CNMC found that online platforms managing food deliveries compete with restaurants which manage the food orders themselves, since consumers perceive them as substitutes. While in the former market

---

[34] Similarly, the UK Office of Fair Trading (as it then was) found two relevant markets in *MasterCard*, Case No CA98/05/05.

[35] The summarised argument was taken from L Filistrucchi et al (n 26) 312.

[36] See eg L Filistrucchi et al (n 26) 315.

[37] *Google Search (Shopping)* (Case COMP/39740); see Press Release IP/17/1784 of 27 June 2017, 'Antitrust: Commission fines Google €2.42 billion for abusing dominance as search engine by giving illegal advantage to own comparison shopping service'; also pending are *Google's* Android operating system and *Google's* AdSense. On the relevant market in the case of *Google* see G Luchetta, 'Is The Google Platform a Two-Sided Market?' (2014) 10 *Journal of Competition Law & Economics* 185; see also H Hobbelen, N Lorjé and A Guenay, 'Selected recent developments in the application of EU competition law to online platforms' (2016) *Mediaforum* 20–22, available at www.eui.eu/Projects/ENTRANCE/ Documents/NewEntrance/Workshops/AnnualConference/Recent-Development-in-the-Application- of-EU-Competition-law-to-Online-Platforms-Hobbelen-Lorje%CC%81-Guenay.pdf.

[38] Comisión Nacional de los Mercados y la Competencia (CNMC), *Just Eat/La Nevera Roja*, Case No C/0730/16, available in Spanish at www.cnmc.es/expedientes/c073016. For a short description of the case in English see OECD, 'Annual Report on Competition Policy Developments in Spain—2016' (2017) paras 38–41, available at www.oecd.org/officialdocuments/publicdisplaydocumentpdf/?cote= DAF/COMP/AR(2017)15&docLanguage=En.

[39] *Just Eat/La Navera Roja* (n 38), paras 26–28.

(for restaurant intermediation), the market share of the resulting entity would amount to nearly 80 per cent, in the latter (for consumer intermediation) it would only have a 10 per cent market share. In view of this, the CNMC cleared the merger with commitments.[40]

Theoretical Foundations

It should be remembered that according to the dominant economic analysis, cross-subsidisation between the two sides of the market in order to achieve optimal participation and maximise externalities is one of the defining elements of two-sided markets.[41] Indeed, according to Filistrucchi et al, two interconnected markets should be characterised as part of a single market whenever 'the demands on the two sides of the market are linked by *indirect network effects* and the firm recognises (ie *internalises*) these indirect network effects'.[42] As these authors explain 'one of the consequences of defining only one market is that a firm would be either on both sides of the market or on none'.[43]

This is certainly true for those collaborative platforms where a transaction between the two groups (ie suppliers and consumers) is concluded. Therefore, the platform operator has to be active in both sides of the platform at the same time, since it would be impossible to process the transaction if it was only active in either one side (that of the supplier or that of the consumer) of the platform. Accordingly, it would be incorrect to evaluate the transaction under the hypothesis that there are two separate markets for intermediation. In view of the above, a collaborative platform, similarly to a payment card provider, 'only experiences competitive pressure from other providers which are also active on both sides of the platform'.[44] Thus, it has been argued that, while non-transaction markets (eg media) form two separate and connected markets, only one market is to be found in the markets where a transaction is concluded between the two sides through the platform (eg credit cards), and a 'two-part tariff' can be applied by the platform ('i.e. the possibility for the platform to impose a price both for membership and for usage').[45] Or, to use the expression of Evans and Schmalensee writing

---

[40] For the commitments imposed and the rationale of the CNMC see section II.E.ii.

[41] See Ch 1 above. According to JC Rochet and J Tirole, 'Two-Sided Markets: A Progress Report' (2006) 37 *The RAND Journal of Economics* 645, for a market to be two-sided it is enough that the price structure is not neutral; see also Filistrucchi et al (n 26) 301–303 taking up this point.

[42] Filistrucchi et al (n 26) 296–97, note omitted; the same idea is also expressed in 300–301.

[43] ibid 301.

[44] I Graef, 'Stretching EU competition law tools for search engines and social networks' (2015) 4(3) *Internet Policy Review* 4, available at https://ssrn.com/abstract=2655555; see also Filistrucchi et al (n 26) 301.

[45] M Colangelo and V Zeno-Zencovich, 'Online Platforms, Competition Rules and Consumer Protection in Travel Industry' (2016) 5 *EuCML* 75, 77; see also Filistrucchi et al (n 26) 293.

about credit card fees, 'the interchange fee is not an ordinary price; its most direct effect is on price structure, not price level'.[46]

Thus, the definition of a market as a two-sided one not only allows for a more accurate depiction of market power, but also for the proper understanding of the platforms' economic choices. Therefore 'transaction platforms' (ie where the parties transact through the platform) should, in principle, be analysed as single two-sided markets, as opposed to non-transaction ones (ie where no transaction takes place or the platform only intermediates without participating in the actual transaction).[47]

Antitrust Consequences of Defining Two-sided Markets

The finding of one (two-sided) or two separate markets has practical implications for the definition of the relevant market, and therefore of market power, dominance, and for merger assessments.[48] As explained,

> [a]s one side of the market is usually subsidized, the antitrust authorities may be inclined to define the relevant product market solely based on the paying side. Each side of a multisided market, paying or non-paying, could also theoretically constitute a separate product market, which in turn creates difficulties in seeing the broader, multisided picture.[49]

In that sense, secondly, if competition authorities find two separate but connected markets and examine those independently, the *free* provision of (intermediation) services on one side of the platform could be considered as predatory pricing. On the other hand, in a single two-sided market, such a pricing structure is frequently necessary to activate indirect network effects, achieve balance between the two groups and thus an optimal match of supply and demand. This is why, even if two separate, but interrelated, relevant markets are found in a two-sided system, the examination of potential anti-competitive practices must take into consideration the broader economic context and the interactions between the two sides in determining whether there is an antitrust violation.[50]

---

[46] DS Evans and RL Schmalensee, 'The Economics of Interchange Fees and their Regulation: An Overview' (2005) *MIT Sloan Working Paper* 4548-05, available at www.kansascityfed.org/publicat/pscp/2005/Evans-Schmalensee.pdf, 76.

[47] On the same hypothesis see Lougher and Kalmanowicz (n 7) 92; Graef, 'Stretching EU competition law tools for search engines and social networks' (2015) 3.

[48] In that regard, economists argue that a correct analysis of multi-sided markets must take into account all groups served by the platform. See DS Evans and RL Schmalensee, 'The Antitrust Analysis of Multi-Sided Platform Businesses' in RD Blair and DD Sokol (eds), *Oxford Handbook on International Antitrust Economics* (New York, Oxford University Press, 2015); and (2012) Coase-Sandor Institute for Law & Economics Working Paper No 623, available at http://ssrn.com/abstract=2185373.

[49] G Gürkaynak et al, 'Multisided markets and the challenge of incorporating multisided considerations into competition law analysis' (2017) 5 *Journal of Antitrust Enforcement* 100, 108, note omitted.

[50] See Case T-491/07 *Groupement des cartes bancaires* EU:T:2012:633; and on appeal Case C-67/13 P *Groupement des cartes bancaires* EU:C:2014:2204.

More generally, taking into account the network effects between the two sides of the market can justify activities that would otherwise be anticompetitive.[51] Put in a more normative way:

> restrictions of competition on one side of a two-sided market could not be folded in the *'object'* box, if there was a *prima facie* justification for them pertaining to the other side of the market. However, this did not mean that they are immune of prosecution under the *'effects'* analysis.[52]

b. Relevant Product Market for Platform Intermediation

Irrespective of whether it is one two-sided market for intermediation (for both sides simultaneously) or there are two separate markets (for intermediation services for the supplier and intermediation services for the recipient), the relevant product market/s of platform intermediation should be specified by reference to such underlying service.[53] Thus, in *Travelport/Worldspan* the Commission identified a relevant market for electronic travel distribution services through a GDS; in *Google/DoubleClick* it established a market for intermediation in online advertising, and confirmed it in *Microsoft/Yahoo*.[54] Similarly, collaborative platforms should be found to be active in the intermediation market for each respective sector. Therefore, prima facie, *Uber* and *Lyft* would be active in the market of intermediation for transportation, *Airbnb* and *HomeAway* in the market of intermediation for short-term accommodation and so on. Considering the myriad of the business models and the variety of levels of services provided by collaborative platforms, this delineation may not be so simple. For instance, *Couchsurfing* and *Airbnb* provide completely different services, even though they both technically operate on the relevant market of intermediation for short-term accommodation. Similarly, a question arises as to whether collaborative platforms belong in the same relevant market as traditional intermediaries (brokers): do *Airbnb*, *Booking. com* and tourist agencies matching their clients with hotel accommodation belong to the same relevant market? Does *Uber* compete in the same relevant market as traditional taxi operators or dispatch centres? Further, are all services offered by a single collaborative platform to be included in the same relevant product market? Could the least expensive levels of service, such as *UberPOP* or the ride-sharing service of *UberPOOL* be considered as substitutes of luxury transportation

---

[51] See, inter alia, M Schanzenbach, 'Network Effects and Antitrust Law: Predation, Affirmative Defenses, and the Case of U.S. v. Microsoft' (2002) 4 *Stanford Technology Law Review* 3; WJ Kolasky, 'Network Effects: A Contrarian View' (1999) 7 *George Mason Law Review* 577, 578; GL Priest, 'Rethinking Antitrust Law in an Age of Network Industries' (2007) 4 *Yale Law & Economics* Research Paper No 352 at 4; and N Van Gorp and O Batura, 'Challenges for Competition Policy in a Digitalised Economy' (2015) Study for the ECON Committee, 59.
[52] D Auer and N Petit, 'Two-Sided Markets and the Challenge of Turning Economic Theory into Antitrust Policy' (2015) 60 *The Antitrust Bulletin* 426, fn 138.
[53] Lougher and Kalmanowicz (n 7) 93.
[54] *Microsoft/Yahoo! Search Business* (Case COMP/M.5727) [2010] OJ L 24/1.

services offered by *UberLUX*; and how do these compete with *Lyft Premier* and *Lyft Lux*? The answer here largely revolves around demand substitutability.[55] The latter is determined mainly by the consumers' reactions to the products/services' prices, which are revealed through the SSNIP test.

According to this hypothetical test, if a small but significant non-transitory increase in prices (SSNIP) proved unprofitable for the business, the services to which consumers would turn would be included in the relevant market.[56] However, the SSNIP test was intended for traditional one-sided markets, while platforms are two-sided; its applicability here is thus questionable.[57] Firstly, in two-sided markets there are two 'demand-sides' and platforms set two prices (one on each side), thus raising the question which one should be taken into account under the SSNIP test. Even more so, secondly, given the indirect network effects between the two sides, which side's profitability would be taken into consideration under the test? Further, with regard to indirect network effects, the SSNIP test would not

> account for the fact that a reduction of the number of customers on side A is likely to lead to a reduction of the number of customers on side B such that, if the price on side B is kept constant, there would be a loss in profits also on side B.[58]

Thirdly, the SSNIP test is not designed for markets where the provision of services is free, as is the case with certain collaborative platforms (on both or on one side).

---

[55] The Commission identifies three main sources of competitive constraints upon undertakings: demand substitutability; supply substitutability; and potential competition. Supply substitutability may also be significant here. In its Notice on the definition of relevant market, the Commission acknowledges that supply-side substitutability may also be taken into account in situations 'when companies market a wide range of qualities or grades of one product; even if for a given final customer or group of customers, the different qualities are not substitutable, the different qualities will be grouped into one product market provided that most of the suppliers are able to offer and sell the various qualities immediately and without the significant increase in costs …'; see Commission Notice on the definition of relevant market for the purposes of Community competition law [1997] OJ C 372/5, para 21; see also AJ Padilla, 'The Role of Supply-Side Substitution in the Definition of the Relevant Market in Merger Control' (2001) Report for DG Enterprise A/4, European Commission, available at http://ec.europa.eu/DocsRoom/documents/2658/attachments/1/translations/en/renditions/pdf.

[56] The so-called 'Small-but-Significant-Non-Transitory-Increase-in-Price-Test' (SSNIP test) is a fundamental tool for the definition of the relevant market. According to the test, it is examined whether an increase in price (5–10%) would result in a significant number of consumers switching to readily available substitute products. If substitution were enough to make such increase unprofitable for the business, then the substitutes are included in the relevant market.

[57] For the applicability of the SSNIP test in multi- (or two-) sided markets see, inter alia, DS Evans and MD Noel, 'Defining Antitrust Markets When Firms Operate Two-Sided Platforms' (2005) 3 *Columbia Business Law Review* 101, 133; by the same authors, 'The Analysis of Mergers that involve Multisided Platform Businesses' (2008) 4 *Journal of Competition Law & Economics* 663, 667; DS Evans, 'Two-Sided Market Definition' (2009) *Market Definition in Antitrust: Theory and Case Studies, ABA Section of Antitrust Law* 20, available at https://ssrn.com/abstract=1396751; RB Hesse, 'Two-Sided Platform Markets and the Application of the Traditional Antitrust Analytical Framework' (2007) 3(1) *Competition Policy International* 191, 192–93; Colangelo and Zeno-Zencovich, 'Online Platforms, Competition Rules and Consumer Protection in Travel Industry' (2016) 77. The test has been invoked in few cases concerning two-sided transaction markets; see Filistrucchi et al (n 26) 329–38 and the cases referenced and analysed therein.

[58] Filistrucchi et al (n 30) 330–31.

It also fails to take into account non-monetary value, paid by the recipients of the intermediation services in another form, namely in the form of data ('freemium'). Fourthly, the SSNIP test:

> which is designed to assess to what extent products and services are currently substitutes to each other—is unlikely to capture the changes in substitutability brought by technological developments that may occur in the next two to three years (i.e. the time span relevant for the assessment of a merger).[59]

Further, fifthly, even though the 'price' criterion is always significant, collaborative economy participants value the special collaborative services' characteristics and intended use as well.[60] Therefore, apart from the SSNIP test, which is based on price elasticity, other indicia may be useful in the collaborative economy.

In line with this position, in the recent *Microsoft/LinkedIn* merger,[61] the Commission explored and took into account the *intended use* of the social networking services and answered the question whether they could be segmented according to their intended use.[62] Thus, it defined a distinct narrow market for professional social networks based on functionality, use and scope. A similar approach was followed in *Facebook/Whatsapp*, where 'the Commission looked beyond substitutability between consumer communications apps and mobile telecoms services based on their general purpose (communication). The Commission's investigation examined the specific product features and the (added) value communications apps can provide to customers', thus defining a narrow market.[63]

Thus, in the above example of various levels of transportation services: (a) the distinct characteristics of such services; (b) the intended end-use; (c) the price difference; and (d) consumer preferences, all point to the conclusion that (final) consumers, ie riders, would not use those services interchangeably. Similarly, suppliers (ie drivers) would not be able to easily substitute one service with the other, since for instance driving for the luxury version of a platform means that the driver owns a luxurious car of a certain type, year, with certain amenities and so on. Therefore, different levels of collaborative services would probably constitute different relevant markets.

---

[59] European Commission, 'Competition merger brief' (2015) Issue 1—February, fn 15, available at http://ec.europa.eu/competition/publications/cmb/2015/cmb2015_001_en.pdf.

[60] The Commission in its Notice states: 'A relevant product market comprises all those products and/or services which are regarded as interchangeable or substitutable by the consumer, by reason of the products' characteristics, their prices and their intended use'; However, 'product characteristics and intended use are insufficient to show whether two products are demand substitutes'; see Commission Notice on the definition of relevant market for the purposes of Community competition law [1997] paras 7 and 36 respectively. See also C Ortiz, 'Market Definition and the Sharing Economy' *Developing World Antitrust* (19 August 2016), available at https://developingworldantitrust.com/2016/08/19/market-definition-and-the-sharing-economy/#_edn12.

[61] *Microsoft/LinkedIn* (Case COMP/M.8124) [2016] OJ C 388/4.

[62] A question touched upon but ultimately left open in the *Facebook/Whatsapp* merger (Case COMP/M.7217) [2014] OJ C 417, paras 59–60.

[63] European Commission, 'Competition merger brief' (2015) 3.

To make market definition even more complex, collaborative platforms are beginning to expand their services in different market sectors. *Airbnb*, in addition to accommodation, provides intermediation for 'touristic experiences', while *Uber* has been engaging in intermediation for (food, medicines, and even kittens')[64] deliveries along with the rides, and the list goes on. Such services are clearly not interchangeable, but then again the myriad of business models, the variations of services and the multitude of complementary services provided by collaborative platforms would—under current competition law tests—paradoxically lead to a myriad different relevant product markets, with very few—if any—competitors.

In view of this, traditional methods and tools for the definition of the relevant market may be inadequate due to: (a) the two-sided nature of the intermediation market/s; and (b) the disruptive innovation that collaborative economy brings. The SSNIP test should, therefore, at least be revised to account for the undertaking's total profitability after the hypothetical increase in price, taking into account both sides of the market.[65]

ii. *Defining the Market for the Underlying Service*

In defining the relevant market for the underlying service, the main issue is whether the collaborative services can be included in the same relevant markets as traditional services. In the affirmative: (a) mergers between traditional firms and collaborative platforms will be treated as horizontal; and (b) more importantly, incumbents and collaborative suppliers (whether it be merely peers or the platform as well) will be treated as competitors. Though the definition of the relevant product market for the underlying services is largely contingent upon the specific conditions of each respective market sector and requires a case-by-case analysis, in what follows general observations are made with regard to the relationship between incumbents and collaborative players in the accommodation and transportation sectors.

In the accommodation market, according to the demand substitutability test, if *Airbnb* (and any similar platform) is found to exert competitive restraints to hotels, then it will be included in the same relevant market. In applying the test, apart from price elasticity, other characteristics shall also be taken into account with regard to determining the competitive restraints. Thus, '[p]ast substitution, comparisons of the room capacity of hotels versus the growing supply of Airbnb, the impact of Airbnb on hotel's revenues, uniqueness of Airbnb service, consumer's preferences, could all constitute evidence that supports demand substitutability'.[66]

---

[64] *UberKITTENS*; see https://newsroom.uber.com/uberkittens-are-back.
[65] Filistrucchi et al (n 26) 332–33; see also Russo and Stasi, 'Defining the relevant market in the sharing economy' (2016) 7–8.
[66] Ortiz, 'Market Definition and the Sharing Economy' *Developing World Antitrust* (19 August 2016), notes omitted.

Generally speaking, *Airbnb* exerts competitive restraints upon the hotel industry; it 'can affect hotel room revenue through lower occupancy rates, decreased hotel room prices, or a combination of these two factors'.[67] However, two considerations need to be made in including *Airbnb* in the relevant market. Firstly, *Airbnb*—unlike hotels—is characterised by great heterogeneity in the accommodation offered. It does not just list rooms or apartments, but rather it lists anything from tree houses to houseboats, castles and private islands. The Commission in its merger assessments has considered whether short stay residencies should be included in the same relevant market as hotel accommodation services, but has not yet reached a conclusion on the exact relevant product market.[68] At the same time, the Commission has entertained the possibility of further segmentation of the relevant market for hotel accommodation services and with regard to that it has examined criteria such as price rates, services and amenities, access to customer base, access to centralised reservation platforms, loyalty schemes and comfort/price level, on the basis of the star rating system. However, it has left the definition of the exact relevant product market open.[69] Secondly, the customer base of hotels—or certain hotels for that matter—is quite different from that of *Airbnb*: 'business travellers whose hotel expenses will be reimbursed and vacationers who frequent high-end hotels are two examples of consumers we view as much less likely to substitute a hotel stay with an Airbnb stay'.[70] Therefore, the demand substitutability test could lead to different results for different price/level hotel categories; while *Airbnb* can be a substitute for middle-priced and budget-friendly hotels, it is questionable if this will also be the case in relation to upper scale hotels. However, thirdly, in view of *Airbnb*'s dynamic model and the adaptability of the supply on the platform, demand substitutability may alter in a matter of months. Indeed, 'seeing a growth opportunity in the business travel segment, Airbnb recently launched an initiative to attract more business travelers'.[71] Within a year, 'the number of people using the site for business purposes tripled and is expected to quadruple this year'.[72] Same goes for luxury accommodation. *Airbnb* has been investing in high-end vacation rentals through the acquisition of *Luxury Retreats*,[73] and has been piloting a

---

[67] G Zervas, D Proserpio and J Byers, 'The rise of the sharing economy: Estimating the impact of Airbnb on the hotel industry' (2016) Boston University School of Management, Research Paper No 2013-16, 10. The research shows (at 3) that 'in areas [of Texas] where Airbnb is most popular the revenue of the most vulnerable hotels in our data has decreased by about 8–10% over the past five years'.

[68] See *Marriott International/Starwood Hotels & Resorts Worldwide* (Case COMP/M.7902) [2016] OJ C 192/4, paras 64–69; *Accor/Pierre et vacances/Newcity* (Case COMP/M.4612) [2007] OJ C 193, Recital 15 ff; *Ascott Group/Goldman Sachs/Oriville* (Case COMP/M.3068) [2003] OJ C 52, Recital 13 ff.

[69] As above.

[70] Zervas, Proserpio and Byers, 'The rise of the sharing economy: Estimating the impact of Airbnb on the hotel industry' (2016) 22.

[71] ibid 24, note omitted. *Airbnb* has incorporated a feature marking certain apartments as 'Business Travel Ready', if they have relevant amenities.

[72] O Zaleski, 'Airbnb Goes After Business Travelers With New Booking Tool' *Bloomberg Technology* (28 April 2017).

[73] D Ting, 'Airbnb Acquires Vacation Rental Company Luxury Retreats, Officially Moves Into Luxury' *Skift* (16 February 2017).

'premium' programme in order to attract higher-paying visitors, whereby it inspects homes that can be offered through this programme and encourages their hosts to act as 'hoteliers'; [74] meanwhile Marriott during the *Marriott/Starwood* merger assessment, submitted to the Commission that a portion of its customer base is turning to non-traditional lodging providers such as *Airbnb*.[75]

In the transportation market, collaborative platforms facilitating transportation services have faced accusations of posing unfair competition to transportation incumbents. Here again, substitutability does not always accurately reflect the relevant market in which collaborative platforms compete.

> A ridesharing app's closest competitor in this context may be a bus, train, or airplane—none of which looks or operates anything like a ridesharing app. In fact, in France, the national state-owned railroad provider, SNCF, sees the online long-distance carpooling platform Blablacar as its main competitor.[76]

Uber has been considered to pose unfair competition to traditional taxis and has been (entirely or partly) banned in a number of cities.[77] The innovation brought by the collaborative platforms sometimes makes it difficult to include the services in an existing relevant market; *Uber*'s services seem to fall between the licensed taxis services and private hire vehicles (PHVs), since *Uber* rides are being 'hailed' on the basis of proximity but are also pre-booked.[78] In the *Uber* NY court case (*Meyer v Kalanick*) it was argued that neither licensed taxis nor traditional cars for hire could be considered as reasonable substitutes, because of the differences of the *Uber* model from those (the ride can be tracked on the mobile, no need to carry cash or credit card, availability of driver's ratings, etc);[79] the alleged market in which *Uber* competes is the 'new mobile app-generated ride-share service market', of which *Uber* has an approximately 80 per cent market share.[80] However, in practice *Uber* competes with both taxis[81] and PHVs, from which it has drawn market share and customers.[82] 'In any case, even if Uber drivers were not considered to actually compete on the licensed taxi market in all jurisdictions, they must

---

[74] O Zaleski, 'Airbnb Readies a Premium Tier to Compete More With Hotels, Sources Say' *Bloomberg* (22 June 2017).

[75] *Marriott/Starwood* (Case COMP/M.7902), para 201.

[76] D O'Connor, 'Understanding Online Platform Competition: Common Misunderstandings' in A Ortiz (ed), *Internet: Competition and Regulation of Online Platforms*, e-book (Competition Policy International, 2016) 12, available at www.competitionpolicyinternational.com/wp-content/uploads/2016/05/INTERNET-COMPETITION-LIBRO.pdf.

[77] See Ch 7 below.

[78] For more on this see Lougher and Kalmanowicz (n 7) 94.

[79] *Meyer v Kalanick* Case No 1:15-cv-09796 US District Court for the Southern District of New York.

[80] In the US, *Uber*'s chief competitor in this market, *Lyft*, has only a 20% market share, and a third competitor, *Sidecar*, left the market at the end of 2015.

[81] It has been indicated that between January 2012 and August 2014, the use of taxis in San Francisco declined 65%. See Geradin, 'Should Uber be Allowed to Compete in Europe? And if so How?' (2015) 6.

[82] In the UK, *Uber* is treated as a private hire operator and *Uber* drivers are required to have a private hire licence; see www.uber.com/en-GB/drive/london/get-a-license/london-ignition.

be regarded as posing at least significant competitive constraints on licensed taxi services'.[83]

Allegations of 'unfair competition' have been raised not only by private drivers and their associations, but also by public transportation operators. The French ride-sharing company, *BlaBlaCar*, was accused by the Spanish confederation of bus transportation (*Confebus*) of unfair competition on the grounds that (inter alia) *BlaBlaCar* behaved as a public transporter without any relevant authorisation and that its drivers benefited from illegal profits. In its judgment, Madrid's commercial court ruled in favour of the platform by clarifying that it is not active in the transportation market, but rather in the intermediation market, and that its drivers' activity is restricted exclusively in the sector of private transportation, since the platform 'does not attempt to organise commercial transportation but to connect private individuals who wish to travel together and share the costs', and does not compete with buses.[84] Rather, the Court comes to the impressive conclusion that 'the platform BlaBlaCar not only is not infringing the public interest, but rather that such interest benefits from development of these new technologies that allow proliferation of new, more competitive markets'.[85] Therefore, 'setting limits for collaborative economy platforms is not only contrary to the public interest and would be unjustified, but would also be discriminatory'.[86]

Indirectly, the above finding also bears with it the question of the role of regulation as an element determining the boundaries of the relevant market. In other words, should the mere fact that *BlaBlaCar* and *Uber* are not subject to the same regulatory requirements as traditional cab drivers be enough to distinguish the corresponding product markets? To the extent that the services' characteristics need to be taken into account in order to determine the relevant product market, and given that these characteristics are, to a large extent, shaped by regulation, an affirmative answer could be given; at least in the cases where such characteristics are perceived as being important by consumers. This, however, would mean that regulators would have a free hand in artificially defining relevant product markets through regulation, an assumption which most competition lawyers would find counterintuitive. Prior experience in the field of network-bound industries (telecoms, gas etc), where incumbents had to face new entrants unconstrained by past regulation and (labour law etc) commitments, is of little help here, since

---

[83] Lougher and Kalmanowicz (n 7) 95, note omitted.

[84] Sentencia caso *Blablacar*, No 30/2017 del Juzgado Mercantil No 2 de Madrid, available in Spanish at www.lenguajejuridico.com/sentencia-del-juzgado-madrid-caso-blablacar; quote taken from F Jenny, 'Enforcement issues in rapidly changing/high tech markets (Presentation Slides)' (2017) Melbourne University Law School Seminar, slide 63, available at https://ssrn.com/abstract=2951135; see also R Guirado, 'What has a Spanish Court said about BlaBlaCar?' *Legal Sharing* (4 February 2017), available at www.legalsharing.eu/single-post/2017/02/04/BlaBlaCar-Judgement.

[85] R Guirado, 'What has a Spanish Court said about BlaBlaCar?' (2017).

[86] ibid.

liberalisation there was organised through formal re-regulation setting the rules of a (tentative) level playing field for all participants. In the collaborative context, absent such sector-specific regulation, it would be somehow far-fetched to say that the existing regulatory differences, on their own, define different product markets. In any event, the difference of regulatory burdens imposed on incumbents and on new entrants could be taken into account under the state aid rules.[87]

iii. Defining the Geographic Market

Defining the geographic market is also complex. While most collaborative platforms, like traditional electronic platforms, are present and active globally via the internet, the provision of the underlying services often entails an element of location and requires physical proximity of supplier and consumer.

The Commission Notice's test for geographic market is based on the question '[w]hether the customers of the parties would switch their orders to companies located elsewhere in the short term and at a negligible cost'.[88]

The specific business model of each platform is highly relevant for the definition of the relevant geographic market; while for example on *Fiverr*, the provision of the underlying services (translations, freelance writing etc) operates globally without any restriction of locality or need for physical presence at a certain place, in *Uber* or *Lyft* the proximity of the suppliers (drivers) to consumers (riders) is significant.[89] In the merger examination between *Just Eat* and *La Nevera Roja*, the Spanish National Authority for Markets and Competition found that the intermediaries offer their services of intermediation and management of online food delivery nationally, since they (each) provide their services through a single IT platform across Spain and their advertising campaigns and commercial policies towards restaurants are national.[90]

Unlike the provision of the underlying service, the relevant geographic market for the intermediation, as it is performed digitally, does not necessarily depend on the platform's location. Criteria such as language or country specificities, content differentiation and cross-border provision of the intermediation services through technological means may be taken into consideration. In the *Google/DoubleClick* case, the geographic market for intermediation in online advertising was defined as at least the European Economic Area (EEA).[91] The same geographic market was found in *Microsoft/LinkedIn*,[92] and in the recent *Google Search (Shopping)* case, for

---

[87] For which see section III below.
[88] Commission Notice on the definition of relevant market (n 55) para 29.
[89] The same distinction is further discussed in Ch 5 below, where a distinction between Online Labour Markets (OLMs) offered globally and Mobile Labour Markets (MLMs) offered locally is made for labour law purposes.
[90] CNMC, *Just Eat/La Nevera Roja* Case No C/0730/16, para 38.
[91] *Google/DoubleClick* (Case COMP/M.4731).
[92] *Microsoft/LinkedIn* (Case COMP/M.8124).

internet search engines.[93] In its decision in the *Microsoft* case,[94] the Commission found that the relevant geographic market for client PC operating systems (OSs) was worldwide. Similarly, in *Google/Motorola Mobility* and *Microsoft/Nokia*, which concerned mobile OS, the Commission found that the relevant geographic market was at least EEA-wide, or even worldwide, in scope, but ultimately left the question open.[95]

iv. Concluding Remarks

Traditional definitions of the relevant market revolve largely around price. However, the collaborative economy is based on quality, trust and innovation and occasionally on the free provision of services. While the collaborative economy generally exerts competitive restraints on traditional businesses to the point that it is being characterised as a 'disruptive innovation', the inclusion of such innovative services in traditional relevant markets does not always fit organically, but rather seems artificially propelled. A stiff application of classic tests, such as the SSNIP, may lead to manipulation of the markets' realities in favour of dogmatism and convenience. Nonetheless, so far 'the Commission implicitly chooses to focus on preserving innovation in existing markets rather than encouraging disruptive innovation in new markets'.[96] This is ascertained from the Commission's practice of defining narrow markets on the basis of the features available to consumers, as seen for example in the *Microsoft/Skype* and the *Facebook/Whatsapp* mergers. However, '[i]f the relevant market is defined around the specific functionality offered, potential competitive constraints from related or future services are not taken into account',[97] thus 'ignoring' the inherent innovative element. In view of the above, it might be time for an altogether new approach in relevant market definition. A shift towards a more modern, innovative and holistic approach in market definition has shyly emerged in the more recent assessments of mergers in the digital environment, thus raising expectations for things to come.

C. Market Power

Even though the collaborative economy is fairly new in the EU, some platforms have already gained market power (or at least market dynamic) that has caused

---

[93] The Commission found that *Google* is dominant in general internet search markets throughout the European Economic Area (EEA), ie in all 31 EEA countries; see *Google Search (Shopping)* (Case COMP/AT.39740), Press Release IP/17/1784 of 27 June 2017.

[94] *Microsoft* (COMP/C-3/37.792) [2004] OJ L 32/23.

[95] *Google/Motorola Mobility* (Case COMP/M.6381) [2012] OJ C 75, paras 33–35; *Microsoft/Nokia*, (Case COMP/M.7047) [2014] OJ C 44, paras 74–77.

[96] Graef (n 44) 5, with reference to C Ahlborn, DS Evans and AJ Padilla, 'Competition policy in the new economy: is European competition law up to the challenge?' (2001) 22(5) *European Competition Law* 156, 161–62.

[97] ibid.

speculations of dominance, especially if the relevant market is defined narrowly. While market power itself is not condemned nor prohibited under EU competition law, it has implications both for Article 101 TFEU and 102 TFEU assessments, as well as for merger controls.

Dominance has been defined by the Court as a:

> position of economic strength enjoyed by an undertaking, which enables it to prevent effective competition being maintained on a relevant market, by affording it the power to behave to an appreciable extent independently of its competitors, its customers and ultimately of consumers.[98]

While market power and dominance are determined largely by market shares in the traditional economy,[99] for collaborative businesses market power does not necessarily coincide with market share. While in traditional markets, businesses compete mainly on price, in the collaborative economy platforms compete on innovation as well, a factor not measured by market shares.[100] Both the Commission and the General Court have recently acknowledged that market shares are not necessarily indicative of market power in dynamic, innovative contexts.[101] The General Court in *Cisco*, confirming the Commission's approach in the *Microsoft/Skype* merger decision,[102] acknowledged that 'the consumer communications sector is a recent and fast-growing sector which is characterised by short innovation cycles in which large market shares may turn out to be ephemeral. In such a dynamic context, high market shares are not necessarily indicative of market power and, therefore, of lasting damage to competition'.[103] Similarly, the German Monopolies Commission (*Monopolkommission*) acknowledged with regard to digital markets that '… it would be premature to associate [a] high user share with corresponding market power'.[104]

Thus, in the evaluation of market power in the collaborative economy, elements other than market shares need to be taken into account. Some of them reinforce market power (see section i below), while others act as limitations thereto (see section ii below).

---

[98] See Case 27/76 *United Brands Company and United Brands Continentaal BV v Commission* EU:C:1978:22, para 65, and Case 85/76 *Hoffmann-La Roche & Co AG v Commission* EU:C:1979:36, para 38.

[99] For a discussion on market share thresholds see L Kaplow, 'Market Share Thresholds: On the Conflation of Empirical Assessments and Legal Policy Judgments' (2011) 7 *Journal of Competition Law & Economics* 243.

[100] Graef (n 44) 2–3.

[101] This was the case in the Commission's *Microsoft/Skype* merger evaluation; confirmed by the General Court in Case T-79/12 *Cisco Systems Inc and Messagenet SpA v Commission* EU:T:2013:635.

[102] *Microsoft/Skype* (Case COMP/M.6281) [2011] OJ C 341.

[103] Case T-79/12 *Cisco*, para 69.

[104] German Monopolies Commission, 'Competition policy: the challenge of digital markets' (2015) Special Report 68, para S27, available at www.monopolkommission.de/index.php/en/home/84-pressemitteilungen/285-competition-policy-the-challenge-of-digital-markets.

i. Reinforcing Market Power

a. Network Effects

Network effects often lead to a 'winner-takes-all' dynamic, which allows the first, most active, most efficient player to attract the biggest number of participants, in both markets, thus marginalising all other players. This in turn attracts even more participants, thus reflecting the 'positive feedback loop'. Therefore, once the platform has accumulated a significant mass of users, it reaches a 'tipping point', becomes incumbent and shows a tendency towards 'superstar economics' and dominance. Potential lack of interoperability can further reinforce the impact of network effects.

b. Possession of Big Data

Big data at the disposal of the 'established' platform can exert an important lock-in effect, especially in view of potential lack of interoperability.[105] The role of vast amount of data in the establishment of market power has been addressed by US and EU competition authorities in the context of merger control.[106] So far they have found the potential advantages from aggregation of data not to pose any risk for competition, but rather to help platforms provide better services.[107] Indeed, the Commission has been very demanding in order to find that possession of big data constitutes a competitive advantage. In *Facebook/Whatsapp*, in line with its previous practice in *Google/DoubleClick*, *Telefónica/Vodafone/Everything Everywhere* and *Publicis/Omnicom*,[108] the Commission found that data would not provide a unique, non-replicable advantage, in view of the fact that competitors could still obtain large amounts of data through data brokers or data analytics service providers or by collecting and analysing them themselves. Further, it has found that the scope of data is limited, as the 'benefits from additional data scale tend to increase at a decreasing rate'.[109] The Commission has been similarly reticent in finding potential infringements of competition law by data paid as exchange for free access to a platform's services ('freemium'). Even though it recognises that possession of big data can indeed amount to competition law infringement, it has not found any (infringement) in any of the related merger cases it has reviewed.

However, the data accumulated by collaborative platforms are of different nature and type than those already examined. For instance, in the *Facebook/Whatsapp* merger, the Commission concluded that 'communication via apps

---

[105] For further reading on the interaction of big data with competition see M Stucke and A Grunes, *Big Data and Competition Policy* (Oxford, Oxford University Press, 2016).

[106] ibid ch 6 for an overview on '[t]he US's and EU's Mixed Record in Assessing Data-Driven Mergers'.

[107] For eg see *Google/DoubleClick* (Case COMP/M.4731), para 360; and *Facebook/Whatsapp* (Case COMP/M.7217), para 180.

[108] *Telefónica UK/Vodafone UK/Everything Everywhere/JV* (Case COMP/M.6314) [2013] OJ C 66; *Publicis/Omnicom* (Case COMP/M.7023) [2014] OJ C 84.

[109] European Commission, Competition merger brief (n 59) 6.

[...] do not necessarily carry long-term value for consumers'.[110] On the contrary, the data accumulated by collaborative platforms, which include the users' reviews, preferences, commercial and otherwise behaviour and so on, do create lasting effects, as: (a) they reflect an 'investment' of some sort in the platform; and (b) they incentivise users to remain with the same platform. Therefore, big data gathered create a competitive advantage over new collaborative platforms. Given the significance of data, these may create barriers to entry, when new entrants are unable to collect or obtain access to the same kind of data as established platforms.[111] The joint report of the French and German Competition Authorities on 'Competition Law and Data' highlights two important factors with regard to data contributing to market power: 'the scarcity of data (or ease of replicability) and whether the scale/scope of data collection matters to competitive performance'.[112] With regard to the former, even though data are 'non-rivalrous' as such, access to those data may be prohibitively costly, since new entrants would have to invest significantly, and even so, factors such as network effects, switching costs and scale economies may impede them from creating the large customer base needed to gain the same data as incumbents.[113] Further, even though nowadays it appears that 'data is everywhere', and the costs of collecting data has decreased due to technological progress, the various types of data are not always substitutable. With regard to the latter, ie scale and scope of data collection, the potential advantage from data depends 'on the volume levels: (i) at which a firm can reap the economic benefits of data; (ii) beyond which these benefits decline or cease to exist altogether'.[114]

It remains to be seen whether the disruptive nature of the collaborative economy will tilt the Commission's and Court's approach, so far, according to which 'any possible issues relating to the sensitivity of personal data are not, as such, a matter for competition law, they may be resolved on the basis of the relevant provisions governing data protection'.[115]

---

[110] European Commission Decision, Case M.7217—Facebook/ WhatsApp. Brussels, 03.10.2014 C(2014), 7239 final, para 113.

[111] For the opposing view see O'Connor, 'Understanding Online Platform Competition: Common Misunderstandings' (2016) 25–26, where he argues that data: (a) 'is just one of many inputs that dictate success for online businesses', (b) 'is non-rivalrous and non-exclusive', (c) 'quickly becomes stale', and (d) 'has diminishing returns to scale'.

[112] Autorité de la Concurrence and Bundeskartellamt, 'Competition Law and Data' (2016) 35, available at www.autoritedelaconcurrence.fr/doc/reportcompetitionlawanddatafinal.pdf.

[113] The development of data brokers could increase availability of data, but still these would not amount to the incumbents' data quality and quantity; see Autorité de la Concurrence and Bundeskartellamt, 'Competition Law and Data' (2016) 38–42.

[114] ibid 54.

[115] See Case C-238/05 *Asnef-Equifax v Asociación de Usuarios de Servicios Bancarios (Ausbanc)* EU:C:2006:734. See also European Commission, Competition merger brief (n 59) 6–7. However, in May 2017, the Commission decided to fine *Facebook* €110 million for providing incorrect and misleading information during the *Facebook/Whatsapp* merger procedure, according to which *Facebook* 'would be unable to establish reliable automated matching between Facebook users' accounts and WhatsApp

c. High Switching Costs

As a result of the above (network effects and possession of big data), the switching costs in the collaborative economy are relatively high. Suppliers have invested time and effort, have gained reputation and reviews,[116] have potentially undergone training and learning costs, and may even have built a 'client base' who work with them regularly. Similarly high are the costs for (end) consumers, who have entered their data onto the platform, such as their frequent routes on *Uber* or dietary preferences on *Eatro* etc, receive personalised offers, have built their reputation through reviews and have become familiar with the system. '[D]ata collection may increase switching costs as the provider most used by an individual has more information on him or her and is able to tailor his service offerings to that particular individual'.[117] Further, the lower the cost of the service offered, the more unlikely it will be for consumers to switch from the search habits, history, cookies etc which link them to their preferred site to one which offers (insignificantly) lower prices thus making switching or multi-homing unattractive. High switching costs may lead to 'lock-in' of users and establishment of dominance.

All the above can create entry barriers and establish dominance of those incumbent collaborative platforms. Additional factors such as the community of reference, reputation and trust,[118] 'reliability of the service, functionalities offered, size of the underlying network, trendiness, etc' play a fundamental role.[119] Thus, in the *Uber* NY case (*Meyer v Kalanick*), the Court found that 'Uber's market position has already helped force Sidecar out of the marketplace', while 'Uber's dominant position and considerable name recognition has also made it difficult for potential competitors to enter the marketplace'.[120]

ii. Constraining Market Power

a. Temporal Market

The 'temporal market' also needs to be considered. In view of the innovative and 'disruptive' character of the collaborative economy, such a 'superstar' lead may

---

users' accounts', a practice effectively followed post-merger. Such fine, imposed after the clearance of the merger, could indicate a shift of the Commission towards a more 'data-sensitive' philosophy. See Commission's Press Release of 18 May 2017, 'Mergers: Commission fines Facebook €110 million for providing misleading information about WhatsApp takeover', IP/17/1369.

[116] See US Federal Trade Commission (FTC) Staff Report, 'The "Sharing" Economy: Issues Facing Platforms, Participants and Regulators' (2016) 46–47 available at www.ftc.gov/reports/sharing-economy-issues-facing-platforms-participants-regulators-federal-trade-commission; the FTC Staff Report also provides an interesting overview of reputation systems at 35–47.

[117] Autorité de la Concurrence and Bundeskartellamt, 'Competition Law and Data' (n 112) 28.

[118] Russo and Stasi (n 22) 5.

[119] Factors considered in *Whatsapp/Facebook*. See European Commission, Competition merger brief (n 59) 6.

[120] *Meyer v Kalanick*, Case No 1:15-cv-09796 New York Southern Court, Opinion and Order of Judge Rakoff (31 March 2016) 21–22.

be extremely short-lived. In the fast-paced digital economy, market dynamics have shown that '[n]ew rivals can emerge from unexpected places'[121] and displace established companies.[122] This was acknowledged in the *Microsoft/Skype* merger, where the Commission and the General Court found that even though *Microsoft* would have high market share after the merger, the dynamic character of the sector and the existence of sufficient competitors to which consumers could easily switch eliminated the competitive concerns.[123] In the same way, in *Facebook/Whatsapp*, the dynamic and fast-moving market acted as a mitigating effect on the negative impact of network effects on competition.[124]

b. Multi-homing

Multi-homing, ie the ability to switch between different platforms and use those at the same time, mitigates market power.[125] The

> actual scope of multi-homing can reveal further information on the mode of competition and the relevance of indirect network effects. In particular, multi-homing on one side A of a platform reduces the relevance of network effects emanating from this side A towards other sides: if the same users from side A are present on all platforms, the number of these users does not affect the decision between platforms of users from other sides.[126]

For example, if the same drivers are available both through *Uber* and *Lyft*, consumers can use both and alternate indiscriminately between the two platforms. Therefore, it has been suggested that the number of 'multi-homed' users of a platform should not count at all in its market share, as any minor deterioration of the service would send them off to the competitors.[127] From this perspective, multi-homing appears as a major instrument for preventing a dominant position from ever coming to existence. Thus, (exclusivity or other) agreements with the suppliers which restrict multi-homing are to be viewed with great suspicion; the same is true for other CRR vertical agreements,[128] whereby suppliers are bound to offer the same prices in all other platforms, thus rendering multi-homing pointless.

---

[121] O'Connor (n 76) 17.

[122] For eg *Google* and *Facebook* displaced *Yahoo* and *MySpace* respectively, within a matter of a few years, even though until then, the latter were dominating the respective markets.

[123] *Microsoft/Skype* (Case COMP/M.6281) paras 120–32 and Case T-79/12, *Cisco*, paras 68–95.

[124] See European Commission, Competition merger brief (n 59) 5.

[125] See *Facebook/Whatsapp* (Case COMP/M.7217).

[126] S Wismer, C Bongard and A Rasek, 'Multi-Sided Market Economics in Competition Law Enforcement' (2017) 8(4) *Journal of European Competition Law & Practice* 257, 262.

[127] See eg M Colangelo, 'Parity Clauses and Competition Law in Digital Marketplaces: The Case of Online Hotel Booking' (2017) 8(1) *Journal of European Competition Law & Practice* 3, 12; and before that, M Armstrong, 'Competition in Two-Sided Markets' (2006) 37 *The RAND Journal of Economics* 668, 688.

[128] For which see section II.E.ii below.

Similarly, the locking-in of consumers should be avoided; platform interoperability, data portability and reputation transfer from one platform to the other are ways of enhancing multi-homing, thus preventing the creation of a dominant position.

In view of the novelty of many of the factors mentioned above and the uncertainties surrounding their actual application, it is submitted that a strong indication of a platform's dominance would be its reluctance to innovate. Amidst the existing vivid competition and the fast-paced digital environment, platforms must constantly innovate, provide new and/or improved services, employ various marketing strategies and react to consumers' demand fast and effectively. Given that a multitude of products and services are offered for free, platforms must compete on quality and innovation in order to survive. Therefore, if a platform stops innovating, competition authorities should be alarmed.[129]

D. Practices Coming under Article 101 TFEU

The three-party relationships in the collaborative economy, while corresponding to a new business model, are not entirely unknown to competition law. Restrictions to inter-platform collusion (see section i below) and intra-platform collusion (see section ii below) are discussed.

i. *Inter-platform Competition: Collusion between Collaborative Platforms*

What makes collusion between collaborative platforms 'innovative' in relation to traditional practices violating Article 101 TFEU are algorithms. The use of algorithms and the way that use may impact competition law has been an issue of intense research and debate in recent years.[130] The fact that collaborative platforms

---

[129] For the interrelation of innovation and competition see D Vitkovic, 'The Sharing Economy: Regulation and the EU Competition Law' (2016) 9 *Global Antitrust Review* 78, 109 ff, available at https://ssrn.com/abstract=2926852; see also P Ibáñez Colomo, 'Restrictions on Innovation in EU Competition Law' (2016) 41 *European Law Review* 201; and (2015) LSE Law, Society and Economy Working Papers No 22, available at www.lse.ac.uk/collections/law/wps/WPS2015-22_Colomo.pdf. As P Ibáñez Colomo puts it: 'reduced competitive pressure can be expected to reduce firms' incentives to invest in the development of new products' 8.

[130] See, among many, M Stucke and A Ezrachi, 'Artificial intelligence and collusion: When computers inhibit competition' (forthcoming) University of Illinois Law Review; and (2015) University of Tennessee Legal Studies, Research Paper No 267, available at http://ssrn.com/abstract=2591874; A Ezrachi and M Stucke, *Virtual Competition: The Promise and Perils of the Algorithm-Driven Economy* (Cambridge MA, Harvard University Press, 2016); and more recently by the same authors, 'Algorithmic Collusion: Problems and Counter-Measures' (2017) OECD, Roundtable on Algorithms and Collusion; SK Mehra, 'Anti-trust and the Robo-Seller: Competition in the time of algorithms' (2017) 100 *Minnesota Law Review* 1323; and (2015) Temple University Legal Studies, Research Paper No 15, available at https://ssrn.com/abstract=2576341; JE Gata, 'The sharing economy, competition and regulation' (2015) Competition Policy International, available at www.competitionpolicyinternational.com/assets/Europe-Column-November-Full.pdf; PL Parcu and ML Stasi, 'The role of intent in the assessment of conduct under Article 102 TFEU' in PL Parcu, G Monti and M Botta (eds), *Abuse of Dominance in EU Competition Law: Emerging Trends* (Cheltenham, Edward Elgar, 2017).

rely on algorithms not only in order to define their prices, but, more fundamentally, in order to perform their basic functions, makes the collaborative economy the perfect showcase of all the emerging issues. Price fixing remains, however, the most salient one. Stucke and Ezrachi have found four (non-exclusive) categories of possible collusion facilitated by algorithms:[131] (a) the 'Messenger', whereby humans agree on the collusion and employ computers/algorithms to implement and monitor the cartel; (b) 'Hub and Spoke';[132] (c) 'Predictable Agent'; and (d) 'Autonomous Machine'.[133] Given that platforms may reach comparable prices as a result of processing comparable data with similar algorithms, horizontal collusion may be very difficult to establish under traditional competition law: collusive 'intent' would be altogether absent, as would any explicit 'agreement'.[134] Some authors, therefore, propose that the fundamental role played by big data and its use by 'robo-sellers' in determining market prices, should lead the enforcement authorities to revisit the above two concepts in order to apprehend indirect intent enshrined in the coding of algorithms and 'agreements' which are reached without the parties ever colluding.[135] In the US such developments have, discretely, emerged.[136]

More specifically, the literature has identified that the sophisticated algorithms employed by collaborative platforms could either constantly monitor competitors' prices and automatically adjust to them, or, worse, function as 'predictable agents' designed to predict and react to changing market conditions in a predetermined way. For instance, they can predict the competitors' changes in pricing and adjust respectively, especially if the algorithms are similarly built and the products/services are relatively homogeneous. Ezrachi and Stucke observe that 'the nature of electronic markets, the availability of data, the development of similar algorithms, and the stability and transparency they foster, will likely push some markets that were just outside the realm of tacit collusion into interdependence'.[137] While the market may be influenced by this interdependent action of competing platforms, this action could only be classified as conscious parallelism/tacit

---

[131] See Stucke and Ezrachi, 'Artificial intelligence and collusion: When computers inhibit competition' (2015).

[132] For which see section II.D.ii.a.

[133] For (c) and (d) see immediately below.

[134] It should be noted that both under the Sherman Act and under EU law, oligopolists that achieve price coordination interdependently, without communication or facilitating practices, may escape enforcement, even when their actions yield supra-competitive pricing that harms consumers.

[135] See Mehra, 'Anti-trust and the Robo-Seller: Competition in the time of algorithms' (2015); see also Stucke and Ezrachi, 'Artificial intelligence and collusion: When computers inhibit competition' (2015).

[136] The US Department of Justice, in a case involving *Amazon* and price-fixing in the area of posters, found that the conspirators 'adopted specific pricing algorithms for the sale of certain posters with the goal of coordinating changes to their respective prices and wrote computer code that instructed algorithm-based software to set prices in conformity with this agreement'; see www.justice.gov/atr/public/press_releases/2015/313011.docx; for a discussion of this and other cases, see Stucke and Ezrachi, 'Artificial intelligence' (n 130).

[137] Ezrachi and Stucke, 'Algorithmic Collusion: Problems and Counter-Measures' (2017).

collusion—considering there is no agreement—and therefore be legal.[138] The case would be different if the platforms consciously decided in advance to develop similar algorithms with the objective of influencing the market. 'Condemned actions may include signalling, exchange of information, agreement to engage in common strategy, manipulation through the sharing of data pools and other collusive strategies'.[139]

Further, algorithms used by collaborative platforms often have the self-learning abilities of 'autonomous machines'.[140] Machines can determine themselves the means to achieve the inserted target, for instance, profit optimisation. They do so through self-learning and experimentation. Since this scenario involves minimal human intervention it would be extremely difficult for competition authorities to find any anticompetitive practice by applying the existing rules.

In view of the above, commentators suggest even broader adaptations to legal reasoning by, for instance, 'reconsidering the relationship [and respective responsibility] between humans and machines' and looking into 'the relevant algorithm to establish whether any illegal action could have been anticipated or was predetermined'.[141] Indeed, EU Commissioner for competition, Margrethe Vestager, has recognised that 'there are many ways that collusion can happen, and some of them are well within the capacity of automated systems' and has made clear that 'pricing algorithms need to be built in a way that does not allow them to collude'. Further, she warned industry 'that companies can't escape responsibility for collusion by hiding behind a computer programme'.[142] Hence, developments are forthcoming in this area, especially so after the Commission decision imposing a record fine on *Google* for an abusive practice perpetrated through its search algorithm.[143]

ii. Intra-platform Competition

Collaborative platforms typically run electronic applications and offer intermediation, while the underlying services are offered by the suppliers, owning the cars, houses, skills, and so on, necessary for such services. Therefore, platforms and suppliers operate, in principle, in different markets, and any agreement between them is a vertical one. Moreover, it is by virtue of such vertical agreements that

---

[138] ibid 16 ff.

[139] See Stucke and Ezrachi, 'Algorithmic Collusion: Problems and Counter-Measures' (n 130) para 74.

[140] Stucke and Ezrachi, 'Artificial intelligence' (n 130) 22 ff.

[141] ibid 31.

[142] Commissioner M Vestager, Speech delivered on 16 March 2017 as reported by M Levitt et al, 'EU Antitrust enforcement 2.0—European Commission raises concerns about algorithms and encourages individual whistleblowers' in *Kluwer Competition Law Blog* (21 March 2017), available at http://kluwercompetitionlawblog.com/2017/03/21/eu-antitrust-enforcement-2-0-european-commission-raises-concerns-about-algorithms-and-encourages-individual-whistleblowers/; see also S Lawrance and M Hunt, 'Will pricing algorithms be the European Commission's next antitrust target?' *Bristows CLIP Board* (21 March 2017), available at www.bristowsclipboard.com/post/will-pricing-algorithms-be-the-european-commission-s-next-antitrust-target.

[143] *Google Search (Shopping)* (n 37).

the collaborative economy, with all its benefits for consumers, employment etc, has been able to emerge and flourish. It is essential to keep this in mind when evaluating, under Article 101(1), then 101(3) TFEU, any agreement between the platforms and their suppliers.

The literature and case law have identified the possibility of anticompetitive behaviour in the collaborative economy in the form of horizontal co-operation of service suppliers with the facilitation of the collaborative platform with which they are connected vertically.

The above two observations, ie that restrictions to competition are feasible at the intra-platform level, but that they may be necessary or else overall beneficial, raise at least four questions, which are briefly discussed in what follows: (a) to what extent are (horizontal) agreements between peers relevant for competition law?; (b) to what extent does the central role occupied by platforms affect the 'verticality' of the relations easily ascertained in the previous paragraph?; (c) how are established competition tools for the analysis of vertical agreements to be used in the collaborative economy; (d) and what is the role of Article 101(3) TFEU in the collaborative economy?

a. Collusion between Service Suppliers: Horizontal Verticality?

The exploration of a possible collusion among the individual service providers is contingent upon their qualifying as separate undertakings in the first place.[144] Even if two separate undertakings are found to exist, it may be generally difficult to apply (traditional) competition law to individual service providers, since it would be difficult to establish collusion: (a) they do not enter into horizontal contracts with any competitor, but into a vertical one with a (and occasionally several) platform/s; and (b) their agreement with the platform is individual and not directly or explicitly connected with those of the other providers. However, there are some indications that could prove otherwise.

Individual service providers may have indeed entered in a *horizontal agreement*, either by clearly intending to collude or by accepting the probability of collusion. While the case is still pending,[145] the NY District Court during the preliminary proceedings found that the probability of a horizontal agreement between drivers was evidenced by their signing up for *Uber* 'precisely "on the understanding that the other [drivers] were agreeing to the same" pricing algorithm', especially considering that their agreements with *Uber* 'would "be against their own interests

---

[144] See section II.A above.
[145] In the ongoing case *Uber* NY (*Meyer v Kalanick*), *Uber* has moved to compel arbitration instead of undergoing a jury trial, according to the company's Terms and Conditions accepted by the plaintiff. See A Denney, 'Appeals Court Set to Eye Uber's Drive to Steer Price-Fixing Dispute to Arbitration' *New York Law Journal* (22 March 2017), available at www.newyorklawjournal.com/id=1202781782290/Appeals-Court-Set-to-Eye-Ubers-Drive-to-Steer-PriceFixing-Dispute-to-Arbitration. This matter is discussed further in Ch 6 on dispute resolution.

were they acting independently".[146] The ability to benefit from reduced price competition plausibly constitutes 'a common motive to conspire'. Moreover, it has been argued that the conclusion of a horizontal agreement among *Uber* drivers may be evidenced by the organisation of events and meetings for *Uber* drivers in several cities, where they meet up in person.[147] This is plausible especially considering that in *T-Mobile*, the Court held that a single meeting between undertakings may ground a concerted practice.[148] If intent is found, then the individual service providers and the platform will be participating in a hub-and-spoke type conspiracy.[149]

The instrument of such a horizontal agreement is *Uber's* pricing algorithm, which exclusively determines the rates practised by all drivers. 'The common algorithm which traders use as a vertical input leads to horizontal alignment'.[150] Indeed, *Uber* drivers do not compete on price and do not negotiate fares, but rather 'automatically' charge the fares set by the algorithm, thus creating suspicions of price-fixing.[151] Even though *Uber* has claimed that the company's terms allow drivers to charge less than the algorithmically suggested price, the app lacks the mechanism to do so, thus rendering that option practically impossible.[152] However, *Uber's* recent move to emulate *Lyft* and allow users to tip drivers through the app, may constitute a more plausible argument against price uniformity.[153] In any case, *Uber's* algorithm 'has been referred to as "algorithmic monopoly" as it is controlled by *Uber* and may mimic a perceived competitive price rather than the true market price'[154] therefore raising suspicions of 'manipulation' of the perceived market price,[155] facilitating a 'techno-cartel'[156] and 'classic hub-and-spoke conspiracy'.[157]

---

[146] *Meyer v Kalanick* (n 120) 12–13.

[147] ibid. In that regard, *Uber* and *Lyft* drivers were prohibited from unionising in fear of their colluding after the relevant law was blocked by a Seattle Judge. The US Chamber of Commerce, which brought the request before the Court, claimed the law in question 'turns labor law on its head, treating independent businesses as employees, and flouts antitrust law, allowing independent economic actors to fix prices'; see *Chamber of Commerce of the United States of America v City of Seattle et al*, Case No 2:17-cv-00370 US District Court for the Western District of Washington. See J Rosenblatt and E Amon, 'Judge Blocks Seattle Law Allowing Uber and Lyft Drivers to Unionize' *Bloomberg Technology* (4 April 2017).

[148] Case C-8/08 *T-Mobile Netherlands BV* EU:C:2009:343.

[149] As was found probable in *Meyer v Kalanick* (n 120). It should be remembered that in the hub-and-spoke type of collusion, the competing companies (spokes) are not in direct contact with each other but rather interact via a common trading party (hub).

[150] Stucke and Ezrachi, 'Artificial intelligence' (n 130) 14.

[151] On this issue see Gata, 'The sharing economy, competition and regulation' (2015) 4.

[152] The argument was made by *Uber* during the court proceedings of *Uber NY* case (*Meyer v Kalanick*) fn 3, and was rejected by the Court.

[153] See A Hawkins, 'You can now tip your Uber driver in the app' *The Verge* (6 July 2017).

[154] Stucke and Ezrachi, 'Artificial intelligence' (n 130) 14.

[155] *Uber* has contested that, by claiming '[w]e are not setting the price. The market is setting the price. We have algorithms to determine what that market is'; statement made by *Uber's* former CEO and Co-Founder. See J Priluck, 'When Bots Collude' *The New Yorker* (25 April 2015).

[156] Mehra (n 130) 2.

[157] Stucke and Ezrachi, 'Artificial intelligence' (n 130) 15.

The above can be held true all the more so in the EU, especially in view of the recent judgments of the CJEU on collusion in the digital environment.[158] The CJEU has found that the individual service providers may be found to participate in concerted practices by silently accepting the platform's anticompetitive terms. In its recent judgment in *Eturas,* the Court held that the clients of a platform who learned of and did not act against the application of a uniform discount decided unilaterally by the platform, could be held liable for collusion.[159] It further explained that even without any direct contact, a presumption of awareness and therefore collusion is possible on the basis of objective and consistent indicia.[160] In other words, the presumption of awareness established means that if an anti-competitive message is being sent to the platforms' users, the latter:

> are presumed to: (i) have knowledge of the communication; (ii) have subscribed to the infringement in the content of the communication provided that they did not publicly distance themselves from the conduct; and (iii) have used that knowledge when determining market behaviour (i.e. the Anic presumption).[161]

Such presumption shall be combined with other indicia in order to reach a conclusion on the existence (or lack) of collusion. This development may greatly facilitate the finding of concerted practices between collaborative economy participants.

Some authors have identified price signalling between suppliers as a potential antitrust concern for the collaborative economy.[162] The announcement of individual service providers' prices, availability and other sensitive information which is relevant for competition, may raise suspicions for facilitation of anti-competitive price signalling. According to the Guidelines on horizontal co-operation agreements, 'artificially increasing transparency in the market' may facilitate coordination depending on the specific market's conditions.[163] Further, '[i]nformation exchanges between competitors of individualized data regarding intended future prices or quantities should therefore be considered a restriction of competition by object'.[164] However, at the current stage of development of the collaborative economy, it is unlikely that price signalling occurs between the suppliers considering that: (a) there is great heterogeneity among the products/services offered on each platform; (b) the provision of the underlying services is not characterised

---

[158] Namely Case C-74/14 *Eturas* EU:C:2016:42 and Case C-194/14 P *AC-Treuhand v Commission* EU:C:2015:717, which are further discussed below.

[159] Case C-74/14 *Eturas*.

[160] In view of the effectiveness principle, the Court clarified that an infringement may be proven not only by direct evidence, but also by valid and consistent indicia.

[161] Hobbelen, Lorjé and Guenay, 'Selected recent developments in the application of EU competition law to online platforms' (2016) 14. However, the Court decided that platform users cannot be required to take excessive or unrealistic steps so as to rebut the presumption; see Case C-74/14 *Eturas* (n 158) para 41.

[162] Lougher and Kalmanowicz (n 7) 100–101.

[163] European Commission, 'Guidelines on the Applicability of Article 101 of the Treaty on the Functioning of the European Union to horizontal co-operation agreements' [2011] OJ C 11/1, para 65.

[164] ibid para 74.

by oligopoly, but rather by zillions of peers; (c) the announcement of the prices/rates on the platform does not refer to future pricing intentions, but rather reflects the price at real-time conditions, since most services offered are ready to be purchased; and (d) there is a legitimate underlying reason for the announcement of such information by platforms, as it facilitates the matching between suppliers and consumers. Further, the overall benefits for the consumers would probably trigger the exception of Article 101(3),[165] thus rendering the announcement legal.

b. Collaborative Platforms as Facilitators of Collusion

In view of the above, the question arising is whether the platform may be found to be orchestrating or else facilitating the concerted practices. The platform may not itself qualify as an association of undertakings, since it is connected only contractually with the service providers, it does not promote their interests but its own, and the providers have no say whatsoever in determining the platform's policies and decisions.[166] However, platforms may be found responsible for collusion of undertakings operating in a completely different market segment.

Both issues have been addressed by the CJEU in the *Treuhand* judgment.[167] The Court held that a consultant company, operating in a completely distinct market from the one where the collusion took place, but which actively and positively coordinated and facilitated the collusion, may be held liable together with the participating undertakings.[168] Even more so, '[p]latforms can be held liable for behaviour that enables others to coordinate their behaviour anti-competitively, even if the platform does not directly benefit itself'.[169]

The platform's anticompetitive behaviour is contingent upon the degree of the participation it exerted in the concertation. In its *Treuhand* judgment, the Court refers to the 'essential role' played by the platform, the 'full knowledge' and active participation. Similarly, the Commission in its *JPY Libor* decision clarified that the broker facilitated cartels by: (a) acting as a communications channel between traders; (b) disseminating misleading information to the cartel's competitors; and (c) using its contacts with non-participants in the cartel in order to influence

---

[165] For which see section II.D.iv.

[166] In Case C-382/12 P *MasterCard* EU:C:2014:2201, the Court found that Art 101 catches all forms of cooperation—no evasion on account simply of form of coordination.

[167] Case C-194/14 P *AC-Treuhand v Commission* EU:C:2015:717.

[168] It should be noted, however, that the test used by the Court in order to hold the 'facilitator's' liability is quite strict, since it requires that its conduct should be: (a) directly connected to the negotiation and implementation of the agreement between the parties; and (b) have as its very purpose 'the attainment, in full knowledge of the facts, of the anticompetitive objectives', see para 38. For a brief and concise note on the case, see G De Stefano, 'AC-Treuhand Judgment: A Broader Scope for EU Competition Law Infringements?' (2015) Editorial, 6 *Journal of European Competition Law & Practice* 689–90.

[169] R Wezenbeek, 'Platforms as facilitators of concerted practices; Lessons from the payments sector', presentation for *ENTraNCE Workshop: Antitrust Enforcement in Traditional v Online Platforms* (4 December 2015) Florence, 15, available at www.eui.eu/Projects/ENTRANCE/Workshop/Antitrust EnforcementinTraditionalvOnlinePlatforms.aspx.

their behaviour.[170] Though it is still unclear which actions (or omissions?) would constitute an active or essential role of the platform,[171] in view of the recent approach of the Commission and the Court towards intermediaries as facilitators of cartels, as well as the *Uber* NY case (*Meyer v Kalanick*), whereby facilitation by *Uber's* ex CEO was found probable, collaborative platforms may need to be extra cautious of any anti-competitive practices.

However, the two-sided nature of collaborative markets may act as a mitigating factor of any liability pinned on them in view of the above.[172] Thus, when examining potential collusion, the general economic context of the two-sided market needs be taken into account, as discussed above.[173]

c. Vertical Practices

Antitrust issues in the collaborative economy could emerge through vertical pricing restrictions. First, a potential violation of antitrust rules concerning the collaborative economy is through contracts that reference rivals (CRRs).[174] Such contracts could be exclusivity agreements, most-favoured-nation (MFN)[175] or meet-the-competition (MTCs)[176] clauses. These may be imposed on suppliers by platforms to ensure that the former provide their services exclusively for the platform, instead of multi-homing or, at least, that they provide their services on the best possible terms and most competitive prices. In this way, for instance, *Uber* could enter into exclusivity agreements with its drivers, so as to prevent them from driving for a competitive company; *Airbnb* could enforce such clauses to homeowners so as to require them not to rent their apartments at a lower price on any other competitive platform, and so on. Such clauses could give rise to both anti-competitive behaviour in the form of collusive agreements (Article 101 TFEU) and abuse of dominance (Article 102 TFEU).[177] CRRs have already been found to restrict competition in the digital platform environment, thus creating precedent that collaborative platforms should take into account.

---

[170] *Yen interest rate derivatives (YIRD)* (Case COMP/AT.39861) Decision of 4 February 2015 (not yet published); see http://europa.eu/rapid/press-release_IP-15-4104_en.htm.

[171] On this question see Hobbelen, Lorjé and Guenay (n 37) 19.

[172] In that respect, see Case T-491/07 *Groupement des cartes bancaires*; and on appeal Case C-67/13 P *Groupement des cartes bancaires* (n 50).

[173] See section II.B.i.a above.

[174] On these see S King, 'Sharing Economy: What Challenges for Competition Law?' (2015) 6 *Journal of European Competition Law & Practice* 729; see also Vitkovic, 'The Sharing Economy: Regulation and the EU Competition Law' (2016) 109ff; see also A Ezrachi, 'The Competitive Effects of Parity Clauses on Online Commerce' (2015) 11 *European Competition Journal* 488. CRRs have particularly been addressed in the case of online travel agents as well as the online banking sector. On this see UK House of Lords, 'Online Platforms and the Digital Single Market' (2016) 10th Report of Session 2015-16, paras 107–25; see Hobbelen, Lorjé and Guenay (n 37) 7–9.

[175] These require the seller to offer the product/service at the lowest price to a particular customer. Also known as parity clauses.

[176] These provide that if a customer receives a better price from an alternative seller, the current seller will have to match that price. King highlights that such clauses could lead to collusion.

[177] CRRs as a form of abuse of dominance will be discussed in section II.E.ii below.

An example of restriction to competition via CRR clauses is the *Apple e-books* case, whereby *Apple* signed agreements including CRR clauses with certain book publishers.[178] The CRR clauses in question required publishers to ensure that the retail price of an e-book listed on *Apple* would not be greater than the price on any other competitor's platform, including *Amazon*, thus forcing publishers to re-negotiate their agreements with *Amazon* and to increase retail prices for e-books. The US District Court found the CRRs to be a key element of the collusive behaviour of *Apple*. Accordingly, in the EU *e-books* antitrust case, even though the clauses themselves were not found incompatible with Article 101 TFEU, they certainly caused the Commission's concern. Thus the Commission, in finding a coordination between *Apple* and the publishers, and imposing commitments on the parties, obliged the company to terminate existing agreements and refrain from using price MFNs.[179]

Second, resale price maintenance (RPM) may occur if platforms and suppliers agree that the underlying services will not be provided below a set minimum price; this scenario is relevant when platforms exert some control over the price.[180] RPM may occur in the form of: (a) price fixing, where the service is provided only at a certain price (enforced, as the case may be, by the use of a pricing algorithm or other technical means); (b) an obligation not to provide services below a certain price; and/or (c) an obligation upon suppliers to observe a recommended price. With regard to the latter, price recommendations are permitted only insofar as they involve true recommendations and do not effectively constitute RPM. Thus, for instance *Airbnb's* practice of suggesting a 'recommended price' is prima facie innocuous, as long as home-owners fix their prices freely. However, the Commission in its Final Report on the E-commerce sector inquiry expressed concern that increased price transparency and the use of pricing software could enable platforms to monitor any deviations from recommended prices, to the point where price recommendations essentially could work like RPM.[181] Further, collaborative platforms may be incentivised to enter into such agreements considering that they receive a percentage of the price paid for each transaction.

All in all, in view of the emerging number of vertical agreements in the online environment, the Commission has expressed its intention to pursue action

---

[178] See *United States of America v Apple Inc, et al*, 12-cv-02826-DLC, US District Court for the Southern District of New York (filed 7 October 2013); *United States of America v Apple Inc*, 13–3741-cv, US Court of Appeals for the Second Circuit (30 June 2015); and *Apple Inc, v United States*, 15-565, Supreme Court (7 March 2016). The Supreme Court left intact the lower court ruling without comment and without a noted dissent. For further analysis on this with regard to the collaborative economy see King (n 174) 733.

[179] *E-books* (Case COMP/39.847) [2013] OJ C 378/25.

[180] See Australian Competition and Consumer Competition (ACCC), 'The sharing economy and the Competition and Consumer Act' (2015) *Deloitte Access Economics*, 23, available at www.accc.gov.au/system/files/Sharing%20Economy%20-%20Deloitte%20Report%20-%202015.pdf.

[181] EU Commission, 'Final report on the E-commerce Sector Inquiry' COM(2017) 229 final, para 13: 'With pricing software, detecting deviations from "recommended" retail prices takes a matter of seconds and manufacturers are increasingly able to monitor and influence retailers' price setting'.

against vertical restraints in the online space and make it an enforcement priority.[182] Therefore, collaborative platforms should be wary of not restricting competition through vertical agreements with their suppliers.

iii. Bringing Intra-platform Agreements under Established Categories of EU Competition Law

The practices discussed and the issues raised above beg a more horizontal and normative question: are pre-established categories and solutions reached in other economic fields directly transposable to intra-platform agreements in the collaborative economy? In this respect: (a) the Vertical Agreements Regulation; (b) specific forms of vertical agreements; and (c) the ancillary restraints doctrine are briefly discussed.

a. Regulation 330/2010 on Vertical Agreements

Regulation 330/2010,[183] replacing Regulation 2790/99 is supposed to help undertakings structure their vertical agreements, by offering a block exemption under Article 101(3) to all those agreements which come within its scope and which are entered into by undertakings having moderate market power, not exceeding 30 per cent.[184] In view of the 'superstar economics' and other market power characteristics of the collaborative economy (discussed at section II.C.i above) it is highly likely that the agreements which eventually reach the competition authorities, at the national and even more so at the EU level, do have over 30 per cent market share. Further, while the Regulation applies only to vertical agreements, the collusion-enhancing role of the platforms (discussed at section II.D.ii above), combined with the cumulative effect of the zillions of similar agreements concluded between the platform and the suppliers of underlying services, is likely to bring such agreements outside the scope of the Regulation.

b. Agreements Falling outside Article 101(1)

Franchise agreements and the clauses which are necessary for the agreement to operate are altogether outside Article 101(1), according to the Court's judgment in *Pronuptia*.[185] It would be tempting, in order to ensure legal certainty, to find that *Uber* drivers, and especially *Deliveroo* bikers, operate under a franchise agreement

---

[182] ibid.

[183] Commission Regulation (EU) No 330/2010 of 20 April 2010 on the application of Article 101(3) of the Treaty on the Functioning of the European Union to categories of vertical agreements and concerted practices [2010] OJ L 102/1.

[184] Although from a normative point of view it is somehow peculiar to start with a Regulation applying the exception of Art 101(3) before examining forms of agreements which would be altogether outside the rule of Art 101(1), the presentation here follows a more positivist/realistic approach, the one which is likely to be followed by undertakings themselves when trying to structure their agreements.

[185] Case 161/84 *Pronuptia de Paris v Schillgalis* EU:C:1986:41.

with the corresponding platform: they operate in a framework set up by the plat-form, use its app, logos and other IPR and conform with its instructions on core features of the service provided, and pay a fee (or commission) proportional to the number of transactions concluded.

There are, however, at least four grounds on which franchise agreements do not seem to fit the collaborative paradigm. Firstly, the award of a franchise is typi-cally associated with services of some technicality, reposes on specific qualification criteria which need to be satisfied by the franchisee, and concerns a restricted or else limited number of franchised outlets. Two-sided markets, on the other hand, typically work efficiently on the basis of externalities created by the large numbers of users, on both sides. Secondly, in franchise agreements, the role of IPR rights, know-how etc is core, not just incidental, as it is in the collaborative context. Thirdly, as Advocate General Szpunar puts it in his Opinion in *Uber France*:

> the role of the franchisor is limited to providing services (such as trade mark licences, know-how, the supply of equipment and the provision of advice) to the franchisees. It will have no relationship with the users of the final services, which will be provided solely by the franchisees. The services of the franchisor are therefore independent of the final services.[186]

This condition is certainly not met in the case of *Uber*, as with most other plat-forms that play some active role in the delivery of the underlying service. On the other hand, platforms which operate as mere billboards or, in any event, do not exercise a decisive role in the provision of the underlying service (such as eg *Airbnb, BlaBlaCar, TaskRabbit, MTurk* etc) may not qualify as franchisors in the first place, for lack of substantial input. Fourthly, and as a direct consequence of the previous objection, while franchisees get the money from the users and then return a proportion to the franchisor, in the collaborative context the opposite is true, ie the platform receives the money and 'pays' the suppliers.

This last characteristic of the collaborative economy could point towards the existence of an agency agreement, which also falls outside the scope of Article 101(1).[187] The function of a commercial agent is to negotiate business and to enter into contracts on the principal's behalf in exchange for a commission for every transaction concluded or for a salary. Here the big question would be 'who is the agent of whom'? Given that in the agency model the agent is being paid by the principal, are *Uber* drivers or *Airbnb* hosts agents of the platform, trying to sell a service that the platform itself does not—and is not able to—provide? Certainly not! Then are the platforms agents of the services provided by drivers and home-owners? That would make economic sense, but in this configuration the money flows would be in the reverse order, that is, from the principal (supplier) to the agent (platform), while in reality the opposite is true.

---

[186] Opinion of AG Szpunar in Case C-320/16 *Uber France SAS* EU:C:2017:511, para 22.
[187] Joined Cases 40/73 etc, *Suiker Unie v Commission* EU:C:1975:174, para 480.

Therefore, neither of the two categories contemplated—which would provide a safe harbour from the application of Article 101(1)—seem to be accommodating the realities of the collaborative economy. Indeed, if anything, the case law on copyright collecting societies, which are traditional two-sided markets, could be relevant for collaborative platforms.[188]

c. Ancillary Restrictions Doctrine

Since none of the above works, the third question which needs to be answered, is whether it is possible, in each case, to distinguish the core agreement from ancillary agreements and/or restrictions and uphold the latter in view of the beneficial effects of the former, in the sense of the *Nungesser* and *Remia and Pronuptia* case law.[189] The answer is a qualified yes.

Most agreements contain core and ancillary terms. However, in the collaborative economy, agreements tend to be minimal and simpler than those typically signed between undertakings, and tend to contain only the core terms. The agreements themselves need not contain all the ancillary terms, as many of them tend to be enforced directly through the application or other software run by the platform. Therefore, subject to the Court's judgment in *Eturas*,[190] the boundaries between agreed and unilateral practices are blurred further than they already are in the offline context.[191] If the terms were indeed to requalify as unilaterally imposed, rather than agreed between the parties, it could be more difficult to show their indispensability, as they may correspond to the interests of only one party to the detriment of those of the other.

Moreover, in an environment as fluid as that of the collaborative economy it may be difficult to show that one or the other term is not core, but is nonetheless indispensable. It is no coincidence that it was in examining an agreement in a two-sided market, in *MasterCard*, that the Court noted that where the agreement in question 'is simply more difficult to implement or even less profitable with the restriction concerned' the test of objective necessity would not be satisfied.[192]

Therefore, although the doctrine of ancillary restrictions could serve to uphold some agreements and/or restrictions judged as indispensable, the specific characteristics of the collaborative economy make its application quite unpredictable.

---

[188] See eg Case 395/87 *Ministère Public v Tournier* EU:C:1989:319; Joined Cases 110/88, 241/88 and 242/88 *Lucazeau v SACEM*, EU:C:1989:326; and more recently Case C-351/12 *OSSA v LIML* EU:C:2014:110.

[189] Case 258/78 *Nungesser v Commission* EU:C:1982:211; and Case 42/84 *Remia and Pronuptia v Commission* EU:C:1985:327.

[190] Discussed in section II.D.ii.a above.

[191] Indeed this is a distinction which has occupied the EU Commission and Courts for a long time, and where the lines are still not clearly set; see eg for a very large concept of unilaterally imposed terms as caught by Art 101 TFEU, Joined Cases 25/84 and 26/84, *Ford v Commission*, EU:C:1985:340, partly overturned by Joined Cases C-2/01 P and C-3/01 P *Bayer* EU:C:2004:2; see also the discussion by R Wish and D Bailey, *Competition Law*, 8th edn (Oxford, Oxford University Press, 2015) 110–15.

[192] Case C-382/12 P *Master Card v Commission* EU:C:2014:2201, para 91.

iv. The Role of Article 101(3) TFEU

Provided that the above behaviours are found to restrict competition under Article 101(1) TFEU in the first place, an assessment of their overall economic benefits according to Article 101(3) TFEU is due before judging whether the agreement is illegal.[193] In general, the collaborative economy is based on and promotes technical and economic progress and improves the distribution of products and the provision of services, thus creating a richer market and a plurality of choices of both services and prices for consumers. Therefore, the pro-competitive effects may outweigh the anti-competitive effects and the prohibition of the anti-competitive practices of Article 101(1) may be lifted.

Further, the special characteristics of collaborative platforms as two-sided markets marked by network effects create an environment where certain technically anticompetitive practices may benefit the market and potentially consumers. Hence, even horizontal agreements (or else co-ordination) between competing platforms, which 'talk to each other', could, under certain circumstances, benefit consumers and the market: interoperable platforms serve more users on both sides and therefore secure better matching. In that regard, co-operation may be more beneficial than competition. Similarly, vertical restrictions, such as exclusivity agreements, may be beneficial for the market overall, since concentrated market power on one or few competing platforms may have better economic results due to network effects. In this respect some platforms present the same characteristics as natural monopolies.

It is, therefore, worth examining the possible application of Article 101(3) in the case study of *Uber's* algorithm discussed above. Even though such a hub-and-spoke agreement can be classified as an 'object restriction' or else fall within the scope of 'hard-core restrictions',[194] the application of Article 101(3) is not altogether excluded.

The first condition of Article 101(3), according to the Guidelines, ie an improvement in the production or distribution of goods or in technical or economic progress,[195] is probably met.

The second and third conditions, ie fair share to consumers and indispensability of the restriction, need to be examined in view of *Uber's* business model. The surge pricing algorithm aims to balance supply and demand by closing the gap and thus to provide better outcomes for both sides, ie drivers who make more profit and riders who find rides easier and quicker. Even though one side of this two-sided market suffers from paying higher prices, the overall ecosystem has

---

[193] In view of the two-sided nature of collaborative platforms, a restriction on one side may not even qualify as a restriction under Art 101(1) when taking into account the two-sided market as a whole. See case C-67/13 P *Groupement des cartes bancaires* EU:C:2014:2204, esp paras 78–79. See also Hobbelen, Lorjé and Guenay (n 37) 10.

[194] Wish and Bailey, *Competition Law* (2015) 127–28.

[195] Commission Communication, Notice—Guidelines on the application of Article 81(3) of the Treaty [2004] OJ C 101/97, para 34.

economic advantages. It has been argued that when the surge pricing mechanism is absent, as occurred in New Year's Eve 2014–15 in New York, 'key indicators of the health of the marketplace deteriorated dramatically'.[196] Because of the failure of the surge pricing mechanism on that occasion, 'completion rates fell dramatically and wait times increased, causing a failure of the system from an economic efficiency perspective'.[197] The market does, in a way, therefore benefit from *Uber's* pricing mechanism. The question is whether a fair share of benefits accrue to consumers.[198] As was decided by the European Court of Justice in *MasterCard*,[199] subsidisation of the benefits between the two sides of the market is not sufficient; nor is the argument that the network effects will *eventually and indirectly* benefit the side which suffers from the restriction. On the contrary, the Court (on appeal) clarified that

> efficiencies must relate to the market on which the restriction of competition is established. Advantages found only on one market of a two-sided system and not on the market where the restriction of competition takes place, cannot compensate for the restriction of competition, in particular where the purchasers on both markets are not substantially the same.[200]

This condition will certainly be fulfilled for drivers, since they receive surged prices. The outstanding question is whether this is enough for the second condition of Article 101(3) to be met, irrespective of any benefits accruing for riders, who are effectively shouldering the price increase. It could be argued that they benefit in terms of waiting time or even finding transportation in the first place.[201] Further, in certain circumstances even with the higher (surged) prices, the *Uber* rides may be more economical with regard to other possible transportation options, such as traditional taxis or private car hiring. This issue is highly circumstantial but in general the argument that the second condition is met may very well be accepted. Besides, for these same reasons, *Uber's* pricing mechanism may be deemed indispensable, based on its business model and the general objective of collaborative platforms, which is none other than to facilitate matching between supply and demand.[202]

---

[196] See J Hall, C Kendrick and C Nosko, 'The Effects of Uber's Surge Pricing: A Case Study' (2015) 8, available at http://economicsforlife.ca/wp-content/uploads/2015/10/effects_of_ubers_surge_pricing.pdf.

[197] ibid.

[198] Both suppliers (drivers) and recipients (riders) can qualify as consumers with regard to their relationship with the platform.

[199] Case C-382/12 P *MasterCard* (n 166).

[200] See Hobbelen, Lorjé and Guenay, (n 37) 12, commenting the *MasterCard* case referenced above. Thus, as far as Art 101(3) is concerned, the question whether there are two separate markets or one two-sided market is irrelevant.

[201] In *REIMS II*, the Commission accepted that even though some consumers may pay higher prices, the overall benefits were sufficient to offset this; *REIMS II* (Case No IV/36.748) [1999] OJ L 275/17.

[202] Discussion on the indispensability of the restriction here presupposes that the *Uber* surge pricing algorithm is not considered as 'ancillary' in the sense of Art 101(1).

However, the last criterion for the application of Article 101(3), ie no substantial elimination of competition, would be more difficult to meet than the above three conditions.[203] The pricing algorithm indeed eliminates all price competition between *Uber* drivers, ie between all parties of the agreement, as demonstrated above.[204] It remains to be evaluated if other forms of competition, eg through quality (of the cars), qualifications (of the drivers), politeness, flexibility etc, remain possible or if, on the contrary, they are also eliminated through the access and/or conduct conditions that *Uber* imposes on its drivers; and whether such forms of competition are deemed important by consumers.

Considering that the four conditions set by the Guidelines must be cumulative, the application of Article 101(3) TFEU in the case of *Uber's* pricing algorithm is unlikely. *Uber*, however, is an extreme example of automatic, uniform and inescapable price fixing. Other platforms which are less aggressive in the way they fix, propose or else impact on prices may be better candidates of an exemption under Article 101(3).

E. Practices Coming under Article 102 TFEU[205]

Once market power has been established,[206] it might still be difficult to establish abuse. Technology and the data gathered by platforms provide them with the capacity to monitor customers' activities, accumulate data and react to market changes in real time. Computer algorithms may be used to optimise behavioural advertisements, individualised promotions and targeted, discriminatory pricing.[207] Would such 'market-driven' adjustment qualify as 'abuse'? In other words, if *Uber's* surge pricing perfectly reflects the supply and demand conditions of the market at a given moment,[208] is this not what competition law is all about? Even more so, applying different prices for different consumers based on real-time market conditions may be optimal for balancing the supply and demand sides, and thus for the very health of the platform. Indeed, it may be the way for achieving Pareto optimal effects, by having individual market participants paying exactly the price they are willing to for the services offered by platforms.

---

[203] This view is also supported by Nowag, 'UBER between Labour and Competition Law' (2016) 95–104.

[204] See section II.D.ii.a above.

[205] This section focuses on platforms, since the complete absence of any commonality of interests and any real means of directly coordinating among themselves would mean that the suppliers could not possibly be found collectively dominant under Art 102 TFEU.

[206] See section II.C above.

[207] Stucke and Ezrachi, 'Artificial intelligence' (n 130) 4.

[208] According to *Uber's* Q&A webpage, prices may temporarily increase on the occasion of sports events, bad weather, public holidays etc, the purpose being to secure adequate supply at all times; see www.help.uber.com/h/34212e8b-d69a-4d8a-a923-095d3075b487.

i. Tying and Bundling

Similar questions would arise in the event of dominant platforms performing tying and bundling practices, ie supplying a product/service only in a bundle with some other product/service.[209] While competition law does not prohibit every bundling practice, in view of the *Microsoft* saga it is possible that a violation of Article 102 TFEU could be raised, eg if *Airbnb* started imposing its own photographers and obliged hosts to pay extra for the photography service, or if *DogVacay* obliged dog-sitters to use *DogVacay's* own dog supplies, such as dog food or collars, toys etc, for which an extra charge would be made to the consumer. As platforms grow, they pursue the provision of additional services either in different markets (horizontal integration) and/or in upstream and downstream markets (vertical integration). Platforms may either force such additional services upon consumers as complementary/tied services or incentivise their users (both suppliers and consumers) to promote the complementary services. Further:

> [i]ncreased integration could also allow an integrated platform to cross-subsidise across the different arms of its business—making it difficult for non-integrated platforms to compete on the basis of price (such as is seen in the supermarket and petrol station markets). Importantly though, in order for the platform to engage in this type of 'leveraging', it must have a degree of market power in at least one of the markets it operates in.[210]

Data is relevant here as well, considering that the platform tying its products may use valuable information gathered from its initial service for the complementary services as well:

> A ride-sharing platform, for example, has intrinsic knowledge of a consumer's regular whereabouts and spending patterns. It could use this knowledge for offering complementary or synergistic P2P services, such as grocery shopping or dry-cleaning delivery. As other platforms competing for these related markets do not benefit from such knowledge, the information asymmetry places them at a significant competitive disadvantage.[211]

This concern has been raised in the ongoing case against *Google*, where the Commission has expressed its concern that consumers may be using certain applications not on the basis of quality, but rather on the basis of easier access.[212]

---

[209] For an overview of the anti-competitive practices of tying and bundling in relation to servitisation, see J Hojnik, 'The servitization of manufacturing: EU law implications and challenges' (2016) 53 *CMLR* 1575.

[210] See ACCC, 'The sharing economy and the Competition and Consumer Act' (2015) 22.

[211] Lougher and Kalmanowicz (n 7) 100.

[212] See *Google Android* (Case COMP/40099). As of the time of writing no decision has been issued. However, such concern has been expressed in Press Releases and Memos made publicly available, and especially Commission's Fact Sheet of 20 April 2016, 'Antitrust: Commission sends Statement of Objections to Google on Android operating system and applications', MEMO/16/1484, whereby the Commission states that its 'analysis has shown that consumers rarely download applications that would provide the same functionality as an app that is already pre-installed (unless the pre-installed app is of particularly poor quality)'.

Further, the big data and/or meta-data owned by a dominant firm, may, under circumstances, qualify as 'essential facilities'[213] and refusal to grant access to newcomers or other competitors may qualify as abusive.[214] This scenario presupposes that the data, to which access is denied by the incumbent, is indispensable for carrying on the competitor's business in question, ie that there are no alternative data and there are technical, legal or economic obstacles to collecting (or otherwise acquiring) these data.[215] This requirement would be met if the data owned by the dominant platform are 'truly unique and that there is no possibility for the competitor to obtain the data that it needs to perform its services'.[216] Even if indispensability is proven, 'it would still need to be demonstrated that refusal to access would be likely to prevent any competition at all'.[217] A potential obligation enforced by competition authorities to provide access to those data would also raise concerns in terms of data protection and privacy rules. Further, obliging companies to reveal their data and/or algorithms would create artificial transparency, facilitating collusion or other anti-competitive practices.[218]

ii. Locking-in of Peers through CRRs

Another issue arising from the potential dominant position of a platform is, as mentioned above, the use of vertical agreements to lock-in suppliers, ensure the best possible prices and conditions of the services and exclude rival platforms from competition. Thus, in the recent *e-book MFNs and related matters* case against *Amazon*,[219] the Commission found that by virtue of a number of MFN clauses in distribution agreements with e-book publishers, *Amazon* had abused its dominant position. The Commissioner for Competition, Margrethe Vestager, stated that 'Amazon used certain clauses in its agreements with publishers, which may have made it more difficult for other e-book platforms to innovate and compete effectively with Amazon'.[220] The clauses included the requirement that publishers

---

[213] For the economic advantage drawn from data, see section II.C.i above.

[214] Under the logic of Case C-418/01 *IMS Health* v *NDC Health* EU:C:2004:257, commented by V Hatzopoulos (2004) 6 *CMLR* 1613. For a general overview of this doctrine, see V Hatzopoulos, 'The evolution of the essential facilities doctrine' in G Amato and DC Elhermann (eds), *EC Competition Law: A Critical Assessment* (Oxford, Hart Publishing, 2007); more specifically on the issue of data as an essential facility, see I Graef, *EU Competition Law, Data Protection and Online Platforms: Data as Essential Facility* (Wolters Kluwer, 2016).

[215] See Case C-7/97 *Bronner* EU:C:1998:569 paras 4–45.

[216] Autorité de la Concurrence and Bundeskartellamt, 'Competition Law and Data' (n 112) 18.

[217] D Geradin and M Kuschewsky, 'Competition law and personal data: preliminary thoughts on a complex issue' (2013) *Discussion Papers Tilburg Law and Economics Center* No 10, 15 available at https://ssrn.com/abstract=2216088.

[218] Such a development may already be underway following Commission's antitrust decision on *Google Search (Shopping)*.

[219] *E-book MFNs and related matters* (Case COMP/AT.40153) Decision of 4 May 2017, not yet published.

[220] See European Commission, Press Release, 'Antitrust: Commission accepts commitments from Amazon on e-books' (4 May 2017), available at http://europa.eu/rapid/press-release_IP-17-1223_en.htm.

offered to *Amazon* similar or better terms and conditions as those offered to its competitors, not only in terms of prices but also of other aspects that a competitor could use to gain advantage, such as alternative distribution models and innovative e-books or promotions.[221]

At the national level,[222] a number of jurisdictions have identified anticompetitive effects of MFN clauses used in agreements between online travel agents (OTA) and hotel suppliers.[223] The business model of those platforms is based on providing cheaper prices to customers, offering deals and matching demand and supply—much like collaborative platforms. The lack of such clauses and the possibility of hotels to provide better prices on their own websites or on other platforms could undermine the very business model of OTAs. Competition authorities have, therefore, been performing a pro- and anti-competitive effects balancing act, resulting mainly in commitments of OTAs to restrict the use of such clauses.

As the collaborative economy expands and competition becomes fiercer, it is possible that such clauses could be employed by platforms to ensure the best possible prices for the services listed on their websites. Similarly, collaborative platforms may 'lock' their users using CRRs so as to limit competition by forbidding or weakening a user's multi-homing behaviour and thus hinder new entry.[224] In that regard, '[e]xclusivity requirements may be a device to reinforce tipping and create barriers to entry',[225] as well as influence a platform's market power. This is further reinforced by the existence of network effects that may lead to a snowball effect and even monopoly.

---

[221] The Commission and *Amazon* agreed on commitments including the termination of existing contracts with publishers entailing MFNs and the obligation to refrain from '(i) relevant clauses requiring publishers to offer Amazon similar non-price and price terms and conditions as those offered to Amazon's competitors or (ii) any such clauses requiring publishers to inform Amazon about such terms and conditions'. See the relevant Press Release (n 220).

[222] National cases including such clauses in other fields refer to: (a) price comparison websites in the UK: Competition and Markets Authority (CMA), 'Private Motor Insurance Market Investigation, Final Report', 24 September 2014, available at www.gov.uk/cma-cases/private-motor-insurance-market-investigation#finalreport; (b) the field of energy in Germany: Bundeskartellamt, Press Release, 'Verivox Vows to Stop Using 'Best Price' Clauses', 3 June 2015, available at www.bundeskartellamt.de/SharedDocs/Meldung/EN/Pressemitteilungen/2015/03_06_2015_Verivox.html; and c) *Amazon* marketplace in the UK and Germany: see Bundeskartellamt, Press Release, 'Amazon Abandons Price Parity Clauses for Good', 29 August 2013, available at www.bundeskartellamt.de/SharedDocs/Meldung/EN/Pressemitteilungen/2013/26_11_2013_Amazon-Verfahrenseinstellung.html%3Fnn%3D3599398; OFT Press Release 60/13, 'OFT Welcomes Amazon's Decision to End Price Parity Policy', 29 August 2013, available at http://webarchive.nationalarchives.gov.uk/20140402160400/http://oft.gov.uk/news-and-updates/press/2013/60-13.

[223] Namely UK, Germany, Italy, France, Sweden, and the US. For a thorough analysis of parity clauses and OTAs see Colangelo, 'Parity Clauses and Competition Law in Digital Marketplaces: The Case of Online Hotel Booking' (2017) 3–14.

[224] On this see section II.C.ii above.

[225] King (n 174) 732.

In view of the above, in the *JustEat/La Nevera Roja* merger, the CNMC expressed its worries that the resulting entity could exclude other platforms from competition if it concludes exclusivity or other CRR agreements with the suppliers (ie restaurants). Thus, 'in order to guarantee effective competition, the acquirer undertook not to apply exclusivity obligations to the restaurants using the service, nor to link the fees to the percentage of orders made through the platform'.[226]

On the other hand, incumbents may use their dominant and longstanding position to restrict the dynamic competition introduced by collaborative platforms. One way they can do this is by expanding and establishing themselves in the collaborative environment. For example, in the accommodation market, traditional hotel chains heavily invest in or acquire platforms.[227] If the traditional businesses combine their dominant position with CRR agreements, they may achieve dominance in the collaborative economy as well. Another way incumbents may abuse their dominant position to the detriment of collaborative platforms is through lobbying, and achieving regulation that will burden or even altogether block collaborative activities.

* * *

All in all, it may be said that while the collaborative economy and its players are still young, the speed with which this segment of the economy evolves, the 'superstar economics' that it entails through externalities and the role of data as a multiplier of market power, makes it relatively easy for collaborative platforms to gather market power; the temptation of abusing it is made greater by the fact that they operate in a regulatory grey area. Article 102 TFEU and the corresponding Commission and Court case law do provide for the necessary instruments to deal with such abuses, if used in a flexible manner.

III. State Aids

A. Fiscal Indeterminacy as Economic Advantage?

Collaborative platforms are a new thing in the economy. They lack the links that traditional entrepreneurs have with the government and State agencies. Their relationship with power is mostly one of suspicion, if not plain animosity. The most powerful collaborative platforms, such as *Airbnb*, invest human and financial resources to make governments listen (also) to them and not fight them.

---

[226] N Parr and C Hammon (eds), 'Merger Control' 5th edn (Global Legal Group) 188, available at http://www.uria.com/documentos/publicaciones/5014/colaboraciones/1868/documento/GLI-MC5_Spain.pdf?id=6435.

[227] See King (n 174) n 23 therein.

The others are either trying to comply with restrictive regulation pushed through by the incumbent traditional providers, or to pursue their activities virtually unnoticed by the authorities. For the time being, the risk of public money being directly transferred to a collaborative platform is quite low.

However, concerns under Article 107 ff TFEU may be raised. Collaborative economy participants enjoy an economic advantage in the form of: (a) tax payment facilities; and (b) 'forgiveness' of liabilities.

With regard to tax payment facilities, some Member States have already enacted tax relief measures especially for collaborative economy actors,[228] while others silently allow the non-payment of several taxes. Most Member States are, therefore, currently not collecting from collaborative economy participants, inter alia: (i) VAT by any of the parties involved; (ii) local or sector-specific taxes (eg tourist tax); (iii) personal income tax from prosumers, since most of them avoid declaring income they gain from collaborative practices; (iv) corporate income tax,[229] etc.

With regard to the 'forgiveness' of liabilities, most Member States are currently allowing the operation of collaborative companies, such as *Uber*, without claiming any social security payments for suppliers/workers[230] or any licence fees.[231] Considering that the concept of aid embraces not only positive benefits, such as subsidies themselves, but also interventions mitigating the burdens normally included in the budget of the beneficiary,[232] the above economic privileges, specifically awarded to/allowed for collaborative platforms, grant them a competitive advantage that could constitute 'State aid'.

---

[228] See Commission Staff Working Document 'European agenda for the collaborative economy—supporting analysis' SWD(2016) 184 final, at 5.2.2, Table 6.

[229] The Commission found that Ireland granted undue tax benefits to *Apple*, which is illegal under EU State aid rules, because it allowed *Apple* to pay substantially less tax than other businesses (Case No SA.38373) [2017] OJ L 187; both Ireland and *Apple* have challenged the Commission's decision in Case T-778/16 *Ireland v Commission* [2017] OJ C 38/35 and Case T-892/16 *Apple Sales International and Apple Operations Europe v Commission*, respectively: these are pending at the time of writing. Similarly, the Commission has opened an investigation on whether the corporate income tax payable by *Amazon* in Luxembourg complies with the EU rules on State aid (Case No SA.38944); see www.europa.eu/rapid/press-release_IP-14-1105_en.htm. It is worth noting that those two companies operate under a similar tax model to those of several collaborative platforms, such as *Airbnb*.

[230] The CJEU has ruled that tolerance by the responsible public body of late payment of social security contributions gives the beneficiary a significant commercial advantage by mitigating the burden associated with normal application of the social security system: see Case C-256/97 *DM Transport* EU:C:1999:332, para 19.

[231] In fact, Member States have withdrawn or amended existing laws in order to legitimise the lack of licences. See eg in Greece the abolition of provisions requiring a tourist accommodation licence for short-term rentals (Art 2(4) of Law 4336/2015, Official Gazette A 94).

[232] See, inter alia, Case C-387/92 *Banco Exterior de Espana v Ayuntamiento de Valencia* EU:C:1994:100, paras 13–14; Case C-256/97 *DM Transport* para 19; Case C-276/02 *Spain v Commission* EU:C:2004:521, para 24; Joined Cases C-128 and 129/03 *AEM* EU:C:2005:224, para 38; Case C-522/13 *Navantia* EU:C:2014:2262, paras 22–23.

B. Regulatory Void as Regulatory Advantage?

Additionally, collaborative platforms enjoy a regulatory advantage, since they operate on preferential terms, thus disrupting equality of treatment between operators. Indeed, collaborative economy participants face fewer (if any) complex and time-consuming regulatory requirements, such as undergoing authorisation/licensing procedures, being registered with the competent professional body, passing capacity tests, being subject to professional disciplinary rules, having to underwrite professional insurance policies etc. Such requirements have a cost for the professionals and are a source of revenue for the State. The Court has already held that procedural advantages selectively awarded, which favour the cost structure of an undertaking in relation to its competitors, may constitute State aid.[233] Could that case law expand and also cover more broadly 'regulatory advantages'? Article 107 ff TFEU could, then, assume a function similar to that played by national rules on 'fair competition'.

The question has already been brought before the European Parliament, in a petition on alleged abuses of competition law by *Uber*.[234] The question posed was whether *Uber* and/or *Uber* drivers in the UK were benefiting from 'contravening licensing law through allowing bookings relating to one licensed area to be served by vehicles and drivers licensed in another area'.[235] The Commission acknowledged that it was a matter 'primarily related to question of compliance with the applicable national and/or local regulatory framework'[236] and found 'no indications that any State resources have been used or have been foregone by the State in the course of the licensing procedures for provision of taxi and PHV services in the United Kingdom'.[237] It is unfortunate that the issue of regulatory advantages as a state aid measure was only brought in the context of a petition briefly addressed by the European Parliament's Petitions Committee, and it is even more unfortunate that the Commission's response is summary, if not erroneous: it is worth asking how it is ever possible to lift an authorisation requirement without foregoing the corresponding licensing fees. Hence, the issue of regulatory permissiveness as a state aid is bound to re-emerge.

IV. Conclusions

The rapid expansion of the collaborative economy has awaken competition with incumbents in the offline world. While in some markets the new services have a

---

[233] See Case C-690/13 *Eurobank* EU:C:2015:235.
[234] European Parliament, Committee on Petitions, Notice to members on the subject: Petition No 1173/2015 by Neil Warwick (British) on behalf of Campaign Against Unlawful Taxis In Our Nation Limited (CAUTION), on alleged abuses of competition law by Uber (29 June 2016).
[235] ibid.
[236] ibid.
[237] ibid.

complementary effect on traditional businesses, in others incumbents fear they will become entirely obsolete—if not driven out of the market altogether. The ground for fierce competition is set. National regulators have already been called on to ensure a level playing field, and the courts have been asked to eliminate any 'unfair competition', while the EU has, as yet, taken a back seat approach.

Nonetheless, sooner rather than later, the Commission will have to evaluate mergers and acquisitions between collaborative platforms or collaborative platforms and incumbent businesses, examine collusion, abuse of dominance and even state aids. This brings up the question whether the Commission is prepared and whether it has a proper toolkit at its disposal. The conundrum of the two-sided nature of markets has not as yet been resolved with consistency by the Commission and the Courts. Market definition for intermediaries has not yet been treated with confidence. The role of algorithms and their effects in competition is new territory and finding of dominance in a fast-paced and constantly evolving environment will be challenging. By definition, innovative competition does not limit itself to existing norms and 'boxes', thus creating doubt as to whether classic competition tools are sufficient to deal with such issues. As Ezrachi and Stucke note '[a]ntitrust law is not fixed. With new harms come new laws to prevent that harm'.[238] As the advancement of technology 'need not leave antitrust law behind',[239] the Commission may have to be prepared to be more radical than in the past, to treat issues with a 'fresh eye' and react to the realities instead of applying known and tried approaches. For one thing, the collaborative economy is about to test the reflexes of the Commission and the Courts, as it is expected that they will be called on to draw lines in a field resembling moving sand.

---

[238] Ezrachi and Stucke, 'Algorithmic Collusion: Problems and Counter-Measures' (2017) para 96.
[239] As was observed by Judge Rakoff in *Uber* NY (Meyer Kalanick) (n 120).

5

Labour Relations in the Collaborative Economy

I. Introduction

Unbeknown to her, Jennifer Guidry has become the symbol of the dark face of the collaborative economy. Her story of working for four different collaborative platforms, seven days a week, twenty (four) hours a day, after being published in the *New York Times*,[1] has been the red flag for several authors writing on employment in the collaborative economy.[2] Mother of three, suffering from a back and hip condition from her previous employment in the US Navy, Jennifer cobbles together a living which is neither pleasant nor sustainable; more importantly she lacks any benefits of a traditional full-time employee such as health insurance, paid holidays, training, retirement saving plans and tax withholding. She had to take up this kind of living upon losing her proper job during the recession of 2009—birthday of many important platforms such as *Uber, RideCell* and others.

If Jennifer is an extreme and clearly negative case of a collaborative worker, her case is nonetheless interesting, as it may be pointing to the shape of things to come in the field of employment. In the first chapter of this book the positive effects that the collaborative economy can deliver to individuals have been discussed: the use of idle capacity, spare time and skills; the topping up of revenues; flexibility; the joy of participating in socially and environmentally friendly activities and so on.[3] In this chapter the question is: has the collaborative economy actually delivered upon its promises? If not, what has gone wrong? And how could it be made better?

The chapter has both a positivist and a normative ambition. In order to fulfil this ambition and to answer the above questions, three issues will be discussed in turn: how does the collaborative economy transform employment conditions

---

[1] N Singer, 'In the Sharing Economy Workers Find Both Freedom and Uncertainty' *NY Times* (16 August 2014).
[2] See, inter alia, M Carboni, 'A New Class of Worker for the Sharing Economy' (2016) 22(4) *Richmond Journal of Law and Technology* 1; see also D Das Acevedo, 'Regulating Employment Relations in the Sharing Economy' (2016) 20 *Employee Rights and Employment Policy Journal* 1, 17 and 35.
[3] See Ch 1 above.

(section II); is such transformation aptly captured by existing legal categories (section III); and what could be done in order for this new form of economic activity to deliver the promised advantages (section IV)?

II. The Transformative Effect of the Collaborative Economy on Employment

A. Employment in the Collaborative Economy—Basic Characteristics

An examination of the transformative effects of the collaborative model on the economy in general and on employment conditions in particular, needs to start with an important disclaimer: while it is possible to gather evidence through qualitative methods, case studies and content gathered from the internet,

> the important data that would show economic effects are those gathered by the platforms, which so far have been made available only to selected researchers … It would provide evidence on costs and benefits for different categories of stakeholders, from which aggregate net effects could be estimated.[4]

Further, for the purposes of the present chapter a distinction so far implicit needs to be made out.[5] On the one hand, there are activities which are offered and performed electronically, at a distance, also called Online Labour Markets (OLMs) and which are potentially global: high-skilled ones, such as legal advice, business consulting, design, coding and translation; and lower-skilled ones, such as administrative support, data entry, tagging, or indeed any other task of 'artificial artificial intelligence' as *Amazon* brands the human micro-tasks performed eg in *Amazon Mechanical Turk (MTurk)*.[6] The two large platforms in this area are *Upwork* and *Freelancer*, with over 35 million registered users (in 2015).[7] On the other hand, there are activities which are based on electronic matching but the performance of which is physical and requires direct interaction, also called Mobile Labour

---

[4] C Codagnore, F Abadie and F Biagi, 'The Future of Work in the "Sharing Economy": Market Efficiency and Equitable Opportunities or Unfair Precarisation?' (2016) EU Commission JRC Science for Policy Report No 27913, 4, available at http://publications.jrc.ec.europa.eu/repository/bitstream/JRC101280/jrc101280.pdf.

[5] This is a standard distinction made by the Organisation for Economic Co-operation and Development (OECD), 'New Forms of Work in the Digital Economy' (2016) OECD Digital Economy Papers, No 260, 9–10, available at www.oecd-ilibrary.org/science-and-technology/new-forms-of-work-in-the-digital-economy_5jlwnklt820x-en; and by the EU Commission JRC, see Codagnore, Abadie and Biagi, 'The Future of Work in the "Sharing Economy": Market Efficiency and Equitable Opportunities or Unfair Precarisation?' (2016).

[6] OECD, 'New Forms of Work in the Digital Economy' (2016) 22.

[7] ibid.

Markets (MLMs); these are by definition local and include low-skilled services such as driving, cleaning, baby/dog-sitting and other errands, as well as higher-level interactive services, such as the delivery of lessons; home-sharing is also in this category. OLMs tend to be more P2B while MLMs more P2P.[8]

The above distinction is crucial, firstly because OLMs are subject to fiercer, more globalised, competition—although the 'flat world' axiom is still far from being confirmed:[9] 'different prices, currencies, languages, time zones, and other factors such as cultures, create barriers for the theoretically global reach of such platforms'.[10] Secondly, MLMs are by definition easier to capture by locally applicable regulation, which OLMs may evade altogether. The distinction between low and high skill activities is also important, since the former are more likely to be performed by an employee while the latter by an independent contractor.

Micro-entrepreneurs, on-demand workers, freelancers, contractors, etc, as those working in the collaborative economy are called, are typically self-employed and under-employed, while a smaller number is altogether unemployed.[11] The way they perform their duties clearly enters—and considerably broadens—the category of Non-Standard Work (NSW), consisting of: (a) the self-employed, as well as by employees who are (b) temporary full-time, (c) permanent part-time, and (d) temporary part-time.[12]

It is very difficult to know the exact number of people working in the collaborative economy as estimates in the US vary from 600,000 or just 0.3 per cent,[13] to 14 million or 9 per cent of the working population.[14] According to the same 'conservative' survey, above, (of 0.3 per cent) the number of collaborative workers in the EU would be estimated at 100,000 (0.05 per cent of all EU employees).[15] A total of 52.6 million contractors worldwide is estimated to exist, with few European platforms having more than 100,000 contractors.[16] Still, in 2015 gross revenue from collaborative platforms was estimated at €28 billion, almost doubling from 2014.[17]

---

[8] Codagnore, Abadie and Biagi (n 4) 5.

[9] ibid 7 and, more extensively, 40–42.

[10] OECD (n 5) 17. It is interesting to note however that the top 10 countries using *Upwork* are, on the employer side exclusively developed countries, while on the provider side essentially low-cost countries such as the Philippines, Bangladesh, India, Pakistan; the US, the UK and Canada also figure on the provider side; see OECD (n 5) 19.

[11] ibid 6.

[12] NSW accounts for 33% of total employment in OECD countries, ranging from as low as 17% in Eastern Europe, up to 58% in the Netherlands; see OECD (n 5) 22–28.

[13] WP De Groen and I Maseli, 'The Impact of the Collaborative Economy on the Labour market' (2016) Centre for European Policy Studies (CEPS) Special Report, 20 available at http://ec.europa.eu/DocsRoom/documents/16953/attachments/1/translations.

[14] Codagnore Abadie and Biagi (n 4) 22, with further references to the original sources.

[15] De Groen and Maseli, 'The Impact of the Collaborative Economy on the Labour Market' (2016) 20.

[16] ibid 22.

[17] M Schmid-Drüner, 'The situation of workers in the collaborative economy' (2016) Employment and Social Affairs, European Parliament, available at http://www.europarl.europa.eu/RegData/etudes/IDAN/2016/587316/IPOL_IDA(2016)587316_EN.pdf.

Earnings of collaborative workers may vary from a mean of US$3,380 per year for the average *Airbnb* host,[18] to US$475 per year for the average tasker working (four to five times a year) for the French *YoupiJob* platform.[19] People working for *MTurk* can hardly make more than US$5 per hour (against the US$7.25 minimum wage)[20] while *Uber* drivers, after allowing for idle times and running costs make around US$7.20 per hour.[21] Typically suppliers of MLMs receive more per hour for their activities than the average 'offline' worker,[22] but work less and, overall, make less money; suppliers of OLMs, who are in competition with those from developing countries, receive clearly less per hour than 'offline' workers in their (developed) country.[23] Overall, therefore, suppliers in the collaborative economy earn less than they would have earned if they performed the same work under proper employment conditions.

The above finding should be combined with the cost, in terms of time, effort and money, of constantly looking up for jobs and submitting offers, often in the form of tenders (such as in *CoContest*, where the projects not selected are not being paid for),[24] in different platforms and of communicating with different tentative clients (directly or through the platform). Indeed, according to an ILO study,[25] OLM workers spend an average of 18 minutes of unpaid work for every hour of paid work. As a supplier has put it 'I'm essentially competing for every hour of my employment'.[26] Things may be even worse for workers offering MLMs, who physically need to commute between platform allocated jobs.

If the above data is correct, then all the flexibility-and-autonomy fuss of the collaborative economy is a big fail: not only would crowdworkers have to work more than 12 hours a day to cobble together a decent income, but also these hours would be neither fixed nor conveniently spread within the day, as they are strictly demand-dependent.[27] This means that any other job, or other occupation and family engagement would suffer accordingly.

---

[18] OECD (n 5) 13.

[19] ibid 15.

[20] Which corresponds, however, to 14 times the minimum wage in India; see De Groen and Maselli (n 13) 10.

[21] Codagnore, Abadie and Biagi (n 4) 36.

[22] See the figures reported in Schmid-Drüner, 'The situation of workers in the collaborative economy' (2016) 10.

[23] OECD (n 5) 12–14; see also Schmid-Drüner (n 17) 10, where it is explained that designers from Italy (with a monthly average of €1,477) are unlikely to participate in the *CoContest* platform, which pays €5 per hour, while designers from Serbia (with a monthly average of €334) are more than happy, since they can make 7.6 times the minimum wage and 3.2 times the average wage; see also De Groen and Maselli (n 13) 11.

[24] In fact the three best projects get 70%, 20% and 10% respectively and all the rest get nothing.

[25] The results of which are reproduced in Schmid-Drüner (n 17) 11.

[26] Quote taken by S Kessler, as reproduced by MA Cherry, 'Beyond Misclassification: The Digital Transformation of Work' (2016) 37(3) *Comparative Labor Law and Policy Journal* 544; *Saint Louis University Legal Studies* Research Paper No 2016-2; available at https://ssrn.com/abstract=2734288, 26, with reference to S Kessler, 'Pixel and Dimed: On (Not) Getting By in the Gig Economy' *Fast Company* (18 March 2014) available at www.fastcompany.com/3027355/pixel-and-dimed-on-not-getting-by-in-the-gig-economy.

[27] Codagnore, Abadie and Biagi (n 4) 37.

The firms that do have recourse to such services gain in many ways. While some of the gains follow a win-win logic, some others are part of a zero-sum game, in the sense that gains for the one side are losses for the other. In the former category one can put down the possibility of finding talented people, unrestricted by geography, within a very short period of time, chosen upon merit from a large pool of candidates, allowing the searcher to face temporary demand surges. In the latter category (of zero-sum gains), firms may be said to draw advantages in at least four ways. Firstly, they are able to break down complex tasks into several simpler ones and allocate each one of these to different, lower-skilled people; in this way, objectively, firms lower their costs. Secondly, many of these tasks may be performed at a distance by lower-wage workers; therefore, firms gain from the legitimate-but-controversial wage differential, with all the social dumping and race to the bottom that this may entail. Thirdly, they gain because they replace proper employees, for whom they pay social security charges, health insurance, holidays, training etc, with individual 'micro-entrepreneurs' who shoulder all the above on their own—or not.[28] By the same token, fourthly, they break any collective bargaining framework.

B. From Micro-entrepreneur to '*Lumpen-cognitariat et Salariat Algorithmique*'?[29]

As stated in the previous section, employment in the collaborative economy has all the characteristics of NSW (non-standard work) and beyond. Similarly, it raises all the well-documented problems of NSW (see section i below), and many more, more (or not so) original ones. The latter revolve around the way that work is broken down and awarded to crowdworkers (see section ii below), the role of algorithms and ratings (see section iii below), the general insecurity and uncertainty surrounding work (see section iv below), health safety and security (see section v below) and, even, fundamental rights (see section vi below).

i. Non-standard Work (NSW) Issues—Made Worse

Since the adoption of the Lisbon strategy back in 2000, and the introduction of the concept of 'flexicurity', the problems ensuing from NSW have been discussed at length both in academia and by political institutions at the national, EU and OECD level.[30] In the latest OECD report discussing NSW matters, specifically in

---

[28] According to data reported in Codagnore, Abadie and Biagi (n 4) 36, from US taskers having *MTurk* and *CrowdFlower* as their primary source of income, only 8.1% make regular payments into private pensions and only 9.4% contribute to social security.

[29] Expression borrowed by O Ertsscheid, 'Du digital labor à l'uberisation du travail' *Numerique* (25 January 2016), available at www.inaglobal.fr/numerique/article/du-digital-labor-l-uberisation-du-travail-8747#intertitre-5.

[30] In the EU context see S Peers, 'Equal Treatment of Atypical Workers: A New Frontier of EU Law?' (2013) 32(1) *Yearbook of European Law* 30.

relation to 'New Forms of Work in the Digital Economy',[31] its authors make the following points. Firstly, they emphasise that temporary or else NSW is often not entered into voluntarily, but as a substitute to, or as a waiting-room for, more permanent employment.[32] The effects of NSW include, according to this report: (a) the fact that NSW workers earn less than full-time employees; (b) that NSW workers are less likely to receive employer-sponsored training; (c) that NSW workers are likely to receive less work-related benefits in the form of unemployment benefits, eligibility for work-injury, sickness and maternity benefits. The authors conclude by finding that NSW is more of a 'trap' into precarity than a 'bridge' towards standard work. This, in turn, tends to aggravate rather than limit inequalities.[33]

Crowdworking simply exacerbates all the above: workers, often completely unknown to the platform, receive nothing by way of health insurance coverage, social security pay, or, indeed, any other kind of employment-related benefit.

ii. Breaking Down of Work—Taylorism[34] Revamped

All the above effects are made worse in the context of the collaborative economy because of the breaking down of bigger projects and working activities to smaller, often mindless, tasks. Cherry, based on previous literature, puts forward the idea that the passage from an industrial, manufacturing-based economy to a knowledge-based one, in the late twentieth century, is now taking a further step towards platform-based crowdwork.[35] And while at first sight it would seem that this third phase is a normal evolution from the second digital-based one, in actual fact several 'aspects of crowdworking look more like a throwback to the earlier industrial model'.[36]

According to this view, in the industrial model workers typically had a life-long job, were specialised in the specific tasks allocated to them, and expected to evolve within the strict hierarchy of the firm, which granted them corresponding benefits (in terms of training, bonuses etc); in the knowledge-based economy workers navigate their professional life by moving horizontally between different firms, in which they are typically hired on project/s basis, thus acquiring different and wider skills, which they use to ascend professionally and claim better positions and better pay in every subsequent firm; the crowdworking economy, on the other hand, is based on micro-labour which 'is identified for its small scope, short duration, tiny output, and limited remuneration'[37] and by its massive scale, in the sense that it is performed by huge numbers of micro-labourers. Or to put it in Cherry's words:

> if the digital era broke schedules down into part-time or project-based shifts, crowdwork breaks those schedules down even further into the micro-level. It moves from 'project'

---

[31] OECD (n 5).
[32] OECD (n 5) 25.
[33] See also Schmid-Drüner (n 17) 9.
[34] See Frederick Winslow Taylor, *The Principles of Scientific Management* (Harper & Brothers, 1911).
[35] Cherry (n 26).
[36] ibid 20.
[37] ibid 22.

based work (with coherent aims and stages) occurring over a duration of weeks, months or years, into 'task' based work (the purpose of which may not ever be explained to workers) occurring in just hours, minutes or seconds. Micro labor is described as 'taking the division of labor to once unthinkable extremes',[38]

in a way Taylor would envy.

Therefore, not only the firm has no reason whatsoever to invest into the micro-workers, but the workers are completely cut off from the purpose of their work and, of course, from any guidance, team-working, or else human interaction; they are even more alienated than Ford's chain workers, who at least could physically communicate and professionally unionise. Add to this the possibilities of automatic, impersonal and often ruthless management, through algorithms or otherwise (discussed in the following paragraphs), the low levels of pay (already discussed) and the complete absence of social or other benefits, and you have a nightmarish pre-industrial setup. Indeed 'the crowdwork model may be more of a throwback to the industrial model, incorporating the efficiency and control of automatic management, without the industrial model job security or stability'.[39]

iii. Algocracy

Taylorism is being pushed to unprecedented lengths by the use of technology and algorithms, which operate as substitutes to direct managerial control and create power asymmetries between the platform and the worker. Such—typically opaque—algorithms may be used, as is the case with *Uber*,[40] in order to assign work (as they perform the matching), in order to fix prices (eg in case of surge) and in order to evaluate the worker in a semi-automated manner, on the basis of users' ratings, acceptance/cancellation rate,[41] and other, more opaque criteria. Other platforms, such as *Upwork*, are able to control their on-demand workers by measuring their productivity in terms of keystrokes, while other platforms use even more intrusive virtual office applications, such as regular screen shots and activity logs.[42] Algorithms may be further used in order to perform a series of managerial and/or supervisory tasks such as speeding up the work process, determining the timing and length of breaks, monitoring quality, ranking employees and more. 'Code makes crucial on-the-spot decisions about individualized employees and what they need to be doing in real time'.[43] Such algorithm-based governance, alternative to both markets and hierarchy, has been dubbed as 'algocracy'.[44]

---

[38] ibid 24–25.

[39] ibid 26.

[40] Codagnore, Abadie and Biagi (n 4) 40.

[41] It has been documented eg that *Uber* in San Francisco requires drivers to have cancellation rates below 5% and an acceptance rate of 90%, see Codagnore, Abadie and Biagi (n 4) 39.

[42] Codagnore, Abadie and Biagi (n 4) 39.

[43] Cherry (n 26) 21.

[44] A Aneesh, 'Global Labour: Algocratic Modes of Organization' (2009) 27(4) *Sociological Theory* 347; it is interesting to note, from an etymological point of view, that although the term algorithm sounds as if it is of Greek origin, in fact it comes from the medieval Latin word 'algorismus', itself inspired from the name of the Persian mathematician Al-Khwārizmī; in Greek, the word 'algos', stands for 'pain', 'sufferance' or 'evil'.

The automatic 'termination'[45] of workers when their ratings fall below a certain level (4.6 out of 5 stars in the case of *Uber*, with small variants across cities), or else 'firing by algorithm',[46] is the most extreme manifestation of algocracy; and one that has been explicitly abandoned in the settlements reached in cases *O'Connor v Uber* and *Cotter v Lyft*, whereby an arbitration procedure, at the charge of the platform, has been instituted.[47]

There is, however, more evil into algocracy. Ratings, posted by the platform, do play a very important role in the professional life of collaborative workers; having high ratings is their way to out-perform one another. This pushes workers to be constantly alert, and is a means of permanent, omni-present, surveillance. To the extent that ratings also take into account the response rate and speed, ie activities which do not necessarily occur during working hours—but supposedly during rest or family time—such surveillance runs around the clock and also covers private life.

Such surveillance is occasionally made worse by the workers themselves, in their efforts to counter the platform's surveillance methods. *Uber* drivers, for instance, in order to be able to prove that complaints by customers are unfounded, have started to install dash-cams in their cars,[48] thus further jeopardising both their own and their customers' privacy.

iv. Uncertainty, Insecurity, Isolation and Precarity

Algocracy has a further, but not less important, consequence in the area of pay. *Uber* and *Lyft* drivers do not know in advance either the destination they will be going to, or the fee they are going to get for it; on top of surge pricing, *Lyft* also practises a 'happy hour' when traffic is low. Drivers often go to a 'surge' area, only to find out that the offer there has been increased and that surge prices no longer apply. *CoContest* participants know that if they are not chosen through their project, they will receive no payment—but do not know exactly on what basis their project is being evaluated. Moreover, many collaborative workers complain that it is not always clear what commissions, charges etc apply to their fees.[49]

All the above make for a toxic working environment, whereby uncertainty as to the kind of work and the level of pay is common, there is insecurity as to the next micro-task to be performed, or more generally the existence of employment and isolation reign: we have the expansion of precarious labour, with all the social risks and downturns that this entails.[50]

---

[45] As the word is appropriately used in the contract signed between *Uber* and its drivers; a brush of humour from *Uber's* lawyers, a tribute to the ex-governor of California, or a truthful expression of the platform's attitude towards its workers?

[46] Cherry (n 26) 22.

[47] For a brief discussion of these cases see section III below.

[48] Schmid-Drüner (n 17) 14.

[49] De Groen and Maselli (n 13) 11.

[50] A Kalleberg, 'Precarious Work: Insecure Workers: Employment Relations in Transition' (2009) 74 *American Sociological Review* 1; see also Cherry (n 26) 22; see also Schmid-Drüner (n 17) 15.

v. Health and Safety Issues

The toxic working environment described above cannot possibly leave workers' health unaffected. On top of health risks connected with online work, such as stress, visual fatigue, musculoskeletal problems, and the risks connected with the specific physical activity performed (in case of MLMs), collaborative workers run a host of psychosocial risks unknown to date, connected to the factors already discussed: precariousness of work, continuous real time evaluation and impact of ratings, around-the-clock short notice work, mixing up of work and non-work activities, rapid pace of work without breaks, isolation.[51]

Moreover, especially for OLMs, offered at a distance, firms can afford to be completely agnostic as to the safety and security norms under which micro-workers perform their duties: ergonomic seating, protection from radiation and the like are all 'externalised' to the individual worker. Similarly, for the risks associated to the provision of MLMs, platforms typically require the workers to be individually insured and rarely do they offer some supplementary insurance:[52] while *Uber* has taken an insurance policy up to a US$ million for its customers, its drivers need to be individually insured against work accidents, assault etc.[53]

vi. Discrimination, Child Labour, Forced Labour: The Issue of Fundamental Rights

Discrimination in the 'workplace' has been documented in the form of clear statements posted on platforms, directly based on nationality (eg 'this job is not for people from Bangladesh or Pakistan') or indirectly based on language and accent (eg 'female caller with a British, or Australian or New Zealand accent').[54] Gender discrimination also occurs, since many employers due to information overload, choose to ignore the data concerning skills, merit and value for money and fall back on stereotypes: for instance they tend to choose men for programming and women for customer service.[55] Further, racial discrimination has been documented on the basis of the users' profiles, photos etc.[56] *Airbnb's* initiative to introduce a strict anti-discrimination policy[57] is welcome, but so far it is rather the exception than the rule. Indeed, authors comment that discrimination thrives in the collaborative economy because of the regulatory vacuum in which it operates.[58]

---

[51] See Schmid-Drüner (n 17) 15.

[52] See also Das Acevedo, 'Regulating Employment Relations in the Sharing Economy' (2016) 30.

[53] *Airbnb*, on the other hand, has initiated an insurance scheme covering damage to both guests' and to hosts' property.

[54] Schmid-Drüner (n 17) 16.

[55] ibid.

[56] ibid.

[57] *Airbnb*, 'Airbnb's Nondiscrimination Policy: Our Commitment to Inclusion and Respect', available at www.airbnb.com/help/article/1405/airbnb-s-nondiscrimination-policy--our-commitment-to-inclusion-and-respect.

[58] Codagnore, Abadie and Biagi (n 4) 42.

There are issues, however, that even a strict regulatory regime would have difficulties facing. Child labour and forced labour, both prohibited, inter alia, by the 1998 ILO Declaration on Fundamental Principles and Rights at Work, supposedly monitored in physical form, may easily reappear in the context of micro-work. Already documented virtual 'sweatshops' for 'gold-farming' in online games (ie advancing quickly in order to build a high-level character),[59] leave little doubt that basic micro-work may be performed in 'click factories' under similar circumstances.[60]

C. Room for Optimism?

The 'e-topia', apparently driven by an altruistic spirit (as the *Wikipedia* example seemingly suggests), could eventually become a social 'downward spiral' when risks traditionally borne by firms are being 'pushed back' to individuals—shifting costs to workers [and, in Europe, ultimately the welfare state, which offers health-coverage, unemployment benefits and the like]. Hence, the rise of the sharing economy can also act as a midwife for further growth of 'precarious employment'. The boundary between 'micro-entrepreneur' and 'precariat' (or rather 'cybertariat') has never been so blurred.[61]

In view of the above developments, the gloomy vision set out above seems to be fully justified. It should be kept in mind, however, that the collaborative economy is still in its early infancy, that current participants are exploring new ground and that pioneers are likely to suffer. Some steps in the right direction, by means of self-regulation, are already being made: *Lyft* and *Uber* have set aside the automatic 'termination' clause; *TaskRabbit*, in 2015, set a wage floor of US$12.80 per hour; platforms such as *Munchery* (food preparation and delivery), *Qii* and *MyClean* (house cleaning), *Luxe* (valet parking), *Shyp* (mailing) and *Hello Alfred* (errands and chores) hire their workers as employees, while *Instacart* (groceries) has reclassified several of its workers.[62] Evidence shows that, despite the above 'costly' initiatives, most of these platforms are doing well economically—and the same has been confirmed by *Deliveroo*, *Amazon* and *Uber* before the UK House of Commons.[63] Other platforms, such as *Even*, have put into place savings accounts for their providers, perequating bad with good months in order to make sure they receive a fixed monthly income.[64]

---

[59] Schmid-Drüner (n 17) 9.

[60] See also the OECD (n 5) 33.

[61] A Aloisi, 'Commoditized Workers: Case Study Research on Labor Law Issues Arising from a Set of "On-Demand/Gig Economy" Platforms' (2016) 37 *Comparative Labor Law and Policy Journal* 653, 683.

[62] Codagnore, Abadie and Biagi (n 4) 49.

[63] UK House of Commons, Work and Pensions Committee, 'Self-employment and the gig economy' (2017) 13th Report of Session 2016–17, 12, available at https://publications.parliament.uk/pa/cm201617/cmselect/cmworpen/847/847.pdf.

[64] Das Acevedo (n 2) 33.

The above measures, partly at the platforms' initiatives, partly as a response-settlement to judicial 'misclassification' actions, are intended both to make collaborative workers happier and, to a large extent, to keep platforms outside the focus of the judiciary and the regulators. Indeed, most of the problems mentioned above would be remedied if collaborative workers were afforded the status of 'employee', which explains why both individual and class actions have been brought to this effect. There is only so much that courts can do, however, without breaking into the territory of the regulator.

III. Courts Struggling on a Binary Logic: Self-employed versus Employees

The collaborative economy developed out of private initiative and entrepreneurship in order to make better use of idle capacity, so 'most of the workers in the digital labour market should be considered freelancers, since they make money from labour outside an employee-employer relation'.[65] This somehow 'easy' assertion, however, needs to be checked against actual realities. Indeed as explained in Chapter 2, where the platform exerts control over the important aspects of the service provided, and the supplier only has a secondary role, the latter may legally qualify as an employee of the former. This legal classification is supported by—so far limited and non-conclusive—empirical research, which shows that an increasing number of suppliers in the collaborative economy work in conditions that in the traditional economy would qualify as 'employment'.

In the absence of any special legal category specifically corresponding to the characteristics of the collaborative economy, courts on both sides of the Atlantic have struggled to apply old rules to new realities. They have tried to fit atypical and extremely variable tripartite contractual relations into the typically binary distinction between employees and self-employed persons. Or, as Judge Chhabria put it in the *Lyft* litigation in California 'in this case we must decide whether a multifaceted product of new technology should be fixed into either the old square or the old round hole of existing legal categories, when neither is a perfect fit'.[66]

The discussion of major US cases showcases the very real risks of divergent and, indeed, inconsistent decisions in the field of employment law (see section A below). Then the EU, more limited, experience is discussed (see section B below). Further, the EU Commission's approach is outlined (see section C below), before, lastly, a brief comment is added on EU labour law rules (see section D below).

---

[65] De Groen and Maselli (n 13) 12.
[66] *Cotter v Lyft Inc* 60 F Supp 3d 1067, ND Cal 2015.

A. US Case Law

In the California *Uber (Berwick)* case[67] the Los Angeles County Court made reference to a California Supreme Court ruling,[68] according to which the factors that should be taken into account in the assessment of the employer/employee relationship are the following:[69] whether the supplier's occupation is distinct from the platform's business; whether the supplier provides the instrumentalities, tools and the place for the supplier (or whether these are provided by the platform); whether the service requires special skills from the supplier (and is not supervised by the principal); whether the suppliers have an opportunity for profit or loss depending on their managerial skills; whether the job is only for a short time and/or not permanent; whether the payment is per job and not per hour; and whether the parties believe that they are entering an employment relationship. If some of the above criteria are fulfilled then the supplier should not qualify as an employee.[70] The Los Angeles County Court further made reference to the California Courts of Appeal in *Yellow Cab*, where the criteria used in order to qualify cab drivers as employees were that the 'platform' found the passengers for them and broadly controlled their operation.[71]

Applying the above criteria in the case of *Uber* drivers the Los Angeles Court found that 'by obtaining the clients in need of the service and providing the workers to conduct it, Defendants [*Uber*] retained all necessary control', while being 'involved in every aspect of the operation [as they] vet prospective drivers [who] cannot use Defendant's [*Uber's*] application unless they pass Defendant's [*Uber's*] ... checks'; the Court also held that 'Defendants [*Uber*] control the tools the drivers use; for example drivers must register their cars with Defendants [*Uber*], and none of their cars can be more than ten years old' and that 'ownership of the vehicle ... may be a much less important factor'. Moreover, the Court held that 'the passengers pay Defendants [*Uber*] a set price for the trip, and Defendants

---

[67] *Uber Technologies Inc v Barbara Berwick* Case No 11-46739 EK California Labor Commissioner, 2015 (Berwick), available at cdn.arstechnica.net/wp-content/uploads/2015/06/04954780-Page0-20.pdf.

[68] *SG Borello and Sons Inc v Dept of Industrial Relations* (1989) 48 Cal 3d, 341.

[69] The case did not concern electronic platforms, thus the language used is 'adapted' to the present context.

[70] For a discussion of these judgments and of the criteria set, see MJ Sorensen, 'Private Law Perspectives on Platform Services: Uber—a business model in search of a new contractual legal frame?' (2016) 5 *Journal of European Consumer and Market Law* 15, 16–17.

[71] *Yellow Cab Coop v Workers Compensation Appeals Board* (1991) 226 Cal App 3d, 1288; US case law on whether cab drivers are in an employment relationship with the dispatching platform/call-center is quite extended; in cases where the cab is not owed by the cab driver it is easier to establish the existence of an employment relationship, see eg *HT Cab Co v Ginns* 280 SW 2d 360 (Tec Civ App 1955) and *Scott v Manzi Taxi and Transportation Co* 179 AD 2d 949 (NY App Div 1992), but the same conclusion may also be reached in cases where the cab driver owns the vehicle, see eg *Weingarten v XYZ Two Way Radio Service Inc* 183 AD 2d 964 (NY App Div 1992); for a discussion of these cases see A McPeak, 'Sharing Tort Liability in the New Sharing Economy' (2016) 49 *Connecticut Law Review* 171, 206–209, available at https://ssrn.com/abstract=2776429.

[*Uber*], in turn, pay their drivers a non-negotiable service fee. Defendants [*Uber*] alone have the discretion to negotiate this fee with the passenger'; further the Court held that

> Plaintiff's [driver's] car and her labor are her only assets. Plaintiff's [driver's] work did not entail any 'managerial' skills that could affect profit or loss ... But for the Defendant's [*Uber's*] intellectual property, Plaintiff [driver] would not have been able to perform the work.

Thus, the Los Angeles County Court found that *Uber* drivers are employees of the platform.

The complete opposite conclusion was reached by the Florida Court of Appeal in the *Uber (McGillis)* case.[72] Broadly the same criteria as the ones ensuing from the California Supreme Court ruling (discussed above) are set under Florida law,[73] in order to characterise an employment relationship. On the basis of those the Florida Court upheld the decision of the Department of Economic Opportunity, denying Mr McGillis reemployment assistance on the basis of: (a) the clear terms of the contract and the fact that *Uber* acts on reliance upon it (for its fiscal and social obligations); (b) the fact that drivers supply the most essential equipment of their work, the car; (c) drivers choose whether, when, where to drive; (d) drivers are not subject to direct supervision by *Uber*; and (e) drivers are allowed to work for other competing platforms. The Court dismissed as being irrelevant the right of *Uber* to 'terminate' drivers and held that the fact that *Uber's* principal business is to provide transportation does not affect the above assessment.

On the basis of this judgment (at least presumably), in May 2017, Florida's governor signed into law a Bill establishing that drivers of transportation platforms (such as *Uber* and *Lyft*) are independent contractors—and not employees—provided that this is clearly stipulated into their contract, that they are free to choose when to work, and that they are free to work for competing platforms, or indeed, pursue any other economic activity. It should be noted, however, that such law only shields platforms from the application of State, not Federal, employment laws, such as the Fair Labor Standards Act.[74]

The above two examples, taken from the *Uber* litigation,[75] make clear that employment law issues raised by collaborative platforms are certain to yield different solutions in different jurisdictions. More surprisingly still, they are likely to reach different solutions under US Federal laws, given that, as Carboni

---

[72] *Darrin McGillis v Department of Economic Opportunity and Rasier/Uber* Florida DC Appeal, 3d N. 3D15-2758, delivered in February 2017.

[73] (Second) Restatement of Agency, para 220 id at 174–75.

[74] See AP Lazarus and KJ White, 'Florida Legislation Establishes That Ride-Sharing Drivers Are Independent Contractors, Not Employees' *Hunton Employment & Labor Law Perspectives Blog* (23 May 2017), available at www.huntonlaborblog.com/2017/05/articles/employeeindependent-contractor/florida-legislation-establishes-ride-sharing-drivers-independent-contractors-not-employees.

[75] There are more 'reclassification' cases concerning *Uber* in the US, as well as *Lyft* and other—non-driving—platforms, such as *CrowdFlower, Handy, Homejoy* and *Postmates*; see Codagnore, Abadie and Biagi (n 4) 48.

convincingly shows, 'under several federal statutes, definitions of what constitutes an employee versus an independent contractor differ'.[76] As she puts it,

> companies wishing (or more realistically, needing) to analyze whether their workers are properly classified as employees or independent contractors, they must look at a myriad of tests that pair with the appropriate statute regulating certain segments of business, labor and employment law. For instance there is the Internal Revenue Service's 'right to control' test used for federal tax purposes [20 criteria]; the common law right to control test used for federal discrimination law [11 criteria]; the Employment Retirement Income Security Act of 1974 (ERISA); a modified Treasury version of the common law right to control test used for Affordable Care Act purposes; a newly modified version of common law right to control test formulated for National Labor Relations Act; and the economic realities test applied to Fair Labor Standards Act [6 criteria].[77]

In view of the above exasperating uncertainty, it is plainly regrettable, from a legal point of view, that *Uber* has chosen to settle all its employment court cases,[78] therefore precluding guidance from the US Supreme Court. It is worth noting that in the *Uber (O'Connor)* case the California District Court has mooted the idea that established jurisprudence for defining employment (ie the *Borello* test)[79] should be revised by higher courts, in order to take into account the characteristics of the collaborative economy;[80] and that legal doctrine has put forward alternative criteria.[81]

B. EU Case Law

The situation in the EU is hardly any better. In the first *Uber* case to be published concerning labour law, the Central London Employment Tribunal, in case *Aslam, Farrar et al v Uber* found in favour of the drivers.[82] Judge Snelson held that reality could not be bound by 'armies of lawyers'[83] who resort to 'fictions, twisted language and even brand new terminology'[84] in order to contrive

---

[76] Carboni, 'A New Class of Worker for the Sharing Economy' (2016) 13.

[77] ibid 13–14; the number of criteria in square brackets are taken from the analysis following this excerpt.

[78] See Codagnore, Abadie and Biagi (n 4) 49.

[79] For which see above n 66.

[80] *O'Connor v Uber Technologies, Inc et al*, C13-3826 EMC, 2015 WL 1069092, N.D. Cal; however such an approach has been criticised as being 'techno-determinist' in the sense that it is based on the (false) idea that pre-existing laws cannot rule a set of social phenomena, see Aloisi, 'Commoditized Workers: Case Study Research on Labor Law Issues Arising from a Set of "On-Demand/Gig Economy" Platforms' (2016).

[81] See eg GE Brown, 'An Uberdilemma: Employees and Independent Contractors in the Sharing Economy' (2016) 75 *Maryland Law Review* 15, available at http://digitalcommons.law.umaryland.edu/cgi/viewcontent.cgi?article=1042&context=endnotes.

[82] See Case Nos 2202551/2015 & Others, *Aslam, Farrar v Uber*, Judgment of 28 October 2016, available at www.judiciary.gov.uk/judgments/mr-y-aslam-mr-j-farrar-and-others-v-uber.

[83] ibid para 78.

[84] ibid para 87, notes omitted.

documents 'in their clients' interests which simply misrepresent the true rights and obligations in both sides'.[85] He further took into consideration that although the contracts signed between *Uber* and its drivers made it plain that no employment relationship existed, all other *Uber* literature, whereby it provided guidance to drivers (through written instructions, email and messaging), did in fact point in the opposite direction.[86] Third, Judge Snelson took into consideration that the services—and the brand—being promoted by the platform were those of the platform, not of the individual drivers, and agreed with the North Carolina District Court in finding that 'Uber is no more a "technology company" than Yellow Cab is a "technology company" because it uses CB radios to dispatch taxi cabs'.[87] Moreover, he found *Uber's* argument that it is a mosaic of 30,000 linked small businesses, consisting of 'a man in a car seeking to make a living by driving it' as he put it, 'faintly ridiculous'.[88] He further ridiculed *Uber's* argumentation in the following words:[89]

> Uber's case is that the driver enters into a binding agreement with a person whose identity he does not know (and will never know) and who does not know and will never know his identity, to undertake a journey to a destination not told to him until the journey begins, by a route prescribed by a stranger to the contract [*Uber*] from which he is not free to depart (at least not without risk), for a fee which a) is set by the stranger, and b) is not known by the passenger (who is only told the total to be paid), c) is calculated by the stranger (as a percentage of the total sum) and d) is paid to the stranger.

The learned judge further based his assessment that an employment relationship exists between *Uber* and its drivers on the facts that *Uber*: (a) interviews and recruits drivers; (b) controls key information concerning clients and excludes the drivers from it; (c) pushes, under the menace of 'termination', drivers to accept/not to cancel trips; (d) sets the default route; (e) fixes the fare; (f) imposes conditions, instruct and controls drivers; (g) subjects drivers, through the rating system, to performance management/disciplinary procedure; (h) handles complaints about the drivers; and (i) reserves the power to amend the driver's terms unilaterally.[90]

In view of the above, and other elements, the Employment Tribunal reached the conclusion that 'the terms on which Uber rely do not correspond with the reality of the relationship between the organisation and the drivers. Accordingly, the Tribunal is free to disregard them'.[91] So much so that the Tribunal also plainly set aside a contractual clause subjecting all disputes to Dutch law, stating that the contract in which this clause was included (the formal one, in which *Uber* was supposed to be working for the drivers) had the complete opposite content from

---

[85] ibid para 96.
[86] ibid para 88.
[87] ibid para 89.
[88] ibid para 90.
[89] ibid para 91.
[90] ibid para 92; the judgment uses 13 criteria, which are here presented in a more summary way.
[91] ibid para 96.

the (unwritten) employment contract actually concluded between *Uber* and its drivers.[92] This judgment has been appealed by *Uber* and judgment is awaited.[93]

In other cases concerning other collaborative platforms, the Central London Employment Tribunal has again found in favour of the existence of an employment relationship. This was so in case *Dewhurst v Citysprint*, concerning a cycle courier,[94] were Judge Wade (sitting alone) found the contract between the platform and the supplier to be 'window dressing' for an employment relationship,[95] given that 'the claimant [was] both economically and organisationally dependent upon *Citysprint* not only for her livelihood, but also for how it is earned'.[96] The judge held that in construing contracts relating to work, which are typically concluded between unequal parties, 'whilst the express terms of the contract are key pieces in the jigsaw, the bar is low before the true situation can be explored';[97] even if this amounts to a 'purposive approach to the problem'.[98] Similar logic has been followed by the London Central Employment Tribunal in relation to cycle couriers employed by *Excel*.[99] In a more nuanced, and extremely well-reasoned judgment, the UK Court of Appeal held that a plumber engaged by *Pimlico Plumbers* (which intermediated between him and the clients) was not an 'employee' but was, nonetheless, entitled to 'worker' status, which is more protective than that of the 'self-employed'.[100] Further, at the time of writing, the Central Arbitration Committee was expected to rule on whether *Deliveroo* riders are to be considered as 'workers' and may unionise or not.[101] This litigation has been initiated by the Independent Worker's Union of Great Britain, but if worker status were recognised, then every individual rider could claim all the statutory benefits accruing to this legal category. In the meantime, in a move to appease its drivers and MPs complaining about the way *Uber* treats drivers, *Uber* announced that it would offer insurance to UK drivers in case of injury or sickness.[102]

---

[92] ibid para 105.

[93] C McGoogan and J Yeomans, 'Uber loses landmark tribunal decision over drivers working rights' *The Telegraph* (28 October 2016).

[94] Case No 2202512/2016 *Ms Dewhurst v Citysprint UK Ltd*, Judgment of 5 January 2017, available at www.egos.co.uk/ir35_cases/Dewhurst_v_City_Sprint_2016.pdf.

[95] ibid para 55.

[96] ibid para 57.

[97] ibid para 60.

[98] ibid para 61, citing Lord Clarke of the Supreme Court; in favour of a purposive approach see G Davidov, 'The Status of Uber Drivers: A Purposive Approach' (2017) 6(1–2) *Spanish Labour Law and Employment Relations Journal* 6; Hebrew University of Jerusalem Legal Research Paper No 17-7; available at https://ssrn.com/abstract=2877134.

[99] C McGoogan, 'Blow for "gig economy" as tribunal rules Excel must pay courier holiday' *The Telegraph* (24 March 17).

[100] *Pimlico Plumbers Ltd v Gary Smith* [2017] EWCA Civ 51, available at www.judiciary.gov.uk/wp-content/uploads/2017/02/pimlico-plumbers-v-smith.pdf; the Court of Appeal upheld the judgment of the Employment Appeal Tribunal, itself upholding the judgment of the Employment Tribunal.

[101] C McCoogan, 'Tribunal to rule on Deliveroo riders' employment status' *The Telegraph* (6 March 2017).

[102] S Gosh, 'Uber will offer insurance to UK drivers in case they are injured or sick' *Business Insider* (27 April 2017).

In France, the Paris Labour Tribunal (Prud'hommes) in December 2016 reclassified the relation between *LeCab* (one of *Uber's* competitors) and one of its drivers from a commercial to an employment contract.[103] This judgment, however, which concerned the individual driver, was to a large extent based on the exclusivity clause contained in the contract, a clause which has since been eliminated—and no longer figures in *Uber's* contracts. In view of this, in a special mediation concluded in February 2017, and in view of avoiding a collective finding that its drivers are all employees, *Uber* offered to provide transitional financial aid to its drivers in difficulty, thus simulating a minimum guaranteed income scheme.[104] Further, *Uber* won, on technical grounds concerning the administration of proof, a case brought against it by the Employees' Social Security Fund (URSSAF, Ile-de-France), whereby URSSAF was claiming the reclassification of *Uber* drivers and the payment of social security charges for them.[105] An appeal against this judgment, as well as URSSAF's criminal action against *Uber* for contribution-evasion,[106] are pending.

In Spain, on the other hand, the Second Commercial Tribunal of Madrid, in a judgment delivered in the framework of unfair competition (thus not specifically concerned with labour law relations) incidentally held that *BlaBlaCar* drivers—which contrary to *Uber's* go to their destination and only take 'passengers' in order to share the costs of the trip—are in no employment relationship with the platform.[107]

A preliminary question concerning the status of *Uber* drivers has been submitted to the CJEU by the Brussels District Commercial Court, only to be turned down by the CJEU as being inadmissible.[108] At the time of writing no other case concerning the (employment/freelancer) status of *Uber*—or any other collaborative platform's suppliers—was pending before the CJEU. This means that in the years to come, different Member State jurisdictions are likely to reach different conclusions on this issue: it is true that the evidence adduced and the arguments put forward by the Central London Employment Tribunal are difficult to ignore, but it is also true that national labour laws differ and that different collaborative platforms—and even *Uber* itself—use different agreements in different jurisdictions; the US experience briefly sketched above only confirms this danger. Therefore, the risks of fragmentation and of unjustified discrimination between people performing the same tasks (under contract law), and people harmed by those (under tort law—since vicarious or other strict liability applies to employers for the deeds of their employees), are present.

---

[103] C Crouzel, 'Pour la première fois, un chauffeur de VTC est reconnu salarié par la justice' *Le Figaro* (27 January 2017).

[104] 'VTC: la proposition d'Uber clôt la médiation' *Le Figaro* (7 February 2017).

[105] G Sebag, 'Uber Wins Driver-Status Case in France on Legal Technicality' *Bloomberg* (15 March 17).

[106] I de Foucaud, 'L'Urssaf lance une bataille juridique pour requalifier les chauffeurs Uber en "salarié 3"' *Le Figaro* (17 May 2016).

[107] *Confebus v BlablaCar* SJM M 6/2017 (2 February 2017) ECLI:ES:JMM:2017:6, 8.

[108] Case C-526/15 *Uber Belgium v Taxi Radio Bruxellois* EU:C:2016:830; for a brief discussion of this case see Ch 7 below.

C. The EU Commission's Approach

Such fragmentation and discrimination is undesirable not only in terms of national contract and tort law, but also—and more importantly—for the purposes of applying national and EU labour protection rules.[109] EU 'labour law' rules come into play when a 'worker' may be said to exist.[110] The Commission in its Collaborative Economy Communication has tried to illustrate the way in which the three criteria set out by the case law and the doctrine, ie the existence of subordination, the pursuance of genuine work and the existence of remuneration, apply in the collaborative economy.[111] In respect of the first criterion the Commission distinguishes situations where the platform determines the choice of the activity, remuneration and working conditions, from those where it merely processes the payment deposited by the receiver and passes it on to the provider. In relation to the second criterion the Commission distinguishes effective and genuine work from work which is purely marginal and accessory. Lastly, remuneration is used in order to differentiate work from volunteering.

The above criteria have been developed by the CJEU in order to define, in an extensive way, the scope of one of the fundamental freedoms, the free movement of workers. They are bound to lead to the qualification of an employment relationship in as many situations as possible. It is questionable, therefore, whether it is helpful/desirable to directly transpose them in the context of the collaborative economy, as they risk denaturing the essence of the relations there developed; by the same token it would risk creating a straightjacket to the further development of the collaborative economy. What is more, if such an over-expansive approach to the concept of 'worker' and 'employment' were to be followed it would lead to holding the platforms as employers in the vast majority of cases. This, however, would be directly contrary to the Commission's tendency described above, ie to apply very strict criteria for holding a platform as the supplier of the underlying service. In other words, if the Commission were to follow the criteria it has enunciated in its 2016 Communication, on the one hand it would find that most

---

[109] The fact that labour law remains essentially a matter of national regulation should not overshadow the fact that there are EU rules, inter alia, on working time (Directive 2003/88/EC), information on individual working conditions (Directive 91/533/EC), posted workers (Directives 96/71/EC, 2014/67/EU and Regulation 883/2004/EC), anti-discrimination for non-standard forms of employment (eg part-time, fixed-term or workers employed under temporary agencies, Directives 97/81/EC, 1990/70/EC and 2008/104/EC respectively), anti-discrimination on grounds of gender, ethnicity, sexual orientation (Directive 2000/78/EC), protection in case of insolvency of employers (Directive 2008/94/EC), protection in case of collective redundancies (Directive 98/59/EC), in case of transfer of undertakings (Directive 2001/23/EC) or in case of cross-border mergers (Directive 2005/56/EC).

[110] On working time see Case C-428/09 *Isère* EU:C:2010:612; on collective redundancies see Case C-229/14 *Balkaya* EU:C:2015:455; and on employment equality see Case C-432/14 *O* EU:C:2015:643.

[111] Commission Communication, 'A European Agenda for the collaborative economy' COM(2016) 356 final, 13.

platforms are mere intermediaries (since they do not own the assets etc) but, at the same time, they employ the suppliers of the underlying service. In this way the Commission would be taking with the one hand what it would be giving with the other in terms of the platforms' involvement and liability towards consumers. This inconsistency may be helping consumers, but it is certainly prejudicial to platforms which will not only be held liable towards the consumers, but will also be subject to the full constraints of labour legislation. Such an effect cannot possibly correspond to the Commission's intentions.

D. EU 'Labour Law' Secondary Legislation

Once a supplier in the collaborative economy does qualify as a worker, then s/he is subject to EU labour law rules.[112] From these EU rules of secondary legislation two, at least, merit special attention in the collaborative framework.

Firstly, the Working Time Directive (WTD), for the purposes of which it is crucial to identify which activities do count as working time. According to this text 'working time' is defined as 'any period during which the worker is working, at the employer's disposal and carrying out his activity or duties, in accordance with national laws and/or practice'.[113] Working time has been extensively construed by the CJEU to cover 'working time spent on call or on stand-by where the worker concerned must be physically present at his place of work',[114] in relation to medical doctors and firemen. Moreover, the Court has held that for those workers who do not have a fixed or habitual place of work, travelling to work at the beginning and the end of the day, is 'work'.[115] Further, the Court has held that Article 6(b) of the Directive, setting the maximum ceiling of hours that may be worked weekly at 48 hours, 'constitutes a rule of EU social law of particular importance from which any worker should benefit'[116] and, therefore, it may not validly be derogated to, even with the worker's consent.[117] Also, the Court has held that this same article has direct effect and may be invoked by individuals even where no such right is specifically accorded to them by national legislation.[118] Moreover, the Court has

---

[112] See above n 9.

[113] European Parliament and Council Directive 2003/88/EC of 4 November 2003 concerning certain aspects of the organisation of working time (Working Time Directive—WTD) [2003] OJ L 299/9; Art 2(1).

[114] See interpreting Directive 2003/88, Case C-429/09 *Fuss v Stadt Halle* EU:C:2010:717, para 55, with further references to Case C-303/98 *Simap* EU:C:2000:528, the order in Case C-241/99 *CIG* EU:C:2001:371, and the judgment in Case C-151/02 *Jaeger* EU:C:2003:437, all interpreting the previous WTD.

[115] Case C-266/14 *Fedéracion de servicios privados v Tyco* EU:C:2015:578.

[116] ibid para 33; see also para 49.

[117] ibid para 33; see also para 49.

[118] ibid para 35; see also para 49.

held that workers whose rights under the Directive have been violated may claim damages from their States.[119] Therefore, the Court is quite serious about having the rules on working time, especially Article 6(b), respected in all circumstances.

Would the above jurisprudence also cover on-demand workers available on-call—but not on a shift basis, while waiting in their own homes or private cars?[120] Would it cover only the seconds, minutes or hours that crowdworkers spend performing the actual task assigned to them? Or would it also cover the time they spend waiting for a call, preparing their offer or commuting between different tasks? Would the communication, exchange of information, time spent in rating users etc be accounted for? Further, given that the 48-hour limit imposed by the WTD encompasses work offered for any number of employers, multi-homing, in the way Jennifer Guidry does, would need to be accounted for. These are issues which will certainly need to be answered once it is recognised that crowdworkers are 'workers' in the sense of EU law.

The second big question is to know which Directive (or indeed Directives) on NSW are applicable to collaborative workers: both the Fixed Term Work Directive[121] and the Part-Time Work Directive[122]—and occasionally also the Temporary Work Agency Directive[123]—could be applied to platforms and their workers. It is true that all three directives are animated by the same objective, ie to make sure that workers falling within their respective scope are not ill-treated and discriminated against. It is also true, however, that their actual form (the first two give binding force to an agreement previously reached by the social partners, while the latter is in the form of a 'traditional' European Parliament and Council Directive), their timing and their content differ to a large extent. It is also true that while collaborative working has many resemblances to the above forms of NSW, it is nonetheless different from any of them. Therefore, it would be important for workers in the collaborative economy to know which text/s of secondary legislation, if any, they may validly invoke in their relations with platforms.

---

[119] ibid various paras and operative part.

[120] At present the answer seems to be in the negative; according to a briefing circulated by the UK public service Union, 'when workers are on-call but based at home or somewhere other than their workplace, on-call time only counts as working time from the time they are called out'; see Unison, 'Working Time Directive—On Call and Sleeping In' (2013), available at www.unison.org.uk/content/uploads/2013/06/Briefings-and-CircularsWorking-Time-Directive-On-call-and-Sleeping-in-ver12.pdf; while according to RMT, Britain's specialist Transport Union, working time does not include time spent on-call unless actually working, see RMT, 'Working Time Regulations—Your Questions Answered', available at www.rmt.org.uk/about/policies/research/employment-law/working-time-regulations-your-questions-answered/?preview=true.

[121] Council Directive 1990/70/EC of 28 June 1999 concerning the framework agreement on fixed-term work concluded by ETUC, UNICE and CEEP [1995] OJ L 175/43.

[122] Council Directive 97/81/EC of 15 December 1997 concerning the Framework Agreement on part-time work concluded by UNICE, CEEP and the ETUC [1998] OJ L 14/9.

[123] European Parliament and Council Directive 2008/104/EC of 19 November 2008 on temporary agency work [2008] OJ L 327/9. This is supposed to apply to 'contracts of employment or employment relationships with temporary agency workers in order to assign them to user undertakings to work there temporarily under their supervision and direction', see Directive 2008/104, Art 3(1)(b).

IV. Beyond the Binary Logic: Tentative Regulatory Interventions

From all the above it becomes clear that, while some suppliers in the collaborative economy make easy money with little effort, truly valorising their idle capacity—or that of their homes—others struggle under inhuman conditions to make ends meet. Most of the latter do not qualify as 'employees', as this legal category is currently defined by most legal orders, and may not claim the corresponding rights. In the meantime, courts on both sides of the Atlantic are struggling to square new realities with old rules, in an unforeseeable and, necessarily, contradictory manner, thus resolving some problems but creating new ones.

This, in turn, begs the question whether it would be worth discussing specific 'employment' rules, applicable in the field of the collaborative economy. If the survey according to which the collaborative economy only employs 0.4 per cent in the US and 0.05 per cent of the workforce is accurate, then the simple answer would be that such an initiative seems premature.[124] If, however, other surveys showing much higher percentage of the labour force (up to 9 per cent)[125] involved into collaborative activities are closer to reality, and in view of the sharp yearly increase of both people working in, and revenue generated from the collaborative economy, a different approach may be justified.

More than the numbers, however, what needs to be addressed is the more fundamental question: are we ready to endorse the substitution of people working normal hours under normal conditions with workers like Jennifer?[126] Or, to use Cherry's words, 'the question is whether the crowdwork model that the on-demand economy moves us into is a sustainable and desirable future for work'.[127]

Most authors agree that some kind of regulatory intervention should take place. The second thing they mostly agree upon is that, in the 'employees or nothing at all' dilemma, collaborative workers should not be fully assimilated as 'employees'. Several arguments are put forward to that effect: that this would be discriminatory against other, part-time or else temporary workers;[128] that it would be unjustifiably stretching legal categories;[129] that it would be difficult to implement;[130] that it would not correspond to the 'workers' state of mind, since a large proportion remain as occasional suppliers;[131] that it would put unjustifiable

---

[124] V Hatzopoulos and S Roma, 'Caring for Sharing? The Collaborative Economy under EU Law' (2017) 54 *CMLR* 81, 119.

[125] See n 14 above.

[126] See also Das Acevedo (n 2) 35.

[127] Cherry (n 26) 27.

[128] Das Acevedo (n 2) 32.

[129] ibid.

[130] ibid.

[131] M Cohen and A Sundararajan, 'Self-Regulation and Innovation in the Peer-to-Peer Sharing Economy' (2015) 82 *The University of Chicago Law Review Dialogue* 116, 122–23.

costs on the platforms and would endanger their very business model.[132] All the authors just cited are US-based; the UK House of Commons, in its 2017 Report on 'Self-employment and the Gig Economy', on the other hand, recommends that 'an assumption of the employment status of "worker" by default, rather than "self-employed" by default, would protect both those workers and the public purse'.[133] Therefore, this perceived 'unanimity' among authors needs to be relativised, and possibly reviewed, in the EU context.

Agreement among the authors stops there. Several ideas have been put forward by them, which are briefly discussed below.

One idea that seems to have wide support is that of creating a new, intermediary, special status for collaborative economy workers, between employees and independent contractors: that of the 'dependent contractor'.[134] This status would have some basic rights (eg basic expenses connected to the activity, mandatory insurance), but not others (eg social security) and would strike a middle way between workers' protection and platforms' interests. Carboni, and Harris and Krueger, carry out a comparative analysis and find that such a third category already exists, in different versions, in Italy (para-subordinate), Germany, France (micro-entrepreneur), Spain (economically dependent autonomous employee) and Canada. Those authors do concede, however, that these institutions are subject to critique in their respective legal orders. The main critique of this proposal is that it would cover more people, but would create fresh grey areas at the edges of this new category.[135] Moreover, it would put at peril the status of several people currently classified as 'employees'.[136]

A second idea is that of 'portability' of welfare rights:[137] instead of being dependent on employers, personal security accounts should be made portable.

---

[132] On this point see, among others, Codagnore, Abadie and Biagi (n 4) 50, who explain that a regulatory solution mid-way between the complete lack of protection and the judicial recognition of a full employee status would be much preferable.

[133] See n 63 above; it should be further noted that this Report is highly critical of the practices and contractual clauses used by platforms in relation to suppliers working for them.

[134] SD Harris and AB Krueger, 'A Proposal for Modernizing Labor Laws for Twenty-First Century Work: The "Independent Worker"' (2015) The Hamilton Project Discussion Paper 2015-10, available at www.hamiltonproject.org/assets/files/modernizing_labor_laws_for_twenty_first_century_work_krueger_harris.pdf; A Hagiu and R Biederman, 'Companies Need an Option Between Contractor and Employee' *Harvard Business Review* (21 August 2015), available at https://hbr.org/2015/08/companies-need-an-option-between-contractor-and-employee; Carboni (n 2); A Bolton, 'Regulating Ride-Share Apps: A Study on Tailored Reregulation Regarding Transportation Network Companies, Benefiting Both Consumers and Drivers' (2015) 46(1) *Cumberland Law Review* 101, 141–42.

[135] See Codagnore, Abadie and Biagi (n 4) 50; and V De Stefano, 'The rise of the "just-in-time workforce": On-demand work, crowdwork and labour protection in the "gig-economy"' (2016) ILO, Conditions of work and employment series No 71, 19 available at http://www.ilo.org/travail/whatwedo/publications/WCMS_443267/lang--en/index.htm.

[136] De Stefano, 'The rise of the "just-in-time workforce": On-demand work, crowdwork and labour protection in the "gig-economy"' (2016) 20.

[137] J Berg, 'Income Security in the On-Demand Economy: Findings and Policy Lessons from a Survey of Crowdworkers' (2016) 37(3) *Comparative Labor Law and Policy Journal* 543; Harris and Krueger, 'A Proposal for Modernizing Labor Laws for Twenty-First Century Work: The "Independent Worker"' (2015); Aloisi (n 61).

'Benefits (wage insurance, health insurance, disability and injuries insurance) should be designed universally and not being tied to specific employers'.[138]

> Every worker would hold an account regardless of the number of businesses they work for or the nature of the contractual agreement. For each job, the client would have to pay a proportion of the earnings into this account, thus having the same obligation vis-à-vis its platform workers as with its employees.[139]

The OECD in its 2016 Report on 'New Forms of Work in the Digital Economy'[140] seems to be embracing this solution, and one would have thought that the EU— used as it is to the principle of social security portability through Regulations 1408/71 and 883/2004—would do so too.

A report prepared by the Research Service of the European Parliament, however, mooted the idea of including collaborative economy service providers in the scope of the general rules applicable to self-employment and allowing platforms to develop their own benefits policies in competition with other insurance options otherwise available.[141]

With the same logic, but pushing it further, others have proposed to set a time-constrained 'safe harbour' for platforms to develop their own protective policies before imposing any rules on them.[142]

Apart from this last option, all other proposals argue in favour of some regulatory intervention in order to make sure that the collaborative economy does not lead to an employment middle-ages, but does indeed manage to deliver most of its potential, not only for consumers and firms, but also for those who make it happen.

Further, according to the European Commission JRC report,[143] endorsed by the EP report,[144] a Fair and Dignified Support Infrastructure should be adopted which should include the following pillars:[145] (a) minimum wage, coupled with maximum number of hours worked per day and a prohibition on deactivating worker's accounts if their acceptance rate falls; (b) a minimal form of social protection and health insurance; (c) liability insurance for damage to third parties; (d) regulation of privacy protection; and (e) algorithms that do not produce discrimination. Further ideas, such as the prohibition of exclusivity clauses, thus allowing multi-homing, and the non-applicability of cartel prohibitions in order to enable platform workers to coordinate have been put forward.

Many of these issues are further discussed in Chapter 7 below.

---

[138] Codagnore, Abadie and Biagi (n 4) 51, with reference to Berg and other sources.
[139] Schmid-Drüner (n 17) 21, also with reference to Berg.
[140] OECD (n 5) 30–31.
[141] P Goudin, 'The Cost of Non-Europe in the Sharing Economy: Economic, Social and Legal Challenges and Opportunities' (2016) European Parliament, European Parliamentary Research Service, available at www.europarl.europa.eu/RegData/etudes/STUD/2016/558777/EPRS_STU(2016)558777_EN.pdf.
[142] A Sundararajan, *The Sharing Economy, The End of Employment and the Rise of Crowd-Based Capitalism* (Cambridge MA, The MIT Press, 2016).
[143] Codagnore, Abadie and Biagi (n 4) 58.
[144] Schmid-Drüner (n 17) 7.
[145] These are freely represented here.

6

Dispute Resolution

I. Introduction

Complex legal issues, novel problems, ambiguous relations, fragmented regulation and battles of users with platforms for undertaking responsibility: all of these call for effective and flexible dispute resolution mechanisms. The collaborative economy is based on trust. Thus, apart from effective preventive measures, such as reputation systems and other self-regulatory mechanisms, it is also necessary to provide for effective and 'fit' dispute resolution systems that will provide redress to those aggrieved.

Due to the multi-faceted character of the collaborative economy, the avenues for dispute resolution depend on several factors: the business model of the collaborative platform; the parties to the dispute; the identity of the aggrieved (eg consumer or provider, freelancer or worker), and so forth.

Firstly, disputes could emerge between peers with regard to the performance of the underlying service. As opposed to sale of goods, the performance of services entails more factors that can go wrong and disputes are bound to occur. For example, an *Airbnb* host could forget to let the guest into the apartment on time, resulting in the guest staying at a hotel for the first night in town, a babysitter at *TaskRabbit* could accidentally break a high-value vase, an *Uber* driver could have an accident during an *Uber* ride, a customer at *Fiverr* could claim that the designing services ordered were of poor quality and thus end up not paying the designer for the project, and the list goes on.

Secondly, disputes could occur between peers with regard to participation on the platform, namely with regard to the reputation system. For example, an *Uber* driver could receive a wrongful or unfair review that his driving was reckless, thus causing the deactivation of his account by *Uber*; an *Airbnb* guest could post a review containing sensitive personal information about the host, and so on.

Thirdly, disputes in the collaborative economy could be between peers and platforms, concerning the platform's intermediary services. Peers could, therefore, potentially claim the platform was liable for misleading or insufficient information, unfair Terms and Conditions, unlawful data processing, insufficient background checks etc.

Fourthly, platform and peers could be parties to disputes arising from the underlying service, considering that the role of the platform is as yet hazy, and relationships are still undefined. Thus, peers could be claiming employment benefits from the platform or claim the latter's exclusive or shared liability for the performance of the underlying service.

Fifth, third parties influenced by the collaborative economy, such as *Airbnb* neighbours or competitive unions and associations, could be involved in dispute resolution with either collaborative platforms and/or peers.

These are only a few examples of disputes potentially arising in the collaborative economy. Such disputes can be resolved either through traditional judicial dispute resolution, or through alternative and online dispute resolution mechanisms. These are most likely to be approached in reverse order. The collaborative economy offers the perfect ground for examining disputes in the digital era and further promotes embedded dispute resolution systems. Further, the platform economy raises all the difficulties of private international law connected to internet transactions, with the additional difficulties that these are multi-sided markets and that it is not clear which party, if any, is a consumer. In what follows, the most common disputes arising in the collaborative economy are discussed, ie mainly of civil and/or commercial nature, while discussion of other more rare disputes, such as criminal cases, are outside the scope of the present chapter.

II. Judicial Dispute Resolution

The traditional avenue for disputes such as those described above is none other than litigation. Indeed, collaborative economy disputes have reached both national courts and the CJEU. Class action lawsuits have been brought to national courts, particularly for the 'reclassification' of collaborative economy participants (eg *Uber* drivers) as employees, while unions and individuals have also resorted to litigation to protect their rights and interests.[1]

A. Applicable Law and Jurisdiction

Due to the cross-border—and sometimes global—reach of collaborative platforms, the applicable laws governing the disputes arising and the courts' jurisdiction are not always apparent. While in some disputes between peers the local element is predominant, in others, as many as five jurisdictions and applicable legal regimes may be relevant; parties to the transaction may each reside in different countries (or continents for that matter), while the platform is headquartered in another

---

[1] See Ch 5 above.

country (typically in the US) and maintains some sort of establishment in an EU Member State (eg Ireland for *Airbnb*, the Netherlands for *Uber*) and runs subsidiary local branches. Further, the lines between online and offline disputes are often intertwined, thus causing headaches for all parties involved and most importantly peers, who may suddenly find themselves involved in cross-border, lengthy and costly judicial proceedings. The most complex problems arguably arise in Online Labour Markets (OLMs),[2] such as for example, providing writing or translation services through *Freelancer* or *Upwork*, due to the fact that the provision of the service happens 'online' rather than in a specific country.[3] In such a complex system, the applicable law and jurisdiction further depend on which parties are involved and how their respective role is outlined within the tripartite collaborative relationship, as discussed in Chapter 2 above.

i. Disputes between Peers

As explained below,[4] disputes between peers and the platform are often largely governed by the choice of law and jurisdiction inserted in the Terms or else Agreement of the platform with its users. Transactions between peers will rarely (if ever) involve such a choice, let alone in writing, while the platform generally does not set any terms for disputes between users.[5] In that respect, private international law, namely the rules of Brussels I Regulation (recast)[6] on jurisdiction and the rules of the Rome I Regulation on applicable law[7] provide valuable guidance.

The most salient issue arises in terms of contractual obligations and largely depends on the characterisation of the parties involved. Generally speaking, the party that qualifies as a 'consumer' will be entitled to the more favourable rules on jurisdiction and applicable law. Therefore, the key question of which party qualifies as a professional (trader) and which as a consumer comes to haunt us once again (see Chapter 2). Three scenarios are prevalent.

---

[2] For further analysis on MLMs and OLMs see Ch 5 above.

[3] Such issues in the context of online transactions are well documented; see inter alia LE Gillies, *Electronic Commerce and International Private Law, A Study of Electronic Consumer Contracts* (Hampshire, Ashgate, 2008); FF Wang, *Internet Jurisdiction and Choice of Law: Legal Practises in the EU, US and China* (New York, Cambridge University Press, 2010).

[4] See section II.A.ii immediately below.

[5] Some collaborative platforms provide online dispute resolution mechanisms, as discussed in section V.B below, but they have little or no contribution to peers' judicial dispute resolution.

[6] European Parliament and Council Regulation (EU) No 1215/2012 of 12 December 2012 on jurisdiction and the recognition and enforcement of judgments in civil and commercial matters (Brussels I Regulation (recast)) [2012] OJ L 351/1. The recast Regulation applies to legal proceedings instituted on or after 10 January 2015, while the repealed Regulation applies to judgments given in proceedings instituted before that date (Art 66).

[7] European Parliament and Council Regulation (EC) No 593/2008 of 17 June 2008 on the law applicable to contractual obligations (Rome I Regulation) [2008] OJ L 177/6.

Firstly, both the supplier and the recipient of the underlying service act within their trade or profession, ie not as consumers, and are therefore in a B2B contractual relationship. Being in a B2B relationship, the two parties are, generally speaking, free to choose a jurisdiction for any contractual claims that may come up. However, in practice collaborative participants rarely (if ever) discuss, decide upon and designate jurisdiction. The provision of such freelance services usually takes place in a fast-paced, informal environment with little communication prior to the conclusion of the contract. For example, freelance writers or designers on *Freelance* or *Fiverr* do not normally enter into much discussion with their clients about the terms for the provision of their services and even less so about the jurisdiction and applicable law in case of future disputes. In that event, the applicable law is that of the country where the service provider habitually resides,[8] regardless of whether that country is an EU Member State or not.[9] Further, the 'special jurisdiction' of matters relating to a contract of the Brussels I Regulation (recast) fall into play.[10] Thus, either one of the parties can be sued in the Member State where 'the services were provided or should have been provided'.[11] This is a contentious issue in the provision of online services, since there are three possible jurisdictions: the place of uploading, the place of downloading, and 'the closest connecting factor'.[12] Most likely the place where the services are (or should have been) provided is the place of downloading, ie the Member State where the recipient is domiciled, since this solution better reflects the objective of the contract.[13] This is particularly burdensome for suppliers who, under this provision, may be sued in the Member State of the consumer's residence.

Secondly, provided that a 'consumer contract' has been concluded, and in the absence of any choice of applicable law and prorogation of jurisdiction, the relevant special protective provisions for 'consumers contracts' shall be triggered[14] so as to offer added protection to the consumer, who presumably is the weaker party. This will be the case if the contract is concluded between: (a) a natural person who acts for purposes outside of his/her trade or profession, ie the consumer; and (b) 'a person who pursues commercial or professional activities in the Member State of the consumer's domicile or, by any means, directs such activities to that Member State or to several States including that Member State, and the contract

---

[8] Rome I Regulation 593/2008, Art 4(b).

[9] ibid Art 2.

[10] Brussels I Regulation (recast) 1215/2012, Art 7(1).

[11] ibid point (b), in the case of the provision of services.

[12] See Wang, *Internet Jurisdiction and Choice of Law: Legal Practises in the EU, US and China* (2010) esp 53–57.

[13] Similarly on the determination of the place of performance of obligation in the case of delivery of goods see Case C-381/08 *Car Trim* EU:C:2010:90; for a more extensive analysis of this issue and the relevant case law see D Vrbljanac, 'International jurisdiction for Internet disputes arising out of the contractual obligations' *Proceedings, 6th International Conference on Information Law & Ethics (ICIL 2014): Lifting the Barriers to Empower the Future of Information Law & Ethics* (Thessaloniki, University of Macedonia Press, 2015).

[14] Rome I Regulation 593/2008, Art 6 and Brussels I Regulation (recast) 1215/2012, Section 4.

falls within the scope of such activities'.[15] In that case the supplier (eg freelance writer) qualifies as a person 'pursuing or directing' his or her commercial or professional activities towards the recipient's Member State,[16] while the recipient qualifies as a consumer (B2C).[17] If these conditions are met, then the consumer will be protected by the special provisions; the dispute will be governed by the law of the consumer's country of residence and the consumer will be able to commence proceedings either before the courts of the Member State where the supplier (defendant) is domiciled or, before the courts of the Member State where the consumer is domiciled, even if the supplier is non-EU domiciled.[18] Further, the supplier may bring proceedings against the consumer only before the courts of the Member State where the consumer is domiciled.[19] In practical terms this means that an occasional freelancer on *Fiverr* providing writing, editing, translating and similar services could be sued in another Member State under the law of that country and that s/he would only be able to sue the consumer in the latter's Member State.

Thirdly, both parties to the dispute act outside their profession/trade, ie they are consumers, and their relationship is a C2C one. In that case, since both parties fall in the same category and presumably possess similar skills, knowledge and experience, the reasons for the special protection of the rules governing 'consumer contracts' are absent, and their relationship will governed by the general rules on contracts, as in a B2B relationship. Therefore, the above analysis under the first scenario applies here as well.

From the above, it is clear that different rules apply to collaborative suppliers depending on whether they act within or outside their trade/profession. The CJEU jurisprudence shows that the special protection is not be offered where it is not justified.[20] Thus, it has been adjudicated that 'those provisions cover only a private final consumer, not engaged in trade or professional activities',[21] involved in a transaction not 'having any connection whatever with his trade or profession'.[22]

---

[15] Art 17(1)(c).

[16] On the concept of 'directing activities' see Vrbljanac, 'International jurisdiction for Internet disputes arising out of the contractual obligations' (2015) at 2.2, and the case law analysed therein.

[17] On rarer occasions it is possible that the supplier will be treated as a mere 'prosumer', while on the receiving end the client is a company acting within the purposes of its commercial/professional activities (C2B).

[18] This is one of the main changes that the updated Brussels I Regulation (recast) 1215/2012 brings; see Arts 6(1) and 18(1).

[19] Art 19 allows an agreed upon forum, but only in view of an agreement '(1) which is entered into after the dispute has arisen; (2) which allows the consumer to bring proceedings in courts other than those indicated in this Section; or (3) which is entered into by the consumer and the other party to the contract, both of whom are at the time of conclusion of the contract domiciled or habitually resident in the same Member State, and which confers jurisdiction on the courts of that Member State, provided that such an agreement is not contrary to the law of that Member State'.

[20] See Case C-89/91 *Shearson Lehman Hutton v TVB* EU:C:1993:15; Case C-269/95 *Benincasa v Dentalkit* EU:C:1997:337; Case C-96/00 *Gabriel* EU:C:2002:436; Case C-27/02 *Engler* EU:C:2005:33.

[21] Case C-96/00 *Gabriel*, para 39.

[22] ibid para 47.

In *Gruber*, the CJEU ruled that the special protection of the Brussels I Regulation should not be extended to persons concluding a contract for purposes partly within and partly outside their trade or profession, 'unless the trade or professional purpose is so limited as to be negligible in the overall context of the supply, the fact that the private element is predominant being irrelevant in that respect'.[23] In view of this strict interpretation of 'consumer contracts', collaborative economy suppliers will probably be treated as acting within their profession/trade, even though in practice they may be mere prosumers providing occasional services, who lack expertise, legal and business knowledge and professional resources.

ii. Disputes between Peers and the Platform

Disputes are bound to arise between peers and platforms either with respect to the intermediary services or the nature of the contractual relationship (eg employment or not) or even the underlying service (eg shared liability).

Unlike contracts between peers, contracts of peers with most (or at least the most well-known) platforms usually include clauses on applicable law and court jurisdiction. These clauses generally favour platforms, are included within their Terms and Conditions and usually reflect the place where they are established or else operate through some sort of offices. For example, *Airbnb*, for EU residents, designates Irish law as the applicable law and jurisdiction of Irish courts, while *Uber* designates Dutch law and Amsterdam as the place for its dispute resolution proceedings.

However, the free designation of applicable law and jurisdiction by collaborative platforms does not hinder consumers' rights according to national (and implemented EU) laws. Under Article 6(2) of the Rome I Regulation, consumers enjoy the protection afforded to them under the mandatory provisions of national laws, regardless of the choice of law.

Here again the rules governing the applicable law and the jurisdiction will be dependent on the identity of the peer. As *Airbnb* state:[24]

> If you are acting as a consumer, you agree to submit to the non-exclusive jurisdiction of the Irish courts. Judicial proceedings that you are able to bring against us arising from or in connection with these Terms may only be brought in a court located in Ireland or a court with jurisdiction in your place of residence. If Airbnb wishes to enforce any of its rights against you as a consumer, we may do so only in the courts of the jurisdiction in which you are a resident. If you are acting as a business, you agree to submit to the exclusive jurisdiction of the Irish courts.

---

[23] Case C-464/01 *Gruber* EU:C:2005:32.
[24] Clause 21.3 of the Terms of Service as of the time of writing, available at www.airbnb.com/terms#sec19.

This means that final recipients of the services will certainly be considered as consumers and therefore will benefit from the additional protection. The same goes for service suppliers who qualify as prosumers. On the other hand, service suppliers who qualify as professionals (businesses) will be bound by exclusive jurisdiction of the Irish courts.

Another issue that should be highlighted concerns jurisdiction and applicable law over individual contracts of employment. As explained in the previous chapter, the question of whether collaborative 'workers' are employees or not is as yet unresolved. However, there are indications and case law that point to the existence of an employment relationship with the platform, especially in the transportation sector. Provided that this is the case, then collaborative 'employees' will further benefit from the protective rules of the Brussels I Regulation (recast)[25] and the Rome I Regulation.[26] It is worth mentioning that in that event, the choice of law is of limited effect, since derogation from the protective rules is only allowed after the dispute has arisen or if the agreement allows additional jurisdiction/s for the employee.[27]

B. Is Judicial Dispute Resolution Fit for the Collaborative Economy?

The complexity of the issues discussed above acts as a disincentive for platform users to pursue redress through courts. In reality, litigation is probably the least convenient avenue for those aggrieved and in most cases is not fit for the collaborative economy. Participation in court proceedings is costly and time-consuming and therefore burdensome for most consumers. Especially considering the small amounts involved in most disputes in the collaborative economy and the high costs of litigation, 'the cost of legal redress by litigation is not proportionate to the value of the claim'.[28] It is therefore consequent that peers will most likely not seek redress through courts, even if that means that their loss will not be reimbursed. Further, the above difficulties deriving from the cross-border nature of the disputes, the distance between the parties to the disputes, language barriers and the disincentive to get involved in cross-border court proceedings would deter collaborative peers from resorting to judicial dispute resolution. In that regard also, enforcement will be equally difficult, since transactions in the collaborative economy occur between strangers, who can easily 'disappear' if things go wrong.

---

[25] Section 5.
[26] Art 8.
[27] Brussels I Regulation (recast) 1215/2012, Art 23.
[28] J Hörnle, 'Online dispute resolution in business to consumer e-commerce transactions' (2002) 2 *Journal of Information, Law & Technology (JILT)*, available at http://www2.warwick.ac.uk/fac/soc/law/elj/jilt/2002_2/hornle/#a2.7.

Moreover, traditional judicial justice cannot endorse the tripartite collaborative relationship. For example, the placement of burden of proof on the supplier in a dispute with a consumer would be unfair in view of the platform's control and the information asymmetries therein; *Uber* drivers would be unable to defend themselves in a dispute concerning the fare, as the relevant information on the algorithmic decision-making lays with the platform.[29] Last but not least, the adversarial nature of litigation is at odds with the friendly, community-promoting model of the collaborative economy, especially where there is no exchange of money. Courts are therefore a rather hostile forum for those peers who swap tools or books, share their kitchen or perform tasks for each other in a time-bank platform and so on.[30] Litigation, therefore, is in most cases probably 'the last resort', if alternative and/or online dispute resolution means are exhausted. All these point to the need for effective alternative resolution mechanisms. At the same time, courts are likely to be of help only in a restricted number of cases, namely high monetary value disputes and disputes between parties residing in the same Member State.

III. Alternative Dispute Resolution

In view of the unsuitable nature of judicial justice, it may be beneficial for both platforms and peers to have another avenue by which to resolve their conflicts outside the courtrooms. Therefore, without prejudice to the right of users to proceed to trial if they wish to, or if a solution is not reached by any other option, alternative dispute resolution (ADR) could be a valuable outlet for the collaborative economy. Of course, due to the highly diversified nature of disputes in the collaborative economy, the standard claim of a need for a case-by-case analysis applies, meaning that users' rights under different circumstances may be best protected in court or through other alternative systems.

Arbitration is generally preferred by platforms, for it allows them to treat every dispute individually, as opposed to having to challenge class-action lawsuits. It is less costly and more efficient. Further, arbitration decisions are binding in the sense that there is no subsequent recourse to litigation, while at the same time they do not set legal precedent for future disputes and therefore different users fighting the same issue can achieve different outcomes. Most platforms include in their Terms & Conditions provisions concerning mandatory[31] or optional arbitration and/or mediation.

---

[29] R Calo and A Rosenblat, 'The Taking Economy: Uber, Information, and Power' (2017) 117 *Columbia Law Review* 1623; University of Washington School of Law Research Paper No 2017-08; available at https://ssrn.com/abstract=2929643, 33.

[30] Especially with regard to dispute resolution in those small-sized, true sharing economy models (SEMs): see H Scheiwe Kulp and AL Kool, 'You Help Me, He Helps You: Dispute Systems Design in the Sharing Economy' (2015) 48 *Washington University Journal of Law & Policy* 179.

[31] Such clauses are contentious in both the US and the EU, as explained in section IV below.

While the ADR Directive[32] offers opportunities for the resolution of disputes in C2B relations, it does not apply to B2B or C2C transactions, since it only covers disputes between traders and consumers. This means that a large number of collaborative transactions will fall outside its scope, as constituting either B2B relationships,[33] when the supplier qualifies as a service provider and disputes with the platform, or C2C,[34] when the supplier qualifies as a mere prosumer and his/her interests collide with the consumer's. It further does not cover proceedings initiated by a trader against a consumer, ie B2C relationships.[35] However, in the collaborative economy, suppliers (traders or prosumers) are equally—if not more so—prone to damages as consumers. The ADR Directive also only covers disputes between a consumer resident and a trader established somehow (through offices, agency, branch etc) in the EU. Therefore, this limited scope of the ADR Directive leads to fragmented and potentially unfair implementation of ADR rules across the EU with regard to collaborative activities.[36]

Moreover, even though ADR is generally more 'user-friendly', it is still not an 'exact fit' for the collaborative economy, as its effectiveness in protecting peers' rights is questionable. Firstly, out-of-court procedures such as mediation and arbitration are based on face-to-face interactions. Therefore, considering the cross-border nature of most collaborative transactions, the obstacle of location is a reality. For instance, *Uber* has determined Amsterdam as the place where its arbitration/mediation will take place. However, this would require peers to travel to the Netherlands, and thus investment of time and money.

Secondly, as platforms are the ones who dictate the terms of the dispute resolution system, they are in a position to 'award' themselves the discretion of deciding what type of ADR will be followed (mediation or arbitration) and on important parameters of the process. For example, in the case of arbitration, platforms can decide which arbitrator to use,[37] the rules according to which the arbitration will take place, the location of arbitration, the language of the process, allocation of expenses between parties, and so on. All these factors are expectedly significant for the very outcome, let alone the equality and fairness of the procedure, even before its commencement. In view of the limited bargaining position of peers, the enforcement of all the above factors unilaterally by the platform creates significant imbalance between the parties. This is enhanced in the case of those suppliers who qualify as businesses and are therefore stripped of any consumers' rights.

---

[32] European Parliament and Council Directive 2013/11/EU of 21 May 2013 on alternative dispute resolution for consumer disputes and amending Regulation (EC) No 2006/2004 and Directive 2009/22/EC (Directive on consumer ADR) [2013] OJ L 165/63.

[33] The Directive explicitly mentions that it does not apply to disputes between traders; Art 2(2)(d).

[34] Art 2(1).

[35] Art 2(2)(g).

[36] Health services, which are also part of the collaborative economy, are excluded from the scope of the ADR Directive as well.

[37] Such a practice was employed by *eBay* but was later corrected in order to be aligned with the rules on unfair terms; see C Riefa, *Consumer Protection and Online Auction Platforms: Towards a Safer Legal Framework* (New York, Routledge, 2016) 138–39.

Thirdly, the recent labour settlements that *Uber* was able to achieve through mandatory arbitration in the US have caused concerns that 'under current law arbitration effectively extinguishes important worker rights'.[38] Collective (or class-action) lawsuits, an important tool for protecting employment rights, are dismantled through arbitration.

On the opposite side of the collaborative economy, in those more 'informal' collaborative environments, such as community platforms for sharing among neighbours, swapping, lending etc, it has been argued that ADR, and more specifically mediation, is the best method of dispute resolution.[39] Due to the interpersonal nature of such interactions, mediation can offer the floor to parties for communicating their issues, adjusting their respective roles and responsibilities and resolving the dispute in an interactive way.

IV. Validity of Dispute Resolution Clauses Employed by Platforms

In their effort to manage millions of users globally, and to avoid finding themselves overwhelmed by a growing number of legal disputes, platforms employ various dispute resolution clauses to tip the scale in their favour and control somewhat the judicial proceedings against them. Some of these clauses are either in the grey zone of legality or categorically illegal.

To begin with, the validity of clauses restricting the users' rights to trial is questionable, especially considering that more often than not they are 'buried' in the fine print that users do not read. Terms are extremely lengthy, in a very small typesize and written in 'legalese', a language that most users find intimidating and confusing.[40] As such they may be held invalid under the consumer protection rules on unfair terms in consumer contracts, as discussed in Chapter 2.[41]

Further, these terms may not be easily accessible to the user. In that case, the specific form of the platform, ie whether it allows for 'click-wraps', 'browse-wraps',

---

[38] KVW Stone, 'Uber and arbitration: A lethal combination' *Economic Policy Institute, Working EconomicsBlog* (24 May 2016), available at www.epi.org/blog/uber-and-arbitration-a-lethal-combination.

[39] See Scheiwe, Kulp and Kool, 'You Help Me, He Helps You: Dispute Systems Design in the Sharing Economy' (2015) 226; see also J Orsi and E Doskow, *The Sharing Solution, How to Save Money, Simplify Your Life & Build Community* (US, Nolo, 2009) 108.

[40] As correctly put by Katsh and Rabinovich-Einy: 'It would not surprise us if the two authors of this book are the only humans (other than Airbnb's lawyers and employees) who have fully read these rules. This user agreement contains over 30,000 words. Much of it is in a very small font, essentially fine print in digital form'; see E Katsh and O Rabinovich-Einy, *Digital Justice: Technology and the Internet of Disputes* (New York, Oxford University Press, 2017) 69.

[41] Council Directive 93/13/EC of 5 April 1993 on unfair terms in consumer contracts (Unfair Terms Directive) [1993] OJ L 95/29.

'scrollwraps' or 'sign-in-wraps'[42] may lead to the conclusion that the user read and agreed to the Terms, or the opposite. In a preliminary ruling on the question whether 'click-wrapping', ie merely clicking on a hyperlink which opens a box with terms including an exclusive choice of forum, qualifies as 'communication' within the meaning of Brussels I Regulation,[43] the CJEU ruled in favour of the validity of such clauses.[44] However, it did so in a case involving a B2B online contract; therefore it is as yet uncertain whether the validity of such clauses can be claimed in B2C relationships.

Content-wise, these dubious clauses may include provisions for exclusive jurisdiction, mandatory arbitration, waiver of the right to participate in class-action lawsuits, unfair allocation of arbitration costs, withholding of the right to unilaterally modify the terms on dispute resolution, and so on.

Most notably, 'exclusive jurisdiction' clauses that array dispute resolution to specific courts, which are usually favourable to the platform but not to the consumer, may be unfair. This is especially so since the terms were not negotiated but rather were offered on a 'take it or leave it' basis. In that regard, the CJEU has ruled that:

> where a jurisdiction clause is included, without being individually negotiated, in a contract between a consumer and a seller or supplier within the meaning of the Directive and where it confers exclusive jurisdiction on a court in the territorial jurisdiction of which the seller or supplier has his principal place of business, it must be regarded as unfair within the meaning of Article 3 of the Directive in so far as it causes, contrary to the requirement of good faith, a significant imbalance in the parties' rights and obligations arising under the contract, to the detriment of the consumer.[45]

Another widely used dispute resolution clause is the agreement on mandatory arbitration. Many platforms require peers to agree (by accepting the platform's Terms while signing up) to resolve any future dispute through arbitration as opposed to in court. For example, *Airbnb* enforces an arbitration agreement on parties who: (a) reside in the United States; or (b) do not reside in the United

---

[42] Browse-wrap agreements usually include a hyperlink titled 'Terms and Conditions' or 'Terms of Use' etc and they do not require affirmative consent by the user. On the contrary, click-wraps require the user to click on a box under an expression such as 'I agree' or 'I agree on the Terms' etc or click on a hyperlink that opens a window. Scroll-wraps require the user to scroll through the Terms and click on an 'I agree' box to express his/her consent. Finally, sign-in wraps intertwine signing up for using the website's services with consent to the website's Terms. For further reading see ML Rustard, *Global Internet Law*, 2nd edn (US, Hornbook Series, 2016) 235–37; NS Kim, *Wrap Contracts: Foundations and Ramifications* (New York, Oxford University Press, 2013); and A Gatt, 'Electronic Commerce—Click Wrap Agreements, The Enforceability of Click-Wrap Agreements' (2002) 18(6) *Computer Law & Security Review* 404.

[43] Art 23(2).

[44] Case C-322/14 *El Majdoub* EU:C:2015:334.

[45] Joined Cases C-240/98 to C-244/98 *Océano Grupo Editorial and Salvat Editores* EU:C:2000:346, para 24; see also Case C-137/08 *VB Pénzügyi Lízing* EU:C:2010:659, para 54; Case C-237/02 *Freiburger Kommunalbauten* EU:C:2004:209 para 23; Case C-243/08 *Pannon GSM* EU:C:2009:350, paras 41–43.

States, but bring any claim against *Airbnb* in the United States. Similarly, *Upwork* states that '[t]his Mandatory Binding Arbitration and Class Action/Jury Trial Waiver provision ("Arbitration Provision") applies to all Users except Users located outside of the United States and its territories'. Most notably, *Uber's* Terms require users (even EU residents) to waive their right to trial and arbitrate any dispute that may occur between them and the platform concerning the Terms.[46] Such clauses may deprive consumers of their right to trial. Thus, despite their wide use by platforms, the validity of exclusive arbitration clauses, especially when agreed upon before any dispute arises, is contentious in the US and plainly forbidden in many EU jurisdictions.[47]

According to the Directive on unfair terms in consumer contracts, terms which have the object or the effect of 'excluding or hindering the consumer's right to take legal action or exercise any other legal remedy, particularly by requiring the consumer to take disputes exclusively to arbitration not covered by legal provisions' may be unfair.[48] Similarly, the Brussels I Regulation (recast) states that derogation from the jurisdiction laid down in consumer contracts before the dispute arises is void.[49]

In the EU such pre-dispute clauses are widely forbidden by Member States. The CJEU too has stated that national courts must be able to examine the unfairness of arbitration clauses even after the arbitration decision is final.[50]

In the US, *Uber's* arbitration clause has been dealt with inconsistently by courts.[51] However, it is interesting to note Judge Rakoff's reasons for denying *Uber's* motion to compel arbitration in the antitrust case *Meyer v Kalanick*.[52] The Judge stated that

> [w]hen contractual terms as significant as the relinquishment of one's right to a jury trial or even of the right to sue in court are accessible only via a small and distant hyperlink titled 'Terms of Service & Privacy Policy,' with text about agreement thereto

---

[46] For *Airbnb* see section 19 of its Terms, available at www.airbnb.com/terms#sec19. For *Upwork* see section 21.4 of *Upwork's* User Agreement (emphasis omitted), available at www.upwork.com/legal. For *Uber* see *Uber's* Terms, at point 6 on governing law and arbitration, available at www.uber.com/legal/terms/fr-en (as at July 2017).

[47] See, inter alia, P Cortés, *Online Dispute Resolution for Consumers in the European Union* (New York, Routledge, 2011) 107–12; see, inter alia, J Hörnle, 'Legal controls on the use of arbitration clauses in B2C e-commerce contracts' (2006) 8 *EBL* 8, 9; C Riefa, 'Uncovering the dangers lurking below the surface of European consumer arbitration' (2008) 4 *Consumer Journal* 24, 25; and by the same author, *Consumer Protection and Online Auction Platforms, Towards a Safer Legal Framework* (2016) 136–39.

[48] Unfair Terms Directive 93/13, Art 3(3) and Annex, 1(q).

[49] Art 19.

[50] See Case C-168/05 *Mostaza Claro* EU:C:2006:675, para 39; Case C-40/08 *Asturcom Telecommunicaciones* EU:C:2009:615, para 59.

[51] See T Higgins, K Mantoan and D Corbett, 'Uber Rolls Along, Despite Driver Challenges to its Arbitration Agreement' *Orrick Employment Law and Litigation Blog* (14 February 2017), available at http://blogs.orrick.com/employment/2017/02/14/uber-rolls-along-despite-driver-challenges-to-its-arbitration-agreement; see also T Dickerson, 'Uber On the Brink' *Law360 Expert Analysis* (8 May 2017), available at www.law360.com/articles/921141/uber-on-the-brink.

[52] For which see Ch 4 above from a competition law point of view.

presented even more obscurely, there is a genuine risk that a fundamental principle of contract formation will be left in the dust: the requirement for 'a manifestation of mutual assent'.[53]

Even in the case that an opt-out option is given to parties, as claimed by *Uber* in the US, such provisions are, in the words of Judge Chen, often 'inconspicuous, inadequately explained, and onerous to use'.[54]

In view of the above, '[r]estricting consumers to one form of redress in online contracts is a subtle but highly effective form of "digital injustice"'.[55] Indeed, even if they did read and accept the Terms, which is highly unlikely, consumers are generally unaware of and/or underestimate the significance of such pre-dispute arbitration clauses. As the weaker party, they typically cannot understand the practical implications arising from such a clause and their effects on them. Apart from end consumers, this may be true for collaborative economy suppliers as well, since their skills, knowledge and expertise do not differ significantly from those of mere consumers, even if they, for example, systematically rent out their apartment on *Airbnb*, or drive full-time for *Uber*.

V. Online Dispute Resolution

'No one—neither the courts, nor alternative processes—is prepared to handle the volume, variety, and character of disputes that are a by-product of the levels of creative and commercial activity happening online today'.[56] This is especially true in view of the mounting importance of the collaborative economy. It is estimated that the number of disputes from e-commerce disputes will rise to a billion disputes in a few years, in view of *Airbnb's*, *Uber's* and other platforms' growth.[57]

In that respect, it is widely argued that online—or even virtual—dispute resolution (ODR) is the future.[58] Indeed, the characteristics of ODR systems fit perfectly in the innovation brought by the collaborative economy. It capacitates resolution

---

[53] *Meyer v Kalanick*, Case 1:15-cv-09796-JSR Opinion and Order of 29 July 2016, 28. The question was brought—and was still pending at the time of writing—before the US Court of Appeals for the Second Circuit; see A Frankel, 'Uber's arbitration appeal at the 2nd Circuit is big test for Internet businesses' *Reuters* (30 November 2016).

[54] *Abdul Kadir Mohamed v Uber Technologies Inc*, Case No 15-16178, *Ronald Gillette v Uber Technologies Inc*, Case No 15-16181, and *Abdul Kadir Mohamed v Hirease LLC*, Case No 15-16250, in the US Court of Appeals for the Ninth Circuit.

[55] Katsh and Rabinovich-Einy, *Digital Justice, Technology and the Internet of Disputes* (2017) 46.

[56] ibid 14.

[57] ibid 67.

[58] See, inter alia, L Victor, 'Is Online Dispute Resolution the Wave of the Future?' *ABA Online Journal* (18 March 2015), available at www.abajournal.com/news/article/is_online_dispute_resolution_the_wave_of_the_future; E Katsh and C Rule, 'What We Know and Need to Know About Online Dispute Resolution' (2016) 67 *South Carolina Law Review* 329, 332.

of cross-border conflicts at a distance, without any inconvenience to the parties; it allows for utilisation of useful software applications, easily accessed and used by peers; it may make great use of the large databases already available in the digital sphere; and in general it has the capacity to yield technology to the service of justice. Besides, the online resolution of disputes generating from online activity seems highly appropriate. In some regards, ODR is to traditional justice systems what *Airbnb* is to the accommodation and *Uber* to the transportation industries; a fast, cheap and convenient alternative solution.[59] In fact, some collaborative platforms providing the forum and connecting peers in order to resolve their disputes have already emerged.[60] In that sense, ODR is part of the collaborative economy in the broader meaning.

A. EU ODR

In line with the European Regulation on ODR,[61] platforms must include in an easily accessible way an electronic link leading to the EU Commission's ODR platform.[62] Failure to do so may bring significant penalties and even prohibition from further trading online on the grounds of unfair competition.[63]

The ODR platform started operating in February 2016 and is still in its infancy. Thus, assessing its effectiveness for the collaborative economy is still premature.[64] However, two observations need to be made; firstly, the ODR Regulation (and the ODR platform) only apply to disputes between a trader and a consumer, which means that suppliers that qualify as professional service providers will be treated as traders with regard to the ODR and will not be able to resort to the ODR website to solve their complaints against the platform. Similarly, it mainly covers disputes initiated by consumers against a trader, and only rarely will it resolve disputes

---

[59] See RJ Condlin, 'Online Dispute Resolution: Stinky, Repugnant, or Drab' (2016) University of Maryland Francis King Carey School of Law Legal Studies Research Paper No 2016–40, available at http://ssrn.com/abstract=2873918.

[60] Such as eg *FairClaims*.

[61] European Parliament and Council Regulation (EU) No 524/2013 of 21 May 2013 on online dispute resolution for consumer disputes and amending Regulation (EC) No 2006/2004 and Directive 2009/22/EC (Regulation on consumer ODR) [2013] OJ L 165/1.

[62] ODR Regulation 524/2013, Art 14(1). The term 'easily accessible' is bound to cause controversy; is it sufficient to include the ODR link in the platform's Terms, usually at the bottom of a lengthy legal document, as eg *Airbnb* does?

[63] M Munz and S Lorenz, 'Online Traders: New Obligation in EU for Provision of Link to Online Dispute Resolution (ODR) Platform' *White & Case* (9 June 2016), available at hwww.whitecase.com/publications/article/online-traders-new-obligation-eu-provision-link-online-dispute-resolution-odr.

[64] As of the time of writing, no report has been issued from the Commission on the functioning of the platform. However, in its Press Release of 24 March 2017, 'Buying online and solving disputes online: 24,000 consumers used new European platform in first year', IP/17/727, the Commission comments on the positive results of the ODR platform and states that in the first year of its existence it has received 24,000 consumer complaints; however, no statistics are currently available on how many of them have actually been resolved.

initiated by traders,[65] even though—as noted above—this is highly usual in the collaborative economy. Secondly, the ODR Regulation and the EU ODR platform only apply when both the consumer and the trader are EU-based, meaning that if one of the parties to the dispute is domiciled (or is established) outside the EU, the platform cannot be used.[66] This limits significantly the application of the ODR platform in the collaborative economy. Therefore, despite the welcome innovation brought by the ODR Regulation, it still does not take into consideration the special relations of the collaborative economy.

B. Internal Platform Dispute Resolution

Most platforms boldly claim that they do not get involved in disputes between users. They rather follow a back-seat approach when it comes to conflicts between users, and encourage them to reach a solution on their own. Indicatively, *Kickstarter* in its Terms of Use highlights under the title 'Stuff We Don't Do and Aren't Responsible For' that the company does not become involved in or mediate disputes between users.[67] Platforms still aim to establish themselves as mere intermediaries that do not get involved in the activity of peers; however, in reality platforms go to great lengths to impose an array of self-regulation measures, they control important aspects of the transaction, such as payment, insurance, matching, promotion, training of suppliers, background checks, insurance and so on,[68] and they even participate (some more actively than others) in the provision of the underlying service. Another example of self-regulatory measures, is *Airbnb's* 24-hour refund policy, which prevents a vast majority of disputes from ever arising.[69] Thus, platforms have already endorsed some dispute prevention measures through self-regulation.[70] In the future, the need for further involvement of platforms in both the pre-dispute and the post-dispute phase will increase. As put by Rabinovich-Einy and Katsh,[71]

> Even for those platforms, which claim to occupy an intermediary role of 'merely' connecting users with one another, it is no longer tenable to keep them from addressing problems and complaints. Several of the large 'sharing economy' and social media

---

[65] Art 2(2) of the ODR Regulation 524/2013 states: 'This Regulation shall apply to the out-of-court resolution of disputes referred to in paragraph 1, which are initiated by a trader against a consumer, in so far as the legislation of the Member State where the consumer is habitually resident allows for such disputes to be resolved through the intervention of an ADR entity'.

[66] ODR Regulation 524/2013, Art 2(1).

[67] *Kickstarter*, Terms of Use, para 6, available at www.kickstarter.com/terms-of-use?ref=footer.

[68] See Ch 7 below.

[69] *Airbnb*, 'What is Airbnb's Guest Refund Policy?', available at www.airbnb.com/help/article/544/what-is-airbnb-s-guest-refund-policy.

[70] On the various measures used by platforms to ensure trust, prevent and resolve disputes, see O Lobel, 'The Law of the Platform' (2016) 101 *Minnesota Law Review* 87, 146–56.

[71] O Rabinovich-Einy and E Katsh, 'Access to Digital Justice: Fair and Efficient Processes for the Modern Age' (2017) 18 *Cardozo Journal of Conflict Resolution* 637, 645, notes omitted.

platforms have learned over time that they must address such problems if they are to keep their status as market leaders. Whether they do so in a manner that truly enhances access to digital justice is a key question for the future.

Indeed, platforms are in a unique position to assist parties to resolve their disputes. Even more so they are capable of complementing the self-regulatory measures put in place in order to prevent disputes. They are in possession of vast amounts of personal and non-personal data and they can design their algorithms with dispute prevention and resolution in mind. According to Katsh and Rabinovich-Einy[72]

> dispute prevention is also occurring at the data (or, Big Data) level, at the predispute resolution stage, and even at predispute phase, where data allows megaplatforms to structure interactions in a way that reduces the likelihood of disputes occurring. Airbnb, for example, may base its decision on which listings to display first, on data analysis that indicates that such transactions are less likely to generate problems.

Some collaborative platforms, and most notably *Airbnb*, have introduced in-house dispute resolution systems.[73] *Airbnb* encourages peers ('host' and 'guest' in its own terminology) to carve out a solution by themselves. They can do so through *Airbnb's* Resolution Center, whereby parties can submit their requests from the other party, such as for example requests for refunds, claim of the security deposit, request compensation for damages, and so on. If the parties are unable to come to an agreement within 72 hours from the request's submission, they may ask for *Airbnb* to step in. A member from the *Airbnb* team will then be involved in review-ing all the information provided by the parties and according to the platform's policies, the *Airbnb* 'arbitrator' will make a final decision.[74]

Apart from money-related matters, a major source of disputes in the collabora-tive economy concerns peer reviews. An unfair or untrue guest review significantly impacts on the host's reputation within the *Airbnb* community, challenges his/her status (eg 'super host') and reduces prospective revenue. *Airbnb* provides for a primitive resolution process concerning disputes over reviews, whereby '[i]f you disagree with a review your host wrote about you, you can write a response that will post directly below the review and will be visible by the rest of the *Airbnb* community'.[75] *Airbnb's* arbitration process can only be employed after 14 days of trying to resolve the dispute. *Airbnb* does not edit, delete or censor reviews, unless they violate the platform's content policy.

---

[72] Katsh and Rabinovich-Einy (n 40) 72.

[73] *eBay* is a pioneer in establishing an internal dispute resolution process, with its highly successful 'community court', which processes an impressive number of over 60 million disputes a year, 'essentially making it the largest small claims court in the world'; see E Katsh and O Rabinovich-Einy, 'Dispute Resolution in the Sharing Economy' (2014) in U Gasser et al, *Internet Monitor 2014: Reflections on the Digital World: Platforms, Policy, Privacy, and Public Discourse*, Research Publication No 2014-17, 59.

[74] *Airbnb*, 'What is the Resolution Center', available at www.airbnb.com/help/article/767/what-is-the-resolution-center?locale=en.

[75] *Airbnb*, 'How do I handle a disagreement with my host after a trip?', available at www.airbnb.com/help/article/1423/how-do-i-handle-a-disagreement-with-my-host-after-a-trip?topic=203.

The benefits of internal platform ODR are potentially great. Firstly, it gives peers an equal standing, in that final consumers, as well as prosumers and service providers, can seek dispute resolution under the same terms. While in all other dispute resolution systems, the service providers are faced with reduced protection, internal platform ODR can accommodate perfectly the special tripartite relations of the collaborative economy, thus providing a system 'tailored' to the needs of the peers. Secondly, it can restore trust to peers that if a dispute arises, their damage will be remedied. Thirdly, in-platform ODR is fast, cheap and easy to access, and alleviates difficulties created from the cross-border nature of the transactions.

Even though such initiatives offer great opportunities, they still need refinement. For instance, it has been observed that some of *Airbnb's* policies, according to which the final decision will be made, 'are not sufficiently detailed or comprehensive to cover specific disputes'.[76] 'It remains a bit of a gamble, therefore, to submit a dispute to Airbnb's team. Since parties agree that the decision is final, it will be very hard to contest it in court if one disagrees with the outcome'.[77] Further, the lack of effective intervention with regard to peer reviews creates frustration for parties who often cannot 'undo' the damage caused by negative reviews.[78] Another concern with in-house ODR is transparency and fairness. When platforms play the role of an arbitrator/mediator, neutrality must be maintained for it to be successful; the possibility of partial dispute resolution in favour of the one group or the other is present for a number of reasons, including network effects and the need of the platform to always regulate the balance between the two groups.

Further, platforms have not fully exploited the technological tools at their disposal in order to solve disputes between their peers. In that respect, they could follow the examples of *eBay's* and *Alibaba's* ODR mechanisms, whereby the first stage of dispute resolution includes automated processes, such as online forms, 'technology-assisted negotiation',[79] data and algorithmic decision-making for simple and 'popular' disputes, where precedent can easily be fed into the algorithm; in that regard, platforms could promote virtual dispute resolution, as well as ODR.[80] However, in view of the risky nature of decision-making by algorithms, without any human intervention, internal platform ODR should entail a second stage of dispute resolution, including either employees of the platform or members of the platform acting as juries, as in the examples of *eBay* and *Alibaba*.

---

[76] V Mak, 'Private Law Perspectives on Platform Services Airbnb: Home Rentals between AYOR and NIMBY' (2016) 5 *EuCML* 19, 23.

[77] ibid.

[78] Such frustration is very vividly depicted on a website solely created to channel *Airbnb* participants' anger towards *Airbnb*; see www.airbnbhell.com.

[79] See Katsh and Rabinovich-Einy (n 40) 34 and again 65–66.

[80] On the relationship of artificial intelligence with dispute resolution see AR Lodder and J Zeleznikow, 'Artificial Intelligence and Online Dispute Resolution' in MA Wahab, E Katsh and D Rainey (eds), *Online Dispute Resolution Theory and Practice: A Treatise on Technology and Dispute Resolution* (The Hague, Eleven International Publishing, 2011).

VI. Conclusion

'The sharing economy has reached a sort of "headache" phase, wherein regulatory crackdowns and competition between rival companies spawn dispute-related headlines'.[81]

Since the collaborative economy is drifting away from its original purpose and (most) platforms cannot justify the 'mere intermediary' claim anymore, it is high time platforms dealt with dispute resolution in a more mature, sophisticated and effective manner. Dispute prevention self-regulatory measures can go a long way to preventing disputes from arising in the first place, in view of the tools in possession of platforms, namely big data and smart algorithms. This should be complemented by effective and flexible 'peer-oriented' ODR systems, either provided within and by the platform or facilitated by the platform.

Platforms must, therefore, take a more 'hands-on' approach in dispute resolution, if not out of ethics and a sense of legality, then out of pure self-interest. Experience has shown that peers react badly to unfair practices and/or distrust and in a 'peer' economy this could be a major problem for platforms; in order to ensure their viability, platforms must inspire trust among peers. This can only happen if they assume responsibility for providing effective outlets for aggrieved peers to claim their redress.

Further, in any case, due to the multi-faceted character of the collaborative economy, and the variety of types of disputes arising, a mix of different avenues for dispute resolution should be available to peers, both consumers and suppliers, irrespective of their status as service providers or prosumers. Disputes against the platform can only be fairly resolved by a third party. This means that peers should have some sort of ODR and/or ADR outlet, as well as the right to proceed to trial. In that regard, platforms, and especially those based in the US which generally lack European law experience, should be wary of unfair or else illegal dispute resolution terms restricting EU residents' right of trial.

Last but not least, a final conclusion in terms of regulation needs to be made. The reasons for the special protective dispute resolution rules are present not only for end consumers, but also for providers of the underlying service. Therefore, a regulatory extension of the above protective status to also cover suppliers that technically qualify as 'professionals' against the platform would better reflect the needs and protect the rights of collaborative participants.

---

[81] Scheiwe Kulp and Kool (n 30) 197, note omitted.

7

The Regulation of the
Collaborative Economy

I. Introduction

Collaborative platforms exist amidst self-regulation, public regulation and no regulation at all. While they spend a great amount of time and resources negotiating for lighter, favourable regulation with public regulators, fending off legal actions and defending themselves against incumbent firms, most platforms do support some regulation, essentially in the form of self-regulation.[1] They do so for a number of reasons, including to: (a) protect their users and their rights; (b) prevent any potential liability pinned on them; (c) avoid bad reputation and therefore loss of value and revenue; (d) appear responsible and generally show a good face to regulators, and so on. While no regulation is by no means a viable option, self-regulation appears as a valid alternative and/or complement to traditional top-down regulation.

In what follows I first explore, in an empirical manner, the ways in which collaborative platforms have been using self-regulatory methods to make up for the current regulatory void, as well as the ways in which (selected) national authorities have dealt with this void. The Commission's action plan affecting the collaborative economy is also briefly discussed. Building on this first part, in the second, more normative part of this chapter, I discuss the ways in which the collaborative economy could be efficiently regulated, by answering three core questions: whether regulation is desirable in the first place; what kind of regulation is desirable; and which are the areas that need to be regulated.

---

[1] An interesting categorisation of self-regulation has been made by J Black, who has identified four types of self-regulation: 'voluntary self-regulation', which involves no direct governmental involvement; 'coerced self-regulation', when the industry formulates and imposes rules due to the threat of governmental regulation; 'sanctioned self-regulation', when the industry formulates rules subject to governmental approval; and 'mandated self-regulation', which refers to self-regulation imposed upon governmental request; see J Black, 'Decentering Regulation: Understanding the Role of Regulation and Self-Regulation in a "Post-Regulatory" World' (2001) 54 *Current Legal Problems* 103, 118; see also M Cohen and A Sundararajan, 'Self-Regulation and Innovation in the Peer-to-Peer Sharing Economy' (2015) 82 *The University of Chicago Law Review Dialogue* 116, 123–24.

II. An Empirical Approach—What about the Current Regulatory Void?

A. Self-regulation by Collaborative Platforms

The collaborative economy is based on trust, both in the platform and in peers; activities (such as hospitality, transportation) which were previously offered only to family members, neighbours, friends or friends of friends are now offered to complete strangers. The platform's role is precisely that of making, through their intermediation, strangers trust each other and share with one another. Thus, trust has become some kind of 'valuable, marketable good'.[2] If the user (consumer) has a negative experience from participating in the platform, not only will the platform lose business, but also it may trigger governments' reactions, due to safety, security and consumer protection concerns. This is especially true considering the high risk of some collaborative activities, such as sharing a ride or a room with a stranger. Therefore, 'platforms are often highly incentivised to regulate the quality of services on their platform'.[3]

   Collaborative platforms not only have the incentives to impose self-regulation mechanisms but also the means to do so; they possess great amounts of data, useful for identifying negative behaviour, and are in the best position to exert some control over their users. Platforms have the ability (or, as has been explained in Chapters 2 and 3, the obligation) to 'notice-and-take-down' negative content, flag or forbid access to certain users.

i. *Mechanisms Employed by Platforms to Impose Self-regulation*

a. Enforced Quality

Collaborative platforms have employed various self-regulatory mechanisms to enhance trust among users, either by standardising exchanges or offering quality and/or safety guarantees. These emanate from the platform itself and result in the so-called 'enforced quality'. These mechanisms reflect a centralised approach on behalf of the platform, since it assumes and exercises some control itself in order to enhance trust primarily in itself and secondarily in peers. Such control on behalf

---

[2] T Teubner, 'Thoughts on the Sharing Economy' (2014) 11 *Proceedings of the International Conference on e-Commerce* 322; see also T Slee, 'Some Obvious Things About Internet Reputation Systems' *Whimsley Blog* (29 September 2013), available at http://tomslee.net/2013/09/some-obvious-things-about-internetreputation-systems.html.

[3] U Gasser, 'The Sharing Economy: Disruptive Effects on Regulation and Paths Forward' *Swiss Re— Centre for Global Dialogue, Risk Dialogue Magazine* (6 June 2016), available at http://institute.swissre.com/research/risk_dialogue/magazine/Digital_Economy/sharing_economy_disruptive_effects.html.

of the platforms alleviates users from the burden of 'having to critically evaluate each individual with whom they interact, thus lowering transaction costs'.[4]

Thus, some platforms set quality standards that prosumers must meet as a condition to participate in the provision of services through that platform. For example, *Uber* and many of the transportation platforms[5] impose conditions on the types of cars (only passenger cars, of a certain age etc), as well as the facilities that should be offered (bottle of water, Wi-Fi connection, Bluetooth connection with the passenger's music etc).[6] In so doing, the service provided becomes somewhat standardised and the consumers' expectations correspond to the actual service offered and are therefore more likely to be met.

Most collaborative platforms also use some form of identification system for their users (both consumers and prosumers). While in the early years of peer-to-peer transactions and peer-reviewing (eg on *eBay*) anonymity was a common practice, nowadays anonymity or ambiguity as to the identity (and even personality) of the user is suspicious if not dangerous. Information increases trust.

Thus, most ride-sharing platforms (such as *Lyft*) have implemented both screening of criminal records and driving background checks to block prospective drivers from joining the platform as providers in the first place. The criminal checks exclude anyone with a record of violent crimes, sexual offences, theft, property damage, or drug-related offences, while the driving checks will firstly confirm a valid driving licence, and secondly, 'flag' anyone with certain relevant violations (driving on a suspended licence, reckless driving, drug-related driving violations, etc).

Following the same logic but from the opposite (suppliers') side, *Airbnb*, for example, gives hosts the option to hire out their properties only to 'verified' users, who have previously registered with the platform some photo of their official ID documents, such as driver's licence or passport.

Platforms encourage the sharing of as much information as possible concerning a person's identity and personality. Many collaborative platforms have even incorporated a social network log-in feature. Therefore, a cross-verification process between the user's online imprint and offline identity is possible. The collaborative platform users can articulate connections to other users' profiles and search their connections.

Moreover, some collaborative platforms have also introduced 'personality checks' to ensure that the suppliers qualify to provide the relevant service.

---

[4] A Thierer et al, 'How the Internet, the Sharing Economy, and Reputational Feedback Mechanisms Solve the "Lemons Problem"' (2016) 70 *University of Miami Law Review* 830, 859.

[5] The examples which follow are not necessarily taken from *Uber*, but rather illustrate the practices of various transportation platforms.

[6] See eg the different quality standards depending on the different types of services provided in *Uber*. The quality conditions for the standard service differs greatly than those for the lux service; see www.ridesharingdriver.com/uber-vehicle-requirements-can-you-drive-for-uber-with-your-car.

Lyft has instituted a 'Mentor Session', where an experienced *Lyft* driver rides with the 'prospect' and performs a 19-point vehicle inspection. Prospective drivers must pass in order to be approved as *Lyft* drivers.[7] Similarly, *DogVacay* gives badges to dog-sitters, which improve their search results rankings following reading, watching training videos, and taking tests to improve their dog care knowledge, or undergoing a phone interview with the company.[8]

Although this data collection may seem intrusive (and risky), it undoubtedly increases safety for all users. It may, therefore, be a 'necessary evil' for participation in the collaborative economy. However, it goes without saying that data protection and privacy should not be compromised from potential data spills or privacy intrusions in the name of increasing trust.[9]

Further, collaborative platforms often rely on the 'big data' analytics mechanism. This mechanism uses computer algorithms to monitor transactions and either block or flag any suspicious activity, which is subsequently investigated and evaluated by a human employee. An example of such a mechanism is the *Airbnb* 'trust score' algorithm. *Airbnb* monitors all transactions, including the profiles, the listings, the communications between supplier and consumer and so forth. When the algorithm picks up suspicious activity, such as key-words indicating attempt to circumvent the *Airbnb* payment system, or fake reviews, or even money laundering, the case is further investigated by humans. Therefore, big data analytics is a useful tool collaborative platforms use to combat fraud, abuse and violation of their policies.[10]

Moreover, the payment for the collaborative services normally takes place: (a) digitally; (b) via the collaborative platform; and (c) (typically) in advance. Therefore, platforms act as intermediaries in the *completion* of the transaction as well as the *initial connection* of the parties. The platform acts, therefore, as a 'guardian' of security of transactions, which is immensely increased compared to payment in person, in cash at the end of a ride. The platform also assumes the responsibility of allocating the payment to the supplier itself, or even withholding it and refunding the customer in cases of abnormal development of the transaction.

Insurance coverage offered by the platform to the users minimises uncertainty, increases digital trust and may incentivise regular people to join the platform. The risks in providing some collaborative activities are especially high, since the costs from potential damage can be considerable. Indeed 'insurance cover seems specifically relevant in many cases of P2P collaborative consumption platforms due to

---

[7] See https://help.lyft.com/hc/en-us/articles/214219507.

[8] Thierer, 'How the Internet, the Sharing Economy, and Reputational Feedback Mechanisms Solve the "Lemons Problem"' (2016) 861.

[9] In this case, self-regulation is not sufficient. Effective public regulation protecting personal data in the digital context must be in place in order to complement self-regulation. For an overview of the data protection regime, see Ch 3 above.

[10] Thierer (n 4) 862–63.

the fact that services rather than goods are provided by private people rather than professionals'.[11]

In 2011, *Airbnb* guests vandalised an apartment in San Francisco, causing great damage to the hosts/prosumers and raising fear and uncertainty among the *Airbnb* community. Thus, *Airbnb* announced the implementation of a sort of insurance policy, called 'Host Guarantee Programme', which protects home-owners (suppliers) for up to one million dollars in damages in some countries.[12] The Host Guarantee Programme is complemented by the Host Protection insurance programme, which aims to protect hosts from third-party claims of bodily injury or property damage, claims brought against landlords and home-owners' associations in cases where guests suffer injury during a stay, and may also cover claims if a guest damages building property.[13] Accordingly, collaborative platforms in the transportation market have implemented insurance policies for their customers covering, for example, third party liability, uninsured or underinsured motorist bodily injury coverage, contingent collision and comprehensive coverage while driving for the platform.[14]

Lastly, some platforms exert a certain (greater or lesser) degree of control of the price for the service provided. While *Airbnb* hosts determine the price for their services themselves, *Uber* sets the price for each ride without any input from the driver. This, on one hand, may be perceived as a guarantee of transparency and objectivity in the determination of prices, considering that a centralised business is generally more trustworthy than an individual stranger, but on the other hand raises issues of competition, employment and liability of the platform, as have been already discussed in the relevant chapters of this book.

b. Reputational Quality

Reputation is the branding of the collaborative economy. Participating in the collaborative economy inherently entails the risk of the unknown. The same goes for concluding any transaction online, ie at a distance, without direct knowledge of the product/service or the provider. As explained above, the existence of information asymmetries between platform and users and among users can cause distrust and result in bad experiences for the collaborative participant. The difficulty of distinguishing good quality from bad is found in the traditional economy as well and has been expressed in the well-known Akerlof's 'bad lemons' theory.[15]

---

[11] M Möhlmann, 'Digital Trust and Peer-to-Peer Collaborative Consumption Platforms: A Mediation Analysis' (2016) 8, available at https://ssrn.com/abstract=2813367.

[12] See *Airbnb*, 'The $1,000,000 Host Guarantee' at www.airbnb.com/guarantee. In the words of Katsh and Rabinovich-Einy '[t]his is the process that looks like—but is not—insurance'; see E Katsh and O Rabinovich-Einy, *Digital Justice: Technology and the Internet of Disputes* (New York, Oxford University Press, 2017) 71.

[13] See *Airbnb*, 'Host Protection Insurance' at www.airbnb.com/host-protection-insurance?locale=en.

[14] See, for example, *Uber's* insurance policy, available at www.uber.com/drive/insurance.

[15] GA Akerlof, 'The Market for "Lemons": Quality Uncertainty and the Market Mechanism' (1970) 84 *The Quarterly Journal of Economics* 488.

According to this theory consumers who do not have sufficient information about the goods offered in a market (Akerlof based his argument on the market for second-hand cars) tend to assume that these are of the lowest quality (bad lemons) and are unwilling to pay the price that high quality goods would cost; this in turn expels high quality goods from the market and is detrimental to all the parties involved.

The Way Reputational Quality Works

It has been argued that the reputational system, on which the collaborative platforms rely, offers a solution to the 'lemon problem', since via reviews or ratings, the potential customers can gain information about the quality of the product or service prior to them using it.[16] The reputation of a supplier in the collaborative economy is, therefore, the equivalent to the brand name in the traditional economy. Research shows that digital reputation 'ratings' could form a 'functional substitute for personal trust, making more, and more credible, transactions possible'.[17] Despite their importance and function, reputation systems have, so far, not been addressed by regulators.

Reputation mechanisms were introduced by the early e-commerce platforms (eg *Amazon*, *eBay*). Since then, the evolution of technology, with the expansion of smart devices, has made it easier for users to post a review at any time and any place. Further, the collaborative economy shows an extra advantage in using reputational mechanisms; direct, and instantaneous interaction between users. Contrary to 'enhanced quality' self-regulation, 'reputational quality' is a matter of peers. The platform plays only a secondary role, while peers, amateurs or not, take the front seat. Their feedback can not only inform other users of the same group, but also influence the contracting parties' activity and even participation in the collaborative platform.

Two types of reputation mechanisms are mainly used. The first one is the qualitative review system, whereby the consumer writes a review of the product or service, describes the quality of the service and is free to commend on (almost) anything related to the product or service. This system is used for service activities having many variants, such as for example, accommodation, writing or designing services etc. The second type is the numerical ratings system, whereby the consumer rates the service or product in a numerical scale (rating stars). The rating system is mainly used for simpler services with not too many variants, such as by transportation platforms. Several platforms, such as *Airbnb*, use a combination of the two.

---

[16] See Thierer (n 4).
[17] DE Rauch and D Schleicher, 'Like Uber, But for Local Governmental Policy: The Future of Local Regulation of the "Sharing Economy"' (2015) George Mason University Law & Economics, Research Paper No 15-01, 9 (note omitted), with reference to L Strahlevitz, 'How's My Driving? for Everyone (and Everything)' (2006) 81 *NYU Law Rev* 1661.

Most collaborative platforms require some form of peer-review following the completion of the transaction within the website, which complements the user's profile. In most platforms, both consumer and supplier receive reputational feedback. *Airbnb* has implemented simultaneous reviews (double blind reviews),[18] which are revealed concurrently after being submitted by both consumer and supplier. Double blind reviews can prevent potential retaliation of negative feedback and therefore secure the integrity and truthfulness of the reviews.

Truthful feedbacks are especially critical, considering that both consumer and supplier reputations can determine access to the platform. Indeed, many collaborative platforms may terminate or block suppliers who have scored low, and suppliers may refuse to accept requests from consumers who have received negative feedback. That is why ratings and reviews are often referred to as 'collaborative sanctioning'.[19] Moreover, high reputational score is essential for both groups. Suppliers build a stronger position within the platform (eg *Airbnb's* 'super-hosts') and therefore increase their customers and revenue, while consumers may gain access to higher quality services. This is why platforms forbid fake reviews in their codes of conduct and investigate potential violations, which may lead to termination of users' accounts.

Nonetheless, even if the peer-reviews are truthful and accurate, scepticism towards the reputation system is not at all unjustified. Several shortfalls of peer-review systems have been identified.[20]

Problems Raised by Reputational Quality Mechanisms—and Tentative Solutions

Firstly, peers are typically able to assess the 'visible' part of the service (eg the cleanliness of the car, the good humour of the driver and the like) but may be completely ignorant as to the 'invisible' parts of it, typically connected with formal qualifications of the supplier and the respect of health, safety and security regulations.

Secondly, reputation mechanisms constitute an ex post evaluation of the service, meaning that their protective role is limited, since they cannot always prevent 'the unexpected' worst-case scenario from happening in a way that proper regulation can.

Thirdly, the creditworthiness of peer-reviews is questioned since studies show that they often are biased. A paper assessing peer-reviews on *eBay* has found that

---

[18] Möhlmann, 'Digital Trust and Peer-to-Peer Collaborative Consumption Platforms: A Mediation Analysis' (2016) 8.

[19] Thierer (n 4) 864, fn 247 therein.

[20] On the problems raised by peer-review mechanisms, see the US Federal Trade Commission (FTC) Staff Report, 'The "Sharing" Economy: Issues Facing Platforms, Participants and Regulators' (2016) available at www.ftc.gov/reports/sharing-economy-issues-facing-platforms-participants-regulators-federal-trade-commission, where very rich references to further sources is to be found.

99.1 per cent of comments by buyers were positive, 0.6 were negative and 0.3 were neutral.[21] Other studies have found that more than 80 per cent of *Airbnb's* stays are above average and that 95 per cent of the listings score between 4.5 and 5 (out of 5) stars.[22] This, may be due to the fact that (mildly) deceived consumers prefer to forget an unpleasant experience and tend not to rate it. Further, regular users of a platform may prefer to avoid confrontation with users from the other side, thus avoiding bitter or else negative comments. This upwards bias is likely to become even more intense in services where the supplier and the consumer share something or become friends, as may be the case with home-sharing platforms. Several solutions have been proposed to counter this problem: that the rating should not only be based on the evaluations submitted, but also on those not submitted;[23] that percentile rating be used in order to give consumers a more accurate view of the supplier's standing;[24] that narrative reviews be shown together with raw reputation score.[25]

Fourthly, ratings can be manipulated by the posting of fake reviews, which can either bolster or tarnish a supplier's reputation. To counter this problem platforms tend to tie evaluations with some verification system and/or with other means of ensuring that the evaluation corresponds to an actual transaction.

Fifthly, peer-based reputational systems pose the problem of the 'cold start', ie the difficulty of new entrants to obtain consumers' trust and gain some market share. In this sense, ratings constitute an important barrier to entry. Also the opposite problem has been identified, that of 'reputation milking': during the last period before quitting a platform, suppliers tend to sit on their acquired reputation 'cheat a few times and then … exit gracefully and take a one way ticket to Brazil'.[26] Against such practices, it has been proposed that newer transactions should weigh more in defining a user's reputation score than older ones. A further idea, against both cold start and milking problems, is that the score is always calculated on the basis of transactions concluded within the last six months.

Some of these problems may be resolved from an 'external', third party, review. This is an option essentially with regard to B2C relations, since professional suppliers have a long, systematic or else permanent presence in the market. Further, for evaluating the business's reputation, feedback provided through social media and online (specialised) review websites is possible.[27] Such websites allow both

---

[21] P Resnick and R Zeckhauser, 'Trust Among Strangers in Internet Transactions: Empirical Analysis of ebay's Reputational System' (2002) 11 *Economics of the Internet and E-Commerce* 127; quoted in the FTC Report, 'The "Sharing" Economy: Issues Facing Platforms, Participants and Regulators' (2016) 40.

[22] G Zervas, D Prosperio and J Buyers, 'A First Look at Online Reputation on Airbnb, Where Every Stay is Above Average' (2015), available at http://ssrn.com/abstract=2554500.

[23] See FTC Report (n 20) 45.

[24] ibid.

[25] ibid.

[26] ibid 44

[27] Most businesses offer specific webpages and social media outlets for customer service concerns.

professionals and amateurs to rate goods and services. For example, *e-Food* is a B2C collaborative platform connecting customers with restaurants delivering in their region. The providing restaurant may receive feedback both within the platform and externally through other comparative platforms, such as *TripAdvisor*.

A further option in order to counter some of the above problems are reputation aggregators, based on social media or otherwise, where the parties' reputation from different platforms would be gathered. This would also foster the practice of multi-homing and platform mobility—a precious instrument for fostering competition in the platform economy,[28] since the reputation concentrated in one platform could be used in all others. This, however, could also have negative implications as people who have scored low in one platform would be excluded from starting over in any other platform—in the same or a different sector.[29]

Uber has argued that the combination of internal oversight with reputational feedback exceeds the regulator's goals in terms of public safety protection and that it (*Uber*) does a better job than taxi licensing boards.[30] Even if this claim may be somewhat exaggerated, it may nonetheless be said that, all in all, 'reputation rating systems seem to solve information asymmetry problems in online transactions':[31] the few horror stories which see the light from time to time compare favourably to the zillions of transactions successfully concluded.

ii. More than Self-regulation: Voluntary Actions

In addition to the above self-regulatory tools employed by the collaborative platforms to improve quality of their (intermediary) services, some platforms have also taken voluntary actions complementary to regulators' efforts. In such cases, it becomes apparent that despite the disruption that the collaborative phenomenon causes, it may also be seen as an opportunity for governments and the EU. Collaboration of public authorities with collaborative players may result in effective enforcement of public policies.[32] The European Economic and Social Committee has recognised that self-regulation and co-regulation 'should be viewed as important instruments for complementing or supplementing hard law, but not as an alternative to it unless there are "fundamental rules" providing a sufficient enabling basis'.[33]

---

[28] For the competition law issues raised by the collaborative economy and the pivotal role of multi-homing see Ch 4 above.

[29] See Organisation for Economic Co-operation and Development (OECD), 'New Forms of Work in the Digital Economy' (2016) OECD Digital Economy Papers, No 260, 32, available at www.oecd-ilibrary.org/science-and-technology/new-forms-of-work-in-the-digital-economy_5jlwnklt820x-en.

[30] See D Das Acevedo, 'Regulating Employment Relationships in the Sharing Economy' (2016) 20(1) *Employee Rights and Employment Policy Journal* 1, 10–11, with further references to the original source.

[31] FTC Report (n 20) 39.

[32] See also below nn 221–225 and the corresponding text on public procurement.

[33] European Economic and Social Committee (EESC), 'Opinion on Self-regulation and co-regulation in the Community legislative framework (own-initiative opinion)' [2015] OJ C 291/29, at 1.2.

One example of such voluntary action is tax collection through the collaborative platforms. As the collaborative platforms establish themselves in modern economies, more and more cities (and/or governments) approach them in order to ask help with the salient issue of tax collection. *Airbnb* has already signed tax agreements with numerous cities in the US and is now starting to enter into agreements with EU countries, namely France, the Netherlands and Portugal.[34] This is an early example of: (a) a combination of public regulation and self-regulation; and (b) voluntary assumption of responsibility on behalf of collaborative platforms.

Furthermore, following complaints and researches showing potential discriminatory and racial tensions among *Airbnb* users, the platform took the initiative to enforce an anti-discrimination policy. The information provided in the users' personal profiles may facilitate discrimination on the basis of supplier's race, gender, age, or other aspects of appearance. A study published in 2014 on digital discrimination showed that non-black *Airbnb* hosts were charging approximately 12 per cent more than black hosts for an equivalent rental in New York City.[35] *Airbnb* reacted by enacting its non-discrimination policy, which includes reducing the prominence of photos, introducing new technology, promoting instant booking (ie without the need of prior approval from the host) and asking users to sign an anti-discrimination agreement.[36] In California *Airbnb* has agreed with the Department of Fair Employment and Housing (DFEH) to enforce the policy, and indeed, in July 2017 the State Agency imposed its first fine on a host who cancelled at the last minute a reservation because the guest was 'asian'.[37]

B. Regulatory Gaps and Solutions Reached in Different Jurisdictions

Self-regulation, as described above, is a potent means of regulating the collaborative economy. It is one, however, which has not been fully deployed by the platforms themselves and, more importantly, has not been acknowledged as an alternative to traditional regulation by public authorities. Public, administrative, legislative and judicial authorities have adopted varied approaches in respect of collaborative platforms.

Different sectors in different jurisdictions have provoked different regulatory reactions. The most intrusive approach taken by national jurisdictions is a ban. Partial or overall bans have been imposed on collaborative platforms, or

---

[34] See *Airbnb*, 'In what areas is occupancy tax collection and remittance by Airbnb available?' at www.airbnb.com/help/article/653/in-what-areas-is-occupancy-tax-collection-and-remittance-by-airbnb-available?locale=en.

[35] BG Edelman and M Luca, 'Digital Discrimination: The Case of Airbnb.com' (2014) Harvard Business School NOM Unit Working Paper No 14-054, available at https://ssrn.com/abstract=2377353.

[36] See BBC, 'Airbnb introduces new anti-discrimination policy' *BBC News* (8 September 2016).

[37] D Lee, 'AirBnB host fined after racist comment' *BBC News* (13 July 2017).

certain services of collaborative platforms, especially in the transportation sector. Secondly, national authorities have imposed various requirements on the part of the service providers, such as licences, age limits, registrations, minimum standards, insurance, time restrictions (eg in short-term rentals), etc. Failure to comply with such requirements has resulted in the imposition of fines. Fines have also been set on both service providers and platforms for violation of existing laws and regulations. The following exploration of case studies in the accommodation and transportation sectors provides an indicative overview of the various existing regulatory and judicial approaches and highlights the regulatory gaps and problematic application of existing laws.

i. Case Study 1: Accommodation—Airbnb[38]

In the accommodation sector, *Airbnb* has faced legal actions in numerous states and for various reasons. The main legal issue arises from potential violations of short-term rental laws. In that regard, EU Member States and US states have: (a) imposed regulatory restrictions and requirements; and/or (b) fined both *Airbnb* and hosts for non-compliance with existing regulation. For example, New York imposed fines on *Airbnb* hosts for not complying with local regulations. According to New York short-rental laws, which were last updated in 2010, most apartments cannot be legally rented out for short periods (less than 30 days), unless the renter is present throughout the visitor's stay.[39] This means that most New York rooms and apartments listed on *Airbnb* can be qualified as illegal hotels. To make matters worse for *Airbnb*, New York state passed a new law in October 2016 imposing even heavier fines on *Airbnb* hosts,[40] despite (or because of) *Airbnb*'s aggressive pro-sharing campaign. *Airbnb* contested the law but soon dropped the lawsuit and came to a settlement with New York City, according to which the law would not be enforced against the platform itself, but rather it would only target individual hosts.[41]

As opposed to New York, which put pressure on *Airbnb* hosts, San Francisco turned directly to *Airbnb*. In June 2016, San Francisco passed a law imposing fines on *Airbnb* itself and similar short-rental websites for every host on their platforms not registered with the city's Office of Short-Term Rentals.[42] *Airbnb* filed a complaint against the city, claiming that 'websites can't be held responsible for

---

[38] Other accommodation platforms, such as *HomeExchange* or *HomeAway*, and even *Couchsurfing*, have also been involved—to a lesser extent than *Airbnb*—in legal actions, mainly with regard to taxation.

[39] New York State Multiple Dwelling Law.

[40] J Clampet, 'Airbnb loses a fight in New York as legislature passes strict advertising law' *Skift* (17 June 2016); see also www.nysenate.gov/legislation/bills/2015/S6340/amendment/A.

[41] *Airbnb Inc v Schneiderman et al*, Case 1:16-cv-08239, US District Court for the Southern District of New York.

[42] City and County of San Francisco, Administrative Code—Short-Term Residential Rentals and Hosting Platforms, Ordinance No 104-16 (File No 160423) of 7 June 2016; see https://sfgov.legistar.com/LegislationDetail.aspx?ID=2703562&GUID=AC847364-A46D-4288-80A2-8CCA275FC703.

the actions of the people who use those sites'[43] and eventually settled this case in May 2017, with *Airbnb* agreeing to streamline and make simple the registration process of hosts with the city and having hosts obtain their business licence directly through the *Airbnb* platform; this is already the case in New Orleans, Chicago and Denver.[44] Moreover, *Airbnb* is to supply the city with a monthly list with all the listed homes.[45] In exchange, the city has agreed to drop all judicial cases and to work together with the platform. This is a fine example of how adversarial bargaining may have a 'collaborative' outcome.

In Europe, where *Airbnb* was slower to arrive than it was in the US, it has been treated in a somewhat friendlier way. Member States' regulators have generally endorsed the platform but with certain restrictions, mainly on the number of days per year a host can rent out his/her home.[46] In 2014, Amsterdam became the first city to pass an '*Airbnb* friendly' law: a law allowing short-term rentals by permanent residents, with certain restrictions[47] and subject to the obligation to pay the relevant taxes, including a tourist tax. Similarly, *Airbnb* was endorsed by France, with the adoption of '*loi ALUR*',[48] a law legalising short term rentals of primary residences, and has begun collecting tourist tax in Paris.[49] Accordingly, London housing legislation was amended in order to clarify that short-term rentals are legal.[50] The UK has even launched an initiative to become the 'global centre for sharing economy'.[51] On the other hand, Barcelona has taken a rather hostile standing, by requiring a special licence for short-time rentals, even though it has stopped issuing those since 2014,[52] by fining *Airbnb* for breaching local tourism laws, turning down *Airbnb*'s 'goodwill' offer to limit the number of homes rented through its platform, and doubling the city's inspectors seeking out illegal rentals.[53] Similarly, Berlin has restricted rentals of entire apartments on *Airbnb*, allowing owners to rent only individual rooms.[54]

---

[43] *Airbnb v City and County of San Francisco* Case 3:16-cv-03615, US District Court for the Northern District of California: San Francisco Division.

[44] MR Dickey, 'Airbnb settles lawsuit with San Francisco' *TechCrunch* (1 May 2017).

[45] ibid.

[46] In Amsterdam the limit is 60 days per year, in Paris 120 days per year and in London 90 days per year.

[47] Namely to rent out their homes for up to 60 days per year to up to four people at a time.

[48] The acronym standing for *accès au logement et un urbanisme rénové*.

[49] *Airbnb*, 'Airbnb to Collect and Remit Tourist Taxes in Paris', Press Release of 25 August 2015, available at www.airbnbcitizen.com/airbnb-to-collect-tourist-taxes-in-1-city-paris.

[50] The measures were included in the Deregulation Act 2015; see the relevant Press Release (26 May 2015) at www.gov.uk/government/news/boost-for-londoners-as-red-tape-slashed-on-short-term-lets.

[51] See Press Release (29 September 2014) 'Move to make UK global centre for sharing economy' at www.gov.uk/government/news/move-to-make-uk-global-centre-for-sharing-economy.

[52] A Kharpal, 'Airbnb's growth is slowing because it's being hit by regulation, UBS says' *CNBC* (13 April 2017).

[53] See M Tadeo, 'Barcelona Takes the Wind Out of Airbnb's Sails', *Bloomberg* (8 February 2017); S Burgen, 'Barcelona cracks down on Airbnb rentals with illegal apartment squads' *The Guardian* (2 June 2017).

[54] P Oltermann, 'Berlin ban on Airbnb short-term rentals upheld by city court' *The Guardian* (8 June 2016).

In an effort to ease the tension with regulators, *Airbnb* has agreed with London and Amsterdam to assume the responsibility of enforcing the local limits on the number of nights per year a host can rent out his/her apartment, as of January 2017.[55] This is the first time that the platform has assumed responsibility for law enforcement with its members.

The above developments show that the dynamics of the regulatory 'war' between *Airbnb* and public authorities are shyly transitioning from a head-on adversary relationship against attempted regulations and restrictions, to collaboration, settlements and mutual compromises. As *Airbnb* is growing and becoming a target in an increasing number of jurisdictions, collaboration might indeed be the only viable option for the platform. On the other hand, a UBS report, analysing data from 127 *Airbnb* cities, shows that 'regulation is having a negative impact on the supply and demand growth of Airbnb'.[56]

ii. Case Study 2: Transportation—Uber

In the transportation sector, *Uber* has been fighting legal battles concerning mostly: (a) labour law; (b) public safety concerns; and (c) unfair competition allegations in relation to the traditional taxi industry.

As regards the first, reference is made to the developments in Chapter 5, above. So far *Uber*, in order to avoid classifying its drivers as 'employees', has settled cases—both in the US and in France—where such classification was forthcoming and has appealed judgments where such requalification had been accepted.[57]

As regards public safety reasons, *Uber* (as well as *Lyft* and other similar platforms) has either been obliged to conform to various regulatory restrictions and requirements (such as drivers' age requirements, no criminal record, adequate insurance, yearly inspected vehicles etc)[58] or has faced a full ban or suspended operations in numerous cities across the world.[59] It was even ruled that *Uber* should be subject to 'the same regulations imposed on other for-hire vehicle services in the state since it was "a common carrier"'.[60] Further, *Uber* was heavily fined by regulators for operating illegally in the state of Pennsylvania in 2014 and

---

[55] N Woolf, 'Airbnb regulation deal with London and Amsterdam marks dramatic policy shift' *The Guardian* (3 December 2016).

[56] Kharpal, 'Airbnb's growth is slowing because it's being hit by regulation, UBS says' (n 52).

[57] See the developments in Ch 5 above, on employment.

[58] See eg the 'Vehicle for Hire Innovation Amendment Act of 2014', enacted in October 2014 by the District of Columbia Council. Some regulation has also been put in place in several US cities. See a map of pro-*Uber* regulation and anti-*Uber* regulation US states at www.qz.com/589041/uber-pulled-off-a-spectacular-political-coup-and-hardly-anyone-noticed/.

[59] For a global map of all the cities that *Uber* is banned from, see www.businessinsider.com/heres-everywhere-uber-is-banned-around-the-world-2015-4; for an update see www.cntraveler.com/story/where-uber-is-banned-around-the-world.

[60] Maryland Public Service Commission Finds that Uber Is A Common Carrier (6 August 2014), available at http://webapp.psc.state.md.us/newIntranet/sitesearch/Press%20Releases/Maryland%20PSC%20Finds%20that%20Uber%20is%20a%20Common%20Carrier.pdf.

posing 'a risk to public safety by offering rides without proof its drivers, vehicles and insurance provisions met state standards'.[61] Commissioner John Coleman stated that *Uber* had committed 123,000 violations prior to receiving authorisation. The platform eventually settled this multi-million dollar fine, after having filed an appeal questioning it.[62] In the UK the High Court upheld the obligation imposed by the Transport for London Board, according to which *Uber's* drivers should undertake a language test, both oral and written.[63] This was deemed necessary in order to make sure that they can properly communicate with passengers, police officers etc and understand signs and signposts.

Lastly, *Uber* has been facing legal challenges as regards its relation to the taxi industry. *Uber* and its *UberPOP* service has been either banned or suspended from numerous cities in various jurisdictions, namely Bulgaria, France, Germany, Belgium, Italy, Portugal, Spain, Sweden, Finland, the Netherlands and Hungary on the grounds of unfair competition. The lack of taxi licences and registration of drivers and the non-satisfaction of 'the requirements for the establishment of public transportation enterprises'[64] have been found to constitute breaches of existing regulations.

In a case brought by a taxi operator, the Brussels Commercial Tribunal declared *Uber* illegal and banned its *UberPOP* services, on the basis that *Uber* and its drivers do not comply with existing rules regulating taxi services (licence, registration etc).[65] Similarly, the Dutch courts imposed a ban on *Uber*, first in Amsterdam and subsequently in The Hague and Rotterdam, on the factual grounds of lack of licence.[66] The Dutch court ruled, however, that licensed taxi drivers, and drivers who do not seek payment, can still drive for the service. In Spain, *Uber* was obliged to cease all activities by an interim measure order of the Madrid Commercial Court, ruling that the collaborative platform was exercising unfair competition to taxis;[67] the same order prohibited all credit cards and other online payment providers to accept payments on behalf of *Uber*, as well as all geolocalisation providers to work with the company. This radical order was later partly quashed to the extent

---

[61] J Stempel, 'Pennsylvania reinstates Uber's record $11.4 million fine' *Reuters* (1 September 2016).

[62] D Packel, 'Pa. Regulator OKs $3.5M Settlement With Uber Over Violations' *Law360* (6 April 2017), available at https://www.law360.com/articles/910375/pa-regulator-oks-3-5m-settlement-with-uber-over-violations.

[63] Z Rodionova, 'Uber drivers must pass written English test, High Court rules' *Independent* (3 March 2017).

[64] See 'Many Countries Ban Uber' *Tempo.Co* (12 April 2016) at http://en.tempo.co/read/news/2016/04/12/056761969/Many-Countries-Ban-Uber.

[65] *SPRL Uber Belgium v Sa Taxi Radio Bruxellois* Commercial Tribunal, Tribunal de Commerce Neerlandophone de Bruxelles, Jugement—Chambre Du President Action En Cessation (23 September 2015), available in Flemish and French at www.lcii.eu/2015/10/16/uber-the-decision-of-the-brussels-commercial-tribunal; a decision characterised as 'crazy' by then Vice-President of the European Commission, Neelie Kroes; see the reaction published at www.ec.europa.eu/archives/commission_2010-2014/kroes/en/content/crazy-court-decision-ban-uber-brussels-show-your-anger.html.

[66] See 'Dutch judges ban taxi service UberPOP (Update)' *Phys* (8 December 2014).

[67] See 'Uber taxi app suspended in Spain' *BBC News* (9 December 2014); *Asociacion Madrileña del Taxi c Uber*, Recurso No 707/2014 (9 December 2014) Juzgado de lo Mercantil No 2 Madrid.

that it covered services other than *UberPOP*.[68] Further, in Germany, the Berlin District Court qualified *Uber* as a 'rental car service' that was violating German passenger transport laws, according to which, rental cars are required to return to home basis after completing a ride. Subsequently, the Frankfurt District Court found that *Uber* failed to have the necessary licences and insurance and posed unfair competition to the local taxi industry. It also found that the company did not carry sufficient insurance; it therefore imposed a nationwide ban.[69] France has also followed a rather hostile approach towards *Uber*. Some of the legal issues that incurred are a ban of *UberPOP's* services in Paris, prohibition of advertisement of several of *Uber's* services and arrest of *Uber* managers on charges including 'deceptive commercial practices', complicity in instigating an illegal taxi-driving activity, and the illegal stocking of personal information.[70] In Italy, a Rome court issued a nationwide ban of some premium *Uber* services (eg *Uber BLACK, LUX, SUV, X, XL*) for unfair competition to taxis, but was soon overturned on appeal,[71] while other services (eg *UberPOP*) continue to be banned upon an order of 2015 by the Tribunale di Milano.[72]

Besides judicial battles, some Member States have attempted to regulate *Uber* and similar companies. In an attempt to regulate collaborative companies such as *Uber*, France introduced Law No 2014-1104 on Taxis and Chauffeured Transport Vehicles, commonly known as *Loi Thévenoud*.[73] This Law, inter alia, prohibits chauffeured vehicles other than taxis from charging a per-kilometer fee, requires chauffeured cars to return to their base or stop in an authorised parking place between fares, and prohibits the use of software that shows the location of nearby available vehicles to potential customers in real-time. The Conseil Constitutionnel ruled on the constitutionality of the above provisions, upon actions brought by *Uber*.[74] It found that the first of these—the prohibition to charge on a distance basis—unjustifiably violated the freedom of enterprise and therefore was

---

[68] *Asociacion Madrileña del Taxi c Uber*, Juzgado de lo Mercantil No 2 Madrid, Order of 22 May 2015.

[69] See J Gesley, 'Legal Challenges for Uber in the European Union and in Germany' *Library of Congress* Blog (14 March 2016), available at https://blogs.loc.gov/law/2016/03/legal-challenges-for-uber-in-the-european-union-and-in-germany.

[70] See '2 Uber executives ordered to stand trial in France' *Los Angeles Times* (30 June 2015).

[71] I Binnie and G Jones (D Goodman(ed)), 'Italian court overturns Uber ban' *Reuters* (26 May 2017); see *Uber v Apptaxi*, Ordinanza No 25857/2017, Tribunale di Roma (26 May 2017), available in Italian at http://www.ilsole24ore.com/pdf2010/Editrice/ILSOLE24ORE/ILSOLE24ORE/Online/_Oggetti_Embedded/Documenti/2017/05/26/OrdinanzaUber.pdf.

[72] *Taxiblu v Uber*, Ordinanza No 16612/2015, Tribunale di Milano (25 May 2015), available in Italian at https://www.leggioggi.it/wp-content/uploads/2015/05/UberOrdinanzaMaggio2015.pdf.

[73] Loi No 2014-1104 du 1er octobre 2014 relative aux taxis et aux voitures de transport avec chauffeur (Loi Thévenoud); available in French at www.legifrance.gouv.fr/affichTexte.do?cidTexte=JORFTEXT000029527162&dateTexte=&categorieLien=id.

[74] *Société UBER France SAS et autre*, Decision No 2015-468/469/472 QPC of 22 May 2015, available in French at www.conseil-constitutionnel.fr/conseil-constitutionnel/francais/les-decisions/acces-par-date/decisions-depuis-1959/2015/2015-468/469/472-qpc/decision-n-2015-468-469-472-qpc-du-22-mai-2015.143800.html.

unconstitutional, while the latter two provisions were constitutional, considered to be justified for reasons of public order. Denmark introduced a new taxi law, requiring drivers to fulfil mandatory requirements, such as fare meters and seat sensors. As a result, *Uber* was forced to withdraw its services from the country in April 2017.[75]

In Italy, the Consiglio dello Stato in a consultative opinion to the government has held that the existing framework for transportation services is inadequate to cover collaborative platforms and the Italian government is—at the time of writing—in the process of issuing clearer rules on competition between traditional taxis and transportation apps.[76] France and Hungary have already introduced purpose-made regulations, while in the UK and Ireland collaborative platforms are required to obtain a prior authorisation as transport operators. The Netherlands is contemplating a complete liberalisation of the taxi and car-and-driver sector,[77] while Finland has passed legislation opening the transportation market for novel businesses expected to enter into force in July 2018.[78]

In view of all the above, *Uber* has filed complaints with the European Commission against France, Germany, Spain and Hungary, alleging that they are in violation of Article 49 (freedom of establishment) and Article 56 (freedom to provide services) TFEU.

iii. Preliminary Rulings to the CJEU

The CJEU has received references for preliminary rulings concerning the activities of *Uber* in Belgium, Spain and France and Germany. The questions posed by Member State courts to the CJEU concern, inter alia, whether *Uber* should be considered as merely a transport service, or as an electronic intermediary service or as 'information society service', and accordingly what EU rules apply.[79] Further, the question has been put whether the concept of 'taxi services' applies equally to unremunerated occasional private carriers who engage in ride-sharing (shared transport) as a result of accepting journey requests that are offered to them via *Uber*.[80] Lastly, Germany's highest court referred to the CJEU the question

---

[75] J Henley, 'Uber to shut down Denmark operation over new taxi laws' *The Guardian* (28 March 2017).

[76] J Conditt, 'Uber is free to operate in Italy on a long-term basis' *engadget* (26 May 2017).

[77] For a more detailed discussion of these trends and the references to the relevant documents, see the Commission Staff Working Document, 'A European agenda for the collaborative economy—supporting analysis' SWD(2016) 184 final, 27 ff.

[78] 'Uber Takes Break in Finland Ahead of New Legislation' *Phys* (6 July 2017).

[79] Case C-434/15 *Élite Taxi v Uber Systems Spain*, pending [2015] OJ C 363/21; Case C-320/16 *Uber France* pending [2016] OJ C 296/22; on this very issue, see D Geradin, 'Online intermediation platforms and free trade principles: Some reflections on the *Uber* preliminary ruling case' in A Ortiz (ed), *Internet: Competition and Regulation of Online Platforms*, e-book (Competition Policy International, 2016), available at www.competitionpolicyinternational.com/wp-content/uploads/2016/05/INTERNET-COMPETITION-LIBRO.pdf.

[80] Case C-526/15 *Uber Belgium v Taxi Radio Bruxellois* EU:C:2016:830.

whether it could ban *UberBLACK* (high-end) service on the ground that it is violating national unfair competition law without, however, infringing internal market principles.[81]

At the time of writing, the CJEU has only issued an Order in *Uber Belgium*, where it held the preliminary request to be inadmissible as being hypothetical and as providing inaccurate and insufficient background information. From the Court's (extremely) summary reasoning two interrelated distinctions may, however, be inferred: firstly, between activities which entail remuneration, and those which follow a mere cost-sharing logic;[82] and secondly, more specifically in the area of transportation, between ride-sharing (co-voiturage)[83] where the final destination is decided by the driver, and car-sharing[84] activities, where the destination is each time set by the user.[85]

As to the question whether *Uber* is a mere electronic platform or (also) a provider of transportation services, Advocate General Szpunar in *Asociación Profesional Elite Taxi (Uber Spain)*[86] clearly opined that *Uber* is offering a 'composite service'[87] that 'certainly cannot be considered to be a ride-sharing platform'[88] given that it 'controls the economically significant aspects of the transport service'.[89] He, thus, concluded that 'Uber is a genuine organiser and operator of urban transport services in the cities where it has a presence'.[90]

Advocate General Szpunar has also issued an Opinion in the French *Uber* case, which concerned the question whether the French law making *Uber's* activity into a criminal offence was a technical regulation concerning an information society service, which in order to be enforceable towards third parties needed to be notified according to Directive 98/34.[91] It should be remembered that this Directive only concerns information society (electronic) services. The Advocate General, based on his previous Opinion, said that *Uber* offers a composite service[92] and held that the French ban only concerned the non-electronic part of it, ie the activity of driving around passengers, not the activity of electronic intermediation itself, which was only incidentally affected.[93] Therefore, he concluded that the French authorities were entitled to enforce their ban on *Uber*. If the Court follows its Advocate

---

[81] Case C-371/17 *Uber*, pending [2017] OJ C 318/5; see also 'Germany refers case on Uber sedan service to European court', *Reuters* (18 May 2017).

[82] Case C-526/15 *Uber Belgium*, para 25.

[83] Both terms used by the Court, although the Order is only available in French (and German).

[84] Term not used as such by the Court.

[85] *Uber Belgium*, para 28.

[86] Opinion of AG Szpunar in Case C-434/15 *Asociación Profesional Elite Taxi v Uber Systems Spain* EU:C:2017:364.

[87] ibid para 28.

[88] ibid para 42.

[89] ibid para 51.

[90] ibid para 61.

[91] Opinion of AG Szpunar in Case C-320/16 *Uber France Sas* EU:C:2017:511.

[92] ibid para 15.

[93] ibid para 28.

General in this case, the solution reached will run in parallel with the judgment of the British High Court, where it was held that regulations by the board Transport for London concerning language aptitude tests were also enforceable against *Uber* drivers.[94] In other words, under both jurisdictions *Uber* will be treated as a transportation—and not as an e-commerce—undertaking, subject to the relevant national regulations.

C. The Commission's Regulatory Approach

The above brief description shows that the current regulatory void gives rise to both fragmentation along national, and even local, lines and legal uncertainty. The European Commission has expressed its interest in reaping the full benefits of online platforms and the digital economy in general.[95] So far, however, it has avoided taking legislative initiatives in this specific area. On the contrary, the Commission has offered soft-law guidance for collaborative platforms, while at the same time promoting legislation in neighbouring areas which could prove partly relevant for the collaborative economy.

i. Soft Guidance

The Commission adopted the ambitious Digital Single Market (DSM) Strategy[96] in May 2015 and has identified the completion of the DSM as one of its ten political priorities. The DSM strategy falls within the framework of the Commission initiatives to strengthen the overall competitiveness of industry, by enhancing small and medium-sized enterprises. The DSM thus aims at improving industry digitisation with actions in areas such as the data economy, internet of things (IoT), cloud computing, standards, skills and e-government.

As part of the DSM Strategy, the Commission conducted an assessment of the role of online platforms on the basis of a public consultation and a series of studies. This has led to the publication of a Communication on online platforms[97] complete with a Staff Working Paper.[98]

In parallel, collaborative platforms have especially caught the attention of the Commission, given their growth and importance in recent years. In this direction, in May 2016 the Commission, based on several 'impulse papers' prepared by

---

[94] See above n 63 and the accompanying text.

[95] Commission Communication, 'Digitising European Industry—Reaping the full benefits of a Digital Single Market' COM(2016) 180 final.

[96] Commission Communication, 'A Digital Single Market for Europe' COM(2015) 192 final.

[97] Commission Communication, 'Online Platforms and the Digital Single Market Opportunities and Challenges for Europe' COM(2016) 288 final.

[98] Commission Staff Working Document, 'Online Platforms and the Digital Single Market Opportunities and Challenges for Europe' SWD(2016) 172 final.

academia and professional consultancies in relation to specific issues,[99] published the EU Agenda for the Collaborative Economy.[100] In this well-drafted document the Commission gives some guidance on the way the various rules already in place may apply in the collaborative sector. It touches upon key issues, such as market access requirements, liability regimes, protection of users, employment in the collaborative economy and taxation.

Overall, the regulatory approach followed by the Commission in the above documents corresponds to a qualified 'wait-and-see' attitude. It has avoided legislating anew,[101] but rather has opted for amending existing sector-specific regulation and issuing guidance on the implementation of existing legislation with regard to online platforms in general and collaborative platforms in particular. Moreover, in a 2014 Communication specifically concerning crowdfunding, the Commission announced a quality mark, yet to materialise.[102] At the occasion of a parliamentary question answered on 29 June 2017, ie more than a year after the adoption of the Commission's Agenda,[103] Commissioner Bienkowska confirmed that the Commission's 'wait-and-see' approach remains.

ii. Regulatory Initiatives—Neighbouring Areas

The Commission's regulatory approach in this novel digital platform environment is driven by four objectives: a level playing field for comparable services; responsible behaviour; trust, transparency and fairness; open and non-discriminatory markets and data-driven economy.[104]

Firstly, the Commission aims to ensure a level playing field for similar digital services. To this end it is currently reviewing the EU telecom rules via the 'connectivity package' launched on September 2016[105] and it has already proposed

---

[99] Some highly analytical and rich Impulse Papers have been published on the following topics: market access requirements, liability issues raised by collaborative economy business models and the economic development of the collaborative economy, available at www.ec.europa.eu/growth/single-market/strategy/collaborative-economy_el.

[100] Commission Communication, 'A European Agenda for the collaborative economy' COM(2016) 356 final; see also its corresponding SWD(2016) 184 final.

[101] Such an approach, of not preemptively regulating fluid new industries, has also been commented on by the FTC (n 20) 57 and 62.

[102] Commission Communication, 'Unleashing the potential of Crowdfunding in the European Union' COM(2014) 172 final.

[103] Written question by MEP E Kaili (S&D), n E-002431/2017.

[104] See Commission Communication, 'Online Platforms and the Digital Single Market Opportunities and Challenges for Europe' COM(2016) 288 final.

[105] Commission Communication and Staff Working Document, 'Connectivity for a Competitive Digital Single Market—Towards a European Gigabit Society' COM(2016) 587 final and SWD(2016) 300 final; see also Commission, 'Proposal for a Regulation of the European Parliament and of the Council establishing the Body of European Regulators of Electronic Communications (BEREC)' COM(2016) 591 final; Commission Communication, '5G for Europe: An Action Plan' COM(2016) 588 final; and Commission, 'Proposal for a Regulation of the European Parliament and of the Council amending Regulations (EU) No 1316/2013 and (EU) No 283/2014 as regards the promotion of Internet connectivity in local communities' COM(2016) 589 final.

a new Directive establishing the European Electronic Communications Code.[106] Further, in January 2017, the Commission proposed a Regulation on Privacy and Electronic Communications in order to provide a high level of privacy protection for users of electronic communications services.[107]

Secondly, in order to ensure that online platforms act responsibly, the Commission has: adopted a new proposal for a Directive amending the Audio-visual Media Services Directive, which addresses online video sharing platforms containing illegal and harmful content to minors;[108] presented a new copyright package, fit for the digital age, which comprises of a Communication, two draft Directives and two draft Regulations;[109] published Principles for better Self- and Co-Regulation which help actors achieve better recognition, respect and credibility.[110] Moreover, the Commission is planning to further explore the need for guidance on the liability of online platforms when putting in place voluntary, good-faith measures to fight illegal content online and will review the need for formal notice-and-action procedures.[111]

---

[106] See Commission, 'Proposal for a Directive of the European Parliament and of the Council establishing the European Electronic Communications Code (Recast)' COM(2016) 590 final. See also Commission Staff Working Document, 'Impact Assessment' SWD(2016) 303 final; Commission Staff Working Document, 'Executive Summary of the Impact Assessment' SWD(2016) 304 final; and Commission Staff Working Document, 'Evaluation and Executive Summary' SWD(2016) 305 final.

[107] See Commission, 'Proposal for a Regulation of the European Parliament and of the Council concerning the respect for private life and the protection of personal data in electronic communications and repealing Directive 2002/58/EC (Regulation on Privacy and Electronic Communications)' COM(2017) 10 final. The Regulation was proposed following the ex post Regulatory Fitness and Performance Programme ('REFIT evaluation') of the ePrivacy Directive.

[108] See Commission, 'Proposal for a Directive of the European Parliament and of the Council amending Directive 2010/13/EU on the coordination of certain provisions laid down by law, regulation or administrative action in Member States concerning the provision of audiovisual media services in view of changing market realities' COM(2016)287 final.

[109] Commission Communication, 'Promoting a fair, efficient and competitive European copyright-based economy in the Digital Single Market' COM(2016) 592 final; See Commission, 'Proposal for a Directive of the European Parliament and of the Council on copyright in the Digital Single Market' COM(2016) 593 final; Commission, 'Proposal for a Regulation of the European Parliament and of the Council laying down rules on the exercise of copyright and related rights applicable to certain online transmissions of broadcasting organisations and retransmissions of television and radio programmes' COM(2016) 594 final; Commission, 'Proposal for a Directive of the European Parliament and of the Council on certain permitted uses of works and other subject-matter protected by copyright and related rights for the benefit of persons who are blind, visually impaired or otherwise print disabled and amending Directive 2001/29/EC on the harmonisation of certain aspects of copyright and related rights in the information society' COM(2016)596 final; and Commission, 'Proposal for a Regulation of the European Parliament and of the Council on the cross-border exchange between the Union and third countries of accessible format copies of certain works and other subject-matter protected by copyright and related rights for the benefit of persons who are blind, visually impaired or otherwise print disabled' COM(2016)595 final.

[110] Available at https://ec.europa.eu/digital-single-market/en/news/principles-better-self-and-co-regulation-and-establishment-community-practice.

[111] Such actions are expected by the end of 2017; see Commission Communication 'on the Mid-Term Review on the implementation of the Digital Single Market Strategy' COM(2017)228 final, 8–9.

Thirdly, in the direction of fostering trust, transparency and ensuring fairness, a revision of the Regulation on Consumer Protection Cooperation was proposed, to facilitate more efficient enforcement of EU consumer law in cross-border situations.[112] Moreover, the Commission issued new guidance on the interpretation and application of the Unfair Commercial Practices Directive in the digital context.[113] Lastly, the Commission aims to further promote interoperability actions, through issuing principles and guidance on electronic identification (eID) interoperability[114] and will carry out a targeted fact-finding exercise on B2B practices in the online platforms environment.[115]

Fourthly, one of the pillars of the growth of online platforms is open, non-discriminatory markets and the promotion of a data-driven economy. In this direction, the Commission has already reformed the data protection regime mainly with the adoption of the General Data Protection Regulation (GDPR), due to enter into force in 2018.[116] Additionally, as part of the 'free flow of data' initiative, the Commission issued a Communication on 'Building a European Data Economy'[117] and the relevant Staff Working Paper 'on the free flow of data and emerging issues of the European data economy'.[118]

Lastly, apart from the general initiatives mentioned above, the EU has also taken steps in regulating more specific and technical issues.[119] The European Parliament and the Council have adopted a Network and Information Security Directive,[120] while a draft Regulation on geo-blocking is on the pipeline.[121] Further, the European Parliament and the Council, in order to enhance regulatory oversight of

---

[112] See Commission, 'Proposal for a Regulation of the European Parliament and of the Council on cooperation between national authorities responsible for the enforcement of consumer protection laws' COM(2016)283 final.

[113] Commission Staff Working Document, 'Guidance on the Implementation/Application of Directive 2005/29/EC on Unfair Commercial Practices' SWD(2016) 163 final.

[114] Data interoperability 'enables multiple digital services to exchange data seamlessly, facilitated by appropriate technical specifications', while in the case of online platforms it facilitates 'widespread cross-platform data exchange'; see Commission Communication, 'Building a European Data Economy' COM(2017) 9 final, 16.

[115] See Commission's webpage dedicated on platform-to-business trading practices, available at https://ec.europa.eu/digital-single-market/en/business-business-trading-practices.

[116] For which see Ch 3 above.

[117] COM(2017) 9 final.

[118] Commission Staff Working Document 'on the free flow of data and emerging issues of the European data economy' SWD(2017) 2 final.

[119] For a list of planned actions of the EU with regard to online platforms see Annex: Roadmap for completing the Digital Single Market in Commission Communication, 'A Digital Single Market Strategy for Europe' COM(2015) 192 final.

[120] European Parliament and Council Directive (EU) 2016/1148 concerning measures for a high common level of security of network and information systems across the Union [2016] OJ L 194/1.

[121] See Commission, 'Proposal for a Regulation of the European Parliament and of the Council on addressing geo-blocking and other forms of discrimination based on customers' nationality, place of residence or place of establishment within the internal market and amending Regulation (EC) No 2006/2004 and Directive 2009/22/EC' COM(2016) 289 final.

parcel delivery, proposed a Draft Regulation on cross-border parcel delivery services, already adopted by the Commission.[122] At the same time, the Commission has proposed legislation to modernise the VAT regime in cross-border e-commerce transactions and e-books,[123] has proposed the eGovernment action plan 2016–2020,[124] as well as the European Cloud initiative,[125] and is currently setting up ICT Standardisation Priorities for the DSM.[126] Last but not least, the Commission has attempted to enhance e-commerce by adopting a draft regulation to update the SatCab Directive,[127] a new draft Directive on the online sale of goods,[128] a draft Directive on the supply of digital content,[129] and a Regulation on cross-border portability of online content services.[130] In that regard, it has also conducted a sector inquiry on e-commerce.[131]

A list of the actions taken in support of the realisation of the DSM is annexed to the Commission's mid-term review published in May 2017.[132]

---

[122] Commission, 'Proposal for a Regulation of the European Parliament and of the Council on cross-border parcel delivery services' COM (2016) 285 final.

[123] https://ec.europa.eu/taxation_customs/business/vat/vat-legislation-proposed_en.

[124] https://ec.europa.eu/digital-single-market/en/egovernment-action-plan-digitising-european-industry.

[125] https://ec.europa.eu/digital-single-market/en/%20european-cloud-initiative.

[126] Commission Communication, 'ICT Standardisation Priorities for the Digital Single Market' COM(2016) 176 final.

[127] See Commission, 'Proposal for a Regulation of the European Parliament and of the Council laying down rules on the exercise of copyright and related rights applicable to certain online transmissions of broadcasting organisations and retransmissions of television and radio programmes' COM(2016) 594 final.

[128] See Commission, 'Proposal for a Directive of the European Parliament and of the Council on certain aspects concerning contracts for the online and other distance sales of goods' COM(2015) 635 final.

[129] See Commission, 'Proposal for a Directive of the European Parliament and of the Council on certain aspects concerning contracts for the supply of digital content' COM(2015) 634 final. For an overview of these proposals, see H Beale, 'The future of European contract law in the light of the European Commission's proposals for Directives on digital content and online sales' (2016) *IDP, Revista de Internet, Derecho y Política, Universitat Oberta de Catalunya* 3; see also R Schulze, D Staudenmayer and S Lohsse (eds), *Contracts for the Supply of Digital Content: Regulatory Challenges and Gaps* (Nomos/Hart Publishing, 2017).

[130] See Commission, 'Proposal for a Regulation of the European Parliament and of the Council on ensuring the cross-border portability of online content services in the internal market' COM (2015) 627 final.

[131] Commission Communication, 'Final report on the E-commerce Sector Inquiry' COM(2017) 229 final.

[132] Commission Communication, 'Mid-Term Review on the implementation of the Digital Single Market Strategy A Connected Digital Single Market for All' COM(2017) 228 final; see also the Annex available at https://ec.europa.eu/digital-single-market/en/news/digital-single-market-commission-calls-swift-adoption-key-proposals-and-maps-out-challenges.

III. Regulation of the Collaborative Economy: A Normative Approach

In order to achieve the desirable balance between innovation and regulation, the EU (and Member States' governments) must overcome the specific regulatory challenges posed by this novel phenomenon. These include:

(a) the lack of definition: as explained, the terminology and definition of the 'collaborative economy' are rather hazy. Activities considered as collaborative by some are not necessarily considered as such by others. This difficulty may bring unjustified heavier regulation upon collaborative participants, may cause fragmentation across the EU, and leaves rooms for;

(b) legal grey areas: collaborative economy platforms often operate in legal grey areas, such as tax, insurance, liability etc, whereby complex legal issues arise due to blurred lines between professional and personal, goods and services, providing and consuming;

(c) novelty and evolution: public regulation is traditionally slow, especially at the EU level. The process of legislating is time-consuming. This comes into conflict with the fast pace of evolution of the collaborative economy and rapid technological progress. Collaborative platforms are 'mushrooming' and evolving by the day, as they reflect the peers' desires at a given time, and are flexible and responsive to real-time needs;

(d) national precedent: in the lines of fragmentation, the EU has already been 'left behind' in comparison to national jurisdictions and in some cases seems to be playing 'catch-up'. For example, the UK in the context of its mission to become a harbour for the collaborative economy innovation, has already created an infrastructure supporting collaborative economy entrepreneurship. Such initiatives, however beneficial for the overall economy, increase the difficulty of regulating anew where precedent has already taken place;

(e) possible harness of innovation; if this is not handled carefully, the EU may accidently end up stifling innovation and wasting its opportunity to benefit from the very profitable collaborative economy. Heavy, systemic approaches inherently contradict the innovative, flexible nature of sharing;

(f) contrasting interests: apart from the balancing act between regulation and innovation, the EU must also find the right balance between tendering of incumbents' rights and promoting collaborative actors. The traditional economy is experiencing nothing short of a seismic vibration with the advent of the collaborative economy. This is particularly apparent in regulated sectors, such as the taxi industry. It hence bears the question whether the promotion of innovation is worth (or requires) the de-regulation of certain market sectors, to the detriment of traditional economic players. Such a risk, however regulated it may be, might result in a lose-lose scenario;

(g) differentiated practices: in addition to all the above challenges, the EU must take into account the variety and diversity of the collaborative economy 'family'. A one-size-fits-all approach can hardly be sufficient for tackling such a manifold phenomenon.

In view of the above, three core questions, in relation to regulating the collaborative economy, need to be discussed.

A. To Regulate or Not to Regulate?

i. Regulate or Leave it up to the Invisible Hands?

This first question is common to any economic activity, but re-emerges afresh in the field of the collaborative economy, based on a handful of fresh arguments. These may be categorised broadly in two categories.

Firstly, there is the 'disruption' line of arguments, according to which the collaborative economy is a very dynamic area which is better off remaining shielded from regulation. For one thing, the collaborative economy is fundamentally based on technologic advances and business innovation, and these may be stifled by premature and/or inappropriate regulation, thus blocking, or else artificially affecting an extremely dynamic and efficient sector of the economy.[133] Further, in view of the dynamism of the sector, the stakes and regulatory objectives are under constant evolution. Hence, the regulator risks misjudging the issues which need regulatory intervention, as many of those will have been resolved by technology, the parties themselves, or their competitors (who come up with more efficient, less problematic alternatives).[134]

Secondly is the 'enhanced' invisible hands line of argument, according to which the collaborative economy, more than any other kind of economy previously known, has the appropriate means of handling market failures. Through the reputational ratings system platforms alleviate information asymmetries,[135] while big data analytics make for a personalised level of consumption and price while also allowing for a tailor-made level of (consumer) protection.[136]

---

[133] This is a commonplace among most, if not all, authors; see indicatively, C Koopman, M Mitchell and A Thierer, 'The Sharing Economy and Consumer Protection Regulation: The Case of Policy Change' (2015) 8 *Journal of Business Entrepreneurship and Law* 529.

[134] The EU Commission has been criticised in the framework of some of its merger decisions, that when trying to project the effects of the proposed merger, often approaches problems in a backward looking manner and imposes conditions and/or commitments which are made obsolete by the very market by the time the merger has been completed, see eg I Graef, 'Stretching EU competition law tools for search engines and social networks' (2015) 4(3) *Internet Policy Review* 4, available at https://ssrn.com/abstract=2655555.

[135] See section II.A.i.b above.

[136] See Ch 2 above.

These arguments, convincing as they are, fail to address two main issues. Firstly, the fact that the collaborative economy does indeed possess the above tools, does not mean that day-to-day problems do not surface: collaborative economy actors participate daily in car accidents, damage to life and property, tax evasion, violation of non-discrimination, data protection or other fundamental personal rights. All these issues, together with employment law challenges (discussed in Chapter 5), do reach the courts and do have to be resolved; in the meantime they do have a cost for the individuals involved and for society as a whole. It is crucial that these are resolved in a coherent, consistent, socially acceptable and economically optimal manner. This is unlikely to happen in the absence of *any* rules. The great variety of ways in which local regulators, judges and other authorities have so far reacted to the challenges posed by *Uber* and *Airbnb* (discussed above) give a clear indication of this risk. If such inconsistencies were acceptable at a time when the collaborative phenomenon was really limited, they are not any more. As Ranchordàs has aptly explained, no regulation may be as stifling to innovation as inappropriate regulation.[137]

This last point, of the growing importance of the collaborative economy, brings to the fore the second argument: 'it simply should not be that a growing sector of the economy is illegal'.[138] This is bad for the economy, as it forces economic activity underground; bad for the users of 'illegal' services, as they are less likely to have recourse to public authorities (judges, police etc) in order to claim protection from malicious, exploitative or else dangerous practices; and bad for the platforms, as regulatory risk will make it more difficult and, at any rate, more expensive for them to obtain fresh investment.[139]

A further argument in favour of regulating collaborative platforms is that, because of their electronic nature and the traceability of all transactions, platforms are more amenable to regulation than traditional industries.[140]

Therefore, it may safely be said that the majoritarian view in legal doctrine, for different reasons, is in favour of some kind of regulation.[141] In the previous chapters of this book the conclusion was reached that regulation is necessary in the area of labour law and may be desirable in areas such as consumer and data

---

[137] S Ranchordás, 'Does Sharing Mean Caring? Regulating Innovation in the Sharing Economy' (2015) 16 *Minnesota Journal of Law, Science & Technology* 414, 474, where she postulates that 'Different Game + Same Rules = Game Over'.

[138] S Miller, 'First Principles for Regulating the Sharing Economy' (2016) 53 *Harvard Journal on Legislation* 147, 153.

[139] ibid.

[140] B Edelman and D Geradin, 'Efficiencies and Regulatory Shortcuts: How Should We Regulate Companies Like Airbnb and Uber?' (2016) 19 *Stanford Technology Law Review* 293, 326.

[141] See also A Strowel and W Vergote, 'Digital Platforms: To Regulate or Not To Regulate? Message to Regulators: Fix the Economics First, Then Focus on the Right Regulation' (2015) Written Evidence (OPL0087) found in UK House of Lords, 'Online platforms and the Digital Single Market: oral and written evidence' 788, text accompanying fn 10 therein, available at www.parliament.uk/documents/lords-committees/eu-internal-market-subcommittee/online-platforms/OnlinePlatformsWrittenEv-VolumePublished.pdf.

protection. To use Chang's words 'regulation is an inevitable truth for the collaborative economy, and … it will be a key factor behind smoothing the integration of collaborative platforms into mainstream society'.[142]

ii. Expand or Disrupt: Extend the Application of Existing Rules or Create New Ones?

Legal principles and legal rules tend to be expressed in general and abstract terms in order to encompass an unlimited number of factual situations. They are based on past experience and are meant to cover future problems; they are applied in a dynamic and flexible manner and often cover successfully situations completely unforeseen at the time when the rule was adopted. However, some technological developments—and the corresponding socioeconomic ones—require fresh rules: advances in the telecoms sector, audio-visual services, data manipulation, internet domain names, cyber-security, have called for fresh rules. Is the collaborative economy one of those areas where specific rules are needed?

The fact that the technology used (internet platforms, search and matching machines, big data analytics) is not in itself all new and disruptive seems to be advocating in favour of a negative answer.[143]

It has been convincingly argued, however, that 'legal disruption is not an accident of the platform economy, it is a core feature';[144] and that 'a regulatory response to the sharing economy requires recognition that the types of transactions occurring differ substantially in how they affect the real world and thus require a differentiated regulatory response'.[145] Indeed, the collaborative environment questions some basic hypotheses upon which basic (liability) rules are grounded, and on which the law's 'special relationships' (under common law) and special liability regimes (under continental law) are being built.[146] In this way, for example in the field of insurance, the collaborative economy is straining the limits between personal and commercial activity.[147] The same is true in the area of taxation, where professionals and non-professionals are subject to different fiscal regimes, both concerning revenue and VAT. Similarly, consumer protection, under EU law—and in many US states—is conditional upon the qualification of the supplier as a 'trader'. Last but not least, the respect of fundamental rights,

---

[142] W Chang, 'Growing Pains: The Role of Regulation in the Collaborative Economy' (2015) 9(1) *Intersect* 1.

[143] See eg K Werebach, 'Is Uber a Common Carrier' (2015) 12(1) *Journal of Law and Policy for the Information Society* 135, who argues that 'it makes little sense to enforce a strict separation between the cyber and the physical world when firms increasingly straddle both'.

[144] Strowel and Vergote, 'Digital Platforms: To Regulate or Not To Regulate? Message to Regulators: Fix the Economics First, Then Focus on the Right Regulation' (2015) text corresponding to fn 36 therein.

[145] Miller, 'First Principles for Regulating the Sharing Economy' (2016) 151.

[146] V Katz, 'Regulating the Sharing Economy' (2015) 30(385) *Berkeley Technology Law Journal* 1065, 1079.

[147] ibid 1093.

such as eg of non-discrimination on the basis of colour, race etc do not apply in the same way to those offering goods and services to the public, and to private individuals:[148] one can freely choose whom to exclude from one's house or car, as long as it is used privately, but this changes as soon as these assets are used to offer services to the public.

Therefore, many authors have argued in favour of fresh legal rules, adapted to the characteristics of the collaborative economy.[149] Hence 'new and unique' rules should be enacted.[150] The term 'experimental regulations' has been mooted.[151] The reasons which justify fresh, collaborative-specific rules include, inter alia:[152] (a) the fact that entrepreneurs, imbued as they are with the ethos of disruption and sidetracked by the mismatch between speedy innovation and slow regulation, are unwilling to engage with existing regulatory systems; (b) that platforms follow new business models which are not easily amenable under existing regulatory frameworks; (c) that large user bases provide platforms with political power over regulators;[153] (d) that the newly-created 'micro-entrepreneur' has neither the willingness nor the capacity to comply with overburdening regulations.

Such rules could be 'fresh', 'new' or 'experimental' in that they foresee new legal categories (eg special liability rules for platforms, special new employment category for suppliers, special consumer protection rules); in that they entail new regulatory forms (eg polycentric co-regulation, for which see section III.B.ii below); in that they foresee new procedures and principles for the adoption of such new rules (the participation of platforms, etc); in that they are designed to be 'innovation friendly'.[154] Some of these ideas will be further discussed below.

iii. Now or Later?

It has been observed that 'the sharing economy evokes three kinds of response: regulate it out of existence, don't regulate it at all, and … "wait-and-see."'[155]

---

[148] These thoughts are taken from Katz above, and duly adapted in order to fit into the European context.

[149] See eg Das Acevedo, 'Regulating Employment Relationships in the Sharing Economy' (2016) 27; see also Miller (n 138) 165–67, who posits among his 'ten principles for the regulation of the sharing economy' 'Principle 7: The Sharing Economy Disrupts and Reimagines Established Regulatory Structures' and 'Principle 8: The Sharing Economy Requires a Response Beyond Traditional Regulation'.

[150] A Jonas, 'Share and Share Dislike: The Rise of Uber and AirBNB and How New York City Should Play Nice?' (2016) 24(1) *Journal of Law and Policy* 205.

[151] H Posen, 'Ridesharing in the Sharing Economy: Should Regulators Impose Uber Regulations on Uber?' (2015) 101 *Iowa Law Review* 405, 429.

[152] These are developed by A Armitage, 'Gauguin, Darwin, & Design Thinking: A Solution in the Impasse Between Innovation & Regulation' (2016) University of California, Legal Studies Research Paper No 235, 5–12.

[153] On this specific issue see S Cannon and LH Summers, 'How Uber and the Sharing Economy Can Win Over Regulators' *Harvard Business Review* (13 October 2014), available at https://hbr.org/2014/10/how-uber-and-the-sharing-economy-can-win-over-regulators.

[154] Ranchordás, 'Does Sharing Mean Caring? Regulating Innovation in the Sharing Economy' (2015) 444.

[155] Das Acevedo (n 30) 15, notes omitted.

As has been discussed in the previous parts of the present chapter, different sectors, in different jurisdictions, have provoked different regulatory reactions. The Commission, in its 2016 Agenda for the Collaborative Economy,[156] has opted for the third option: it has tried to offer insights into the ways existing regulation may apply to the collaborative economy, and has reserved the right to intervene punctually, in the future. In a somehow philosophical approach, Armitage has mooted the idea that

> the benefit of the sharing economy is such to society that we should permit companies to work around cumbersome regulations and therefore be unregulated for a period of time, because the innovation that will arise in response will make the world a better place (just as Gaugin's art does).[157]

In academia, however, the number of voices pleading in favour of some kind of immediate regulation of the collaborative economy grows by the day.[158] The wait-and-see attitude should, according to this view, give way to a 'try-and-see' approach.[159] On top of the reasons stated above, under (a), which point to the necessity of regulation (ie that the collaborative segment of the economy has grown and needs to be made visible etc), arguments in favour of such regulation being instituted immediately include:[160] (a) the fact that enough time has passed since major collaborative platforms started operating (2008 for *Airbnb* and *Task-Rabbit*, 2009 for *Uber* and *Getaround*) and that core elements of their business models, as well as the major problems which need to be responded to, have been adequately identified—so much so that several platforms have started devising their own responses; (b) the fact that collaborative platforms have managed to thrive (overall) in the face of often openly hostile and prohibitive government responses, shows that the risk of regulation stifling innovation may be over-stated—indeed regulation may be 'innovation friendly' if it fulfils certain criteria, such as, inter alia, incrementality, flexibility, sunset and rendez-vous clauses;[161] and (c) the fact that municipalities, cities, or individual states are compelled to adapt regulations, thus leading to de facto fragmentation, which, in turn, may negatively affect the development of the collaborative economy—and the same is true for courts which, for lack of any better rule apply the only existing ones;

---

[156] COM(2016)356 final (n 100).

[157] Above n 152; she explains beforehand that while Gaugin's paintings are a great asset for art, they are the fruit of personal and family choices of contested morality—which, however, are being sidestepped precisely in view of the value of his art. And while she discusses this idea, she reaches the conclusion that in 'the real world' this is not an idea likely to succeed, at 29.

[158] See, inter alia, Das Acevedo (n 30); Miller (n 138); Edelman and Geradin (n 140) 31, where they note that 'software platforms need not be in any important sense "above the law"'.

[159] Das Acevedo (n 30) 27.

[160] The reasons stated below are inspired from Das Acevedo (n 30) 25–26 and from Ranchordás (n 137) 450–51 and 470. For a lengthier discussion of the ways in which regulation may promote innovation see, S Ranchordás, 'Innovation Experimentalism in the Age of the Sharing Economy' (2015) 19 *Lewis and Clark Law Review* 1.

[161] For the conditions that should be fulfilled for regulation to be 'innovation friendly' and for the ways this can happen in the collaborative economy see Ranchordás (nn 137 and 160).

(d) that platforms' financial cost and material distraction of continuously fighting legal battles against public authorities and class-actions here and there may be much higher than that of complying with well-designed regulations;[162] (e) the fact that established platforms do, henceforth, possess both the economic weight and the public support to press for favourable regulations.[163]

B. What Kind of Regulation

i. Ex Ante—Ex Post

Most platforms, and several authors, put forward the idea that, if regulation were to be adopted, such regulation should only intervene ex post, ie in order to correct any problems which have arisen from the service supply, and not ex ante, taking the form of an authorisation or licensing procedure or other prerequisite condition.[164] According to these views the emphasis should be in instituting clear and effective tort rules which would allocate liability between the parties involved. The second pillar of this ex post regulation would consist in foreseeing adequate insurance policies in order to cover the risks associated with each specific activity.

The main objection to this view is that ex post rules do not prevent harm from occurring, but merely spread the cost in an equitable way—a cost that could altogether be avoided by ex ante rules. In areas where the life and corporal integrity of humans is at stake, ex post rules are useful as complementary, rather than as substitutes to ex ante protective rules.

ii. Bottom-up, Top-down or Collaborative?

Most authors agree that in a field as technology-driven and dynamic as the collaborative economy, traditional, top-down, regulation should occur only exceptionally and only to complement self-regulatory techniques. Such techniques, based as they are on the technology supporting the matching function of the platforms, are embedded in the collaborative economy and it would be counter-intuitive to neglect them or dismiss them. Thus, reputation rating systems, profiling etc are to be preferred over other more traditional command-and-control means of regulation. The idea prevails that 'platforms should be viewed as part of the solution, rather than as part of the problem, and they should be included as key actors in a self-regulatory regime'.[165]

---

[162] Armitage (n 152) 39.

[163] Das Acevedo (n 30) 25.

[164] Koopman, Mitchell and Thierer, 'The Sharing Economy and Consumer Protection Regulation: The Case of Policy Change' (2015); D Stallibrass and J Fingleton, 'Regulation, Innovation and Growth: Why Peer-to-Peer Business should be Supported' (2016) 7 *Journal of European Competition Law and Practice* 414.

[165] Cohen and Sundararajan, 'Self-Regulation and Innovation in the Peer-to-Peer Sharing Economy' (2015) 119.

A question looms, however, as to whether these self-regulatory techniques should be subject to some kind of formal regulation, or at least supervision, in order to make sure that they do not lead to abusive or else discriminatory conduct. In this respect, the proposal of the Commission to introduce an EU quality mark in relation to crowdfunding platforms may be an indication of the way forward.[166]

Further, several authors put forward the idea that collaborative platforms call for (some kind of) collaborative regulation. Cohen and Sundararajan discuss the conditions under which self-regulatory organisations (SROs) could effectively regulate the collaborative economy.[167] They observe, however, that

> self-regulatory decisions may suffer from a lack of transparency or reviewability ... [and] must therefore have some form of transparency and governmental oversight. One possible regime could involve a tripartite model in which third-party watchdogs evaluate SROs, and the level of government oversight and regulation is determined by a firm's history of compliance.[168]

Dyal-Chand, based on 'varieties of capitalism' analysis, suggests that intermediary institutions collectively representing the interests of 'microentrepreneurs' involved in the provision of services in the collaborative framework, should be created and should actively participate in defining their working environment.[169] Infranca questions whether this could be feasible, or even desirable, in view of the rather liberal (as opposed to coordinated) character of collaborative markets.[170] Instead, he suggests that platforms should acknowledge the existence of users' forums—presumably on both sides of the market—and consult with them in order to guide their self-regulatory activities.[171] Hence, he pleads for an 'institutional turn' based on 'a more collaborative model, in which institutions with a stake in particular legal and social problems partner with regulators to come up with solutions'.[172] Under a more innovative perspective, Armitage suggests that recourse should be had to 'design thinking' which she defines as a 'solution-focused process, which starts with identifying a goal instead of a problem ... uses logic, imagination, intuition and systemic reasoning [and] is user focused'.[173] She further explains that 'the team engaged in the process should be interdisciplinary and all should have the capacity and disposition to think collaboratively'.[174] More recently, Finck explained that the best way to combine flexibility, high quality rules, efficient implementation with democratic accountability is through

---

[166] See COM(2014) 172 final (n 102).
[167] Cohen and Sundararajan (n 1) 123 ff.
[168] ibid 131.
[169] R Dyal-Chand, 'Regulating Sharing: The Sharing Economy as an Alternative Capitalist System' (2015) 90 *Tulane Law Review* 241–308.
[170] J Infranca, 'Intermediary Institutions and the Sharing Economy' (2016) 90 *Tulane Law Review* 29, 35–36.
[171] ibid 37.
[172] ibid 40, note omitted.
[173] Armitage (n 152) 36.
[174] ibid 37.

'polycentric co-regulation' with the participation of multiple stakeholders, hand in hand with public authorities and the EU.[175]

iii. At the Local, National or Supranational Level

'There is significant reason to think that local governments would be the most appropriate regulators'.[176] This is certainly true for underlying services offered at the local level, such as transportation, home-sharing, dog-sitting, meal-sharing, task-performance and the like. Authors who reason on the basis of such services invariably proscribe the local (ie in the United States: sub-national and even sub-state) level as the best suited to intervene, help and reap the benefits of collaborative activities.[177] This makes sense not only because the effects of the activities are primarily being felt at the local level (traffic de/congestion, zoning etc), but also because such activities are traditionally being regulated at the local level.

The opposite view may, however, be convincingly put forward. Big collaborative platforms are global and need to develop global policies. Many of the services offered, such as crowdfunding, design and consultancy services, e-health, freelance services, such as writing and translation, and the like are offered for a global clientele. But even local services, such as transport services, would benefit from unitary and coherent rules.[178] A further argument in favour of centralised regulation is that, henceforth, big platforms are too big and too resourceful, in terms of litigation, lobbying and public support, to be tackled by local regulators.[179]

The above general considerations acquire a much bigger importance at the EU level, where the issues of competence distribution, power grab and subsidiarity are core. Several activities offered through platforms are regulated at the EU level (such as eg financial services), others remain of the remit of the Member States, or even of lower levels of government (such as eg accommodation), while others are regulated by both. Thus, the transport of goods is, in principle, regulated by a series of EU regulations and directives, while taxi services remain at the discretion of the Member States and/or local governments.[180] Given the breadth and variety of collaborative activities, a sector-specific approach, along the lines of the existing competence shared between the EU and its Member States, could be envisioned. Such an approach would be in line with the principle of subsidiarity, but would

---

[175] M Finck, 'Digital Regulation: Designing a Supranational Legal Framework for the Platform Economy' (2017) LSE Legal Studies Working Paper No 15; and (2018—forthcoming) *EL Rev*, available at https://ssrn.com/abstract=2990043.

[176] Infranca, 'Intermediary Institutions and the Sharing Economy' (2016) 40–41.

[177] See eg Rauch and Schleicher, 'Like Uber, But for Local Governmental Policy: The Future of Local Regulation of the "Sharing Economy"' (2015).

[178] J Mastracci, 'A Case for Federal Ride-Sharing Regulations: How Protectionism and Inconsistent Lawmaking Stunt Uber-Led Technological Entrepreneurship' (2015) 18 *Tulane Journal of Law and Intellectual Property* 1.

[179] Armitage (n 152) 6.

[180] See Case C-338/09 *YellowCab* EU:C:2010:814.

be source of regulatory fragmentation. Another nuanced view has been put forward, whereby market access and other operating conditions should be decided at the local (and national level), while protective laws (including consumer protection and competition law) would be within the remit of the national or/and EU authorities.[181] This view too, by delegating market access to the local/national regulator, neglects the fact that the internal market is all about securing market access in all Member States. The Commission, for its part, in its 2016 Agenda for the Collaborative Economy seems to be embracing a horizontal view, grounded on the wish to enhance the development of collaborative platforms in the EU, irrespective of their field of activity.[182] If the Commission decided to further its Agenda and propose horizontal legislation, finding the appropriate legal basis could prove to be a daunting task.

Once an EU measure is adopted, then the question of its implementation becomes crucial: it will be much easier to implement measures which come within the remit of some Commission's Directorates General (such as DG COMP) or of some existing Agency (such as the Data Protection Officer), rather than measures which correspond to more 'shared' competences.[183] This is why the idea has been mooted to create a European rating Agency for platforms,[184] an 'institutionalist' idea (typically French) yet to be explored.

iv. Horizontal Cross-cutting Rules or Sector-specific Ones?

This question rejoins, to a large extent, the discussion under the previous one. Indeed, the lack of precise definition and the fluid nature of the collaborative economy results in an indefinite number of distinct activities being brought under the umbrella of 'collaborative economy'. This, in turn, makes it plain that horizontal, one-size-fits-all regulations would not make much sense, unless they address in a general way platforms' rights and obligations.[185] Such a horizontal rule could be eg the institution of platform liability for all transactions concluded through it, (even/especially) when the supplier of the underlying service is not a trader.[186] Another topic of horizontal interest could be the use of data by collaborative platforms.[187] Further, reputation rating mechanisms could also be subject to some horizontal regulation.[188]

---

[181] Strowel and Vergote (n 141) under section B.
[182] COM(2016) 356 final.
[183] See Strowel and Vergote (n 141) 789.
[184] Rapports du Conseil de la Numérique (FR), 'Ambition numérique, Pour une politique française et européenne de la transition numérique' (2015) available at https://cnnumerique.fr/telecharger-le-rapport-ambitionnumerique-du-cnnum-qui-a-ete-remis-au-premier-ministre-manuel-valls; this idea is briefly discussed by Strowel and Vergote (n 141) 788–89, who also cite some critical articles.
[185] In this sense see also Miller (n 138) 151–52.
[186] An issue discussed in Ch 2 above as 'the Danish model'.
[187] In this sense see Strowel and Vergote (n 141) 792–93.
[188] For reputation mechanisms and the problems they raise see section II.A.i.b.

C. What to Regulate

i. In Terms of Interests

According to basic theory on regulation, regulation is justified by four major reasons: information asymmetries; natural monopolies; externalities; social and equity concerns.

Cohen and Sundararajan,[189] in parallel with Edelman and Geradin,[190] argue that information asymmetries are adequately addressed by rating systems, big data and other means put to work by platforms. Given that 'platforms have a natural incentive to alleviate exchange-deterring forms of information failure',[191] asymmetries need not be specifically regulated upon[192]—it is yet a different question whether reputational mechanisms themselves should be regulated.[193] Stallibrass and Fingleton contend that in relation to information asymmetries, platforms 'may signal different levels of self-regulation, allowing consumers to make choice between protection and price'.[194] Therefore, the bulk of information requirements, typically foreseen in order to address such asymmetries and to protect consumers, need not be imposed on collaborative platforms. This finding fits perfectly with the proposal made in the final part of the consumer protection section (in Chapter 2) of this book: that if a new, more behavioural-centered, approach were to be followed in the field of the collaborative economy, this would tilt away from the extensive information requirements currently imposed on service providers and would fully exploit the information possibilities offered by reputational and other information mechanisms put to work by platforms.

Natural monopolies are sectors of the economy, typically based on heavy infrastructure, where once the initial investment is amortised, the marginal cost of every extra user decreases; therefore, the larger the number of users, the lower the cost, and thus the price, of their services. These rare situations do justify regulatory intervention securing exclusive or special rights, in order to make sure that no other entrants undercut the user-basis of the natural monopoly. In Chapter 1 above, it has been explained that externalities developed by two-sided platforms, instead of decreasing the cost of services, increase their utility to users. Thus, the same logic, of securing platform monopolies through regulation, could be put forward.

---

[189] Cohen and Sundararajan (n 1) 120–22.

[190] Edelman and Geradin (n 140).

[191] Cohen and Sundararajan (n 1) 121.

[192] See, however, contra, K Erickson and I Sorensen, 'Regulating the Sharing Economy' (2016) 5(2) (special issue) *Internet Policy Review* 1, 6, who believe that trust mechanisms alone burden individuals with disproportionate risks and need to be complemented by more traditional regulation.

[193] See n 188 above and the corresponding text.

[194] Stallibrass and Fingleton, 'Regulation, Innovation and Growth: Why Peer-to-Peer Business should be Supported' (2016) 417.

Such an idea, however, should be resisted as any decision creating a monopoly in an area as fluid and as transformative as the collaborative economy would certainly block natural market dynamics and stifle innovation. It is worth noting that today's big electronic platforms (eg *Google*, *Facebook* and *Chrome*) have been late-comers in their respective relevant markets, but have managed to displace—and occasionally drive out of the market—their precursors (*Altavista*, *MySpace*, *Internet Explorer*). In the field of electronic platforms, competition often comes in the form of a new service, from outside rather than from within a market.

On the contrary, the regulator should take care of negative externalities developed by the platforms' activities, given that neither the platforms themselves nor the peers have the incentive, or the means, to internalise them.[195] Thus, increased car traffic and decreased value of taxi medallions due to car-sharing platforms, violations of zoning regulations and noisy guests brought in by home-sharing platforms, smelly cooking connected to meal-sharing platforms, do justify some kind of regulation. The debate is open to whether such regulation should take the form of command and control rules,[196] or whether a market-based solution, in the form of taxes or levies which help price-in the negative impacts of externalities, would be enough.[197]

Equity considerations and social objectives constitute the fourth broad interest which may be pursued through regulation. In the collaborative economy context this may justify regulation on at least two grounds.

Firstly, there is the protection of suppliers as workers. This issue has been extensively discussed in Chapter 5 above and it has become plain that as the number of such 'workers' grows and as their reliance on the collaborative economy to make their living increases, some regulatory intervention is indispensable in order to secure a minimum labour protection.

Secondly, there is the more far-reaching idea that some collaborative activities could qualify as 'public utilities' and be regulated and subsidised as such. According to this view 'Uber [and like platforms] is the invisible platform that provides an essential service, on demand and at a scale, analogous to water, electric and telecommunications providers'.[198] The argument goes on that 'without the Internet, such services would require the kind of direct hierarchical management used in earlier transportation systems such as trains, airplanes, or express delivery services',[199] while *Uber*, through the use of the Internet and smartphones manages, 'to tie together independently operated vehicles into a mass of transportation resources',[200] in a way that 'aggregate[s] pools of physical resources through Internet connectivity'.[201] Internet-enabled utilities is what traditional utility firms

---

[195] Edelman and Geradin (n 140) 15–21; Cohen and Sundararajan (n 1) 122.
[196] As seems to be suggested by the above authors.
[197] In this sense see Stallibrass and Fingleton (n 164) 418.
[198] See, inter alia, Werebach 'Is Uber a Common Carrier' (2015) 138.
[199] ibid 138.
[200] ibid 139.
[201] ibid 140.

will also be offering in the years to come, with the difference that platforms will not be owning the resources put at the consumers' disposal. Indeed, according to this same argument, public utilities display some basic characteristics all of which are shared by (most) collaborative platforms: (a) they correspond to societally significant markets; (b) they are based on some 'connection' infrastructure; (c) they either are natural monopolies, or tend to become de facto monopolies; and (d) they collect personal information and raise acute privacy issues.[202]

This idea has been taken further by other authors, who suggest that once 'sharing wars' are over, government (local or otherwise) is likely to introduce 'complex webs of subsidies, taxes, regulatory redistributions and reliance aimed at using sharing firms to achieve key governmental ends'.[203] Collaborative activities could be subsidised (in the same way as the construction of big stadiums or congress centers are subsidised) in order to raise the prestige of a city and boost all those economic activities which are connected to the collaborative one. Further, collaborative activities, to the extent that they create employment and offer cheaper services, could, if properly funded and regulated (inter alia against socio-economic biases), serve redistributive purposes. Last but not least, collaborative firms could become the government's contractor and provide goods and services either to the government itself or, on its behalf, directly to citizens.[204]

The term 'public utilities' is derived from the common law and the closest—though more far reaching in terms of legal consequences—equivalent under continental law would be the French 'service public';[205] or in the EU context, 'services of general economic interest' (SGEIs).[206] So, would platforms such as *Uber* and *Airbnb*, which have been banned, chased and demonised, be involved in the provision of SGEIs? Although such a prevision is akin to science fiction today, it may well correspond to reality in few years' time. Indeed, several collaborative activities, from their very 'sharing' nature, through being better adapted to the personal needs of both the provider and the recipient, and through the interpersonal exchange they are based on (as opposed to the impersonal contacts with the unpleasant public service), are ideally suited to serve solidarity-based needs. They may also stand for considerable cost-saving results.

SGEIs could benefit from sharing in at least five ways. Firstly, municipalities could share among themselves expensive goods with important idle capacity, such

---

[202] ibid 143–44.

[203] Rauch and Schleicher (n 17) 37; the ideas expressed in the following sentences come from their article.

[204] This last point is further discussed in the section immediately below.

[205] C Harlow, 'Public service, market ideology and citizenship' in M Freedland and S Sciarra (eds), *Public Services and Citizenship in European Law, Public and Labour Law Perspectives* (Oxford, Clarendon Press, 1998) 48–56.

[206] On this concept see, inter alia, the excellent collection of individual contributions in M Krajewski, U Neegraard and J van den Gronden (eds), *The Changing Legal Framework for Services of General Interest in Europe, Between Competition and Solidarity* (The Hague, Asser Press, 2009).

as excavators, paving machines, road stripping trucks etc,[207] while they could be sharing with private entities office and school buildings and (sports) facilities outside operating hours. Secondly, public authorities could have recourse to sharing companies in order to face their own needs, for instance by taking car-share membership for public officials instead of owing cars. Thirdly, public authorities could contract out some of the tasks they should be performing for their populations; in Greece hoteliers and individuals have been paid by the government to use some of their spare space to host Syrian asylum seekers.[208] More recently *Airbnb* has itself taken the initiative to offer as many as three months of hospitality to an estimated 35,000 asylum seekers stranded in Greece over the next five years.[209] In a more organised manner,

> San Francisco's Department of Emergency Preparedness and BayShare, an advocacy group funded by sharing economy firms to deploy privately-owned sharing services in response to citywide crises. For instance, during a natural disaster, the partnership provides AirBnB listings to house those made homeless, food sharing sites to coordinate charitable food offers, and Lyft cars to transport people away from affected areas, all at lower cost and higher efficiency than operating the same services through government coffers.[210]

Fourthly, sharing firms could provide the government with precious data; hence, eg *Uber* could provide 'huge amount of information about where people want to go and leave and when, which could aid everything from public transportation routing to land use planning.'[211] Fifthly, data detained by the platforms could be used by public authorities, as intelligence or otherwise, in order to protect public security and public health.

If collaborative platforms were to be involved into the provision of SGEIs, the EU is ahead of the US in at least three ways. For one thing, the EU has developed over the years a solid intellectual background, an extensive experience and, even, a legal basis (if need be, Article 14 TFEU), in order to help Member States accomplish their SGEI missions towards their citizens. Given that the problem has been framed, regulatory interventions should be more adequate than in other jurisdictions where the same conversation has not taken place. Secondly, the EU has, after some hesitation, defined the conditions which need to be fulfilled by any service which qualifies as a SGEI. Such a service should be offered: (a) continuously or on a permanent basis; (b) throughout the defined territory (which need not be the entire territory of the Member State); (c) at uniform rates; (d) on similar quality; (e) with no discrimination between the users.[212] The EU Charter

---

[207] See eg www.munirent.co, equipment and service sharing for public agencies.
[208] See eg www.cnn.gr/news/ellada/story/33267/refugees-welcome-h-protovoylia-filoxenias-ton-prosfygon-sto-spiti-mas.
[209] See www.keeptalkinggreece.com/2017/06/14/airbnb-refugees-greece.
[210] Rauch and Schleicher (n 17) 58, note omitted.
[211] ibid.
[212] See eg Case C-475/99 *Ambulanz Glöckner* EU:C:2001:577, para 55.

of Fundamental Rights would—to the extent that the activity concerned is some-how connected with the implementation of EU law[213]—further strengthen users' rights: issues such as discriminatory access, accessibility (of disabled persons) and other issues related to human dignity and fundamental rights could be addressed without recourse to any special regulation. Thirdly, in the EU, through the *Altmark* judgment[214] and the Almuna Package,[215] the framework for funding private entities involved in the provision of SGEIs is already set.

ii. In Terms of Areas to be Regulated

In view of the conclusions reached in the previous section and taking into account the concluding remarks of the previous chapters, it may be said that regu-lation of the collaborative economy is needed in the following areas. First and foremost in the area of labour law,[216] where the stark inequality between power-ful platforms and individual—and occasional—suppliers, combined with the lack of any representation system, puts the latter in a position in which may easily be exploited.[217] If situations such as those of Jennifer Guirdy (see Chapter 5) attract vivid criticism in the US, they are plainly intolerable in the EU. If such situations were to multiply, not only would individual rights—recognised as fundamental in the EU—be violated, but also support for the collaborative economy would quickly turn into mistrust, if not disgust.

A second field in need of rules would be platform liability. Without it being necessary to determine, in each case, whether the platform itself is—or is not—the actual provider of the underlying service,[218] platforms should shoulder some kind of third-party or even strict liability: after all they are the most powerful party in the transaction and they make a benefit out of it. A distinction could be made in that respect between (economically driven) collaborative and (socially driven) sharing platforms. Any such system of liability could/should be completed by clear rules on mandatory insurance policies with specific coverage.

Connected to the previous point, a further area in which regulation could be contemplated would be the system of reputation rating, where an equilibrium

---

[213] See Case C-399/11 *Stefano Melloni* EU:C:2013:107.

[214] Case C-280/00 *Altmark Trans and Regierungspräsidium Magdeburg* EU:C:2003:415.

[215] Commission Regulation (EU) No 360/2012 of 25 April 2012 on the application of Articles 107 and 108 of the Treaty on the Functioning of the European Union to *de minimis* aid granted to under-takings providing services of general economic interest [2012] OJ L 114/8; Commission Decision on the application of Article 106(2) of the Treaty on the Functioning of the European Union to State aid in the form of public service compensation granted to certain undertakings entrusted with the operation of services of general economic interest [2012] OJ L 7/3; Communication 'European Union framework for State aid in the form of public service compensation' [2012] OJ C 8/15; and Commission Com-munication 'on the application of the European Union State aid rules to compensation granted for the provision of services of general economic interest' [2012] OJ C 8/4.

[216] Erickson and Sorensen, 'Regulating the Sharing Economy' (2016) 6.

[217] See more in detail Ch 5 above.

[218] The difficulties of which have been discussed at length in Ch 2 above.

should be found between transparency and objectivity on the one hand and the preservation of reviewees' privacy and the platforms' trade secrets on the other.[219]

A further area which may need specific regulation is data usage (as an economic activity) and data protection (as a fundamental right);[220] all the more so given that, as explained in Chapter 3 above, the recently adopted EU General Data Protection Regulation does not seem to take into account the dangers (or the opportunities) opened by the collaborative economy.

Further, in preceding discussion in this and previous chapters, the possibility that collaborative platforms be used for the provision of SGEIs has been raised. It has also been said that the EU does have both the conceptual and the financial instruments to support such a development. What is lacking, however, is the regulatory framework that would allow collaborative platforms to participate in public tenders for the provision of public services. As it has been explained elsewhere,[221] even after the 2014 reshuffle of EU public procurement rules,[222] it would be difficult for platforms to participate in public tenders; obstacles would lie both at the level of the selection and of the award criteria. With regard to the former, platforms would have difficulties in competing with other tenderers on the second criterion set by the EU Directive, ie that of 'economic and financial standing', since they own nothing and their capitalisation is considerably lower than that of their competitors (eg *Airbnb* owing a platform and having few hundreds of employees in California, as opposed to *Hilton Hotels* owing property valued at billions and having thousands of employees around the globe). Similarly, the third selection criterion, namely the 'technical and professional ability' of a platform, which has no employment relationship with the people who will be performing the tasks and where the choice of such people is not determined in advance, will be very difficult to substantiate. Indeed, although it is foreseen in the Directive that the tenderer may rely on the capacities of other 'entities', the wording of the relevant provision seems to imply that such entities should be individualised at the time of the tender and could be made to provide written commitments.[223] To take this point further, when the *award* criterion used is not merely the lowest price, but the most economically advantageous tender, one of the elements which may be taken into account is the 'organisation, qualification and experience of staff assigned to perform the contract'.[224] Therefore, the said staff needs to be determined in advance.[225]

---

[219] This issue has been discussed in Ch 3 above.

[220] Strowel and Vergote (n 141).

[221] V Hatzopoulos and S Roma, 'Caring for Sharing? The Collaborative Economy under EU Law' (2017) 54 *CMLR* 81.

[222] European Parliament and Council Directive 2014/24/EU of 26 February 2014 on public procurement and repealing Directive 2004/18 [2014] OJ L 94/65, Art 58.

[223] ibid Art 63.

[224] ibid Art 67.

[225] The same conclusion is also drawn from the provisions of the Directive on subcontracting, where it is foreseen that the tenderer may be asked to 'indicate in its tender any share of the contract it may intend to subcontract to third parties and any proposed subcontractors'; ibid Art 71(2).

These are a few of the points that indicate that the current framework for public procurement is far from accommodating tenders from collaborative platforms. This, however, is disconcerting in at least two ways. From an economic point of view, as stated in the previous paragraphs, the award authorities could greatly benefit from receiving collaborative services. From a legal point of view, collaborative platforms, especially when they qualify as more than mere e-providers and are subject to the rules and obligations foreseen for the underlying service providers (eg if *Uber* is qualified as a transportation undertaking), should also have the same rights. Failing that, they would be suffering unjustified discrimination.

The last area to be mentioned, which will probably be the first to be regulated because of the immediate interest of local and national governments, is taxation of collaborative platforms. Given that tax is an issue which has not been discussed in this book, the only thing that need be said in this respect is that, because of the electronic nature of the transactions carried out, collaborative activities are easier than any other kind of activity to tax, once the relevant rules have been put in place.

IV. Conclusion

By way of conclusion on the more general issue of regulation, self-regulation, fresh regulation or, indeed, any kind of regulation, one needs to insist on implementation and enforcement of the rules concerned: those have to be strict and effective. Firstly, any self-regulatory or 'alternative' regulatory approach will be automatically discredited if it is not properly enforced.[226] Secondly, in a sector of the economy where price-sensitivity is high, platforms which would (be free to) choose to conform themselves with costly authorisation or tax regulations would automatically lose the market; hence they will only be willing to endorse such regulations if they are sure that other platforms will (have to) do the same—or that non-compliant platforms (and their users) will bear the consequences of non-compliance.[227] Enforcement may be public or private and it may target either the platform or the suppliers of the underlying service, or both.[228] But it has to be strict and efficient.

---

[226] Edelman and Geradin (n 141) 15–21; Cohen and Sundararajan (n 1).
[227] Miller (n 139) 180.
[228] For a discussion of the options and the experience so far see Katz (n 147) 1089–92.

8

Conclusion

The collaborative or sharing economy has grown from *sharing* into *economy* within a few years.[1] It is still in its growth phase, both in the US and even more so in the EU, where it made a late start. Throughout this process, it is transforming the economic landscape and, more importantly, the social one. Particularly in the field of labour, the collaborative economy is testing concepts, structures and systems that have worked for centuries.

At the same time the collaborative economy is itself subject to constant transformation. *Uber* is actively involved in the driverless car sector, thus signalling its will to take urban transport to the next level. At the same time it has experimented in food, medical marijuana, drugs, Christmas gifts and kittens deliveries, while having an eye turned to converting the *Uber* app to a 'content marketplace', including third party apps[2] and developing self-driven, and even, flying cars;[3] thus 'The Uber of Everything' may be forthcoming.[4] Similarly, *Airbnb*, after acquiring the off-line high-end resort operator *Luxury Retreats*, recently announced that it was launching a premium service in order to attract high-end guests and to compete with specialised platforms such as *Onefinestay* and top-end hotels;[5] at the same time it announced that it was considering collaborating with *Marriott Hotels*, themselves active in offering luxury apartments.

Simultaneously, platforms which started off as lonely riders, battling against competitors, regulators and users, are progressively being mainstreamed. Not only do they work together with incumbents in the markets, but they also work with regulators in their respective jurisdictions: the examples of *Airbnb* amassing taxes for local authorities as well as the example of the California state agency fining an *Airbnb* host because she transgressed *Airbnb's* anti-discrimination policy (see Chapter 7) are good examples of the increasingly close bonds that are

---

[1] See, among many, E Katsh and O Rabinovich-Einy, *Digital Justice: Technology and the Internet of Disputes* (New York, Oxford University Press, 2017) 67.

[2] See J Russell and I Lunden, 'Uber plans to turn its app into a "content marketplace" during rides' *TechCrunch* (3 March 2017).

[3] T Lien 'Uber conquered taxis. Now it's going after everything else' *LA Times* (7 May 2016).

[4] According to the book by T Graham, *The Uber of Everything: How the Freed Market Economy is Disrupting and Delighting* (Above All Press, 2017) available at www.uberofeverything.com.

[5] D King, 'Airbnb testing premium listings' *Travel Weekly* (23 June 2017); it is worth noting that *Onefinestay* was itself acquired by *AccorHotels* in April 2016.

progressively built between yesterday's enemies. Further, the concessions unilaterally made (pushed either by litigation or by scandals) by *Uber* in favour of its drivers, combined with stricter self-regulation and more transparent reputational and hiring/firing mechanisms, show that solutions may be forthcoming on many of the issues raised in this book. Hence, for instance, I trust that competition law will navigate through the novelties presented by the collaborative economy, as it has done in the past, and will come up with fresh and adapted solutions (see conclusions in Chapter 4). Similarly, consumer protection law will embed reputational mechanisms in its operations and adapt to the needs of collaborative activities (see Chapter 2).

There are, however, some issues which are inherently linked to the nature and the core characteristics of the collaborative economy and which do not yield to easy solutions. At least four such areas may be identified.

Firstly, as discussed in Chapter 2, the kinds of contractual relationships developing in the collaborative economy are unclear. This core legal qualification, uneasy as it is for every given activity, becomes a true Gordian knot if one considers the variety of activities and variants of business models pursued through collaborative means. This has consequences both for contract and tort law, as a different standard of care and different obligations stem from each set of rules. It also has consequences for the application of EU secondary legislation, especially the one on consumer protection. The same legal qualifications also play an important role under competition law, as they are core in identifying 'undertakings' and 'agreements' (eg single vertically integrated undertaking, as opposed to several undertakings connected between them with vertical/horizontal agreements), as well as market power (Chapter 4). Employment relations also depend on these same basic qualifications (Chapter 5). The great uncertainty thus ensuing is only made worse by the complex rules on dispute resolution arising in three-party virtual relationships, as discussed in Chapter 6. The guidance offered by the Commission in its 2016 Agenda on the Collaborative Economy is of little help—a symptom of the difficulty of imagining solutions for an even more imaginative economic sector. Therefore, the idea of a Platform Directive, either establishing 'artificial' legal qualifications (traders/consumers) or putting into place a specific liability regime protective of consumers, irrespective of specific legal qualifications may be necessary.

The second area where problems inevitably arise is data protection, discussed in Chapter 3. Collaborative platforms rely on the intensive collection and manipulation of data, both personal and general, with means unimagined few years ago. The legal toolkit for data protection does not seem to have taken into account the possibilities thus offered and seems non-adapted to this new data-devouring reality. The CJEU has constantly interpreted the existing legal framework in favour of data subjects and to the expense of the corresponding economic activities. If such an approach were to be followed in the collaborative economy, it could inflict it a major blow. At the same time, platforms' ultra-performing data-processing capacities should somehow be constrained. A fine equilibrium needs to be achieved, whereby the new data-processing functions and needs are acknowledged, specifically authorised and constrained.

The third issue of concern is algocracy, discussed in Chapter 4 in relation to competition, and in Chapter 5 in relation to employment. Algocracy represents automated decision-making based on algorithms and other mechanised and AI applications. The use of such means is core to the collaborative economy, as without those the matching function between like-minded peers, the determination of the proper characteristics of each service provision, the choice of the appropriate price and many more attributes of collaborative transactions would not be possible, at least not at the massive volume that has made the collaborative economy more than a marginal phenomenon. If algocracy is an inherent attribute of the collaborative economy, and indeed of the forthcoming 'bot economy', its scope, in terms of the areas in which algorithms may be used and of the functions they should be allowed to perform, may be limited. The example of *Uber* and *Lyft* agreeing to stop 'firing by algorithm' is an eloquent example, but other areas, especially in the field of employment, should also be subject to human overview, if not decision-making proper. One such other area—but not the only one—is the way reputation rating operates, as this can have potentially devastating effects on ill-treated peers. Thus, precise ex ante rules (hard or soft) concerning what, how, for how long etc reputation may be gathered, while fixing the criteria which may be introduced in the relevant algorithm (as discussed in Chapter 7), combined with an efficient ex post online dispute resolution mechanism (as discussed in Chapter 6), may be the necessary means to 'tame' algorithms in this area.

The fourth attribute of the collaborative economy which is difficult to come to terms with is the extreme fragmentation of tasks attributed to crowdwokers, as discussed in Chapter 5. The platform, with the use of algorithms or other AI applications, may break down complex projects into numerous micro-tasks and reconstruct them in a highly efficient manner. For crowdworkers, however, the fact of being used as if they were interchangeable in this type of repetitive, directionless, invisible and solitary work, offers zero professional stability, while at the same time it is in no way satisfactory, instructive or even useful for their professional or personal development. The above problem, acute in labour-intensive collaborative activities—as opposed to asset-based activities, such as accommodation—may be the most difficult to resolve through regulation or other means, as it corresponds to a fundamental tendency of the collaborative model.

It has been stated throughout the book that collaborative platforms are gradually being mainstreamed and brought into entrepreneurial normality. If measures were to be adopted in the above areas, this mainstreaming would be taken even further. It could even be that platforms in the collaborative economy would lose some—or indeed all—of their competitive advantages once they are fully 'normalised' and subjected to some coherent set of rules (see Chapter 7). It is unclear, at the time of writing, whether by becoming 'mainstreamed' big collaborative platforms will depose all 'collaborative' or 'sharing' attributes and grow into traditional undertakings; if this were the case, then the collaborative economy would prove to be some kind of 'childhood disease', eventually leading to 'normal' adolescent entrepreneurship; or, else, it would be an alternative way of launching a start-up in the business of two-sided platforms. Of course, the sharing ideology would still animate some platforms, but if this is the case for small, communitarian, solidarity-based projects only, then the 'sharing revolution' will have been yet another bubble in the tech industry.

This book is based on the idea that there is more than just start-up dynamics in the collaborative economy; this is why it is worth examining, as the book has, not only the immediate but also the medium- and long-term effects that the collaborative economy may have. Once properly unleashed—and unleashing is under way—it will not be possible to bring such dynamics back into the fold. Indeed, the way that peers have embraced collaborative activities, and the way that collaborative platforms use to their—and others'—benefit the tools offered by technology, makes it unlikely that the collaborative model will become obsolete or abandoned in the near future. 'Natural selection' or 'invisible hands' will distinguish activities which truly benefit from the collaborative model from those which are only incidentally, by way of trend, offered under this model. In the meantime, regulators, judges and platforms themselves will have found more common ground in view of protecting the general interest. Thus, a book on the same topic written in few years' time would probably have a completely different focus and/or content. That is, provided the EU realises that this economic sector is evolving very quickly and decides to come to grips with it. This will be the measure of success of the present book.

BIBLIOGRAPHY

Books

Botsman, R and Rogers, R, *What's Mine Is Yours: How Collaborative Consumption Is Changing the Way We Live* (London, HarperCollins, 2011).

Cortés, P, *Online Dispute Resolution for Consumers in the European Union* (New York, Routledge, 2011).

Davies, L, 'Netflix and the Coalition for an Open Internet' in D Smith-Rowsey (ed), *The Netflix Effect: Technology and Entertainment in the 21st Century* (New York, Bloomsbury Academic, 2016) 15–32.

Evans, DS and Schmalensee, RL, 'The Antitrust Analysis of Multi-Sided Platform Businesses', in RD Blair and DD Sokol (eds), *Oxford Handbook on International Antitrust Economics* (New York, Oxford University Press, 2015).

Ezrachi, A and Stucke, M, *Virtual Competition: The Promise and Perils of the Algorithm-Driven Economy* (Cambridge MA, London, Harvard University Press, 2016).

Gansky, L, *The Mesh: Why the Future of Business is Sharing* (New York, Portfolio Penguin, 2010).

Geradin, D, 'Online intermediation platforms and free trade principles: Some reflections on the *Uber* preliminary ruling case' in A Ortiz (ed), *Internet: Competition and Regulation of Online Platforms*, e-book (Competition Policy International, 2016).

Gillies, LE, Electronic Commerce and International Private Law, A Study of Electronic Consumer Contracts (Hampshire, Ashgate, 2008).

Graef, I, *EU Competition Law, Data Protection and Online Platforms: Data as Essential Facility* (Wolters Kluwer, 2016).

Graham, T, *The Uber of Everything: How the Freed Market Economy is Disrupting and Delighting* (Above All Press, 2017).

Harlow, C, 'Public service, market ideology and citizenship' in M Freedland and S Sciarra (eds), *Public Services and Citizenship in European Law, Public and Labour Law Perspectives* (Oxford, Clarendon Press, 1998) 48–56.

Hatzopoulos, V, 'The evolution of the essential facilities doctrine' in G Amato and DC Elhermann (eds), *EC Competition Law: A Critical Assessment* (Oxford and Portland, Oregon, Hart Publishing, 2007) 317–358.

—— 'Justifications to restrictions to free movement: Towards a single normative framework?' in M Andenas, T Bekkedal and L Pantaleo (eds), *The Reach of Free Movement* (The Hague, TMC Asser Press/Springer, 2017) 131–156.

—— 'The Allocation of Limited Authorisations under EU Internal Market Rules' in P Adrianse, F van Omeren, W de Ouden and J Wolswinkel (eds), *Scarcity and the State* (Cambridge, Intersentia, 2016) 163–186.

—— 'Des marchés publics à la délivrance des autorisations: Spill-over all over?' in I Govaere and D Hanf (eds), *Scrutinizing Internal and External Dimensions of European Law—*

Les dimensions internes et externes du droit européen à l'épreuve—Liber Amicorum Paul Demaret, Tome 1 (Brussels, P.I.E.-Peter Lang, 2013) 325–338.

—— 'Assessing the Services Directive' in C Barnard (ed), *Cambridge Yearbook of European Law 2007–2008*, Vol 10 (Oxford, Hart Publishing, 2008) 215–261.

Irion, K, 'Special Regard: The Court of Justice and the fundamental rights to privacy and data protection' in U Faber et al (eds) *Festschrift fur Wolfhard Kohte* (Baden-Baden, Nomos, 2016).

Katsh, E and Rabinovich-Einy, O, *Digital Justice: Technology and the Internet of Disputes* (New York, Oxford University Press, 2017).

Kim, NS, *Wrap Contracts: Foundations and Ramifications* (New York, Oxford University Press, 2013).

Krajewski, M, Neegraard U and van den Gronden, J (eds) *The Changing Legal Framework for Services of General Interest in Europe, Between Competition and Solidarity* (The Hague, Asser Press, 2009).

Kuner, C, *Transborder Data Flows and Data Privacy Law* (Oxford, Oxford University Press, 2013).

Lessig, L, *Remix: Making Art and Commerce Thrive in the Hybrid Economy* (New York, The Penguin Press, 2008).

Lodder, AR and Zeleznikow, J, 'Artificial Intelligence and Online Dispute Resolution' in MA Wahab, E Katsh and D Rainey (eds), *Online Dispute Resolution Theory and Practice: A Treatise on Technology and Dispute Resolution* (The Hague, Eleven International Publishing, 2011).

Nordhausen Scholes, A, 'Behavioural Economics and the Autonomous Consumer' in C Barnard, MW Gehring and I Solanke (eds), *Cambridge Yearbook of European Legal Studies 2011–2012*, Vol 14 (Oxford, Hart Publishing, 2012) 297–324.

O'Connor, D, 'Understanding Online Platform Competition: Common Misunderstandings' in A Ortiz (ed), *Internet: Competition and Regulation of Online Platforms*, e-book (Competition Policy International, 2016).

Oostveen, M and Irion, K, 'The Golden Age of Personal Data: How to Regulate an Enabling Fundamental Right?' in M Bakhoum et al (eds), *Personal Data in Competition, Consumer Protection and IP Law—Towards a Holistic Approach?* (Berlin, Springer, 2017) forthcoming.

Orsi, J and Doskow, E, *The Sharing Solution, How to Save Money, Simplify Your Life & Build Community* (US, Nolo, 2009).

Parcu, PL and Stasi, ML, 'The role of intent in the assessment of conduct under Article 102 TFEU' in PL Parcu, G Monti and M Botta (eds), *Abuse of Dominance in EU Competition Law: Emerging Trends* (Cheltenham, Edward Elgar, 2017).

Parr, N and Hammon, C (eds), 'Merger Control', 5th edn (*Global Legal Group*).

Pollicino, O, 'The ambition of the Court of Justice of the European Union to be a Constitutional Court in the field of digital law' in E Psychogiopoulou (ed), *European Courts, New Technologies and Fundamental Rights, Workshop Proceedings* (Hellenic Foundation for European & Foreign Policy, 2017).

Riefa, C, *Consumer Protection and Online Auction Platforms: Towards a Safer Legal Framework* (New York, Routledge, 2016).

Rustard, ML, *Global Internet Law*, 2nd edn (US, Hornbook Series, 2016).

Schulze, R, Staudenmayer, D and Lohsse, S (eds), *Contracts for the Supply of Digital Content: Regulatory Challenges and Gaps* (Nomos/Hart Publishing, 2017).

Stucke, M and Grunes, A, *Big Data and Competition Policy* (Oxford, Oxford University Press, 2016).

Sundararajan, A, *The Sharing Economy, The End of Employment and the Rise of Crowd-Based Capitalism* (Cambridge MA, The MIT Press, 2016).

Thuemmler, C and Bai, C (eds), *Health 4.0: How Virtualization and Big Data are Revolutionizing Healthcare* (Switzerland, Springer International Publishing, 2017).

Tor, A, 'Some Challenges Facing a Behaviorally-Informed Approach to the Directive on Unfair Commercial Practices' in T Tóth (ed), *Unfair Commercial Practices: The Long Road to Harmonized Law Enforcement* (Budapest, Pázmány Press, 2014).

Townley, C, 'The Concept of an "Undertaking": The Boundaries of the Corporation— A Discussion of Agency, Employees and Subsidiaries' in G Amato and CD Ehlermann (eds), *EC Competition Law—A Critical Assessment* (Oxford, Hart Publishing, 2007) 3–23.

Twigg-Flesner, C, 'Disruptive Technology—Disrupted Law? How the Digital Revolution Affects (Contract) Law' in A De Franceschi (ed), *European Contract Law and the Digital Single Market, The Implications of the Digital Revolution* (Cambridge, Intersentia, 2016) 21–48.

Van der Sloot, B, 'The ECtHR as constitutional court in the age of Big Data' in E Psychogiopoulou (ed), *European Courts, New Technologies and Fundamental Rights, Workshop Proceedings* (Hellenic Foundation for European & Foreign Policy, 2017) 19–20.

Vrbljanac, D, 'International jurisdiction for Internet disputes arising out of the contractual obligations' *Proceedings, 6th International Conference on Information Law & Ethics (ICIL 2014): Lifting the Barriers to Empower the Future of Information Law & Ethics* (Thessaloniki, The University of Macedonia Press, 2015).

Wang, FF, *Internet Jurisdiction and Choice of Law: Legal Practises in the EU, US and China* (New York, Cambridge University Press, 2010).

Wish, R and Bailey, D, *Competition Law*, 8th edn (Oxford, Oxford University Press, 2015) 110–115.

Witten, IH et al, *Data Mining: Practical Machine Learning Tools and Techniques*, 4th edn (Cambridge, MA, Morgan Kaufmann, 2017).

Zech, H, 'Data as a Tradeable Commodity' and A De Franceschi, 'Data as a Tradeable Commodity and the New Instruments for their Protection' in A De Franceschi (ed), *European Contract Law and the Digital Single Market, The Implications of the Digital Revolution* (Cambridge, Intersentia, 2016) 51–80.

Journal Articles

Ahlborn, C, Evans, DS and Padilla, AJ, 'Competition policy in the new economy: is European competition law up to the challenge?' (2001) 22(5) *European Competition Law* 156.

Akerlof, GA, 'The Market for "Lemons": Quality Uncertainty and the Market Mechanism' (1970) 84 *The Quarterly Journal of Economics* 488.

Aloisi, A, 'Commoditized Workers: Case Study Research on Labor Law Issues Arising from a Set of "On-Demand/Gig Economy" Platforms' (2016) 37 *Comparative Labor Law and Policy Journal* 653.

Aneesh, A, 'Global Labour: Algocratic Modes of Organization' (2009) 27(4) *Sociological Theory* 347.

Armitage, A, 'Gaugin, Darwin, & Design Thinking: A Solution in the Impasse Between Innovation & Regulation' (2016) *University of California, Legal Studies* Research Paper No 235.

Armstrong, M, 'Competition in Two-Sided Markets' (2006) 37 *The RAND Journal of Economics* 668.

Auer, D and Petit, N, 'Two-Sided Markets and the Challenge of Turning Economic Theory into Antitrust Policy' (2015) 60 *The Antitrust Bulletin* 426.

Bar-Gil, O and Ben-Sahar, O, 'Regulatory Techniques in Consumer Protection: A critique of European Consumer Contract Law' (2013) 50 *CMLR* 109.

Beale, H, 'The future of European contract law in the light of the European Commission's proposals for Directives on digital content and online sales' (2016) *IDP, Revista de Internet, Derecho y Política, Universitat Oberta de Catalunya* 3.

Ben-Sahar, O, 'The Myth of the "Opportunity to Read" in Contract Law' (2009) 5 *European Review of Contract Law* 1.

Berg, J, 'Income Security in the On-Demand Economy: Findings and Policy Lessons from a Survey of Crowdworkers' (2016) 37(3) *Comparative Labor Law and Policy Journal* 543.

Black, J, 'Decentering Regulation: Understanding the Role of Regulation and Self-Regulation in a "Post-Regulatory" World' (2001) 54 *Current Legal Problems* 103.

Böckmann, M, 'The Shared Economy: It is time to start caring about sharing; value creating factors in the shared economy' (2013).

Bolton, A, 'Regulating Ride-Share Apps: A Study on Tailored Reregulation Regarding Transportation Network Companies, Benefiting Both Consumers and Drivers' (2015) 46(1) *Cumberland Law Review* 101.

Brown, GE, 'An Uberdilemma: Employees and Independent Contractors in the Sharing Economy' (2016) 75 *Maryland Law Review* 15.

Busch, C et al, 'The Rise of the Platform Economy: A New Challenge for EU Consumer Law?' (2016) 5 *EuCML* 3.

Calo, R and Rosenblat, A, 'The Taking Economy: Uber, Information, and Power' (2017) 117 Columbia Law Review 1623; University of Washington School of Law Research Paper No 2017-08.

Cannon, S and Summers, LH, 'How Uber and the Sharing Economy Can Win Over Regulators' *Harvard Business Review* (13 October 2014).

Carboni, M, 'A New Class of Worker for the Sharing Economy' (2016) 22(4) *Richmond Journal of Law and Technology* (2016) 1.

Chang, W, 'Growing Pains: The Role of Regulation in the Collaborative Economy' (2015) 9(1) *Intersect: The Stanford Journal of Science, Technology, and Society* 3.

Cherry, MA, 'Beyond Misclassification: The Digital Transformation of Work' (2016) 37(3) *Comparative Labor Law and Policy Journal* 544; Saint Louis U Legal Studies Research Paper No 2016-2.

Cohen, M and Sundararajan, A, 'Self-Regulation and Innovation in the Peer-to-Peer Sharing Economy' (2015) 82 *The University of Chicago Law Review Dialogue* 116.

Colangelo, M and Zeno-Zencovich, V, 'Online Platforms, Competition Rules and Consumer Protection in Travel Industry' (2016) 5 *EuCML* 75.

Colangelo, M, 'Parity Clauses and Competition Law in Digital Marketplaces: The Case of Online Hotel Booking' (2017) 8(1) *Journal of European Competition Law & Practice* 3.

Condlin, RJ, 'Online Dispute Resolution: Stinky, Repugnant, or Drab' (2016) University of Maryland Francis King Carey School of Law Legal Studies Research Paper No 2016–40.

Das Acevedo, D, 'Regulating Employment Relationships in the Sharing Economy' (2016) 20(1) *Employee Rights and Employment Policy Journal* 1.

Davidov, G, 'The Status of Uber Drivers: A Purposive Approach' (2017) 6(1–2) *Spanish Labour Law and Employment Relations Journal* 6; Hebrew University of Jerusalem Legal Research Paper No 17-7.

De Franceschi, A, 'The Adequacy of Italian Law for the Platform Economy' (2016) 5 *EuCML* 56.

De Stefano, G, 'AC-Treuhand Judgment: A Broader Scope for EU Competition Law Infringements?' (2015) Editorial, 6 *Journal of European Competition Law & Practice* 689.

Demary, V, 'Competition in the Sharing Economy' (2015) Cologne Institute for Economic Research, IW Policy Paper No 19.

Dyal-Chand, R, 'Regulating Sharing: The Sharing Economy as an Alternative Capitalist System' (2015) 90 *Tulane Law Review* 241–308.

Edelman, B and Geradin, D, 'Efficiencies and Regulatory Shortcuts: How Should We Regulate Companies Like Airbnb and Uber?' (2016) 19 *Stanford Technology Law Review* 293.

Edelman, BG and Luca, M, 'Digital Discrimination: The Case of Airbnb.com' (2014) *Harvard Business School NOM Unit* Working Paper No 14-054.

Erickson, K and Sorensen, I, 'Regulating the Sharing Economy' (2016) 5(2) (special issue) *Internet Policy Review* 1.

Erving, EE, 'The Sharing Economy: Exploring the Intersection of Collaborative Consumption and Capitalism' (2014) Scripps College, Scripps Senior Theses, Paper No 409.

Evans, D (ed), 'Platform Economics: Essays on Multi-Sided Businesses' (2011) *Competition Policy International (CPI)*.

Evans, DS and Noel, MD, 'Defining Antitrust Markets When Firms Operate Two-Sided Platforms' (2005) 3 *Columbia Business Law Review* 101.

—— 'The Analysis of Mergers that involve Multisided Platform Businesses' (2008) 4 *Journal of Competition Law & Economics* 663.

Evans, DS and Schmalensee, RL, 'The Economics of Interchange Fees and their Regulation: An Overview' (2005) *MIT Sloan Working Paper* 4548-05.

Evans, DS, 'Two-Sided Market Definition' (2009) Market Definition in Antitrust: Theory and Case Studies, ABA Section of Antitrust Law.

Ezrachi, A, 'The Competitive Effects of Parity Clauses on Online Commerce' (2015) 11 *European Competition Journal* 488.

Filistrucchi, L et al, 'Market Definition in Two-Sided Markets: Theory and Practice' (2014) 10 *Journal of Competition Law and Economics* 292.

Finck, M, 'Digital Regulation: Designing a Supranational Legal Framework for the Platform Economy' (2017) *LSE Legal Studies* Working Paper No 15.

Gata, JE, 'The sharing economy, competition and regulation' (2015) *Competition Policy International*.

Gatt, A, 'Electronic Commerce—Click Wrap Agreements, The Enforceability of Click-Wrap Agreements' (2002) 18(6) *Computer Law & Security Review* 404.

Geradin, D and Kuschewsky, M, 'Competition law and personal data: preliminary thoughts on a complex issue' (2013) *Discussion Papers Tilburg Law and Economics Center* No 10.

Geradin, D, 'Should Uber be Allowed to Compete in Europe? And if so How?' (2015) *Competition Policy International*.

Graef, I, 'Market Definition and Market Power in Data: The Case of Online Platforms' (2015) 38 *World Competition* 473.

—— 'Stretching EU competition law tools for search engines and social networks' (2015) 4:3 *Internet Policy Review*.

Gürkaynak, G et al, 'Multisided markets and the challenge of incorporating multisided considerations into competition law analysis' (2017) 5 *Journal of Antitrust Enforcement* 100.

Hagiu, A and Wright, J, 'Marketplace or Reseller?' (2014) 61 *Management Science* 184.

Hall, J, Kendrick, C and Nosko, C, 'The Effects of Uber's Surge Pricing: A Case Study' (2015).

Hamari, J, Sjöklint, M and Ukkonen, A, 'The sharing economy: Why people participate in collaborative consumption' (2015) 67 *Journal of the Association for Information Science and Technology* 2047.

Harris, SD and Krueger, AB, 'A Proposal for Modernizing Labor Laws for Twenty-First Century Work: The "Independent Worker"' (2015) *The Hamilton Project* Discussion Paper 2015-10.

Hatzopoulos, V and Roma, S, 'Caring for Sharing? The Collaborative Economy under EU Law' (2017) 54 *CMLR* 81.

Hatzopoulos, V, 'Case C-418/01, IMS Health GmbH v. NDC Health GmbH' (2004) 6 *CMLR* 1613.

Hatzopoulos, V, 'Du principe de non-discrimination (au niveau européen) au principe de bonne administration (au niveau national)?' (2016) *Cahiers de droit européen* 311.

—— 'The Economic Constitution of the EU Treaty and the limits between economic and non-economic activities' (2012) 23 *EBLRev* 973.

Helbing, D, 'Economy 4.0 and Digital Society: The Participatory Market Society is Born' (2014).

Helleringer, G and Sibony, AL, 'European Consumer Protection Through the Behavioral Lens' (2017) *Columbia Journal of European Law* 607.

Hesse, RB, 'Two-Sided Platform Markets and the Application of the Traditional Antitrust Analytical Framework' (2007) 3:1 *Competition Policy International* 191.

Hobbelen, H, Lorjé, N and Guenay, A, 'Selected recent developments in the application of EU competition law to online platforms' (2016) *Mediaforum*.

Hojnik, J, 'The servitization of manufacturing: EU law implications and challenges' (2016) 53 *CMLR* 1575.

Hörnle, J, 'Legal controls on the use of arbitration clauses in B2C e-commerce contracts' (2006) 8 *EBL* 8.

—— 'Online dispute resolution in business to consumer e-commerce transactions' (2002) 2 *Journal of Information, Law & Technology*.

Hustinx, P, European Data Protection Supervisor, 'EU Data Protection Law: The Review of Directive 95/46/EC and the Proposed General Data Protection Regulation' (2014) *Collected Courses of the European University Institute's Academy of European Law*, 24th Session on European Union Law, 1–12 July 2013.

Ibáñez Colomo, P, 'Restrictions on Innovation in EU Competition Law' (2016) 41 *European Law Review* 201; and (2015) *LSE Law, Society and Economy* Working Papers No 22.

Incadrona, R and Poncibó, C, 'The average consumer, the unfair commercial practices directive and the cognitive revolution' (2007) 30 *Journal of Consumer Policy* 21.

Infranca, J 'Intermediary Institutions and the Sharing Economy' (2016) 90 *Tulane Law Review* 29.

Irion, K, 'Special Regard: The Court of Justice and the fundamental rights to privacy and data protection', in U Faber et al (eds) *Festschrift fur Wolfhard Kohte* (Baden-Baden, Nomos, 2016); *Institute for Information Law* Research Paper No 4; *Amsterdam Law School* Research Paper No 35.

Jenny, F, 'Enforcement issues in rapidly changing/high tech markets (Presentation Slides)' (2017) *Melbourne University Law School Seminar*.

John, NA, 'Sharing and Web 2.0: The emergence of a keyword' (2013) 15 *New Media & Society* 167.

Jonas, A, 'Share and Share Dislike: The Rise of Uber and AirBNB and How New York City Should Play Nice?' (2016) 24(1) *Journal of Law and Policy* 205.

Kalleberg, A, 'Precarious Work: Insecure Workers: Employment Relations in Transition' (2009) 74 *American Sociological Review* 1.

Kaplow, L, 'Market Share Thresholds: On the Conflation of Empirical Assessments and Legal Policy Judgments' (2011) 7 *Journal of Competition Law & Economics* 243.

Katsh, E and Rabinovich-Einy, O, 'Dispute Resolution in the Sharing Economy' (2014) in U Gasser et al, *Internet Monitor 2014: Reflections on the Digital World: Platforms, Policy, Privacy, and Public Discourse*, Research Publication No 2014-17.

Katsh, E and Rule, C, 'What We Know and Need to Know About Online Dispute Resolution' (2016) 67 *South Carolina Law Review* 329.

Katz, V, 'Regulating the Sharing Economy' (2015) 30 *Berkeley Technology Law Journal* 1065.

King, S, 'Sharing Economy: What Challenges for Competition Law?' (2015) 6 *Journal of European Competition Law & Practice* 729.

Kolasky, WJ, 'Network Effects: A Contrarian View' (1999) 7 *George Mason Law Review* 577.

Langhanke, C and Schmidt-Kessel, M, 'Consumer Data as Consideration' (2015) 4 *EuCML* 218.

Liu, S and Matilla, A, 'Airbnb: Online targeted advertising, sense of power, and consumer decisions' (2017) 60 *International Journal of Hospitality Management* 33.

Lobel, O, 'The Law of the Platform' (2016) 101 *Minnesota Law Review* 87.

Lombardi, P and Schwabe, F, 'Sharing Economy as a new business model for energy storage systems' (2017) 188 *Applied Energy* 485.

Lougher, G and Kalmanowicz, S, 'EU Competition Law in the Sharing Economy' (2016) 7 *Journal of European Competition Law & Practice* 87.

Luchetta, G, 'Is The Google Platform a Two-Sided Market?' (2014) 10 *Journal of Competition Law & Economics* 185.

Mak, V, 'Private Law Perspectives on Platform Services Airbnb: Home Rentals between AYOR and NIMBY' (2016) 5 *EuCML* 19.

Mastracci, J, 'A Case for Federal Ride-Sharing Regulations: How Protectionism and Inconsistent Lawmaking Stunt Uber-Led Technological Entrepreneurship' (2015) 18 *Tulane Journal of Law and Intellectual Property* 1.

McPeak, A, 'Sharing Tort Liability in the New Sharing Economy' (2016) 49 *Connecticut Law Review* 171.

Mehra, SK, 'Anti-trust and the Robo-Seller: Competition in the time of algorithms' 100 *Minnesota Law Review* 1323; and (2015) *Temple University Legal Studies*, Research Paper No 15.

Miller, BJ, Moore DW and Schmidt Jr, CW, 'Telemedicine and the Sharing Economy: The "Uber" for Healthcare' (2016) 22 *American Journal of Managed Care* 420.

Miller, S, 'First Principles for Regulating the Sharing Economy' (2016) 53 *Harvard Journal on Legislation* 147.

Möhlmann, M, 'Digital Trust and Peer-to-Peer Collaborative Consumption Platforms: A Mediation Analysis' (2016).

Nowag, J, 'UBER Between Labour and Competition Law' (2016) 3 *Lund Student EU Law Review* 95.

Odudu, O and Bailey, D, 'The Single Economic Entity Doctrine in EU Competition Law' (2014) 51 *CMLR* 1721.

Oh, S and Moon, JY, 'Calling for a shared understanding of the "sharing economy"' (2016) *Proceedings of the 18th Annual International Conference on Electronic Commerce: e-Commerce in Smart connected World*, Article No 35.

Peers, S, 'Equal Treatment of Atypical Workers: A New Frontier of EU Law?' (2013) 32(1) *Yearbook of European Law* 30.

Porat, A and Strahilevitz LJ, 'Personalizing Default Rules and Disclosure with Big Data' (2014) 112 *Michigan Law Review* 1417.

Posen, H, 'Ridesharing in the Sharing Economy: Should Regulators Impose Uber Regulations on Uber?' (2015) 101 *Iowa Law Review* 405.

Priest, GL, 'Rethinking Antitrust Law in an Age of Network Industries' (2007) 4 *Yale Law & Economics* Research Paper No 352.

Rabinovich-Einy, O and Katsh, E, 'Access to Digital Justice: Fair and Efficient Processes for the Modern Age' (2017) 18 *Cardozo Journal of Conflict Resolution* 637.

Ranchordás, S, 'Does Sharing Mean Caring? Regulating Innovation in the Sharing Economy' (2015) 16 *Minnesota Journal of Law, Science & Technology* 414.

—— 'Innovation Experimentalism in the Age of the Sharing Economy' (2015) 19 *Lewis and Clark Law Review* 1.

Ranzini, G et al, 'Privacy in the Sharing Economy' (2017) Report from the EU H2020 Research Project Ps2Share: Participation, Privacy, and Power in the Sharing Economy, 3.

Rauch, DE and Schleicher, D, 'Like Uber, But for Local Governmental Policy: The Future of Local Regulation of the "Sharing Economy"' (2015) *George Mason University Law & Economics*, Research Paper No 15-01.

Resnick, P and Zeckhauser, R, 'Trust Among Strangers in Internet Transactions: Empirical Analysis of ebay's reputational system' (2002) 11 *Economics of the Internet and E-Commerce* 127.

Riefa, C, 'Uncovering the dangers lurking below the surface of European consumer arbitration' (2008) 4 *Consumer Journal* 24.

Rochet, JC and Tirole, J, 'Platform Competition in Two-Sided Markets' (2003) 1 *Journal of the European Economic Association* 990.

—— 'Two-Sided Markets: A Progress Report' (2006) 37 *The RAND Journal of Economics* 645.

Russo, F and Stasi, ML, 'Defining the relevant market in the sharing economy' (2016) 5 *Internet Policy Review* 1.

Schanzenbach, M, 'Network Effects and Antitrust Law: Predation, Affirmative Defenses, and the Case of U.S. v. Microsoft' (2002) 4 *Stanford Technology Law Rev* 3.

Scheiwe Kulp, H and Kool, AL, 'You Help Me, He Helps You: Dispute Systems Design in the Sharing Economy' (2015) 48 *Washington University Journal of Law & Policy* 179.

Snell, J, 'The Notion of Market Access: A Concept or a Slogan?' (2010) 47 *CMLR* 437.

Sorensen, MJ, 'Private Law Perspectives on Platform Services: Uber—a business model in search of a new contractual legal frame?' (2016) 5 *Journal of European Consumer and Market Law* 15.

Stallibrass, D and Fingleton, J, 'Regulation, Innovation and Growth: Why Peer-to-Peer Business should be Supported' (2016) 7 *Journal of European Competition Law and Practice* 414.

Strahlevitz, L, 'How's My Driving? for Everyone (and Everything)' (2006) 81 *NYU Law Rev* 1661.

Strowel, A and Vergote, A, 'Digital Platforms: To Regulate or Not To Regulate? Message to Regulators: Fix the Economics First, Then Focus on the Right Regulation', Written Evidence (OPL0087) found in UK House of Lords, 'Online platforms and the Digital Single Market: oral and written evidence' 788.

Stucke, M and Ezrachi, A, 'Algorithmic Collusion: Problems and Counter-Measures' (2017) *OECD, Roundtable on Algorithms and Collusion.*

—— 'Artificial intelligence and collusion: When computers inhibit competition' (2017, forthcoming) *University of Illinois Law Review;* and (2015) *University of Tennessee Legal Studies*, Research Paper No 267.

Sundararajan, A, 'Peer-to-Peer Businesses and the Sharing (Collaborative) Economy: Overview, Economic Effects and Regulatory Issues' (2014).

Sunstein, CR, 'Impersonal Default Rules vs Active Choices vs Personalized Default Rules: A Triptych' (2012), (unpublished manuscript).

Terryn, E, 'The sharing economy in Belgium—a case for regulation?' (2016) 5 *EuCML* 45.

Teubner, T, 'Thoughts on the Sharing Economy' (2014) 11 *Proceedings of the International Conference on e-Commerce* 322.

Thierer, A et al, 'How the Internet, the Sharing Economy, and Reputational Feedback Mechanisms Solve the "Lemons Problem"' (2016) 70 *University of Miami Law Review* 830.

Thierer, A, 'The Sharing Economy and Consumer Protection Regulation: The Case of Policy Change' (2015) 8 *Journal of Business Enterpreneurship and Law* 529.

Tor, A, 'The Methodology of the Behavioral Analysis of Law' (2008) 4 *Haifa Law Review* 237.

Van Gorp, N and Batura, O, 'Challenges for Competition Policy in a Digitalised Economy' (2015) *Study for the ECON Committee* 59.

Vitkovic, D, 'The Sharing Economy: Regulation and the EU Competition Law' (2016) 9 *Global Antitrust Review* 78.

Werebach, K, 'Is Uber a Common Carrier' (2015) 12(1) *Journal of Law and Policy for the Information Society* 135.

Westerlund, M and Enkvist, J, 'Platform Privacy: The Missing Piece of Data Protection Legislation' (2016) 7 *Journal of Intellectual Property, Information Technology and Electronic Commerce Law (JIPITEC)* 1.

Weyl, G, 'A Price Theory of Multi-Sided Platforms' (2010) 100 *American Economic Review* 1642.

Wezenbeek, R, 'Platforms as facilitators of concerted practices; Lessons from the payments sector', presentation for *ENTraNCE Workshop: Antitrust Enforcement in Traditional v Online Platforms* (4 December 2015) Florence.

Wismer, S, Bongard, C and Rasek, A, 'Multi-Sided Market Economics in Competition Law Enforcement' (2017) 8(4) *Journal of European Competition Law & Practice* 257.

Yakovleva, S and Irion, K, 'The Best of Both Worlds? Free Trade in Services, and EU Law on Privacy and Data Protection', (2016) 2 *European Data Protection Law Review* 191.

Zervas, G, Proserpio, D and Byers, J, 'The rise of the sharing economy: Estimating the impact of Airbnb on the hotel industry' (2016) *Boston University School of Management*, Research Paper No 2013-16.

—— 'A First Look at Online Reputation on Airbnb, Where Every Stay is Above Average' (2015).

Zezulka, O, 'The Digital Footprint and Principles of Personality Protection in the European Union' (2016) *Prague Law* Working Papers Series No 2016/III/2.

Reports

United Kingdom Bodies:

UK House of Lords, 'Brexit: the EU data protection package' (2017) 3rd Report of Session 2017–19.

UK House of Lords, 'Online Platforms and the Digital Single Market' (2016) 10th Report of Session 2015–16.

UK House of Commons, Work and Pensions Committee, 'Self-employment and the gig economy' (2017) 13th Report of Session 2016–17.

UK: Competition and Markets Authority (CMA), 'Private Motor Insurance Market Investigation, Final Report', 24 September 2014.

United States Bodies:

US Federal Trade Commission (FTC) Staff Report, 'The "Sharing" Economy: Issues Facing Platforms, Participants and Regulators' (2016).

Australian Bodies:

See Australian Competition and Consumer Competition (ACCC), 'The sharing economy and the Competition and Consumer Act' (2015) *Deloitte Access Economics*.

German Bodies:

German Monopolies Commission, 'Competition policy: the challenge of digital markets' (2015) Special Report 68, para S27.

Autorité de la Concurrence and Bundeskartellamt, 'Competition Law and Data' (2016) 35, available at www.autoritedelaconcurrence.fr/doc/reportcompetitionlawanddatafinal.pdf.

French Bodies:

Rapports du Conseil de la Numérique (FR), 'Ambition numérique, Pour une politique française et européenne de la transition numérique' (2015). Autorité de la Concurrence and Bundeskartellamt, 'Competition Law and Data' (2016) 35, available at www. autoritedelaconcurrence.fr/doc/reportcompetitionlawanddatafi nal.pdf.

European Union Bodies:

Codagnore, C, Abadie, F and Biagi, F, 'The Future of Work in the "Sharing Economy": Market Efficiency and Equitable Opportunities or Unfair Precarisation?' (2016) *EU Commission JRC Science for Policy Report* No 27913.

De Groen, WP and Maseli, I, 'The Impact of the Collaborative Economy on the Labour market' (2016) *Centre for European Policy Studies (CEPS)* Special Report.

Draft Common Frame of Reference (DCFR), outline edn, prepared by the Study Group on a European Civil Code and the Research Group on EC Private Law (Acquis Group) (Munich, European Law Publishers, 2009).

European Commission, 'Competition merger brief' (2015) Issue 1—February.

European Commission, 'Exploratory study of consumer issues in online peer-to-peer platform markets' Task 1 Report (2017).

European Commission, 'Special Eurobarometer 447 on online platforms' (2016).

European Commission's Study on consumers' attitudes towards Terms and Conditions (T&Cs)', Final Report (2016).

European Data Protection Supervisor, 'Report of Workshop on Privacy, Consumers, Competition and Big Data' (11 July 2014).

European Economic and Social Committee (EESC), 'Opinion on Self-regulation and co-regulation in the Community legislative framework (own-initiative opinion)' [2015] OJ C 291/29.

Goudin, P, 'The Cost of Non-Europe in the Sharing Economy: Economic, Social and Legal Challenges and Opportunities' (2016) *European Parliament, European Parliamentary Research Service.*

Jorge Padilla, A, 'The Role of Supply-Side Substitution in the Definition of the Relevant Market in Merger Control' (2001) Report for DG Enterprise A/4, European Commission.

Koolhoven, R et al, 'Impulse Paper on specific Liability Issues raised by the collaborative economy in the accommodation sector, Paris-Amsterdam-Barcelona', upon request by the Commission (2016).

Korff, D, 'Study on the protection of the rights and interests of legal persons with regard to the processing of personal data relating to such persons' prepared for the Commission (2000).

Martins, B, 'An economic policy perspective on online platforms' (2016) *JRC Technical Reports, Institute for prospective technological studies*, Digital economy Working Paper No 5.

Principles of European Tort Law proposed by the European Group of Tort Law.

Schmid-Drüner, M, 'The situation of workers in the collaborative economy' (2016) *Employment and Social Affairs*, European Parliament.

Article 29 Data Protection Working Party:

Article 29 Data Protection Working Party, 'Opinion 01/2016 on the EU—U.S. Privacy Shield draft adequacy decision', adopted on 13 April 2016, (WP238).

Article 29 Data Protection Working Party, 'Opinion 3/2010 on the principle of accountability', adopted on 13 July 2010 (WP173).

Article 29 Data Protection Working Party, Working Party on Police and Justice, 'The Future of Privacy: Joint contribution to the Consultation of the European Commission on the legal framework for the fundamental right to protection of personal data', adopted on 1 December 2009 (WP168).

Article 29 Data Protection Working Party, 'Opinion 06/2014 on the notion of legitimate interests of the data controller under Article 7 of Directive 95/46/EC', adopted on 9 April 2014 (WP217).

Article 29 Data Protection Working Party, 'Opinion 4/2007 on the concept of personal data', adopted on 20 June 2007 (WP136).

Article 29 Data Protection Working Party, 'Opinion 15/2011 on the definition of consent', adopted on 13 July 2011 (WP187).

Article 29 Data Protection Working Party, 'Opinion on the use of location data with a view to providing value-added services', adopted in November 2005 (WP115).

Article 29 Data Protection Working Party, 'Working Document on the processing of personal data relating to health in electronic health records (EHR)', adopted on 15 February 2007 (WP131).

Article 29 Data Protection Working Party, 'Opinion 01/2016 on the EU—U.S. Privacy Shield draft adequacy decision', adopted on 13 April 2016, (WP238).

Article 29 Data Protection Working Party, 'Opinion 1/2010 on the concepts of "controller" and "processor"', adopted on 16 February 2010 (WP169).

Article 29 Data Protection Working Party Annex—health data in apps and devices—, attached to the Working Party's letter dated 5 February 2015.

Article 29 Data Protection Working Party, 'Opinion 8/2001 on the processing of personal data in the employment context', adopted on 13 September 2001 (WP48).

International Bodies:

De Stefano, V, 'The rise of the "just-in-time workforce": On-demand work, crowdwork and labour protection in the "gig-economy" (2016) *ILO, Conditions of work and employment series* No 71.

Information Commissioner's Office, 'Data controllers and data processors: What the difference is and what the governance implications are' (2014).

Organisation for Economic Co-operation and Development (OECD), 'Annual Report on Competition Policy Developments in Spain—2016' (2017).

Organisation for Economic Co-operation and Development (OECD), 'Guidelines on the Protection of Privacy and Transborder Flows of Personal Data'.

Organisation for Economic Co-operation and Development (OECD), 'New Forms of Work in the Digital Economy' (2016) *OECD Digital Economy Papers*, No 260.

Organisation for Economic Co-operation and Development (OECD), 'Protecting Consumers in Peer Platform Markets, Exploring the Issues' (2016) *OECD Digital Economy Papers* No 253.

Organisation for Economic Co-operation and Development (OECD), 'Two-Sided Markets' (2009) DAF/COMP 20.

Organisation for Economic Co-operation and Development (OECD), 'The OECD Privacy Framework' (2013).

Organisation for Economic Co-operation and Development (OECD), 'Guidelines on the Protection of Privacy and Transborder Flows of Personal Data'.

Newspaper Articles

'2 Uber executives ordered to stand trial in France' *Los Angeles Times* (30 June 2015).

'Dutch judges ban taxi service UberPOP (Update)' *Phys* (8 December 2014).

'Germany refers case on Uber sedan service to European court', *Reuters* (18 May 2017).

'Many Countries Ban Uber' *Tempo.Co* (12 April 2016).

'Uber Takes Break in Finland Ahead of New Legislation' *Phys* (6 July 2017).

'Uber taxi app suspended in Spain' *BBC News* (9 December 2014).

'VTC: la proposition d'Uber clôt la médiation' *Le Figaro* (7 February 2017).

Bajpai, P, 'How Uber is Selling all Your Ride Data' *Investopedia* (9 March 2016).

BBC, 'Airbnb introduces new anti-discrimination policy' *BBC News* (8 September 2016).

Binnie, I and Jones G, (D Goodman(ed)), 'Italian court overturns Uber ban' *Reuters* (26 May 2017).

Braun, E, 'Un Français demande 45 millions d'euros à Uber pour avoir précipité son divorce' *Le Figaro* (8 February 2017).

—— 'Un Français demande 45 millions d'euros à Uber pour avoir précipité son divorce' *Le Figaro* (8 February 2017).

Burgen, S, 'Barcelona cracks down on Airbnb rentals with illegal apartment squads' *The Guardian* (2 June 2017).

Carson, B, 'You're more likely to order a pricey Uber ride if your phone is about to die' *Business Insider* (12 September 2016).

Clampet, J, 'Airbnb loses a fight in New York as legislature passes strict advertising law' *Skift* (17 June 2016).

Clark, J, 'Big Data Knows When You're Going to Quit Your Job Before You Do' *Bloomberg* (30 December 2014).

Conditt, J, 'Uber is free to operate in Italy on a long-term basis' *engadget* (26 May 2017).

Crouzel, C, 'Pour la première fois, un chauffeur de VTC est reconnu salarié par la justice' *Le Figaro* (27 January 2017).

De Foucaud, I, 'L'Urssaf lance une bataille juridique pour requalifier les chauffeurs Uber en "salarié 3"' *Le Figaro* (17 May 2016).

Denney, A, 'Appeals Court Set to Eye Uber's Drive to Steer Price-Fixing Dispute to Arbitration' *New York Law Journal* (22 March 2017).

Dickey, MR, 'Airbnb settles lawsuit with San Francisco' *TechCrunch* (1 May 2017).

Ertsscheid, O, 'Du digital labor à l'uberisation du travail' *Numerique* (25 January 2016).

Frankel, A, 'Uber's arbitration appeal at the 2nd Circuit is big test for Internet businesses' *Reuters* (30 November 2016).

Frenken K et al, 'Smarter regulation for the sharing economy' *The Guardian* (20 May 2015).

Gosh, S, 'Uber will offer insurance to UK drivers in case they are injured or sick' *Business Insider* (27 April 2017).

Hawkins, A, 'You can now tip your Uber driver in the app' *The Verge* (6 July 2017).

Henley, J, 'Uber to shut down Denmark operation over new taxi laws' *The Guardian* (28 March 2017).

Kharpal, A, 'Airbnb's growth is slowing because it's being hit by regulation, UBS says' *CNBC* (13 April 2017).

King, D, 'Airbnb testing premium listings' *Travel Weekly* (23 June 2017).

Lauwers, M, 'Airbnb veut préserver la vie privée de ses hôtes' *L'Echo* (20 July 2017).

Lee, D, 'AirBnB host fined after racist comment' *BBC News* (13 July 2017).

Lee, D, 'Anger as US internet privacy law scrapped', *BBC News* (29 March 2017).

Lien, T 'Uber conquered taxis. Now it's going after everything else' *LA Times* (7 May 2016).

McCoogan, C, 'Tribunal to rule on Deliveroo riders' employment status' *The Telegraph* (6 March 2017).

McGoogan, C and Yeomans, J, 'Uber loses landmark tribunal decision over drivers working rights' *The Telegraph* (28 October 2016).

Menn, J and Levine, D, 'Uber, Lyft settlement did not require either side to pay—sources' *Reuters* (1 July 2016).

Oltermann, P, 'Berlin ban on Airbnb short-term rentals upheld by city court' *The Guardian* (8 June 2016).

Perry, D, 'Sex and Uber's "Rides of Glory": The company tracks your one-night stands—and much more' *The Oregonian/Oregon Live* (20 November 2014).

Priluck, J, 'When Bots Collude' *The New Yorker* (25 April 2015).

Rodionova, Z, 'Uber drivers must pass written English test, High Court rules' *Independent* (3 March 2017).

Rosenblatt, J and Amon, E, 'Judge Blocks Seattle Law Allowing Uber and Lyft Drivers to Unionize' *Bloomberg Technology* (4 April 2017).

Russell, J and Lunden, I, 'Uber plans to turn its app into a "content marketplace" during rides' *TechCrunch* (3 March 2017).

Schwab, K, 'The Fourth Industrial Revolution: What It Means and How to Respond' *ForeignAffairs* (12 December 2015).

Sebag, G, 'Uber Wins Driver-Status Case in France on Legal Technicality' *Bloomberg* (15 March 17).

Singer, N, 'In the Sharing Economy Workers Find Both Freedom and Uncertainty' *NY Times* (16 August 2014).

Stempel, J, 'Pennsylvania reinstates Uber's record $11.4 million fine' *Reuters* (1 September 2016).

Stupp, C, 'European Commission paralysed over data flows in TiSA trade deal' *Euractiv* (11 October 2016).

Tadeo, M, 'Barcelona Takes the Wind Out of Airbnb's Sails', *Bloomberg* (8 February 2017).

Ting, D, 'Airbnb Acquires Vacation Rental Company Luxury Retreats, Officially Moves Into Luxury' *Skift* (16 February 2017).

Walsh, B, 'Today's smart choice: Don't own. Share' *Time* (17 March 2011).

Wong, JC, 'Airbnb Is Already Sharing Non-Anonymized User Data with SF', *SF Weekly* (12 November 2015).

Woolf, N, 'Airbnb regulation deal with London and Amsterdam marks dramatic policy shift' *The Guardian* (3 December 2016).

Zaleski, O, 'Airbnb Goes After Business Travelers With New Booking Tool' *Bloomberg Technology* (28 April 2017).

—— 'Airbnb Readies a Premium Tier to Compete More With Hotels, Sources Say' *Bloomberg* (22 June 2017).

Blogs

'Collaborative Consumption Directory' available at www.collaborativeconsumption.com/directory.

'How the Sharing Economy Is Disrupting the Energy Sector' *Thinque* (20 May 2016), available at https://blog.thinque.com.au/how-the-sharing-economy-is-disrupting-the-energy-sector.

Berra, Y; www.goodreads.com/quotes/261863-it-s-tough-to-make-predictions-especially-about-the-future.

Botsman, R and Rogers, R, 'Beyond Zipcar: Collaborative Consumption' (2010) *Harvard Business Review*, available at https://hbr.org/2010/10/beyond-zipcar-collaborative-consumption.

Botsman, R, 'Defining the Sharing Economy: What Is Collaborative Consumption—And What Isn't?' *Fast Company* (27 May 2015), available at www.fastcoexist.com/3046119/defining-the-sharing-economy-what-is-collaborative-consumption-and-what-isnt.

Briggs, L, 'Energy may be ripe for the sharing economy, thanks to Bitcoin's blockchain technology' *Energy Post* (9 December 2016), available at http://energypost.eu/energy-may-ripe-sharing-economy-thanks-bitcoins-blockchain-technology.

Dickerson, T, 'Uber On the Brink' *Law360 Expert Analysis* (8 May 2017), available at www.law360.com/articles/921141/uber-on-the-brink.

Gasser, U, 'The Sharing Economy: Disruptive Effects on Regulation and Paths Forward' *Swiss Re—Centre for Global Dialogue, Risk Dialogue Magazine* (6 June 2016), available at http://institute.swissre.com/research/risk_dialogue/magazine/Digital_Economy/sharing_economy_disruptive_effects.html.

Gesley, J, 'Legal Challenges for Uber in the European Union and in Germany' *Library of Congress* Blog (14 March 2016), available at https://blogs.loc.gov/law/2016/03/legal-challenges-for-uber-in-the-european-union-and-in-germany.

Guirado, R, 'What has a Spanish Court said about BlaBlaCar?' *Legal Sharing* (4 February 2017), available at www.legalsharing.eu/single-post/2017/02/04/BlaBlaCar-Judgement.

Hagiu, A and Biederman, R, 'Companies Need an Option Between Contractor and Employee' *Harvard Business Review* (21 August 2015), available at https://hbr.org/2015/08/companies-need-an-option-between-contractor-and-employee.

Higgins, T, Mantoan, K and Corbett, D, 'Uber Rolls Along, Despite Driver Challenges to its Arbitration Agreement' *Orrick Employment Law and Litigation Blog* (14 February 2017), available at http://blogs.orrick.com/employment/2017/02/14/uber-rolls-along-despite-driver-challenges-to-its-arbitration-agreement.

Keller, D, 'Intermediary Liability and User Content under Europe's New Data Protection Law' (8 October 2015) *The Center for Internet and Society, Stanford Law School, Blog,* available at https://cyberlaw.stanford.edu/blog/2015/10/intermediary-liability-and-user-content-under-europe%E2%80%99s-new-data-protection-law.

—— 'Policy Debates Over EU Platform Liability Laws: New Human Rights Case Law in the Real World' (14 April 2016) *The Center for Internet and Society, Stanford Law School, Blog.*

Kessler, S, 'Pixel and Dimed: On (Not) Getting By in the Gig Economy' *Fast Company* (18 March 2014) available at www.fastcompany.com/3027355/pixel-and-dimed-on-not-getting-by-in-the-gig-economy.

Lawrance, S and Hunt, M, 'Will pricing algorithms be the European Commission's next antitrust target?' *Bristows CLIP Board* (21 March 2017), available at www.bristowsclipboard.com/post/will-pricing-algorithms-be-the-european-commission-s-next-antitrust-target.

Lazarus, AP and White, KJ, 'Florida Legislation Establishes That Ride-Sharing Drivers Are Independent Contractors, Not Employees' Hunton Employment & Labor Law Perspectives Blog (23 May 2017), available at www.huntonlaborblog.com/2017/05/articles/employeeindependent-contractor/florida-legislation-establishes-ride-sharing-drivers-independent-contractors-not-employees.

May, A, 'Power to the People: How the Sharing Economy Will Transform the Electricity Industry' *World Economic Forum* (10 March 2017), available at www.weforum.org/press/2017/03/power-to-the-people-how-the-sharing-economy-will-transform-the-electricity-industry.

Munz, M and Lorenz, S, 'Online Traders: New Obligation in EU for Provision of Link to Online Dispute Resolution (ODR) Platform' *White & Case* (9 June 2016), available at hwww.whitecase.com/publications/article/online-traders-new-obligation-eu-provision-link-online-dispute-resolution-odr.

Ortiz, C, 'Market Definition and the Sharing Economy' *Developing World Antitrust* (19 August 2016), available at https://developingworldantitrust.com/2016/08/19/market-definition-and-the-sharing-economy/#_edn12.

Owyang, J, 'Honeycomb 3.0: The Collaborative Economy Market Expansion' (2016) available at www.web-strategist.com/blog/2016/03/10/honeycomb-3-0-the-collaborative-economy-market-expansion-sxsw.

Packel, D, 'Pa. Regulator OKs $3.5M Settlement With Uber Over Violations' *Law360* (6 April 2017), available at https://www.law360.com/articles/910375/pa-regulator-oks-3-5m-settlement-with-uber-over-violations.

Ramasastry, A, 'Too Much Sharing in the Sharing Economy? Uber's Use of Our Passenger Data Highlights the Perils of Data Collection via Geolocation' *Verdict* (10 February 2015), available at https://verdict.justia.com/2015/02/10/much-sharing-sharing-economy.

Schiller, B, 'The Sharing Economy Takes On Electricity, So You Can Buy Your Power From Neighbors' *Fast Company* (30 September 2014), available at www.fastcompany.com/3036271/the-sharing-economy-takes-on-electricity-so-you-can-buy-your-power-from-neighbors.

Slee, T, 'Some Obvious Things About Internet Reputation Systems' *Whimsley Blog* (29 September 2013), available at http://tomslee.net/2013/09/some-obvious-things-about-internetreputation-systems.html.

Stone, KVW, 'Uber and arbitration: A lethal combination' *Economic Policy Institute, Working Economics Blog* (24 May 2016), available at www.epi.org/blog/uber-and-arbitration-a-lethal-combination.

Torben, R, 'Will the sharing economy approach enter the energy market' (13 February 2017), available at www.torbenrick.eu/blog/technology/sharing-economy-approach-enter-the-energy-market.

Victor, L, 'Is Online Dispute Resolution the Wave of the Future?' *ABA Online Journal* (18 March 2015), available at www.abajournal.com/news/article/is_online_dispute_resolution_the_wave_of_the_future.

INDEX

Lightning Source UK Ltd.
Milton Keynes UK
UKHW022040120719

346067UK00003B/108/P